ROUTLEDGE LIBRARY EDITIONS:
INTERNATIONAL TRADE POLICY

I0130545

Volume 25

TARIFF LEVELS AND THE ECONOMIC UNITY OF EUROPE

TARIFF LEVELS AND THE ECONOMIC UNITY OF EUROPE

An Examination of Tariff Policy,
Export Movements and the Economic
Integration of Europe, 1913–1931

H. LIEPMANN

Routledge
Taylor & Francis Group

LONDON AND NEW YORK

First published in 1938 by George Allen & Unwin Ltd

This edition first published in 2018
by Routledge
2 Park Square, Milton Park, Abingdon, Oxon OX14 4RN

and by Routledge
711 Third Avenue, New York, NY 10017

Routledge is an imprint of the Taylor & Francis Group, an informa business

British Library Cataloguing in Publication Data
A catalogue record for this book is available from the British Library

ISBN: 978-1-138-06323-5 (Set)
ISBN: 978-1-315-14339-2 (Set) (ebk)
ISBN: 978-1-138-29847-7 (Volume 25) (hbk)
ISBN: 978-1-138-29851-4 (Volume 25) (pbk)
ISBN: 978-1-315-09864-7 (Volume 25) (ebk)

Publisher's Note
The publisher has gone to great lengths to ensure the quality of this reprint but
points out that some imperfections in the original copies may be apparent.

Disclaimer
The publisher has made every effort to trace copyright holders and would welcome
correspondence from those they have been unable to trace.

TARIFF LEVELS AND THE ECONOMIC UNITY OF EUROPE

AN EXAMINATION OF
TARIFF POLICY, EXPORT MOVEMENTS
AND THE ECONOMIC INTEGRATION OF
EUROPE, 1913–1931

BY
H. LIEPMANN

WITH AN INTRODUCTION BY
SIR WALTER LAYTON

TRANSLATED FROM THE GERMAN BY
H. STENNING

LONDON
GEORGE ALLEN & UNWIN LTD
MUSEUM STREET

FIRST PUBLISHED IN 1938

PRINTED IN GREAT BRITAIN BY
THE RIVERSIDE PRESS, EDINBURGH

FOREWORD

By Sir WALTER LAYTON

DURING the past two decades rapid and far-reaching changes have been taking place in the character and distribution of the world's trade. The Great War itself shut off many nations from the outside world and threw them on their own resources, while the economic activity of the rest of the world, which until that time had been mainly focussed upon Europe, was violently interrupted and thrown out of gear. No country, for example, was immune from the effect of the famine of ships. In general, the results were similar to those which would have followed the sudden imposition of a régime of extreme protection. Some of these effects would in any case have been lasting, but subsequent developments have tended to create fresh disturbances rather than to restore the pre-War state of things. The export of machinery from old countries and the general extension of technical knowledge has created new centres of industry; the oil age has challenged the dominance of coal in international commerce; science has destroyed Chili's nitrate monopoly; artificial silk factories in the Orient have undermined Lancashire's supremacy. The world had in any case to adjust itself to these new conditions.

It is, however, a commonplace that these changes have not been left to work themselves out under a régime of unrestricted competition. On the contrary, all the governments of the world have intervened in an attempt to mould and control the development of their own economies. Economic nationalism has been carried to a pitch unknown for many decades before the War and has played a most important part in bringing about a highly unsatisfactory and dangerous state of general politics.

Yet, in spite of the political as well as the economic importance of tariff policy and its close connection with the peace of the world, there have been surprisingly few attempts to make factual studies of tariffs or to trace their effects upon the actual course of trade. Dr. Liepmann's book is an important addition to the very limited literature on the subject.

Much the most important attempt to survey the tariff situation and to examine its effects was made in the extensive documentation prepared for the World Economic Conference of 1927. And one of the most interesting and ambitious of the studies then made was the attempt of the Secretariat of the League of Nations to calculate a quantitative estimate of the level of the chief tariffs of the world.

5

This estimate, which was a lengthy and laborious computation and when made was subject to considerable defects of interpretation, has never been repeated by the Secretariat of the League. But students in various countries have submitted the methods then adopted to critical examination and some attempts have been made to produce calculations for later years. One of the most interesting parts of Dr. Liepmann's book is his calculation of the potential and actual tariff level of a number of the countries of Europe for several years ending in 1931, when the break-down of the gold standard threw international trading relations once more into the melting-pot.

Dr. Liepmann's book, however, is by no means only a statistical study, for he has supplemented his calculations by a detailed realistic examination of the trade of the countries of Europe and of changes in the distribution of the exports of each nation. Though this examination is long and detailed, it is a necessary preliminary to understanding the economic changes that are taking place in Europe.

His exposition will no doubt be subjected to criticism in detail and indeed, in an attempt to focus attention on the effect of tariffs, there is almost inevitably a danger that the picture presented may be incomplete. For example, in the case of Great Britain during the nineteen-twenties the protected industries showed a very rapid growth which was in sharp contrast to the experience of the old-established and unprotected industries; but as the former include the artificial silk and motor industries, while the latter include cotton, wool, coal, iron and steel, shipbuilding, etc., the contrast is not mainly or even primarily to be attributed to our tariffs. Again, Dr. Liepmann's study, particularly in relation to recent years, inevitably brings out the very harmful effects which our statistically moderate tariff has produced on many of the nations of Europe. This damage is undoubted; but if the story as told by him gives an impression of great ruthlessness, there is more than one side to this question.

Dr. Liepmann's primary object, however, is not to pass judgment, but to present material for forming an opinion. This he has achieved with great care and skill, and by so doing has produced a book that will be of real value not only to economic students, but to all who wish to understand the economic problems which are so closely interwoven with the politics of the world of to-day.

February 1938.

PREFACE

THIS book was written in the years 1932–35. The manuscript was completed in February 1936. The work was planned for the series: *Zum wirtschaftlichen Schicksal Europas*, Part I: *Arbeiten zur europäischen Problematik*, edited by Alfred Weber. This series was published with the assistance of the *Rockefeller Foundation*. Unexpected difficulties have postponed the publication of the study until to-day, so that it only now appears in an English translation.

Although all the figures in the concluding chapter about the economic development of Europe in 1934–35 are already part of the economic history of Europe, yet the consequences of European protectionist commercial policy, especially since 1929, and all its dangers, which these figures were intended to illustrate, still persist. Owing substantially to public works and growing rearmaments we are witnessing "national recoveries" in many countries, financed by swelling debts. At the same time, however, the development of world trade remains unsatisfactory. The doubts recorded at the beginning of 1936 regarding the stability of such prosperity are justified even to-day. I have therefore allowed the statistics and conclusions of the last chapter to stand in the form in which they appear in this book.

I desire to express my gratitude to Professor *Alfred Weber* of Heidelberg, at whose instigation the study was undertaken, for his friendly advice and assistance in overcoming many difficulties, and my indebtedness to Sir *Walter Layton* and to Mr. *G. K. Logie*, the former for his Introduction and the latter for his constructive criticism of the book in proof.

HEINRICH LIEPMANN.

LONDON, 1937.

CONTENTS

                                           PAGE

FOREWORD 5

PREFACE 7

PART I

OBJECTS, METHODS AND LIMITS OF THE INVESTIGATION

CHAPTER

I. THE OBJECTS OF THE INQUIRY 17

II. THE METHODS OF THE INVESTIGATION 20

    a. Tariffs.
    b. The Selection of Goods and the Conception of the "Potential Tariff Level."
    c. The Averages.
    d. The Prices.
    e. The Duty Rates.
    f. The "Actual Tariff Levels" and the Economic Integration of Europe.

III. THE LIMITS OF THE INQUIRY 31

    a. Inherent Difficulties of Methods.
        aa. Selection of Goods and Structure of Custom Tariffs.
        bb. The Problem of Price Data.
        cc. The Problem of the Averages.
        dd. The Problem of Comparisons.
    b. Decreasing Importance of Tariffs in the System of European post-War Trade Policy.

PART II

OUTLINES OF EUROPEAN TARIFF POLICY AND DEVELOPMENT OF POTENTIAL TARIFF LEVELS BETWEEN 1913 AND 1931. (SEE TABLES AI AND AII OF APPENDIX.)

I. INDUSTRIAL AND AGRARIAN STATES, AGRARIAN AND INDUSTRIAL TARIFFS IN EUROPE 45

II. STRUCTURE AND ARRANGEMENT OF THE GENERAL GOODS LIST (A-LIST) 49

CHAPTER   PAGE
III. OUTLINES OF EUROPEAN AGRARIAN TARIFF POLICY AND
     DEVELOPMENT OF POTENTIAL AGRARIAN TARIFF LEVELS,
     1913–1931 56

   A. Industrial (Central) Europe.
      Preliminary Remark: The Centres of European Agrarian
      Imports.
      1. Germany 56
      2. France 65
      3. Italy 69
      4. Belgium 73
      5. Switzerland. 76
      6. Austria 79
      7. Czechoslovakia 82

   B. Agrarian (Border) Europe.
      Preliminary Remark: Foodstuff—and Raw Material—
      Countries in Agrarian Europe.
      1. Sweden 85
      2. Finland 88
      3. Poland 90
      4. Roumania 93
      5. Hungary 95
      6. Yugoslavia 96
      7. Bulgaria 98
      8. Spain 99

   C. General Tendencies in the Agrarian Tariff Policy of post-
      War Europe compared with 1913. (See graph A and
      Table IVA of Appendix) 102

IV. OUTLINES OF EUROPEAN INDUSTRIAL TARIFF POLICY AND
    DEVELOPMENT OF POTENTIAL INDUSTRIAL TARIFF LEVELS
    BETWEEN 1913 AND 1931 111

    Preliminary Remark: Industrial and Agrarian Countries of
    Europe as Markets for Industrial Products.

   A. Industrial (Central) Europe.
      1. Germany 113
      2. France 120
      3. Italy 126
      4. Great Britain 131
      5. Belgium 133
      6. Switzerland. 136
      7. Austria 140
      8. Czechoslovakia 143

   B. Agrarian (Border) Europe.
      Preliminary Remark: Differences in the Industrial Recep-
      tivity of the Agrarian Countries of Europe.
      1. Sweden 147
      2. Finland 150
      3. Poland 153

CHAPTER   PAGE

    4. Roumania 157
    5. Hungary 162
    6. Yugoslavia 166
    7. Bulgaria 169
    8. Spain 173
  C. General tendencies of European Industrial Tariff Policy
     before and after the War. (See graphs B, C and Table IVA
     of Appendix) 178

PART III

ACTUAL TARIFF LEVELS IN EUROPE, 1913–1931.
(See Tables BI–IV of Appendix.)

I. DETAILS OF THE METHODS OF CALCULATING ACTUAL TARIFF
    LEVELS 189

II. OUTLINES OF THE ECONOMIC INTEGRATION OF EUROPE . 192

III. LIMITS OF THE TEXTUAL ANALYSIS OF THE ACTUAL TARIFF
     LEVELS 199

IV. ACTUAL TARIFF LEVELS FOR THE EXPORTS OF INDUSTRIAL
     EUROPE 201

    1. *Germany* and the Tariffs in Europe . . . 201
      a. Composition and Value of German Exports.
      b. Geographical Distribution of German Exports.
      c. Actual Tariff Levels of the chief Markets of Germany:
        I. *Germany and Industrial Europe.*—(*aa*) Germany and
         Great Britain, (*bb*) Germany and France, (*cc*) Ger-
         many and Italy, (*dd*) Germany and Belgium, (*ee*)
         Germany and Switzerland, (*ff*) Germany and
         Austria, (*gg*) Germany and Czechoslovakia.
        II. *Germany and Agrarian Europe.*—(*aa*) Germany and
         the Netherlands, (*bb*) Germany and the Scandi-
         navian States, (*cc*) Germany and the Baltic States,
         (*dd*) Germany and Poland, (*ee*) Germany and the
         European South-East, (*ff*) Germany and the
         Mediterranean States.
      d. General trend of German Exports, 1913–1934.
    2. *Great Britain* and the Tariffs in Europe . . . 227
      a. Composition of English Exports.
      b. Geographical Distribution of English Exports.
      c. Actual Tariff Levels of the chief Markets of Great
       Britain:
        I. *England and Industrial Europe.*—(*aa*) England and
         Germany, (*bb*) England and France, (*cc*) England
         and Italy, (*dd*) England and Belgium.
        II. *England and Agrarian Europe.*—(*aa*) England and
         the Netherlands, (*bb*) England and the North
         European Countries, (*cc*) England and Spain,

(*dd*) England and Poland, (*ee*) England and the South-Eastern States, (*ff*) England and the Mediterranean States (Greece and Portugal).

d. General trend of English Exports, 1913–1934.

3. *France* and the Tariffs in Europe 241
   a. Composition of French Exports.
   b. Geographical Distribution of French Exports.
   c. Actual Tariff Levels of the chief Markets of France:
      I. *France and Industrial Europe.*—(*aa*) France and Great Britain, (*bb*) France and Belgium, (*cc*) France and Germany, (*dd*) France and Switzerland, (*ee*) France and Italy.
      II. *France and Agrarian Europe.*—(*aa*) France and Spain, (*bb*) France and the remainder of Border Europe.
   d. General trend of French Exports, 1913–1934.

4. *Italy* and the Tariffs in Europe 254
   a. Composition of Italian Exports.
   b. Geographical Distribution of Italian Exports.
   c. Actual Tariff Levels of the chief Markets of Italy:
      I. *Italy and Industrial Europe.*—(*aa*) Italy and Germany, (*bb*) Italy and Great Britain, (*cc*) Italy and Switzerland, (*dd*) Italy and France, (*ee*) Italy and Austria-Hungary (1927–1931: Austria and Czechoslovakia).
      II. *Italy and Agrarian Europe.*—(*aa*) Italy and the South-Eastern States, (*bb*) Italy and Greece.
   d. General trend of Italian Exports, 1913–1934.

5. *Belgium* and the Tariffs in Europe 263
   a. Composition of Belgian Exports.
   b. Geographical Distribution of Belgian Exports.
   c. Actual Tariff Levels of the chief Markets of Belgium:
      I. *Belgium and Industrial Europe.*—(*aa*) Belgium and Germany, (*bb*) Belgium and France, (*cc*) Belgium and Great Britain.
      II. *Belgium and Agrarian Europe.*—(*aa*) Belgium and the Netherlands.
   d. General trend of Belgian Exports, 1913–1934.

6. *Switzerland* and the Tariffs in Europe . . . 269
   a. Composition of Swiss Exports.
   b. Geographical Distribution of Swiss Exports.
   c. Actual Tariff Levels of the chief Markets of Switzerland:
      I. *Switzerland and Industrial Europe.*—(*aa*) Switzerland and Germany, (*bb*) Switzerland and Great Britain, (*cc*) Switzerland and France, (*dd*) Switzerland and Italy, (*ee*) Switzerland and Austria-Hungary (1927–1931: Austria, Czechoslovakia).
      II. General remark on the duties on Swiss Exports imposed by the States of Agrarian Europe.
   d. General trend of Swiss Exports, 1913–1934.

CHAPTER   PAGE

7. *Austria* and the Tariffs in Europe 277
   a. Composition of Austrian Exports.
   b. Geographical Distribution of Austrian Exports.
   c. Actual Tariff Levels of the chief Markets of Austria:
      I. *Austria and Industrial Europe.*—(aa) Austria and
         Germany, (bb) Austria and Czechoslovakia, (cc)
         Austria and Italy, (dd) Austria and Switzerland.
      II. *Austria and Agrarian Europe.*—(aa) Austria and
          Hungary, (bb) Austria and Yugoslavia, (cc) Austria
          and Roumania, (dd) Austria and Poland.
   d. General trend of Austrian Exports, 1927–1934.

8. *Czechoslovakia* and the Tariffs in Europe .   .   . 285
   a. Composition of Czech Exports.
   b. Geographical Distribution of Czech Exports.
   c. Actual Tariff Levels of the chief Markets of Czecho-
      slovakia:
      I. *Czechoslovakia and Industrial Europe.*—(aa) Czecho-
         slovakia and Germany, (bb) Czechoslovakia and
         Austria, (cc) Czechoslovakia and Great Britain.
      II. *Czechoslovakia and Agrarian Europe.*—(aa) Czecho-
          slovakia and Hungary, (bb) Czechoslovakia and
          Yugoslavia, (cc) Czechoslovakia and Roumania.
   d. General trend of Czech Exports, 1927–1934.

V. ACTUAL TARIFF LEVELS FOR THE EXPORTS OF AGRARIAN
   EUROPE 295
   Preliminary Remark: Differences in Composition and Des-
   tination between the Exports from Agrarian and Industrial
   Europe.

   1. *Denmark* and *Holland* and the Tariffs in Europe .   . 296
      a. Composition of Danish and Dutch Exports.
      b. Geographical Distribution of Danish and Dutch
         Exports.
      c. Actual Tariff Levels of the chief Markets of Denmark
         and Holland:
         A. Actual Tariff Levels of the chief Markets of
            Denmark.—(aa) Denmark and Great Britain,
            (bb) Denmark and Germany.
         B. Actual Tariff Levels of the chief Markets of the
            Netherlands.—(aa) The Netherlands and Germany,
            (bb) The Netherlands and Great Britain, (cc)
            Holland and Belgium, (dd) Holland and France.
      d. General trend of Danish and Dutch Exports, 1913-1934.

   2. *Sweden, Norway, Finland* and the Tariffs in Europe . 304
      a. Composition of Swedish, Norwegian and Finnish
         Exports.
      b. Geographical Distribution of Swedish, Norwegian
         and Finnish Exports.
      c. Actual Tariff Levels of the chief Markets of Sweden,
         Norway and Finland:
         (aa) Great Britain as a Market for Sweden, Norway,

and Finland, (*bb*) Germany as a Market for Sweden, Norway, and Finland, (*cc*) Sweden, Norway, and Finland and the rest of Europe.

    d. General trend of Swedish, Norwegian, and Finnish Exports, 1913–1934.

3. The *Baltic States* and the Tariffs in Europe   .   .   312

    a. Composition of Baltic Exports.

    b. Geographical Distribution of Baltic Exports.

    c. Actual Tariff Levels of the chief Markets of the Baltic countries.

    d. General trend of Baltic Exports, 1927–1934.

4. *Poland* and the Tariffs in Europe   315

    a. Composition of Polish Exports.

    b. Geographical Distribution of Polish Exports.

    c. Actual Tariff Levels of the chief Markets of Poland:

        I. *Poland and Industrial Europe.*—(*aa*) Poland and Germany, (*bb*) Poland and Great Britain, (*cc*) Poland and the Tariffs of Austria and Czechoslovakia.

      II. *Poland and Border Europe.*

    d. General trend of Polish Exports, 1927–1934.

5. The *South-Eastern States* and the Tariffs in Europe   .   321

    a. Composition of the Exports of the South-Eastern States.

    b. Geographical Distribution of the Exports of the South-Eastern States.

    c. Actual Tariff Levels of the chief Markets of the South-Eastern States:

        I. *South-Eastern States and Industrial Europe.*—(*aa*) South-Eastern States and Germany, (*bb*) South-Eastern States and Austria, (*cc*) South-Eastern States and Czechoslovakia, (*dd*) South-Eastern States and Italy, (*ee*) South-Eastern States and France, (*ff*) South-Eastern States and Great Britain.

      II. *South-Eastern States and Agrarian Europe.*

    d. General trend of the Exports of the South-Eastern States, 1913–1934.

6. The *Mediterranean Border States* and the Tariffs in Europe   332

    a. Composition of the Exports of the Mediterranean Border States.

    b. Geographical Distribution of the Exports of the Mediterranean Border States.

    c. Actual Tariff Levels of the chief Markets of the Mediterranean Border States:
    (*aa*) Great Britain as a Market for the three countries, (*bb*) France as a Market for the three countries, (*cc*) Germany as a Market for the three countries, (*dd*) Italy as a Market for Greece.

    d. General trend of the Exports of the three countries, 1913–1934.

CHAPTER   PAGE

VI. SUMMARY: THE ECONOMIC INTEGRATION OF EUROPE UP TO 1931 AS AFFECTED BY EUROPEAN TARIFFS. (SEE TABLES BI–IV, IVA, B, OF APPENDIX) 340

 1. The Period of Reconstruction (1925–1929).
 2. The Period of Destruction (1929–1931).

VII. TENDENCIES AND DANGERS OF EUROPEAN POST-WAR TARIFF POLICY 346

 1. Outlines of European post-War Tariff Policy . . 347

  a. Course of Development up to the outbreak of the World Economic Crisis (1929).
  b. The course of Events in 1930 and 1931.
  c. The course of Events in the recent Past (1932–1935).
  d. The result of the European Trade Policy of 1932–1935.

 2. Decisive Factors of European post-War Tariff Policy . 359
  Preliminary Remark: The Gulf between Theory and Practice.
  a. Differences in Costs of Production as causes of Tariff Policy.
  b. Monetary Factors as causes of Tariff Policy.
  c. Population Problems as causes of Tariff Policy.
  d. Military Factors as causes of Tariff Policy.
  e. Fiscal Needs as causes of Tariff Policy.

 3. The Dangers of European Protectionism . . . 367
  Preliminary Remark: Protectionism from the standpoint of Free Trade and the Theory of Location of Industries.
  a. Lowering of the Standard of Life.
  b. Destruction of the Economic Location of Production.
  c. Empire and Regional Tendencies in Europe.
  d. Protectionism and War.

APPENDIX—TABLES AND GRAPHS OF POTENTIAL AND ACTUAL TARIFF LEVELS AND OF FOREIGN TRADE RELATIONS OF THE EUROPEAN STATES 383

BIBLIOGRAPHY 416

INDEX 421

PART I

OBJECTS, METHODS AND LIMITS OF THE INVESTIGATION

I

THE OBJECTS OF THE INQUIRY

PROBLEMS of tariff policy occupy a pre-eminent place in the history of European post-War economy. The number of books and articles in periodicals and newspapers upon tariff questions in the post-War literature of all European countries is beyond computation. An instance of the paramount importance which the tariff problem had attained in questions of post-War economy was the request of the Preparatory Committee of the World Economic Conference of 1927,[1] addressed to the Economic Secretariat of the League of Nations, to make a statistical inquiry into the levels of tariffs throughout the world. This memorandum was prepared under the supervision of Mr. *A. Loveday*, the Director of the Economic Department of the League of Nations, and published in the year 1927 with the title *Tariff Level Indices*.[2] Its statistical statement of the general tariff levels of fifteen European and five overseas countries, 1913 and 1925, to which observations by eminent experts on the methods and the difficulties of such investigations were attached, attracted great attention in economic circles, and caused discussions of the problem, even after the conference had closed.[3]

Voluminous, however, as is the post-War literature upon the tariff problem, especially upon questions of single tariff rates, the number of inquiries which attempt to provide statistical measurements of levels of whole customs tariffs or greater groups of commodities, in the manner of the Geneva investigation, is very small. Only three noteworthy examples of this character may be cited: first, the inquiries of the English

[1] Hereinafter referred to as "W.E.C. 1927."

[2] *Tariff Level Indices*, Geneva, 1927, hereinafter called *Tariff Levels*.

[3] Comp. *Loveday's* London lecture in 1928 and its discussion, "The Measurement of Tariff Levels," in *Journal of the Royal Statistical Society*, vol. cxii, pp. 487–529, hereinafter called "Loveday."

"Committee on Industry and Trade" into the height of duties imposed on England's most important exports between 1914 and 1924 in her chief markets, which was published in 1926 in the second chapter of the Balfour Report (*Survey of Overseas Markets*).[1]   Secondly, the inquiry of the Vienna Section of the International Chamber of Commerce into tariff levels in fourteen European states in the year 1926, which was remitted to the World Economic Conference of 1927.[2]   Thirdly, the report on *The Economic Situation of Austria*, presented in 1924 to the League of Nations by Sir *Walter Layton* and Professor *Rist*.[3]

Moreover, comparative studies of the development of the tariff levels in Europe since 1927 are lacking.   Recently Professor *Condliffe* has complained of this fact in the *World Economic Survey* of the League of Nations, published in 1933.[4]

In the following inquiry an attempt will be made to repair this omission, for the period from 1927 to 1931, at least with regard to tariff developments in Europe.   It will be explained later why the statistical analyses are only continued to the end of the year 1931, and why only the lessons for the present situation (1936) of Europe and the world are drawn from the material discussed in this study.[5]

There are two main questions which we shall endeavour to answer in this work.   These may be quite generally formulated as its two main themes as follows :—

First, statistical bases have been provided for the levels of European tariffs in 1927 and 1931, and for their better appreciation the corresponding figures for the year 1913 are added as a

[1] *Survey of Overseas Markets*, chap. ii, pp. 539 et seq., London, 1926, hereinafter called "Balfour Report."

[2] *Zollhöhe und Warenwerte*, Vienna, 1927, hereinafter called *Vienna Study*.

[3] Comp. W. T. Layton and Ch. Rist, *The Economic Situation of Austria*, Part II, chap. iii, pp. 88–89, Geneva, 1925, hereinafter referred to as the Layton-Rist report.

[4] *World Economic Survey*, 1932–33, p. 194, hereinafter called "Survey I."

[5] Comp. pp. 41–42 of this book.

pre-War comparative basis. This has been done in the tables and graphs of the appendix; and the European tariff policy which is expressed by these figures is elucidated in the second part of this study.

Secondly, the influence of the European tariff policy upon the development of the reciprocal foreign trade relations of Continental countries has been analysed. These intra-European foreign trade relations, investigated by Drs. *Gaedicke* and *v. Eynern* in a manner very valuable for the present book, are called *Die Produktionswirtschaftliche Integration Europas* ("The Economic Integration of Europe"), after the title of the study of these two authors; [1] so that the second main theme of our study consists in an analysis of the effects of European tariff policy upon the economic integration of Europe between 1927 and 1931. The relevant investigations are contained in the third part of the book and are elucidated by numerous smaller tables in the text and a few larger tables in the appendix.

Here important results of recent years (1933–34) are indicated.

The anticipations of the economic future of Europe which are suggested by the individual inquiries in the second and third parts have been summarised in a final chapter on the outlines, causes, and dangers of European post-War commercial policy (between 1927 and 1935).

Before we begin our concrete studies it is necessary, by an examination of the applied methods and limits of such an analysis, to furnish some indication of its very great theoretical and practical difficulties. This will explain why so few statistical inquiries into the levels of whole customs tariffs have thus far been undertaken.

[1] Comp. *Gaedicke* and *v. Eynern*, "Die produktionswirtschaftliche Integration Europas," Text-u-Tabellenband (*Zum wirtschaftlichen Schicksal Europas*, Teil i), Berlin, 1933.

II

THE METHODS OF THE INVESTIGATION

PRELIMINARY REMARK: *Every measurement of a tariff level demands as its data a knowledge of the system of the customs tariffs involved, of the rates of duties of the goods in question, and of the prices of these commodities. Finally, it must be ascertained what kind of averages have been used in the inquiry.*

(a) *Tariffs*

EVERY duty is a tax imposed by a State on the entry of foreign goods into the country, or on the export of its own commodities abroad. In the former case, we are concerned with import, in the latter with export duties. As export duties played a minor part in European commerce both before and after the War, except in a number of the smaller states (e.g. the Balkan States), they will be left out of account in this study.

Two objectives may occasion the imposition of import duties: the state may desire to raise revenue, in which case they become *revenue* or fiscal duties.

The second type of import duty did not develop until the mercantilist age, and only in the nineteenth century did it assume considerable proportions.[1] The purpose of this duty consists in impeding—on urgent occasions—in preventing, the importation of foreign goods which are already produced by home industries or are likely to be produced in the future, although at higher prices than those quoted by foreign competitors. These are the *protective* duties, which, when they prevent import, may be designated *prohibitive* duties. Their intended effect always lies in raising the price level of the goods

[1] Comp. *Bräuer*, article "Zölle," in *Handwörter buch der Staatswissensch.*, vol. viii, p. 1157.

upon which a tariff is imposed above the level which unrestricted foreign competition would bring about in the home
market. Pure fiscal and pure protective tariffs are antagon-
istic. For whereas the former strive after the highest possible
revenue, and therefore the greatest possible importation of
the taxed goods, the latter aim at securing the most comprehensive protection of that branch of home industry which
is protected, and therefore the most effective prevention of
import. The nature of a revenue tariff, free from any protectionist taint, may only be ascribed to those duties which
a country imposes on such imported goods as are neither
'produced by it nor are likely to be produced by it in the
future. (Example: the duties of European countries on colonial
produce.)

In view of the pronounced differences in the productive
possibilities of European climates or European technique, as
well as the frequent admixture of financial and protectionist
motives of the various countries when fixing their tariff rates,
by far the greater number of all duties of the European states
possess a fiscal *and* protectionist character.[1]

Owing to this mutually exclusive nature of revenue and
protective duties, such investigations as those of the League
of Nations Memorandum of 1927, or the *Vienna Study* on the
protectionist nature of tariffs, have omitted the fiscal duties
on alcohol, tobacco and colonial produce,[2] or have subjected
them to special calculations.[3]

In the present study we shall be concerned only with such
duties as those imposed by European countries upon products
of European origin between 1913 and 1931; we shall therefore
have to include duties on *European* alcoholic beverages and
European tobacco.

For, in the first place, it is not correct that these duties have a
purely or primary fiscal importance for *all* European countries,

[1] *Bräuer*, loc. cit., p. 1158.
[2] Comp. *Tariff Levels*, p. 18.
[3] Comp. *Vienna Study*, pp. ix–x and 3.

and are therefore of no significance whatever,[1] in the analysis of the changes in protectionist tariff levels. Secondly, the treatment of the relation between the economic integration of Europe and the development of tariff levels in Europe necessitated their inclusion. For this question involved the discussion of all European tariffs operating to impede the export of important exportable goods of any one European country to any other. Inasmuch as they impede the free exchange of goods, both revenue and protective tariffs have similar effects. Therefore, as was justly stated in the discussion of Mr. *Loveday's* lecture in London, against their omission from such calculations, they are "*both* obstruction to trade."[2]

On the other hand, this study will take no account of duties imposed on products of undoubted non-European origin.

(b) *The Selection of Goods and the Notion of the "Potential Tariff Level"*

We have therefore to investigate the European tariff levels which have impeded the exchange of goods within the boundaries of Europe. By tariff level we understand a magnitude which is equal to the average of the percentages which the duties imposed by any tariff (or group of duties of a tariff) constitute of the values of the commodities subjected to that tariff (or group of duties).[3]

Modern international trade comprises a very great variety of goods. In order to comprehend this variety, modern

---

[1] Rather are they for some countries (e.g. England or the Scandinavian states) pure revenue tariffs; for others, such as France, Spain, Germany, etc., of a definitely protectionist character. Compare discussion of Mr. *Loveday's* lecture, pp. 522 and 501. In order, however, that the duties on alcohol, tobacco, and petrol, imposed often for fiscal reasons, should play no undue part in the calculations, the average figures of their groups of goods were also calculated without them. (See Figures A[1], A[2], B[1], B[2] in the tables of the Appendix.)

[2] See *Loveday*, pp. 494 and 522.

[3] Comp. the definition of the term "tariff level" in *Tariff Levels*, pp. 11, 12, § iii.

tariffs have therefore to contain many divisions and sub-divisions rising from a few hundred items—e.g. the tariffs of Great Britain and the Scandinavian States—to several thousands —e.g. the tariffs of Poland, Roumania, France, etc.[1] Most of these tariffs contain mainly *specific* duties (duties per unit of weight or per piece); while some (e.g. Great Britain and Holland) as a rule impose *ad valorem* duties only. There are also tariff rates, which consist of a combination of specific and *ad valorem* duties, e.g. in the case of Austria, Roumania, etc.

Wherever specific duties are imposed, these must, for the purpose of estimating the tariff levels, be converted into *ad valorem* duties. The theoretically exact level of a whole tariff is a weighted or unweighted average of the height of all the individual duties. As many tariffs consist of thousands of separate rates, an enormous number of separate calculations would have to be made in order to arrive at a correct figure of the tariff level. Such a calculation, however, would be inappropriate. For, besides the duties of imported goods of great importance to the country whose tariff was under investigation, it would also include those hundreds of commodities which play little or no part at all.

Inquiries into the level of a whole tariff or a group of its duties can, therefore, rationally embody nothing more than calculations of the averages of duties upon *selected* goods or groups of goods; these figures are then to be regarded as representative for the level of the *whole* tariff. The selective principle, which determines the admission of any goods into the computation, can only be determined by the purpose of the inquiry.

When the Economic Secretariat of the League of Nations made its inquiry in 1927, it hoped to provide a statistical basis for estimating the hindrance to world trade by tariffs, and therefore tried to determine the tariff levels of the most important importing countries of the *world*. Consequently, it sought, by compiling two lists of 78 or 278 commodities, to provide "fair

[1] See *Loveday*, p. 495.

samples of the whole quantity of goods constituting *inter-national* trade." [1]

In this study we shall apply this method in dealing with the obstructions to the *European* exchange of goods, under the two main headings previously mentioned.

First of all, we shall endeavour to compile a fair sample list of the whole quantity of goods constituting European trade. For this purpose the official export statistics of the European countries for the years 1913, 1927, and 1931 have been examined, and with their aid a list of 144 commodities has been compiled ("A-List," see Appendix of Tables). Each could be regarded as an important export commodity of at least one European country, and several represented important export goods of many others. [2]

This list is arranged into three main groups:

A.—Foodstuffs and live animals (agrarian economy).
B.—Semi-finished industrial goods ⎱ industrial economy.
C.—Manufactured industrial goods ⎰

Each of these three main groups is again divided into 6, 5, 8 classes respectively. The height of the rate of import duty for each of these 144 commodities in fifteen European countries, with respect to the years 1913, 1927, and 1931, has been calculated on the basis of the "normal prices" indicated in the "A-List," which gives the export prices of the leading European export countries in those years. The average duties for each of the nineteen classes, for the three main groups and for the total list, had then to be established, and these average figures had to be taken as representative for the tariff levels of fifteen countries of Europe between 1913 and 1931. [3]

If it be asked whether each of the fifteen countries *really* imported all the 144 goods of the A-List in each of the three

[1] Comp. *Tariff Levels*, p. 12, § iv.

[2] See in Appendix of Tables the A-List, which shows in the case of each commodity, by indicating the price source, for which country it has a special export importance.

[3] See details in section dealing with this list, Part II.

years and actually imposed the estimated duties, the answer is in the negative. For we are concerned with prominent export commodities of the different countries, and for this reason alone their importation into countries where they constitute the most important export commodities is improbable. (E.g. Southern fruit would scarcely be imported into Italy or timber into Finland or Poland.) Other goods in this list have been excluded from the imports of various states owing to prohibitive duties.[1] In all cases where no importation of these goods in the A-List has occurred, such imports have been presumed according to the prices of the A-List and the height of the duties has been calculated according to the rates in operation. In this way, independently of the question of what importation has actually occurred, we have obtained statistical bases for the tariff levels of the principal European export goods in the fifteen most important European importing countries.

As we are concerned to a considerable extent merely with fictitious imports, the tariff levels so determined have been designated "potential tariff levels."

The momentous changes between 1913 and 1931 are shown in Tables AI (absolute figures of the potential tariff levels) and AII (relative figures of the rates of duty and the potential tariff levels in comparison with 1913). In the second part of the study we shall analyse the details of every country.

(c) *The Averages*

The averages derived by adding together the single duties have proved to be useful even without weighting. For the indices of the League of Nations Memorandum calculated with weighted figures show only slight deviations from its unweighted figures.[2] Moreover, it is the opinion of Mr. *Loveday*, who is by far the best authority on these problems, that

---

[1] Partly, of course, for other reasons unconnected with tariff policy, see p. 38 of this study.
[2] See *Tariff Levels*, tables, pp. 15 and 20, § v.

"the practical importance of weighting may not be exaggerated." [1]

Consequently, all the averages of the potential tariff levels in this work are simple arithmetic means.

On the other hand, it would seem very inappropriate to follow the example of the League of Nations Memorandum, and to give only one figure for a whole tariff and another for the duties upon finished goods.

The tables of the potential tariff levels and their textual analysis in Part II of this investigation show very distinctly in almost all tariffs what great differences have developed in the tariff levels of the three main groups, and within their subdivisions.

These differences, only revealed by detailed subdivision of the list of goods, appear both in regional as well as in temporal comparisons. They are an expression of the great differentiation of the general economic structures of the European countries concerned. To ignore them would render all inquiries into the tariff levels of Europe abortive, so that a calculation of merely a few general averages would obscure these differences, which throw light on the tendencies of tariff policy and the real nature of the tariffs of different countries. The lack of further classified figures for the tariff levels of sufficiently homogeneous groups of goods must therefore be regarded as the weakest side of the admirable Geneva study of 1927. Even at that time, this omission prompted the Belgian delegate *Brunet* to declare that such general figures were too vague and took no account of the profound differences which may exist between various systems of protection. [2]

[1] *Loveday*, p. 510.

[2] See *Brunet's* criticism in *Tariff Levels*, p. 26. Perhaps we should add that the special purpose of the Geneva study was the investigation into the disturbances of world trade by tariffs, which precluded detailed inquiries into single tariffs. *Tariff Levels*, pp. 5, 18, § ii.

(d) *The Prices*

The prices of the goods in the A-List were taken from the official export statistics. This method caused a slight increase in the calculated tariff levels. For both specific duties, and, as a rule, the *ad valorem* duties, are imposed upon the prices of the imported goods at the level which they reach at the frontier of the importing country ("cif. prices"). These cif. prices include at least charges for the freight and insurance for the transport of the goods from the frontier of the exporting to the frontier of the importing country, and are therefore higher than the export prices used here; consequently, the tariff rates of the importing countries represent a somewhat slighter burden than the figures here submitted.[1] But these deviations are only slight [2] and are, moreover, present in all tariff calculations in this study. They have been accepted here in view of the great advantage of all export over import statistics.[3]

(e) *The Duty Rates*

The rates of duty which were employed in the computation of the potential tariff levels were the conventional rates in all cases where commercial agreements have turned the autonomous tariffs into conventional tariffs.

In 1913, 1927, and (still) in 1931 Europe was covered with a network of most-favoured nation agreements, which meant that practically every European country enjoyed the benefit of conventional rates.[4] Autonomous rates have only been employed where conventional tariffs did not exist.[5]

[1] See *Tariff Levels*, p. 14, § xv.
[2] See the slight differences between the figures of method A (import prices) and the method B1 (export prices) in *Tariff Levels*, p. 15.
[3] See p. 28 of this study.
[4] With regard to some exceptions, see p. 30 of this study.
[5] Conventional and autonomous rates for the year 1913 were taken from the publication of the "Deutschen Reichsamtes des Innern,"

(f) *The "Actual Tariff Levels" and the Economic Integration of Europe*

The figures of the potential tariff levels have only been obtained with the aid of the "As if" imports of all the 144 goods in the A-List. The official import statistics, which state only actual imports, could not generally be used for a selection of representative European export goods in order to frame such a general list of goods, to serve as the basis of the comparative calculation of tariff levels: for the variation of imports described by the import statistics is, in fact, to a very considerable extent the *result* of that which has first to be investigated, viz. the changes in the tariff levels and their repercussions upon the actual imports of States.[1] Thus, these "As if" imports were essential for understanding the *general* changes and tendencies of European tariff policy *as a whole*, but they could not explain adequately the *concrete* effects of these changes upon the foreign trade position of the single countries.

It was only possible to estimate the different effects upon the exports of the single countries caused by the changes in the tariff policy of the single countries, if the *actual* exports were contrasted with these changes.

Consequently, we shall endeavour (in the third part of this study) to provide a realistic basis for the sometimes hypothetical figures of the potential tariff levels by calculating the duties upon the principal goods *actually* exported by European countries in 1913, 1927, and 1931. By making generous use of the inquiries of *Gaedicke* and *v. Eynern* and the official export

Systematische Zusammenstellung der Tarife des In-und-Auslandes, vol. A-E, Berlin, 1911–13, hereinafter cited as *Zusammenstellung*, for the years 1927 and 1931, from the current publication of the tariffs and commercial treaties of the world in the official *Deutsches Handelsarchiv*, 1919 et seq. (hereinafter cited as *H.A.*).

[1] This is the reason which from the standpoint of method is decisive, why only export statistics but not import statistics were used here. *Loveday* has discussed these reasons with great lucidity in his lecture, pp. 497–498 and 514–515.

statistics, the export connections of twenty-four European countries, with their most important Continental customers, were taken as the starting-point for the comparison of the changes in the duties imposed upon their important exports between 1913 and 1931.

If therefore, in the investigations of the potential tariff levels, the individual countries figured prominently as *importers* of a constructed representative list of goods, we have considered in the third part the various countries, in the first place, as actual *exporters*.

As the tariffs of the chief customers are different, and as the main exports of each country to different customers may belong to distinct groups of commodities, the averages of the duties upon the important exports of a single country to its customers will also vary. The average of the duties upon the important exports of country A to country B, calculated from the duties in the tariff of country B and the prices of the respective goods in country A, may be called the "national index" of the "actual tariff level" of country B for the imports from country A.[1] The actual tariff level of country B then is the simple arithmetic average of all the national indices for the imports of country B. In this way we obtained, first, figures for the height of duties upon important export goods of countries imposed by their most important European markets (Tables D of the sections of Part III); then, in Tables BI–IV of the Appendix, the averages of the national indices of the actual tariff levels of the larger European import countries have been calculated and the figures thus gained are represented in the Tables B of the Appendix as the figures of "actual tariff levels."[2]

For fourteen of twenty-four European states such tables of actual tariff levels could be compiled in accordance with the scheme of commodities used in the A-List.[3]

---

[1] Comp. *Haberler, Internationale Handelspolitik*, p. 265, Berlin, 1933.

[2] Or of all actual imports of a country as far as recorded here.

[3] Comp. more details about actual tariff levels, pp. 189–191 of this study.

With regard to the sources for the selection of data, little need be stated in supplementing what has been said about the calculation of the potential tariff levels.

Here, too, for the reasons above mentioned we were precluded from using import statistics, and only the export statistics for goods and price ascertainments were taken into account.

In every case where a tariff was tied by conventional rates, these again were treated as the rates actually imposed against all importing countries. To this rule there were two exceptions:

(1) In the estimation of German exports to Poland and *vice versa* from 1927 to 1931 only the autonomous duties could be reckoned owing to the absence of a treaty between the two States at this period.[1]

(2) The same applied to exports from Czechoslovakia to Hungary and *vice versa* in 1931, as the commercial treaty between both countries expired on the 15th November 1930.[1]

The rates of duties of all countries were mostly taken from the *Deutsche Handels-Archiv*.[2]

---

[1] For details see Part III, pp. 218–220, 317-318; 291–292, 327–328.

[2] In a number of cases other sources were available, which are indicated in due course.

III

THE LIMITS OF THE INQUIRY

PRELIMINARY REMARK: *An explanation of the methods which have been employed to measure the potential and actual tariff levels would be insufficient without a supplementary description of their chief difficulties and the theoretical limits of the value of the figures obtained.*

Fundamentally the difficulties which prompted the greatest caution when using the tables were twofold: first, sources of error which arose from the methods themselves—that is to say, "inherent" difficulties. Secondly, considerations which were suggested by comparing the relative importance of tariffs in the system of European post-War commercial policy and in that of the pre-War era.

(a) *Inherent Difficulties of Methods*

(aa) *Selection of Goods and Structure of Custom Tariffs*

It is well known that the export and import statistics of the European countries are compiled in accordance with the scheme of their tariffs. As all attempts to assimilate the tariffs of the different countries to each other with reference to the classification of goods have so far failed, there is no agreement between the items of the foreign trade statistics of one country and the goods scheme of the tariff of another. Consequently, all tariff measurements which, like the present, definitely avoid the employment of import statistics encounter extraordinary difficulties when trying to ascertain the precise equivalent items in the corresponding tariffs for the goods selected as important.

Only in the case of plainly defined standard goods is the solution of this problem a simple one; but otherwise "the variety of tariffs is so great that no one has ever succeeded in compiling a synoptic confrontation of various tariffs." [1]

The more detailed the subdivisions of a customs tariff are, then in order to render protection effective, the greater are the difficulties such a tariff system will offer to the classification of goods taken from more comprehensive schemes of foreign trade statistics.

With few exceptions, Europe's post-War tariffs show a tendency towards great subdivision.

List A of the League Memorandum of 1927 mentions the article "Unbleached cotton yarn, single." When the French tariff for this article was checked, it was found that forty rates of duties had to be consulted to discover this "one" article. [2]

From the material collected in this book two examples of the differentiation of European post-War tariffs may be quoted:

In the Polish tariff of 1924 item No. 167, "Machinery and apparatus," was split up into 50 subdivisions, which again were so specialised that the "one" item No. 167 comprised 167 different rates of duty. [3]

In the Italian tariff of 1921 the item No. 301, "Iron pipes," was subdivided into 70 separate rates. Further difficulties resulted from the variety of units of measure for the same goods in export statistics and in tariffs—difficulties which have sometimes been so great as to make it impossible to continue the calculations because no common denominator could be found.

If in calculating potential tariff levels the list of goods were to take full account of the refined subdivision of important tariffs, it would have to consist of a long series of sharply defined commodities in which the different tariffs would permanently

---

[1] See article by *H. Flach*, "Die internationale Vereinheitlichung des Zolltarifschemas in der europäischen Zollunion," in *Europäische Zollunion*, Berlin, 1926, pp. 206–207, and *Loveday*, pp. 506, 514, on the extraordinary difficulties of "marrying" export statistics and tariff items.

[2] See *Tariff Levels*, p. 19, § iv.

[3] Comp. *H.A.*, 1928, pp. 1023–1024.

deviate. And thus the list would not fulfil the essential condition of representing export importance for several countries.

If actual tariff levels for the export goods of a country were to be calculated according to the schemes of tariffs of the chief customers, such a computation would encounter the same difficulties.

Consequently, in the inquiry that follows we had no alternative, in calculating both potential and actual tariff levels, than to employ a minimum and a maximum rate of duty in the case of all those goods in respect of which the duty rates were not perfectly plain. These two rates confined the "space" within the classification of goods of any tariff whose level was to be measured. As, however, double calculations were necessary for almost all goods in groups B and C, also for many of A, the result in nearly all cases has been double figures of the height of duties. This explains why all tables of tariff levels or single duties contain double figures.

(bb) *The Problem of Price Data*

Prices were often a source of considerable miscalculation. They were taken from the export statistics, which in most cases classify goods belonging to closely related branches of production into smaller groups.[1] For any attempt to record the thousands of *individual* export goods—in the strict sense of the word—would be frustrated by the complexity of the material.[2] Further, in most cases these statistics did not indicate the different export prices for the different markets, but provided

[1] Comp. the essay of *Graevell*, "Scheinbare Widersprüche in der Aussenhandelsstatistik," in *Wirtschaftsdienst*, Bd. 19, Heft 3, 1934.

[2] The greater the number of finished goods among the total volume of exports, the stronger is the tendency to classify in groups of goods, as the production of finished goods is the sphere of greatest differentiation. Consequently, the prices of the trade statistics of the great industrial countries represent averages of groups of commodities which often contain a considerable number of single articles.

only a value per unit for a given weight or piece of an export article, arrived at by dividing the amount of total export value by the amount of total weight (or total number of pieces).

In all those countries whose exports consisted mainly of highly manufactured goods, these export values per unit may lead to considerable error in calculating the height of duties. For great variations appear in the prices of these goods in the exports to different countries.

This may be made clear by an example taken from the trade statistics of Switzerland, in which different export prices were given according to different export markets.

The average value of an exported Swiss gold wrist-watch in 1927 amounted to Sw. Fr. 44·30.

But the regional classification of the prices of this "one" article showed:

1. The value of a watch exported to Italy				was Sw. Fr.	66·90
2. "	"	"	Germany	"	"	55·70
3. "	"	"	Great Britain	"	"	28·00

Every calculation based on the average value of 44·30 would show much too high a figure for the German and Italian specific duties on Swiss watches; while, on the other hand, much too low a figure for the amount of the English duty on Swiss watches, if England had a specific duty.

Yet in the present work the value per unit of the export statistics must be taken as the base of price data, just as was done in the *League Study* of 1927. The choice of regionally different values was precluded by the lack of such detailed export prices.[1]

The choice of exact individual prices, however, obtained by inquiries among exporters,[2] is, on the one hand, possible only

[1] Only in the statistics of a few states, e.g. in the Swiss, Belgian, and German export statistics, are such variations in export values given.

[2] This method was employed by the Vienna inquiry upon the tariff level for 402 Austrian export articles, and produced undoubtedly the best price data for inquiries into the hindrances against the export of only one country (see *Vienna Study*, pp. viii, ix).

in the case of strictly defined individual goods; but, on the other hand, cannot be used for investigations which are to comprise more than one country, as it would be impossible to procure the necessary exact price data.[1]

(cc) *The Problem of the Averages*

The manner in which averages are arrived at deserves special attention. It is known that arithmetical averages only give a true picture of the magnitudes of their elements, if the latter are fairly homogeneous. This is well expressed in the statement of the German delegate *Trendelenburg*, contributed to the League Memorandum of 1927: "Between rates of duty of 0 and $33\frac{1}{3}\%$ no average rate can be calculated which can be looked upon as representative." [2]

The classification of potential and actual tariff levels into nineteen subclasses, however, reveals astonishingly great differences in the levels of the various classes and groups, which were more sharply accentuated in 1931 than in 1927 and 1913. The greatest differences are to be found in group A; also groups B and C seldom show homogeneity in the tariff levels of their classes.

Consequently the averages of the general potential and actual tariff levels, regarded as absolute figures, have the least practical value, as they form the average of nineteen, mostly very heterogeneous class averages; therefore these averages can be hardly representative.[3]

Also the averages of the groups A, B, and C are in each case to be tested by the greater or lesser degree of homogeneity of

[1] See *Loveday*, pp. 498–499.

[2] *Tariff Levels*, p. 28.

[3] The exceptional height of the duties on alcohol, tobacco, and mineral oil products was, in addition to their strong fiscal character, the main reason why, on the one hand, they have been omitted in almost all cases when calculating the average of a whole tariff, and why, on the other hand, in calculating the group averages of A and B, they were only employed to ascertain special group averages (A[2] and B[2]). See Tables A and B in the Appendix.

their class averages, before any opinion can be expressed upon their capacity to represent the tariff levels for foodstuffs, semi-manufactured and finished goods of the country concerned. The class averages everywhere have the greatest practical value for appraising the general tendencies of European tariff levels and of European protection. And even with them it is always necessary to pay attention to duties on single commodities differing very much from their class average.

These considerations prompted us, in computing potential tariff levels, to exclude all those countries which admitted the greater part of their imports duty free, but imposed (often very high) duties on a few articles. These duties alone could be utilised in calculating the potential tariff levels, while the majority of imports, admitted duty free, would not enter into the arithmetical average at all. Great Britain is the chief country we have in mind. Before the War she imposed only a few high duties on alcohol, colonial produce and sugar, while in 1927–31, despite the introduction of numerous new duties, she admitted so many goods of the A–List duty free as to render unfair any comparison with the elaborate tariff systems of other countries.

The same applied to Denmark and Norway, as well as to Holland, whose tariff, while admitting a large number of goods in all groups free, never imposed a higher tax than 5% in 1913, and never more than 8% of the value of the goods in 1927–31. (Exceptions: duties on sugar, alcohol, oils, of which indications have been given in the discussion of the actual tariff levels in Part III.)

(dd) *The Problem of Comparisons*

Finally, a warning must be uttered against inferring proportional differences in the *degree of protectionism* from a comparison of the absolute figures for potential and actual tariff levels of various European countries. *Loveday* has convincingly shown that tariff measurements cannot establish anything of the sort.[1] The decisive reason for this lies in the

[1] *Loveday*, pp. 491–493 and 513.

differences in the economic structure of countries. The American delegate, *T. W. Page*, and the Italian delegate, *di Nola*, were right in emphasizing the point (to which *Haberler* has recently called attention [1]) that the same absolute tariff levels may have entirely different effects upon the exclusion of the taxed goods, according to the *purchasing power* of the countries concerned, and the elasticity of the demand for the taxed products.

The foregoing difficulties of the methods of measuring potential and actual tariff levels will have sufficiently indicated with what caution the calculated figures must be used for drawing conclusions.

The inquiry was continually beset by the same danger: the significance of individual duties was often lost in too comprehensive averages. We have therefore frequently returned, in the textual analysis in Parts II and III, to illustrative examples of *single* duties, which the Japanese delegate, *M. N. Sato*, declared in his remarks to the *League Study*, 1927, to be necessary for an " approach to the problem from the economic point of view." [2]

More importance should be attached to the *relative changes* in tariff levels in the course of time than to the absolute figures. For as the same limitations of method were in force during each of the three test years, and therefore had no appreciable influence on the course of development, there is all the greater reality in the changes revealed by the figures—i.e. the broad lines of development of European tariff policy and tariff levels, especially as the intervals between the years are sufficiently wide to allow structural tendencies to emerge.

In whatever manner the problem of tariff level measurement may be approached, it can only be rightly understood if all the figures are interpreted with the necessary circumspection and if its " extreme complexity " [3] be kept constantly in mind. As is

[1] *Haberler*, op. cit., pp. 263–265.
[2] *Tariff Levels*, p. 35.
[3] Phrase used by the Italian delegate *Nola*; see *Tariff Levels*, p. 34.

justly emphasized in the *League Study* of 1927: " Much more important (than the various absolute figures) are the ratios which the figures bear to one another." And Mr. *Loveday* has even denied great significance to the absolute figures.[1]

(b) *Decreasing Importance of Tariffs in the System of European Post-War Trade Policy*

In the foregoing sections we have pointed out why the statistics we have collected should be interpreted with the utmost caution. We have now to touch upon the question of cause and effect as between tariff levels and import movements, and we must show why the whole problem of tariff levels has no longer the same importance as it had in pre-War times.

Generally it should be borne in mind that *many* causes, such as changes in consumption, bad harvests, national boycott movements, and so on, may operate in bringing about changes in the import structure of a country. Here we were only concerned with those import variations which were exclusively produced by means of a restrictive trade policy. So long as the tariff remains the most effective means at the disposal of national trade policy to reduce imports, absolute height and changes in tariff levels of those countries whose production is integrated deserve the greatest consideration. In such cases, obviously changes in imports and exports can be treated as caused by simultaneous changes in tariff levels.

Much greater caution must be observed in applying the relationships of cause and effect when, owing to vital innovations in protectionism, the number and weight of factors restricting imports undergo change.

The axiom of trade policy of pre-War times was, " that

---

[1] *Tariff Levels*, p. 11, § ii, and *Loveday*, p. 499. Recently (1936) Prof. *J. Viner* has again pointed out the difficulties of ascertaining exact figures of Tariff Levels. See his memorandum "On the Technique of Present-day Protectionism," pp. 58–68, in *Improvement of Commercial Relations between Nations*, Joint Committee, Paris, 1936. Hereinafter quoted as *Carnegie Report*.

impediments to the exchange of goods apart from the imposition of tariffs were inadmissible." [1]

With the fundamental change in the relationship of the State and the body economic which has supervened everywhere in consequence of the World War,[2] the preponderant position of the tariff as an instrument of protectionist policy has been diminished. The trade policy of European States in the post-War period produced a number of entirely new kinds of impediment to foreign competition. Their common characteristic is that in the case of imports they do not seek to influence what is the most important sphere of free economic competition, viz. the price mechanism, as every tariff does, but that they seek in a much more drastic fashion to exclude foreign supplies. The importance of tariff policy and tariff levels for preventing imports which are already impeded otherwise, declines in proportion to the degree and extent of these new instruments of protectionism.

If the whole trade policy of a country is determined by such devices, a tariff and the investigation of its level would be futile. Soviet Russia has been a country of this kind since the introduction of the foreign trade monopoly in the year 1917. Imports and exports are regulated by the necessity of national planning. The laws of free competition, and therefore all possibility of import duties to produce an effect on imports, are abrogated. Consequently, post-War Russia is excluded from our investigations, and only the level of the Russian pre-War tariff is calculated for purposes of comparison with its development in Poland from 1927–31.

The importance of tariff policy for the regulation of imports has also considerably diminished in all those European post-

---

[1] Comp. the essay of G. *Stolper*, "State, Nation, Economics," in *Europäische Zollunion*, p. 49. Comp. also Memorandum of Dr. *Leo Pasvolsky* "On the Technique of present-day Protectionism," p. 50 in *Carnegie Report*.

[2] Comp. A. *Bergsträsser's* Introduction to W. *Greiff's* study, "Der Methodenwandel der Europäischen Handelspolitik im Jahre 1931," *Zur handelspolitischen Lage der Gegenwart*, pp. 4–9.

War countries where "laws to protect the home industry" have been passed, embodying regulations for extending preferences to home over foreign products. How far imports can be restricted without tariffs depends on the progress made by state regulation of economic activities and on the extent of legal regulations concerning consumption.

The Spanish law of 1924 to encourage the development of industry, the Hungarian law of 1925, and that of Italy of 1926 are examples of the commercial policy which Dr. *Stolper* had described in 1921 as "administrative protection"; and which, irrespective of any tariff policy, sought to displace foreign goods in favour of home products, a policy which, in Stolper's opinion, was likely to be more effective than tariffs.[1]

It must also be borne in mind that the imposition of taxes upon imports, besides customs duties, during the post-War period meant very high burdens on the imports of a number of countries, which were not perceptible at all in the tariff levels. As an example may be mentioned the taxes upon imports to cover loan-services, or the requirements of municipal finance, as in Greece, which by commercial agreements with Italy and England were fixed at a maximum of 75% of the duty rates.[2]

Since the world economic crisis of 1929, European trade policy has been marked by ever-increasing efforts to restrict imports by other measures than tariffs.

As examples of such novel devices of trade policy, mention need only be made of the introduction of compulsory milling regulations in the most important corn-importing countries in 1929 and 1930; of the French prohibition of mixing French with foreign wines as from 1930, and of regulations for compulsory mixing of alcohol with petrol in Germany and Czechoslovakia.

Instead of the single device of the tariff, a much more com-

---

[1] See *Stolper*, op. cit., p. 57; further *Jones, Tariff Retaliation*, examples of Italian administrative protection, pp. 73–75; also *Greiff*, op. cit., in many places.

[2] *H.A.*, 1926, p. 2267; 1928, p. 253.

plicated trade policy attempted, in an ever greater degree, to regulate the development of European imports. Since the autumn of 1929, it is therefore no longer possible to co-relate striking variations in imports *only* with extreme simultaneous changes in tariff levels, nor to regard them strictly as cause and effect.

Nevertheless, with the exception of Russia, tariffs have been the most important means of regulating imports in Europe [1] until much more effective measures were found in the system of a new commercial protection. Thus, the figures relating to potential and actual tariff levels in 1927 and also in 1931 do retain great importance for an understanding of the protectionist tendencies in Europe.

From about the end of the year 1931, however, quotas or exchange restrictions (or a combination of both) have become the most important instruments of commercial policy, accompanied by numerous new devices of administrative protectionism: such as import preventives, import monopolies for specific goods, preferential agreements, import licences, etc. Tariffs as an instrument of commercial policy have without doubt taken a second place—so that it has been rightly said that "quotas and exchange restrictions, and not tariffs, were now the chief weapons in the commercial war." [2]

Because of this receding of tariffs, it appeared advisable not to carry the present book beyond the year 1931 in so far as its statistical inquiries were concerned. A later evaluation of tariff levels will only be useful when, with the abolition of

---

[1] See *World Trade Barriers in Relation to American Agriculture*, Report, 1933, Washington, hereinafter called *Trade Barriers*, p. 2: "Before the World War and during the prosperous years which preceded the present depression, tariff duties were by far the most important means of restricting imports." Comp. also *Pasvolsky*, loc. cit., p. 51.

[2] See *H. Hauser*: "Des causes économiques de guerre dans le monde actuel," *Revue Economique Internationale*, vol. iv, 1934, p. 239; further, see *Trade Barriers*, pp. 50 et seq., and *L. Robbins, The Great Depression*, p. 115. Comp. also *Pasvolsky*, loc. cit., p. 51, *J. Viner*, loc. cit., p. 72.

quotas and exchange restrictions, some degree of freedom in the exchange of European goods is resumed, wherein tariffs will again play a leading part in regulating imports.

If, after considering all these many factors necessitating a cautious interpretation of the figures marshalled in this study, it be finally asked wherein, then, consists the value of the submitted measurements of tariff levels and their confrontation with the characteristic export and import connections, we would reply:

A knowledge of tariff levels in Europe up to the year 1931 is indispensable to form a judgment on the evolution of protectionist tendencies in post-War Europe, and to perceive the dangers to the economic integration of Europe which grew out of these tendencies even before the world economic crisis, and became much more pronounced after it.

Further, measures which were born of the crisis, or which were deliberately applied to effect a structural change in foreign trade, and which have led since 1931 to an unparalleled shrinkage of foreign trade, may be found to have their roots in changes in tariff levels prior to 1931. We must, however, emphasise our warning—quoting the leading expert on this question, Mr. *Loveday*—against drawing conclusions as to the "degree of protection" in individual countries from the absolute figures of their tariff levels. For this purpose an exact knowledge is required of the *entire* economic structures of the countries concerned.

No measurement of the tariff level of a country is useful, therefore, unless it be regarded as merely one way among others of gaining such knowledge: but it may prove impossible to gain this information without inquiries into tariff levels.[1]

---

[1] See *Loveday's* concluding words on the necessity and limits of measuring tariff levels in his London lecture, op. cit., p. 528.

PART II
OUTLINES OF EUROPEAN TARIFF POLICY AND DEVELOPMENT OF POTENTIAL TARIFF LEVELS BETWEEN 1913 AND 1931

I

INDUSTRIAL AND AGRARIAN STATES; AGRARIAN AND INDUSTRIAL TARIFFS IN EUROPE

IN the following pages we will discuss, country by country, the statistical presentation of the potential tariff levels of thirteen pre-War and fifteen post-War states in Europe (Tables AI). For some countries, comparisons have also been made between the potential tariff levels of 1913, 1927, and 1931 in addition to comparisons between the rates of duties for the same years (Tables AII of Appendix).

The thirteen states of 1913 concerned are the following: Austria-Hungary, Belgium, Bulgaria, Finland, France, Germany, Italy, Roumania, Russia, Serbia, Spain, Sweden, and Switzerland.

The fifteen states of the post-War era are: Austria, Belgium, Bulgaria, Czechoslovakia, Finland, France, Germany, Hungary, Italy, Jugoslavia, Poland, Roumania, Spain, Sweden, and Switzerland.

The reasons why we have omitted Great Britain, Denmark, Norway, and Holland have already been explained.[1] We have also refrained from compiling tables of potential tariff levels for Albania, Greece, and Portugal, owing to the slight importance of these countries as markets for European goods both in pre-War and post-War times.[2] For the same reasons we have compiled no tables for Ireland, Lettland, Estonia or Lithuania; but when discussing the actual tariff levels, the tariffs of these states will be partially taken into account. All comment upon the potential tariff levels of a country takes the year 1913 as the starting-point, in order to emphasize the characteristic changes

---

[1] See p. 36 of this study.

[2] Bulgaria, whose importance as an import market is also very slight, is included in the investigation as the characteristic representative of high protectionism of the Balkan countries.

during the post-War period as reflected in the figures of 1927 and 1931 by comparison with the figures of an economically more stable and better balanced Europe.

The underlying assumption which governed the classification of the whole of our material—both the grouping of the countries and the subdivision of goods—was that basic conception of an agrarian "Border" Europe ("Rand-Europa") and an industrial "Central" Europe ("Kern-Europa"), which was first apprehended in its full significance by Professor *A. Weber*,[1] and subsequently investigated in all its aspects by *Délaisi, Schlier,*[2] *Gaedicke* and *von Eynern*.

We propose to discuss the potential tariff levels *apart* from the detailed and concrete foreign trade connections of the countries concerned, apart from the regional stratification and intensity of the integration of their production with other European countries; thus we can carry through an uninterrupted analysis of the characteristic changes between 1913 and 1931 in the potential tariff levels of the most important groups of European exports and in the tariff policy of all prominent European importing countries. Therefore, it will at first be sufficient to divide the countries generally into agrarian and industrial countries, and to divide the duties into duties upon:

Goods of the agrarian sphere of production (group A, classes AI–VI of the Tables A and B).
Goods of the industrial sphere of production (groups B and C, classes BI–V and CI–VIII of the Tables A and B).

By goods of the "agrarian sphere of production" are to be understood different kinds of foodstuffs as well as live animals, i.e. raw materials and partly and wholly manufactured goods

[1] See *Alfred Weber*, "Europa als Weltindustriezentrum und die Idee der Zollunion" in *Europäische Zollunion*, pp. 122 et seq., and the same in "Industrielle Standortlehre," p. 86, in *Grundr. der Soz.-ok.*, vol. vi.

[2] *Schlier, Aufbau der europäischen Industrie nach d. Kriege*, Berlin, 1932.

which are used for human food.[1] The definition of these goods is that adopted by the Kieler investigation into German foreign trade.[2] Accordingly all duties on the goods in classes AI–VI are designated "agrarian duties."

On the other hand, all agrarian raw materials which are destined for industrial purposes (especially the products of forestry) and all other partially and wholly manufactured goods, as the products of industrial processes, are designated as "industrial goods," and divided into group B (semi-manufactured goods) and group C (finished industrial products).[3]

The duties on the goods of classes BI–V and CI–VIII thus represent the group of industrial duties (duties on semi-manufactured and finished goods).

As regards the classification of the countries investigated into the two groups of industrial and agrarian countries, only the composition of their exports could be decisive for an inquiry into tariff levels and their significance for Europe's foreign trade connections.

All European countries, whose exports of semi-manufactured and finished goods during the years 1913, 1927, and 1931 constituted more than 50% of their total exports, were designated as industrial countries.[4]

According to this selective principle the following countries belonged to "industrial Europe" ("Central Europe" = "Kern-Europa"):

(a) 1913: Belgium, Germany, France, Italy, Switzerland (also Great Britain, which was left out of the inquiries for 1913).

[1] Raw tobacco and some alcoholic beverages also have been included in group A.

[2] *Der deutsche Aussenhandel unter der Einwirkung weltwirtschaftlicher Strukturwandlungen.*" vol. i, p. 9, hereafter cited as *Enquête,* I or II.

[3] A certain arbitrariness of definition is unavoidable in such classifications. Thus, group A must be taken to include a number of semi- and wholly manufactured foodstuffs, but preponderantly it contains raw materials of foodstuff production.

[4] As regards the composition of the exports of European countries, see Table II of the Appendix.

(b) 1927–1931: Belgium, Germany, Great Britain, France, Italy, Austria, Switzerland, and Czechoslovakia.

All the remaining countries of Europe belonged to "agrarian Europe" [1] thus:

(a) 1913: Bulgaria, Finland, Austria-Hungary, Roumania, Russia, Sweden, Serbia, Spain. (Denmark, Greece, Holland, Norway and Portugal are omitted as stated.)

(b) 1927: Bulgaria, Finland, Poland, Roumania, Sweden, Spain, Hungary, and Jugoslavia. In addition to Russia, the countries under (a) are excluded.

In order to elucidate as distinctly as possible the general development of tariff policy and of potential tariff levels in Europe, we shall first discuss concisely the changes in agrarian tariffs, and afterwards deal with the variations in the levels of industrial tariffs, considering first the industrial states and then the agrarian states.

By subordinating in this manner the regional classification to the classification of goods, it was impossible to show all the potential tariff levels and the entire tariff policy of a country at once, but the great differences which have developed between agrarian and industrial tariff levels throughout Europe in post-War times could be demonstrated much better by such an arrangement of the material. Before this, however, the nature and composition of the general goods list must be explained in somewhat greater detail.

[1] Here we have to apologise that in contradiction to the above classification of agrarian raw materials for industrial purposes in the group of industrial economy, the export countries of this raw material (wood)—Sweden, Finland, Norway, Poland, Roumania, Yugoslavia—were included in the "agrarian Europe"; but the main concern was the export of the raw materials of industry, and the countries concerned could not therefore be described as industrial exporting countries. See *Enquête*, II, p. 346.

STRUCTURE AND ARRANGEMENT OF THE GENERAL GOODS LIST (A-LIST)

(See A-List in Appendix)

THE great differentiation of the general economic structure of the European countries and of their exports has produced a great variety in the kind and number of the important European export products. Every type of commodity (agrarian products, raw materials, semi-manufactured and finished goods) is represented in the exchange of European goods. An idea of the magnitude of values involved may be gathered from the table given below.

TABLE: EUROPEAN CONTINENTAL EXPORTS[1]
(In Milliards of M. (Rm.) and %)

Class	Milld. M. 1913	% of C.E.*	Milld. Rm. 1928	% of C.E.
Total Continental exports .	25·6	100·0	40·4	100·0
Divided into:				
Agrarian goods . .	5·9	23·0	9·2	22·8
Raw materials and semi-manufactured goods .	11·2	43·8	17·3	42·8
Manufactured goods .	8·5	33·2	13·9	34·4

* C.E. = European Continental exports = exports of European countries to European markets.
  M = German Mark.
  Rm = German Reichsmark.

Each of the three great production groups comprised goods to the value of many milliards. The A-List sought to do justice to this diversity by a comprehensive division of the three branches of production into classes and by maximal regional distribution of the different goods of the classes selected from the export statistics as being particularly important.

[1] Comp. *Gaedicke*, text volume, pp. 132–133.

As "normal price" of a commodity, i.e. as price of the most rational European producer, we have put in the A-List the export price of that country for whose export the article in question was especially important; in the case of a commodity simultaneously exported by many countries, as far as possible, the price of the largest exporter. Such a normal price was the basis for all calculations of the potential tariff levels of each of the fifteen importing states. For it may be assumed that the largest exporter of a product works in the most favourable natural and technical conditions of production under which with free competition it may be sold in the world market.[1]

The goods selected for ascertaining the potential agrarian tariff levels—viz., the tariff levels of group A—have been divided into six classes.

AI comprises the five most important varieties of cereals, in addition to the two most important semi-manufactured goods of grain production: wheat and rye flour. The countries of east and south-east Europe, and in lesser degree such countries as Germany and France, were particularly interested in this class of exports.

The chief motive in compiling classes AII and AIII was the importance of the export of live stock and dairy produce to the foreign trade of the countries of north and east Europe, as well as Holland, and also Spain and Portugal (sardines in oil).

The chief purpose of class IV was to stress the importance of fruit and vegetable exports for the Mediterranean countries, for France and Holland: with the inclusion of potatoes and hops, important German and Czech export goods were also represented.

Among "other foodstuffs" we have included in Av manufactured foodstuffs, among which sugar represents a very general European export product (e.g. from Germany, Czechoslovakia,

---

[1] See the essay by *H. Gross*: "Strukturelle Voraussetzungen wirksamer Industriezölle," in *Weltwirtschtl. Archiv*, vol. xxxv, 1932, pp. 446–447, on the "Normal structure" of the exports of manufactured goods of a country.

Poland, Belgium, Hungary, etc.), while margarine, cocoa powder, chocolate and olive oil ought to be included in the A-List, owing to the great importance they have achieved among the exports of a number of European countries (Holland, Germany, Italy, Switzerland, Spain, etc.).

Finally, Avi contains four representative commodities which were of vital interest for the export structure of countries in the south and south-east of Europe (Spain, Portugal, Italy, Greece, Bulgaria, Jugoslavia), and also of France. For the reasons mentioned,[1] we have made double calculations in order to arrive at a second figure of the potential tariff levels of group A in all cases where the duties of class Avi have been exceptionally high (averages "A²").

In group B, which related to semi-manufactured industrial goods, we were not interested in goods which entered European countries free of duty—such as skins, hides, ore, wool, flax, logs, etc.

Of great interest, on the other hand, was a tolerably representative selection of those very numerous—and for European exports so representative—semi-manufactured goods which, being 43–44% of the whole of Continental exports, formed the backbone of the European exchange of goods.[2]

Class Bi comprises eleven semi-manufactured textile articles belonging to the cotton, wool, silk, artificial silk, and linen industries, also the leather industry, which were of special importance for the textile exports of Great Britain, France, Belgium, Switzerland, Czechoslovakia, and Italy, and, in a smaller degree, of Germany.

Class Bii comprises four important semi-manufactured wooden and paper goods of the export of the Scandinavian and Baltic countries, of Poland, Roumania, and Jugoslavia; in addition to one semi-manufactured cork commodity, which is very important for Spain and Portugal.

With the selection of fourteen semi-manufactured goods in

[1] See p. 35, note 3.
[2] See *Gaedicke*, pp. 22–23.

class B$_{III}$ we have endeavoured to include at least the most important semi-manufactured products among the highly specialized exports of the great iron and steel industries of Germany, Great Britain, France, and Belgium, and their smaller competitors, Czechoslovakia, Austria, Poland, Sweden, Norway, and Switzerland.

Special difficulties were encountered in making a selection of semi-manufactured chemical products, as has been attempted in class B$_{IV}$. The production of chemical basic materials, of dyes, photographica, fertilizers, cosmetics, and pharmaceutica, is so differentiated as to frustrate any inquiry which attempts to be even approximately comprehensive.

Only eight outstanding products could be selected from the semi-manufactured chemical exports of leading European countries (Germany, Great Britain, France, and Switzerland), to which three finished products—"non-alcoholic perfumes," "sundry medicaments," and "ordinary soaps"—have been added, as their insignificant number and small share of Europe's total chemical exports did not appear sufficient for the compilation of a special class in group C.

Finally, class B$_V$ comprises mineral and coal-oil products, which have been so important in post-War times, owing to the changes in modern power technique. Oil and petrol were important for the exports of Roumania, in a lesser degree of Poland, benzol for the exports of Germany, Belgium, and Great Britain. As these products were nearly everywhere subjected to exceptionally heavy fiscal duties, like the goods in class A$_{VI}$, two average figures have been computed for group B in exactly the same way as for group A.[1]

The greatest difficulty in every selection of goods for calculating representative tariff levels is presented by the group of *manufactured articles*. With the increasing degree of

---

[1] The great difference between the averages for group B in the figures for B^1 and B^2 in the tables A$_I$ show that without this separation a completely misleading increase in the tariff levels of group B would have been the result.

industrialization the differentiation attains an extent that is often hardly conceivable. To mention one example. For the German *small* iron industry alone a range has been ascertained of about 3500 different products.[1]

The present selection of sixty-two manufactured goods of group C, divided into eight classes, could not therefore represent anything more than a list of particularly characteristic export goods of the leading European industrial countries; these were goods the export of which, by its relative proportion to the total export of manufactured goods, was calculated to supply information about the chief industries of finished goods of these countries.

Class CI includes nineteen finished textile goods (besides leather, ready-made and hosiery goods of the cotton, wool, silk, and artificial-silk industries) the export of which was of great importance for the leading European textile-exporting countries such as Germany, France, Switzerland, and Austria, of secondary importance only to Great Britain, Italy, Belgium, and Czechoslovakia.[2]

The three outstanding finished goods of the paper industry are set out in class CII (pasteboard, printing paper, and packing paper). Since the War they were very important export articles of Germany, Great Britain, North Europe, and Austria.[3]

For countries with export industries in the field of cement, glass, and china production (particularly Germany, Belgium, France, and Czechoslovakia) six articles have been selected in CIII.

The production of the iron and steel industry, as well as of industries devoted to the manufacture of copper, aluminium, and precious metals, splits up into so many separate articles that any list of goods claiming to be representative ought to

[1] See *Enquête*, II, p. 242.
[2] On the differentiation in European textile industries see *Enquête*, II, pp. 219 et seq.
[3] See *Enquête*, II, pp. 52–54 and 144–145, as to growth of paper consumption and exports of the world.

contain a very high and very precisely defined number of individual articles. Again, as in the case of the chemical products, the goods selected from the *small-iron* and copper industries in Civ are only some of the biggest items of European exports of this kind. The exporting metal industries of Germany, England, France, Austria, and Czechoslovakia were particularly interested in the development of the duties of this class.

As regards the great engineering industries in Germany, England, Switzerland, Belgium, France, and Sweden, which are old-established, but of which some did not develop a strong export until after the War, a list of fourteen types of machines has been set out in class Cv, which at least aims at representing the biggest export branches of this very differentiated industry, especially the industries concerned with power, textile, and metal machines.

To this class we have added in Cvi the three most important products of the pre-War and post-War vehicle-building industries: railway engines, private cars, and commercial vehicles.[1] The principal export industries of this branch are to be found in Germany, France, Italy, England, and Belgium.

In class Cvii are included nine articles belonging to industries engaged in manufacturing apparatus and instruments, which, owing to the special development of radio and electro exports, played an important part in the export of a number of countries, especially in the relevant industries of Germany, England, Switzerland, Sweden, and Holland.

Finally, class Cviii includes two manufactured articles, tires and toys, the inclusion of which in a representative list of European manufactured commodities is justified by the high proportion of their export to their total output and the growing demand for them in modern economy. The European export centres of these industries are to be found particularly in Germany (toys), France, and England (tires).

To enable us to survey the characteristic changes of the prices of the A-List, the prices of its nineteen classes have been

---

[1] Ships omitted, as they are mostly duty free.

added in the three test years, 1913, 1927, and 1931. For each class the unweighted arithmetical average has been calculated and expressed as a percentage of 1913 (1913 = 100); then group averages were gained by adding the class averages of each of the three main groups, A, B, and C.

From these three group averages finally a total index of the price level of all goods has also been calculated.

In tables AII [1] the relative changes in the duty *rates* for the same classes and groups and in the general potential tariff levels of 1927 and 1931 (1913 = 100) have also been ascertained. These calculations made it easy distinctly to separate the part played by the two factors which alone could cause a change in any tariff level framed by specific duties: the prices on the one hand and the development of rates of duty on the other.

This has been done in the summaries of the study concerning the general trends of the European potential tariff levels.

[1] Although calculated for all fifteen countries, only three of the tables AII are printed here (Germany, Italy, Switzerland).

III

OUTLINES OF EUROPEAN AGRARIAN TARIFF POLICY AND DEVELOPMENT OF POTENTIAL AGRARIAN TARIFF LEVELS, 1913–31

A. INDUSTRIAL (CENTRAL) EUROPE

PRELIMINARY REMARK: *The centres of European agrarian imports*

THE centres of Europe's great agrarian importations both before and after the War were the industrial countries, paramount among which were Great Britain, Germany, France, and Italy. In 1913, Belgium and Switzerland were also important in this respect: after the War, Belgium, Switzerland, Austria, and Czechoslovakia. (We should also mention Holland, which, according to our classification, is part of agrarian Europe.)

In analysing the potential agrarian tariff levels of industrial Europe we have first considered those of the great industrial countries and then those of the smaller countries. As England, the greatest importer of agrarian products, was excluded from our survey we have observed the following order: Germany, France, Italy, Belgium, and Switzerland, and as from 1927 the two succession countries of Austria and Czechoslovakia.

1. GERMANY [1]

(See Tables AI and AII for Germany in Appendix)

The grain duties formed the backbone of German agrarian tariff policy before the War.[2] Table A shows the paramount importance of grain imports to the total of German agrarian

---

[1] Most of the German duty rates brought into calculation were taken from the edition of the German tariff by Hartisch, 1925, and revisions, 1931; supplements from the *Reichsgesetzblatt* and the *H.A.*

[2] Comp. the outline of German agrarian commercial policy by Prof. *W. Röpke* in his book, *German Commercial Policy*, chap. vi, pp. 40–53. London, 1934.

imports, caused by the high deficit in the home production of grain for bread and fodder.

TABLE A: GERMAN AGRARIAN IMPORTS, 1913–1931 [1]

Group	1913 Mill. M.	1913 % of A.I.	1927 Mill. Rm.	1927 % of A.I.	1931 Mill. Rm.	1931 % of A.I.
Total Import . .	10,770	—	14,230	—	6,730	—
Agrarian Import .	3,050	100·0	4,500	100·0	2,025	100·0
Divided into—						
Corn and flour .	960	31·4	1,600	35·6	252	12·5
Butter, eggs, cheese .	351	11·5	755	16·8	453	22·4
Live-stock, meat .	107	3·5	296	6·6	62	3·1
Fruit, vegetables .	282	9·2	565	12·5	455	22·5

A.I. = Agrarian import.

The German grain duties therefore achieved their object: they guaranteed to German agriculture grain prices considerably higher than those in the world market.[2]

The German wheat duty was about 38%, the maize duty about 31%. The highest duty, viz. 45%, was levied on wheat flour. (Thanks to the import certificate system (*Einfuhrscheine*) Germany was an exporter of flour, in spite of the dearness of wheat.) The average of the German grain and flour duties of class AI varied between 27 and 29% in 1913.

Only parts of the second great field where German agriculture had to compete with foreign imports, i.e. dairy farming and meat production, were protected before the War by protectionist duties, especially meat production (duties 26 to 34%). The duties on live-stock were correspondingly high. The great group of dairy products, however, enjoyed but slight protection, and on the average duties were not higher than 20%.

Fruit and vegetables were subjected either to very moderate

---

[1] See *Der auswärt. Handel Deutschlands*, 1913–27, and *Monatl. Nachweise ü.d. ausw. Hand. Deutschl.*, 1931–32. The figures for slaughtered cattle, meat, fruit, and vegetables in *Enquête*, I, S. 208, 202–203.

[2] Comp. *Enquête*, I, S. 170–185.

duties, or, as in the case of a number of southern fruit, to somewhat higher fiscal duties. A number of vegetables, which have become particularly important in post-War times, like tomatoes or cauliflower, were duty free. The tariff level of this class reached, in 1913, 19–20%.

All German agrarian duties of 1913 were surpassed by the duty on raw sugar (90%).

Much higher than any of the other class tariff levels was the German tariff level for alcoholic drinks and tobacco, which amounted to 58–64% in 1913.

The general German agrarian tariff level reached 21–22%, if we exclude class AVI, and of 27–29%, if we include it, although a number of very important duties were considerably above this average; while others, especially on vegetables, fruit, and dairy produce, were appreciably below it (see Table D on p. 64).

The War, the Treaty of Versailles, and the years of inflation up to 1923 brought about a complete change in the agrarian situation. From 1919 until about 1924 Germany became dependent on foreign supplies to an unprecedented extent, so that the removal of duties upon all important classes of agrarian goods during the War remained extensively in force until 1925.[1] When Germany regained her commercial freedom on the 1st January 1925, she had to decide whether she would revert to the system of pre-War protection or not. German economic science decided overwhelmingly against this policy,[2] but the dominant political forces took the contrary view.

The result was the reconstruction of a German agrarian tariff in the years 1925–26, which in 1927 contained higher specific rates of duty for all the six classes of group A than the tariff of 1913.[3]

German agrarian duty rates for 1927 were on the average about 55–65% higher than those of 1913. Within the different

---

[1] See Harms, *Zukunft der deutschen Handelspolitik*, p. 72 and 6ˣ 7ˣ.
[2] Ibid., op. cit., pp. 150–154, and *Röpke*, loc. cit., p. 33.
[3] See for details Table AII.

classes, however, interesting differences may be discerned. While the rates of duty for corn, alcohol, and tobacco remained at almost the 1913 level, the class of dairy produce showed an increase of 35%, and that of vegetables and fruit an increase of 45%.

Even greater, indeed by 80%, was the rise in duty rates for class Av, the rates for chocolate and cocoa being increased by 100 to 200%. The rates for sugar, on the other hand, decreased by 40%. The sharpest increase, however, related to the duty rates for live-stock (150–180% over those of 1913 on the average: horses, 200%; cattle, 100%; pigs, 80%).

As, however, the price level of all classes compared with 1913 had changed in the direction of an almost universal increase of prices (about 29% for all the thirty-eight commodities),[1] the considerably increased agrarian duties of 1927 effected only a moderate increase in the potential tariff level compared with 1913, for which the figures for the general agrarian tariff level of 1927 provided a good basis (25–30%).[2]

It must be borne in mind, however, that in the case of a series of commodities, which were very important, prices rose so much more than the German duty rates that the corresponding duties were considerably lower than in 1913, e.g. for wheat, maize, butter, cheese, pork, sugar, while a number of other articles (barley, wheat, flour, beef, grapes, etc.) were considerably higher taxed (see Table D, p. 64).

The figures of Germany's potential agrarian tariff level in the year 1931 presented a picture of extraordinary changes, whether they be compared with the figures of 1927 or of 1913. They express the complete revolution in German agrarian policy which had taken place between 1927 and 1931, especially since the outbreak of the world economic crisis in the autumn of 1929. Already up to the year 1929, especially under the influence of reparations policy, those forces which insisted upon the utmost self-sufficiency for Germany in the sphere of corn

---

[1] See Index Table of A prices in Appendix.
[2] Including tobacco and alcohol, 30–36%.

production, and strong protection for other agricultural industries such as live-stock raising, meat production, dairy industry, and sugar-growing, had continued to gain ground and had effected the reconstruction of the German agrarian tariff of 1925 et seq. The collapse of the world corn prices, since the autumn of 1929, provoked the attempt to "sever" German agriculture from the world market, and to compel the German consumer to absorb the whole home output of cereals and to use German rye and German potatoes instead of foreign grain food. Consequently, prices were driven up to a level which was far above those of world market prices. Only if the supply of German grain failed should acute needs be covered by imports.

The laws of 22nd December 1929 and 26th March 1930 marked a fundamental change in the existing German practice of fixed corn duties, by establishing a sliding scale in order to keep the home price at a definite level.[1] Since those dates the German corn and flour duties have risen to unprecedented heights in a race with falling world prices; so that, for example, the tariff level of class AI (grain and flour) reached the figure of 186% in the year 1931 (see Table B).

TABLE B: GERMAN CORN DUTIES, 1913–31
(Duty for each Ton shown in M. or Rm.)

Goods	1913 (M.)	1929 (Rm.)	1931 (Rm.)
Wheat	55	65	250
Rye	50	60	200
Barley	13–40	50	180–200
Wheat flour	102	145	430

Already these duties, unexampled as they were in the history of German agrarian duties, would have sufficed to effect a comprehensive restriction of German grain imports. But as world prices for barley and maize constantly fell, and the maize

[1] See *Enquête*, I, pp. 174–177, "Kalender der deutschen Getreidepolitik."

duty was fixed, the desired degree of exclusion as regards German food consumption perhaps would have failed. Further, as regards the stimulation of the consumption of rye for human nourishment, every tariff policy might have proved powerless against the diversion of consumption from rye to wheat, which had begun to show remarkable progress in Germany as well as in western Europe and North America.[1]

Consequently, since the middle of the year 1929 German agrarian policy adopted fresh legal measures to exclude foreign corn supplies from the German market, and these measures have grown more drastic and comprehensive as the world agrarian crisis developed. As early as 4th July 1929 Germany introduced a *compulsory milling* regulation, which prescribed how much German grain German mills had to consume. The quota then amounted (with a duty of 65 Marks per ton) to 40%. Since 16th August 1931 (with a duty of 250 Marks per ton) it was increased to 97%. The effect was the practical exclusion of all imports of wheat and rye.[2] With regard to maize, a selling monopoly was established in 1930, which nearly destroyed those maize imports which could not be prevented by a tied low duty.

The result of this policy was the shrinkage of grain and flour imports, exhibited in Table A, from 1·6 Milld. Rm. in 1927 to a minimum import of 0·25 Milld. Rm. in 1931, while the internal grain price level was kept far above the world market level (see Table C)—in other words, a very far-reaching separation of German grain production from the world market. While in 1913 grain imports accounted for 10·4% of the whole of German imports, this proportion had fallen to 4·4% in 1931.[3]

---

[1] See *Ohlin: Courses and Phases of the World Depression*, p. 21, and *Röpke*, loc. cit., pp. 52, 56–57.

[2] See *Trade Barriers*, pp. 380–381.

[3] The figures taken from *Memorandum sur le commerce extérieur international*, vol. i, Geneva, 1927, hereafter cited as *Memorandum*, and *Statistiques du commerce extérieur*, 1931–32, Geneva, 1933, hereafter quoted as *Statistiques*, ii.

TABLE C: GERMAN AND WORLD MARKET GRAIN PRICES, 1913–31

(In M. and Rm. per 100 kilos (annual average))

Goods	1913 Berlin	1913 World Market	1929 Berlin	1929 World Market	1931 Berlin	1931 World Market
Wheat	18·80	14·90	22·80	19·90	24·90	10·80
Rye	15·50	10·90	19·20	18·50	18·30	7·60
Barley	15·10	12·30	18·50	15·00	18·70	11·10

See *Stat. Jahrbuch für d. dt. Reich*, 1934, p. 161.
World Market = London for wheat, New York for rye and barley.

The protectionist tendencies in the sphere of live-stock breeding and meat production, already observable in 1927, received fresh impetus from the sharp fall in live-stock and meat prices on the world market since the outbreak of the crisis. Between 1929 and 1931, for example, Germany increased the duties on pigs and cattle to such an extent that the average of the rates of duties of class AII was 200% over that of 1913, and the potential tariff level for this class of live-stock in 1931 rose to 40–63% (350–450% of the level of 1913).

The duties on meat were correspondingly raised, in order to prevent a shifting of imports from live stock to meat (duties on fresh beef and pork higher than 50%). These increases were the chief reason why imports of live-stock declined from a value of 78 Mill. Rm. in 1929 to 2·2 Mill. Rm. in 1931, those of fresh meat from 22·4 to 5·5 Mill.[1] On the other hand, the duties on the chief articles in the category of dairy produce up to the year 1931 remained far behind the duties on corn, cattle, and meat (tariff level of class AIII, 28–29% = 44%–45% increase compared with 1913), and the decline in total imports of dairy produce from 755 Mill. Rm. in 1927 to 453 Mill. Rm. in 1931 was much less severe than the collapse of wheat, meat, and live-stock imports.

Not until Denmark, chief supplier of butter to Germany, devalued her currency in October 1931, causing a sharp fall in

[1] See *Enquête*, I, p. 223.

the world butter price and provoking severe competition, at prices with which German butter producers could not compete, did Germany, from 1932 onwards, adopt defensive measures in the sphere of dairy produce as drastic as in other spheres (duty increases, quotas, fat monopoly), measures which need not be more fully described here.

Up to 1931 German tariff policy was also moderate in its dealings with vegetables and fruit imports. Here, too, measures devised to cut imports were not adopted until the years 1932 and 1933, and such measures were particularly directed against vegetable imports (duty increases, quotas, currency restrictions).

On the other hand, the 1927 sugar duty of only 10 Rm., which was nearly 50% below the pre-War rate, did not remain very long at this moderate level. In July of the same year it was increased to 15 Rm.; in the beginning of 1929 to 25 Rm., rising to 32 Rm. at the end of March 1930. It remained at this level throughout 1930 and 1931. As the world sugar price, owing to the competition of Javanese and Cuban cane sugar, had been constantly falling since 1924–25 (in 1927 the world market price of sugar was 24·90 Rm., in 1931 it dropped to 9·25 Rm.),[1] the sugar duty of 25 Rm. represented an enormous protectionist burden on German sugar consumption (height of the duty, 1929 = 98%). The 1931 duty, however, amounted to almost 300% of the raw sugar price and almost 250% of the refined sugar price, the prices at which Germany exported her own sugar to foreign countries. It has only been by a combination of this tariff policy with a rigid regulation of German production and consumption by means of a sugar cartel that the German sugar market has also been cut off from the world sugar market, which so far as the German consumer of 1931 was concerned signified an internal German sugar price of more than 400% above the level of the world market price.[2]

---

[1] Sugar price ex Hamburg. Comp. *Stat. Jahrbuch f. d. dt. Reich*, 1932, p. 127.

[2] See exposition of German sugar policy in *Enquête*, I, pp. 195–203.

In view of such a growth in many duties it is not surprising that Germany's general agrarian tariff level in the year 1931 reached an extraordinary height. Excluding class AVI, the result was a general tariff level for thirty-four goods in group A of from 79–86%—i.e. almost four times the level of 1913.

TABLE D: DUTIES UPON IMPORTANT AGRARIAN
COMMODITIES IN GERMANY, 1913–1931
(*In % of prices*)

Commodity	1913	1927	1931
Wheat . . .	38·0	29·0	212·0
Barley . . .	18·5	25·2	180·0–203·0
Wheat flour . .	45·0	49·0	326·0
Pigs . . .	18·5	16·8	54·0
Fresh pork . .	34·4	23·0	51·0
Butter . . .	8·2	7·9	21·0
Raw sugar . .	91·5	31·6	280·0
Cocoa powder . .	35·0	147·0	214·0
Tobacco (raw) . .	43·5	24·2	63·0
Wine in casks . .	24·5–49·2	30·0–68·0	49·5–69·0

The result of this agrarian tariff policy, combined with a series of other import-restricting measures, was the reduction of imports of those agrarian products which Germany could produce herself from 14·5% of her total consumption in 1926 to 4·8% in 1931.[1]   In other words, there was nearly self-sufficiency in wheat and rye, and small import requirements of grain fodder; imports of live-stock and meat were reduced to insignificant figures, while home sugar supplies were completely sufficient for home demand. On the other hand, imports of dairy produce, vegetables, and fruit still remained large.

The effects of these radical changes in agrarian tariff policy and agrarian tariff levels of the second largest agrarian import market of Europe upon the connections with its chief suppliers must be of an extraordinary character. In Part III of this book

[1] Comp. *Enquête*, I, p. 251.

we shall discuss these questions more fully when we come to analyse the effects of German tariff policy on the exports of the countries concerned.[1]

2. FRANCE [2]
(See Table A1 for France in Appendix)

To a far greater extent than Germany, France, even before the War, was independent of the importation of foreign agrarian products.

In the supplementing of corn, live-stock, and meat requirements—in the post-War era to a somewhat greater extent in the consumption of dairy produce and fruit, too—France, however, relied on large imports (comp. Table A).

TABLE A[3]: FRENCH AGRARIAN IMPORTS, 1913–1931
(In Mill. Francs and %)

Group	1913 Mill. Frs.	1913 % of A.I.	1927 Mill. Frs.	1927 % of A.I.	1931 Mill. Frs.	1931 % of A.I.
Total Imports .	8,420	..	53,000	..	42,200	..
Agrarian Imports .	1,820	100·0	13,950	100·0	14,000	100·0
Viz.:						
Corn . . .	566	31·0	4,550	32·4	3,000	21·4
Fodder and oil seeds	390	21·4	2,320	16·6	1,460	10·4
Meat . . .	39	2·1	840	6·0	920	6·6
Fruit . . .	88	4·8	720	5·2	1,315	9·3

A.I. = Agrarian Imports.
See *Tableau général du commerce extérieur de la France*, 1913/I, 1927/II, 1931/IV.

As with Germany, the pre-War structure of French agrarian imports was largely determined by the requirements for wheat,

[1] See in Part III of this work the description of exports to Germany, especially from the south-east states, Poland, Denmark, and Holland.

[2] For settling French tariff rates use has been made of *Eichhorn, Zollhandb. für Frankreich*, 1929, the *dt. Reichsgesetzbl.*, 1927, Part II, as well as the *Dt. Handelsarchiv (H.A.)*.

[3] In this as in all other tables, imports of colonial produce, being products of countries outside Europe, will, of course, be ignored.

E

barley, and maize, their proportion of total agrarian imports being over 50%. The tariff level of class AI (grain and flour) reached 27-31% in 1913, wheat being considerably over, (35%) and barley and maize considerably below, this average (see Table A on p. 65).

The highest duty was imposed on sugar. In 1913 it amounted to between 100-125%, and, in conjunction with high duties on cocoa powder and chocolate, made the tariff level of class Av, with 45-60%, the highest of all of the six classes of group A, even with the inclusion of alcoholic beverages, which were not taxed highly in France.[1]

On the whole, the French pre-War agrarian tariff, with a general tariff level of 27-31% and its very high duties in a number of cases, presented the picture of a decidedly protectionist agrarian tariff policy, a character which since the effects of the heavy imports of Russian and overseas corn to Europe at the commencement of the eighties of the nineteenth century had grown still more distinct in the new tariff of 1892 and its reform in 1910.[2]

From the troubles of the War and the French post-War inflation a new French tariff emerged at the end of 1927, based upon the Franco-German Commercial Treaty of 1927.[3] Formally, it was only the "changed" tariff of 1910; but in reality it was a completely new instrument of French tariff policy,[4] especially by the revision of hundreds of rates of the French minimum tariff, tied for several years in advance.

The most interesting thing about this new French tariff of 1927 was the fact that its general agrarian tariff level, like the levels of all classes of group A, was considerably *lower* than

[1] We have therefore refrained from calculating a general average figure for France in Table AI, without class AVI.

[2] See *Trade Barriers*, p. 108, and *Nogaro-Moyes, Politique douanière de la France*, pp. 54 et seq.

[3] Supplemented by Commercial Treaties in 1928 with Belgium and Switzerland.

[4] See *Proix, Pol. douanière de la France*, pp. 4-5; *Nogaro*, op. cit., pp. 105 et seq.

the figures of 1913. The new duty rates remained almost the same as in 1913 (the average increase of duty rates in group A was only 5–10%), so that, with the agrarian prices of group A higher by an average of 30%, the tariff level of group A declined to 17·7–20·6% (about 43% below the tariff level of 1913). An enumeration of the various goods and classes of goods is unnecessary (see Table B, p. 68). Manifestly, the protectionist tendencies of the French tariff of 1927 were not to be found in the sphere of agrarian protection.[1]

This was altered at the beginning of the world economic crisis of 1929. By laws dated 3rd December 1929 and 19th April 1931, the French Government, in exercise of powers originating from pre-War times, changed autonomous duty rates *par decret*, an act which required subsequent ratification by parliament, but which avoided time-wasting parliamentary debates; and the duties thus affected increased from 46 items in the year 1929 to 162 items up to the year 1931. It was chiefly agrarian duties, not consolidated by commercial treaties, that were substantially increased by this means up to the end of 1931, prominent among which were the duties on corn, flour, live-stock, meat and milk products, sugar and wine.[2]

As a whole, the agrarian duty rates of group A were in 1931 40–50% higher than in 1913; the rates of duty upon corn and flour duties 80–100% higher; those in respect of class Av and Avi 65–80% higher.

Even sharper was the rise in the tariff levels of single classes, the prices of which had fallen very heavily. Thus the tariff level of class Ai reached 98–102%; of class Av 90–99%; in the case of wine, 35–55%. With a height between 49% and 57%, the general agrarian tariff level was 80% above that of 1913, and had therefore almost doubled. From Table B it can be seen what extremely high duties such important commodities as wheat, maize, barley, pork, sugar, etc., had to pay.

[1] *Trade Barriers*, p. 109, and *Proix*, op. cit., p. 4.
[2] See *Proix*, pp. 22–23.

TABLE B : DUTIES UPON IMPORTANT AGRARIAN COMMODITIES IN FRANCE, 1913–1931
(In % of Prices)

Goods	1913	1927	1931
Wheat . . .	34·5	23·0	180·0
Barley . . .	23·2	13·6	39·2
Maize . . .	25·0	17·0	39·5
Wheat flour . .	39·0–57·0	42·0–56·0	160·0
Pigs . . .	24·0	10·0	36·5
Lard . . .	37·0	27·0	73·0
Fresh pork . .	27·0	14·5	58·0
Raw sugar . . .	125·0	46·0–54·0	200·0–240
Wine in casks . .	51·1	44·0–88·0	59·0–118

These figures showed how strong agrarian protectionist tendencies had become in France under the pressure of falling world prices from 1929 onwards. But they only partially expressed these tendencies. France, too, promptly decided to apply more drastic import restrictions, in addition to tariffs, which were introduced chiefly in respect of wheat and wine, the two most important French agrarian products threatened by foreign competition.

On the 1st December 1929 a compulsory milling regulation of French wheat was introduced, the quota fluctuating between 70% and 97%.[1] The law of 31st December 1929 prohibited the mixing of French with foreign wines, which in the case of Spain, in view of the high alcoholic content of Spanish wines, signified their practical exclusion from the French market.[2]

With the application of a quota system for all imports of live-stock, meat, butter, cheese, and sugar, which was completed by the end of 1931,[3] and the introduction of the licence system for the importation of these groups of goods,[4] France, as one

[1] See *Trade Barriers*, pp. 371–372.
[2] See *Jones*, op. cit., pp. 47–48, as to effects of this policy. See also Part III of this study, pp. 336–337.
[3] See *Greiff*, op. cit., pp. 61–63.
[4] *Trade Barriers*, pp. 374–375.

of the leading European importing countries, resorted distinctly to some of the most drastic of those new commercial devices which have largely pushed tariffs into the background.

The heavy increases in a number of duties and the application of other import-restricting measures, resulted in France, too, in an extensive reduction of imports; especially of corn imports, the absolute value of which declined by 33% compared with 1927, while their share in the total of agrarian imports fell from over 50% in 1913 to 32% in 1931.

At the same time the French price level of the protected goods was kept considerably above the world market level.[1] When, in spite of this protectionist policy, imports of live-stock, meat and fruit, in contrast to the German experience, still showed big increases compared with 1913, the reason was to be sought in the differences of economic conditions. In France the world economic crisis did not make itself felt until 1931,[2] whereas in Germany and in many other European countries, it had been exerting severe pressure since 1929 or 1930.

3. ITALY
(See Tables A1 and A11 for Italy in Appendix)

Despite a preponderantly agrarian population and despite large exports of the products of poultry-farming, of fruit and wines, Italy had to import in pre-War and post-War years large quantities of corn, cattle, dairy produce, and sugar.

Table A contains the most important data of Italian agrarian imports between 1913 and 1931. With a proportion of not less than 67% of agrarian imports, corn imports, which in the case of Italy comprised wheat imports for human, and maize imports for animal consumption, constituted by far the most important item of agrarian imports. In 1913 the total imports of corn and flour reached nearly 13% of the total Italian imports.[3]

[1] See *Proix,* op. cit., pp. 24–27.
[2] *Proix,* op. cit., p. 3.
[3] See Memorandum.

The aim of agrarian tariff policy in pre-War Italy, as in Germany and France, was chiefly to stimulate home corn production by high duties. The Italian wheat duty of 1913

TABLE A: ITALIAN AGRARIAN IMPORTS, 1913–1931
(*In millions of Lire and %*)

Group	1913 Mill. Lir.	1913 % of A.I.	1927 Mill. Lir.	1927 % of A.I.	1931 Mill. Lir.	1931 % of A.I.
Total Imports .	3,650	—	20,400	—	11,640	—
Agrarian Imports .	700	100·0	5,320	100·0	3,000	100·0
Viz.:						
Wheat . . .	400	57·0	3,000	56·5	840	28·0
Other cereals . .	67	9·6	320	6·0	285	9·5
Meat, fresh and manufactured .	? *	? *	240	4·5	170	5·7
Cattle . . .	4	0·6	156	2·9	220	7·3

* No data available.   A.I. = Agrarian Imports.
See *Movimento commerciale del regno d'Italia*, 1913/27/31.

reached the unusual height of 42%. Maize was charged with a duty between 10% and 65%, according to the quality of the product. Wheat flour was likewise strongly protected (41%); the tariff level of class AI stood between 30% and 37%.

Duties on live-stock, meat, dairy produce, fruit and vegetables were very moderate. This also applied to alcoholic beverages,[1] while the import of tobacco was conducted by a monopoly.

But the sugar duty formed a striking exception. For raw sugar, it reached 350–400% (refined sugar 270–300%), a height unprecedented in pre-War times, but fiscal needs, as well as protectionist aims, were responsible for such duties. The tariff level of class Av (114–127%) was only due to these duties.

If we include this class Av, Italy's general agrarian tariff level for 1913 reached 30–40%; but if we exclude it, we get a

---

[1] For this reason, the calculation of double average figures for the agrarian tariff level in Tables AI and AII was unnecessary for Italy, as for France.

figure of 20–24%, which corresponded more nearly to the pre-War agrarian tariff policy of Italy.[1]

With the seizure of political power by Fascism, the character of Italian agrarian policy was completely changed. The movement towards self-sufficiency, especially in the sphere of wheat consumption, the increase of production in all other branches, in order to make the country independent of foreign food supplies, was fostered by entirely novel methods, made possible only by revolutionising the relationship of State and economics. The new policy was inaugurated in the year 1925 under the slogan of "battaglia del grano." Its characteristic features were not the raising of duties, but quite different devices, directly applied in a revolutionary manner to home production, such as confiscation for bad cultivation, production and export premiums, extension of the area cultivated, propaganda of new methods of cultivation, etc., which occupied first place in the endeavour to raise production.[2]

It is true, duties were increased for a number of articles, but were left at the pre-War level in the case of many commodities, which, in view of the rise in prices, mostly meant a fall in the tariff level compared with 1913.

For instance, in the very important class of corn and flour duties no changes in rates occurred, so that the 1927 tariff level of class AI (21–26%) declined by 30% compared with 1913. The same holds good with regard to most articles of classes AII–AIV. If, nevertheless, the figures of their tariff levels were higher than in 1913, this was due to one or two sharp duty increases in each class, which had outweighed the decreases among the rest.

In 1927 Italy's *general agrarian tariff level* reached 21·3–28%, and was therefore about 30% below that of 1913.[3]

The world economic crisis accelerated this relatively stable agrarian tariff policy, although, up to 1931, only in respect of

---

[1] Therefore in Table AI, two average figures for group A in 1913.
[2] Comp. *Trade Barriers*, pp. 410–414.
[3] Or, by excluding class AV in 1913, 10–15% above it.

the corn, flour, and sugar duties. Through various increases between 1929 and 1931 corn and flour duties in Italy, too, reached a prohibitive level. The tariff level of class AI, with 89–131%, was in fact between 200 and 250% higher than in 1913. Wheat was subjected to a duty of 144%; and in June 1931 Italy introduced a compulsory milling regulation for wheat.[1]

The lower sugar duty of 1927 was, as in Germany, of brief duration. With the rapidly falling world price of sugar, the duty increases of the years 1928 and 1930 raised the Italian duty on raw sugar to 200–230%, and that on refined sugar to 160–270%.

In 1931 the general agrarian tariff level reached a height of between 45 and 64% (an increase of between 50 and 60% compared with 1913), for which the exceptional increases in duties on corn, flour, and sugar must be held almost exclusively responsible (see Table B).

TABLE B: DUTIES ON IMPORTANT AGRARIAN COMMODITIES IN ITALY, 1913–1931
(In % of Prices)

Commodities	1913	1927	1931
Wheat .	41·5	27·0	144·0
Wheat flour .	41·0	40·0	186·0
Raw sugar .	346·0–390·0	27·0–40·0	195·0–290
Cocoa powder .	26·0	90·0	150·0
Wine in casks .	48·0	37·0–61·0	37·4–62·0

The result of this combination of duties and other import-restricting measures in Italy, as in Germany and France, was, in the first place, a vast decline in corn imports during the year 1931. The proportion of corn imports decreased from 67% of total agrarian exports to 37·5%, from a value of 467 millions gold lire to 305 millions gold lire between 1913 and 1931.

In 1932 Italy largely increased the duties on other agrarian

[1] Quota 95%, see *Trade Barriers*, pp. 414–415.

products, such as butter, live-stock, and meat. They were combined with the compulsory consumption of Italian live-stock (quota: 85%),[1] and other measures, which here also lessened still more the importance of duties, although the latter, more than in any other country of capitalist Europe, and long before the beginning of the world economic crisis, had become, through the extensive State control of economy, one only of many devices for reducing imports.

4. BELGIUM

(See Table A1 for Belgium in Appendix)

Among the two pre-War and four post-War small industrial states of Europe, Belgium and Switzerland occupied a position of considerable importance for international trade in foodstuffs, thanks to the high purchasing power of their population and their great agrarian import requirements.

In the case of Belgium (like that of Holland), owing to her geographical position, this importance has been increased by the extraordinary transit traffic [2] in large quantities of such agrarian staple products as corn, coffee, etc. Consequently, the agrarian tariff policy of Belgium should first be discussed as that of the greatest importer among the two (or four) smaller industrial countries. In this connection, the effects of this transit trade must not be neglected; these only can explain the astonishingly high import and export figures of Belgium agrarian trade, as they appear in Table A. Dr. *Leener* calculated the proportion of the transit trade at 24% of the total export and 33% of the total import of pre-War Belgium.[3]

Belgian agrarian imports were characterized by a very high percentage of corn and fodder grain. While grain and its products formed 13·3% of the total Belgian imports in 1913,

---

[1] *Trade Barriers*, p. 417.

[2] Greater in pre-War than in post-War times.

[3] Comp. *Leener's* essay, "Commerce" in Mahaim: *La Belgique restaurée*, p. 254.

and as much as 14·4% in 1927, their share was still 8·7% in 1931, in spite of the sharp fall in the price of corn.[1]

TABLE A: BELGIAN AGRARIAN IMPORTS, 1913–1931
(*In Mill. Frs. or %*)

Group	1913 Mill. Frs.	1913 % of A.I.	1927 Mill. Frs.	1927 % of A.I.	1931 Mill. Frs.	1931 % of A.I.
Total Imports .	4,640	..	35,500	..	24,000	..
Agrarian Imports .	1,100	100·0	7,300	100·0	5,700	100·0
Of which:						
Corn . . .	600	54·5	4,000	54·5	2,000	35·0
Fresh meat . .	2	0·2	380	5·2	390	6·8
Butter . . .	21	1·9	30	0·4	380	6·7

A.I. = Agrarian imports.
See *Tableau général du commerce de la Belgique*, 1913/27/31.

In the post-War period imports of live-stock products reached a respectable position, but in spite of that fact most of the demand for meat and dairy produce, as well as for fruit and vegetables, was covered by the highly developed Belgian dairy industry, whilst the densely populated and highly industrialised country was mainly dependent upon imports for supplies of corn and grain fodder.

In these circumstances, and in view of the vital importance of the transit trade, Belgian agrarian policy before the War could only be of a free-trade character.[2] An analysis of the tariff levels of the various agrarian classes of goods was therefore of little interest, especially as the most important goods entered free of duty, while the remainder were subjected to very moderate duties (see Table B, p. 76). Only two characteristic exceptions deserve mention: the duty on raw sugar in this "free trade" country was as much as 80% in 1913, and that on grapes 60%. Both were products of important branches of agriculture, and were exported in considerable quantities.

[1] See *Memorandum et Statistiques*, II.
[2] See *Trade Barriers*, p. 311.

Consequently, protectionist aims must be presumed in this case.

In 1913 the general agrarian tariff level for Belgium, excluding class AVI, reached a height of 25·5%. Including this class, it was 39·5%, owing to the very heavy fiscal duties on wine and tobacco. In connection with these figures, which were surprisingly high for a free-trade country, it must be borne in mind that they were the result of comparatively few duties, some of which were very high, whilst the majority of important goods admitted free did not enter into the calculation at all. In spite of these figures, therefore, it is quite correct to describe Belgium as a free-trade country.

This free-trade policy was reinforced by the new Belgian tariff of 1924, the basis of Belgian commercial policy in post-War times, which appreciably reduced pre-War rates of duty, as the new rates fixed in paper francs mostly failed to catch up with the depreciation of the pre-War franc. Consequently, the Belgian agrarian tariff level of 1927, with a height between 9·9 and 13·7%, was 53–64% below the figures of 1913.

After the beginning of the world economic crisis this moderate agrarian tariff policy was changed in relation to some important commodities, especially as regards live-stock, meat, butter, and sugar. Various duty increases (or the imposition of duties on goods hitherto exempt) in 1930 and 1931 brought the general agrarian tariff level of 1931 up to a height between 21 and 26%, or 26–33%, including class AVI. The raw sugar duty reached as much as 100% in 1931. As nearly all duty increases in these two years took place in the sphere of dairy farming and sugar cultivation, i.e. in the main fields of Belgian agriculture, corn being still admitted free even in 1931, it cannot be denied that Belgian agrarian policy henceforth revealed a protectionist bias. In 1932 Belgium also introduced a *compulsory milling* regulation (albeit on very moderate lines) (quota 5–25%) as well as import licences.[1]

---

[1] See *Trade Barriers*, pp. 311–312.

TABLE B: DUTIES UPON IMPORTANT AGRARIAN COMMODITIES IN BELGIUM, 1913–1931

(*In % of Prices*)

Commodity	1913	1927	1931
Wheat, rye, barley, maize,	Duty free	Duty free	Duty free
Wheat flour . . .	7·1	2·0	3·6
Fresh pork . . .	Duty free	Duty free	14·0
Raw sugar . . .	79·0	29·0	100·0
Raw tobacco . . .	38·0	24·0–47·5	69·0–128·0

5. SWITZERLAND [1]

(*See Tables AI and AII for Switzerland in Appendix*)

Switzerland's agrarian import requirements, both before and after the War, were covered by large grain imports, whilst home agriculture, adapting itself to the qualities of the soil, concentrated upon the production of dairy produce and the finer sorts of fruit, so that a considerable quantity of milk products were exported in the form of cheese and condensed milk (also as milk chocolate), whilst meat, butter, fruit, vegetables, and sugar were imported in considerable quantities. Imports of corn and corn products were 13·1% of the total imports in 1913; 10·5% in 1927, and 8·3% in 1931.[2] Table A contains the most important data in connection with Swiss agrarian imports, 1913–1931.

Before the War Switzerland's agrarian tariff policy was very moderate. Including alcohol and tobacco duties, the general tariff level reached only 12–16%, and the exceptional figures of classes AI and AIV are explained by the height of a single duty in each group, whereas the remaining goods were as lightly taxed as in general the other agrarian products.

The introduction of the new Swiss tariff of 1921 brought about a fundamental change in agrarian tariff policy. Almost

---

[1] For ascertaining Swiss duty rates use has been made of *Napolski, Zollhandbuch d. Schweiz*, 1927; *Zolltarif der Schweiz*, 1931; *Deutsch. Handelsarchiv (H.A.).*

[2] See *Memorandum and Statistiques*, II.

all the rates were increased, some of them very heavily. The tariff then existing was conceived as an adaptation to the great rise in the price level, which was a consequence of the gold inflation during the War, and it was intended that agriculture should, at least, enjoy as much protection as was afforded to it by the pre-War tariff. As, however, its rates remained in force even when prices were falling rapidly after 1922, the agrarian tariff level of Switzerland was bound to show a corresponding rise.[1] These tendencies were well expressed by the increase of duty rates for classes AI–VI, which in 1927 reached on an average 300–500% of the rates of 1913.

TABLE A: SWISS AGRARIAN IMPORTS, 1913–1931
(*In Mill. Francs and %*)

Group	1913		1927		1931	
	Mill. Frs.	% of A.I.	Mill. Frs.	% of A.I.	Mill. Frs.	% of A.I.
Total Import .	1920	—	2560	—	2250	—
Agrarian Import	600	100·0	695	100·0	590	100·0
Of which:						
Corn . .	232	38·6	270	34·0	192	32·4
Animal foodstuffs	99	16·5	120	17·0	127	21·5
Vegetables, fruit .	50	8·3	82	11·8	96	16·2

A.I. = Agrarian imports.
Comp. *Stat. des Warenverkehrs der Schweiz mit dem Ausland,* 1913/27/31.

The wheat and rye purchasing monopoly introduced in the year 1915 was retained, and assured the Swiss farmer stable prices above the world market level; the duties upon these two commodities were not more than statistical fees.[2]

The general agrarian tariff level (excluding class AVI) reached between 17 and 26·5%, and was thus 33–57% higher than in 1913.

Duty increases were particularly heavy in the case of live-

[1] Comp. *Reichlin, Der schweiz Zolltarif u. seine Schutzwirkung,* pp. 11–12, and *Trade Barriers,* p. 499.
[2] *Trade Barriers,* pp. 500–501, and *Reichlin,* op. cit., p. 17.

stock and animal foodstuffs. Slaughtered pigs, cattle, horses, meat, eggs, and cheese had to pay increased duties (compare Table B, below). As the duty increases were definitely confined to the products of Swiss agriculture, the protectionist character of these duties is unmistakable.

Between 1927 and 1931 Swiss agrarian tariff policy, even after the outbreak of the world economic crisis in 1929, remained comparatively stable. The reason being that in these two first years of the crisis especially the corn prices fell very rapidly, but the wheat and rye monopoly, which continued to exist in an altered form from 1929, protected Swiss cereal cultivation. On the other hand, the sharp fall in prices, in the main spheres of Swiss agriculture, did not start, in the case of most of the important commodities, until the middle or the end of the year 1931. Then fresh increases of duty were introduced.

TABLE B: DUTIES ON IMPORTANT AGRARIAN COMMODITIES IN SWITZERLAND, 1913–1931

(In % of Prices)

Commodities	1913	1927	1931
Wheat . . .	1·7	2·0	5·7
Wheat flour . .	9·0–71·0	15·5–138·0	27·5–244·0
Pigs . . .	16·0	26·0–32·5	36·0–48·0
Fresh pork . .	10·6	40·0	65·0
Fresh beef . .	11·6	25·0	32·0
Butter . . .	6·6	4·6	62·0
Raw sugar . .	20·0	5·1	140·0
Raw tobacco . .	13·0	40·0–280·0	50·0–350·0

In particular, it was dairy farming, the most important branch of Swiss agriculture, which was to be protected against foreign competition by high butter duties since 1929, especially since Swiss cheese exports were impeded more and more, and Swiss dairy farming was to be indemnified by closing the Swiss market to foreign butter supplies.[1] The 1931 rate of duty of

[1] Comp. *Reichlin,* op. cit., pp. 15–16.

180 Frs. per 100 kilos represented 900% of the rate of 1913. Very sharp, too, were the duty increases on potatoes, pigs, and sugar. In 1931 the general agrarian tariff level (without AvI) reached 32·5–52%, and was thus 160–210% above the level of 1913. In this connection, such classes as live-stock (29–33½%), dairy produce (43%), other foodstuffs (especially duties on sugar and margarine) (over 50%) showed very high tariff levels.

In the year 1932 Swiss agrarian policy resorted extensively to the new import reducing measures which were everywhere coming into force, by introducing a quota system and licence regulations for nearly all agrarian imports.[1]

6. AUSTRIA[2] (1913: AUSTRIA-HUNGARY)
(*Comp. Table A1 for Austria in Appendix*)

The disintegration of Austria-Hungary by the Peace Treaties of 1919 increased the number of European industrial states by two, compared with the pre-War number. One of the two most important, predominantly industrial, districts, viz. Austria, with its industrial centre of Vienna, became the Austrian Republic, while Bohemia and Moravia became the Czechoslovakia Republic, just as the Hungarian portion of the former empire was incorporated in the new state of Hungary, whilst the remainder of the territory was divided amongst Yugoslavia, Roumania, Poland, and Italy.

In these circumstances we could not furnish comparisons with 1913, so far as the newly formed succession countries were concerned, as the analysis of statistical data pertaining to the same areas for 1913 would have offered insurmountable difficulties. On the other hand, when considering tariff policy and tariff levels, the rates in force in 1913 belonging to the Austro-Hungarian pre-War tariff of 1906, out of which the Austrian, Hungarian, Czechoslovak post-War tariffs arose,

[1] Comp. *Trade Barriers*, pp. 499–500.
[2] For ascertaining Austrian duty rates use was made of: *Müller-Roth-Weiss, Der oesterr. Zolltarif*, 1927, and *Zolltarif für das Gebiet der Republik Oesterreich*, Vienna, 1931; also of the *Dt. Handelsarchiv*.

proved useful when we attempted to throw light on the changes in the tariff policies of the succession countries.

Whereas the Austro-Hungarian monarchy, as a preponderantly agrarian country, with important industrial centres, represented a happily balanced economic area in pre-War Europe, the boundaries drawn by the Treaty of Saint-Germain created in the new state of Austria an area which depended on high agrarian imports. Table A contains the important facts of this situation.

TABLE A: AUSTRIAN AGRARIAN IMPORTS, 1927–1931
(In Mill. Schill. and %)

Group	1927		1931	
	Mill. Schill.	% of A.I.	Mill. Schill.	% of A.I.
Total Import .	3090	—	2160	—
Agrarian Import .	1065	100·0	680	100·0
Of which:				
Corn and flour .	337	31·5	188	27·5
Cattle . . .	277	26·0	168	24·8

A.I. = Agrarian imports.
Comp. *Statistik des auswärtigen Handels Oesterreichs*, 1927–31.

Austria is mainly dependent upon imports for her supplies of corn, live-stock, and meat. Austrian peasant agriculture, like the Swiss, is chiefly devoted to the raising of dairy produce, poultry, vegetables, and fruit.

This was reflected in the Austrian tariff of 1924, and the subsequent tariff changes and commercial treaties.

Compared with the strongly protectionist rates of the Austro-Hungarian tariff of 1906, the duties on corn and flour, on live-stock and meat were greatly reduced, while the duties on dairy produce, vegetables, and fruit were appreciably raised (comp. Table B, p. 81). The potential general agrarian tariff level of Austria in 1927, being 16–17% (excluding the tariff level of class AVI), was between 42 and 45% below the Austro-Hungarian pre-War level. Only one class, "other foodstuffs" (Av), reached a level about 30% above 1913, by reason of heavy duties on sugar, chocolate, and cocoa.

From the beginning of the world economic crisis, Austrian agrarian tariff policy took a protectionist turn, also with regard to goods not hitherto protected. Thus the tariff level of class AI (corn and flour) reached 96% (=200% of the 1913 level). Very heavy increases were also made in the duties on live-stock, meat and butter, especially on sugar (comp. Table B), so that the tariff levels of the classes of live-stock, dairy produce, and other foodstuffs revealed great rises compared with 1927.

TABLE B: DUTIES UPON IMPORTANT AGRARIAN
COMMODITIES IN AUSTRIA, 1927–1931
(1913: Austro-Hungarian Duties)
(*In % of Prices*)

Goods	1913	1927	1931
Wheat	36·0	1·1	72·0
Wheat flour . . .	57·0	4·6	187·0
Pigs	2·5–37·0	8·0	23·2
Fresh pork . . .	33·0	8·1	13·2–28·0
Butter	8·5	20·2	30·5
Raw sugar . . .	21·5	43·0	218·0
Cocoa powder . . .	90·0	118·0	170·0

Austria's general agrarian tariff level in 1931 reached a height of 57–62%, and was thus 100–110% above the 1913 level of the Dual Monarchy. Although Austrian duty rates of 1931 were on the average only 20–40% higher compared with those of 1913, the falling prices of agrarian products brought about this sharp raising of the tariff levels. These duties, however, which were very high for a country needing agrarian imports, were not yet sufficient for Austrian agrarian policy; for in 1932 the quota system was introduced for the most important agrarian products (butters, pigs, beef,. fats, etc.), while drastic currency restrictions for all imports had been in force since October 1931.[1]

[1] See *Trade Barriers*, p. 308.

F

7. CZECHOSLOVAKIA [1]

(Comp. Table A1 for Czechoslovakia in Appendix)

In spite of the fact that Bohemia, with her very important industry, makes Czechoslovakia a member of industrial Europe, a few branches of Czechoslovak agriculture, such as wheat, barley, hops, sugar cultivation, together with related branches of live-stock breeding, are considerably developed. Large quantities of barley, hops, and sugar were exported, whilst other branches of agrarian consumption were dependent on imports. Table A shows the largest of these agrarian import groups.

TABLE A: CZECHOSLOVAK AGRARIAN IMPORTS,
1927–1931
(In Mill. Cz. Crowns and %)

Group	1927		1931	
	Mill. Cr.	% of A.I.	Mill. Cr.	% of A.I.
Total Imports .	18,000	—	11,800	—
Agrarian Imports .	4,480	100·0	2,715	100·0
Of which:				
Corn, flour, pods .	2,170	48·5	1,040	37·4
Cattle . . .	720	16·0	223	8·2
Animal foodstuffs .	560	12·5	480	17·7
Vegetables, fruit .	650	14·6	550	20·2

A.I. = Agrarian imports.

Comp. *Der Aussenhandel der tsch. Republik,* 1927, 1931, and *Memorandum on International Trade,* 1927, 1929, hereafter cited as *Statistiques,* I; and *Statistiques du commerce extérieur,* 1933, hereafter cited as *Statistiques,* III.

In consequence of the political and economic separation of the great agrarian surplus territories of the Austro-Hungarian Dual Monarchy from the dense population of Bohemia, the territory which since 1919 forms the Czechoslovak Republic

---

[1] For ascertaining Czechoslovak duties we have consulted *L. Waertig, Zolltarif d. tsch. Republik,* 1927–30, and the *Dt. Handelsarchiv.*

has been much more dependent upon foreign agrarian supplies than in 1913. This explained, why the Czech customs tariff of 1921 and the following years only incorporated the rates of the old Austro-Hungarian tariff with considerable modifications, which consisted partly of a reduction of the Czech rates compared with the Austro-Hungarian rates of 1913 (comp. Table B, p. 84). The Czech duties on corn, live-stock, and dairy produce in 1927 were considerably lower than those of Austria-Hungary in 1913; in the case of corn and flour, for example, the Czech tariff level of class AI, with 22%, reached only 51% of that of 1913. On the other hand, already in 1927 the Czech duties on vegetables and fruit, as well as on the goods of classes Av and Avi, were considerably higher than in 1913. Nevertheless the general agrarian tariff level of Czechoslovakia in 1927, with a height of 35–38%, was only from 22–30% above the Austrian of 1913, thanks to the retarding influence of the duties of the above-mentioned three classes.[1]

The reactions of Czech agrarian tariff policy to the world economic crisis consisted chiefly of heavy increases in the duties on corn, flour, live-stock, and meat. In 1931 the average of the duties on corn and flour reached a height of 111% (i.e. 260% of the 1913 level), for live-stock 24–63% (or 280–350% of 1913), for animal foodstuffs, owing mainly to very high duties on meat, 56–57% (or 190% of 1913).

By 1931 the general agrarian tariff level had risen to 78–89% (or 270–290% of 1913). Of 38 commodities of group A, only 14 were taxed below 30%, 5 below 50%, 4 had to pay duties between 50 and 100%, 15 duties above 100%. Czechoslovakia also had gone over to an extreme agrarian protectionism.

Moreover, this tariff policy was only a part of Czech commercial policy, which had been employing other protectionist devices long before the outbreak of the crisis. Since 1926 an elaborate import licence system had been in existence for the corn trade, in 1930 a compulsory milling regulation was

[1] The duties on alcoholic drinks and tobacco were excluded from this calculation.

introduced for Czech rye and wheat (quota 75–95%), further, a licence system for imports of cereal, meat, and dairy products, which, without imposing duties, could exclude any undesirable imports. At length, in 1932, the whole of the grain and flour trade was brought under the jurisdiction of a Czech importing syndicate.[1] Thus in Czechoslovakia also, owing to the employment of these devices, tariffs ceased to play the leading part in the regulation of imports since 1931.

TABLE B: DUTIES ON IMPORTANT AGRARIAN
COMMODITIES IN CZECHOSLOVAKIA, 1927–1931
(1913: AUSTRO-HUNGARIAN DUTIES)
(*In % of Prices*)

Goods	1913	1927	1931
Wheat	36·8	16·5	89·5
Rye	34·8	20·5	104·0
Wheat flour . . .	57·0	25·0	127·0
Pigs	2·5–37·0	2·7–10·2	15·1–87·0
Fresh pork . . .	33·0	14·8–24·8	102·0
Cauliflower . . .	Duty free	21·6	40·0
Raw sugar . . .	21·5	133·0	366·0
Raw tobacco . . .	91·5	228·0	340·0

B. AGRARIAN (BORDER) EUROPE

PRELIMINARY REMARK: *Foodstuff and Raw Material Countries in Agrarian Europe*

We have already observed [2] that we have reckoned as part of agrarian Europe also those countries whose exports consisted largely of timber (rough or very little worked). Prominent among these countries were Sweden and Finland, which might better be described as "raw material countries," whilst the rest of the timber-exporting countries of Europe—the Baltic countries, Poland, Roumania, and Yugoslavia—were also such substantial exporters of foodstuffs that they could also be

[1] Comp. *Trade Barriers*, pp. 346–350.
[2] Comp. p. 48, note 1 of this study.

designated as "foodstuff countries," together with the remaining agrarian countries of Europe.

The analysis of the potential agrarian tariff levels in the proper foodstuff countries could usually be made much more summarily than the discussion of the agrarian tariff policy and agrarian tariff levels of the great food-importing countries of industrial Europe. For the tariff policy is of little importance in countries where a product is abundant in relation to the effective home demand and where its internal production and distribution are not artificially restricted by cartels or other devices. But such prospects for a successful tariff policy existed only in a few countries for few products (e.g. sugar in Germany, Hungary, etc.). It was sufficient, therefore, to outline the general tendencies in the agrarian tariff policy of the foodstuff countries of Europe, and to emphasize striking changes that have occurred.

On the other hand, the analysis of the agrarian policy of Sweden and Finland deserved greater attention, as here we were concerned with two raw material countries with large imports of foodstuffs. We have, therefore, begun our exposition with these two Scandinavian countries. Thereafter we have discussed the problems of Poland, the four south-eastern agrarian states of Europe (Roumania, Hungary, Yugoslavia, and Bulgaria), and of Spain.

1. SWEDEN
(Comp. Table A1 for Sweden in Appendix)

Although Swedish agriculture is of great importance in the general economic structure of the country, yielding a large export surplus of butter and a small one of pork, while covering at the same time a great part of rye and wheat consumption, yet Sweden is dependent upon considerable imports in respect of nearly all branches of food production (comp. Table A).

Before the War, Sweden's agrarian tariff policy was very moderate, with notable exceptions in the case of the important group of corn and flour duties, the average height of which (30·3%) was a remarkable one for pre-War times. The duties on rye, barley, wheat, and rye flour, in particular, represented considerable protection for Swedish production (comp. Table B, p. 87).

TABLE A: SWEDISH AGRARIAN IMPORTS, 1913–1931
(In Mill. Swed. Crowns and %)

Group	1913 Mill. Cr.	1913 % of T.I.	1927 Mill. Cr.	1927 % of T.I.	1931 Mill. Cr.	1931 % of T.I.
Total Imports . .	847	100·0	1585	100·0	1430	100·0
Of which :						
Corn, flour . .	65	7·7	127	8·0	54	3·9
Animal foodstuffs .	29	3·4	38	2·4	35	2·4
Vegetables, fruit .	17	2·0	68	4·3	78	5·5

T.I. = Total Imports.
Comp. *Sveriges offiziella Statistik. Handel,* 1913, 1927, and *Statistiques,* III, for the year 1931.

In the case of nearly all the other classes the duties were moderate, with the exception of some fiscal duties, as, e.g., on fruit, alcohol, and tobacco.

These fiscal duties explained the unusually high levels of classes AIV and AVI, so that only by their weight the Swedish general agrarian tariff level (even by excluding the duties on alcohol and tobacco) reached the high figure of 32·5–34% for 1913.[1]

In the post-War period Swedish agrarian tariff policy was unusually moderate compared with European conditions. Until 1929 it maintained the rates of its 1913 agrarian tariff—in some cases even lowered them. Consequently the 1927 general agrarian tariff level fell to about 21% and was thus 37% below the level of 1913.

During the period between 1929 and 1931 Swedish commercial policy showed an even sharper contrast to the agrarian tariff policy of almost all Europe (excluding England, the

[1] Therefore in Table AI two average figures for group A in 1913.

Netherlands, Belgium, Denmark, and Norway). Whereas, in fact, both before and much more after the beginning of the world economic crisis, the latter assumed the drastic protectionist character revealed in the foregoing sections, Sweden, even with her new tariff of 1930, remained true to her liberal agrarian tariff policy by keeping her rates of agrarian duties at the level of 1913, or even below it. If, nevertheless, the general tariff level of 1931 reached 38–40% (=117% of 1913), if the tariff level of class AI (cereals and flour) rose to 54%, of class Av to 47–53% (=167–178% of 1913), this was due almost exclusively to the rapid fall in agrarian prices, especially of the prices of corn, flour, and sugar, while specific duty rates remained stable.

TABLE B: DUTIES ON IMPORTANT AGRARIAN
COMMODITIES IN SWEDEN, 1913–1931
(In % of Prices)

	1913	1927	1931
Wheat	8·6	10·0	26·0
Rye	29·2	18·1	50·5
Barley	40·0	22·8	66·0
Wheat, flour	32·0	31·0	55·5
Rye flour	41·5	27·0	72·5
Raw sugar	43·5–60·0	26·4–37·0	68·0–97·0
Liquors	92·0	89·5	110·0

However, since the outbreak of the world economic crisis, even Sweden resorted to drastic novel protectionist methods in two spheres, in order to shelter certain branches of her agriculture from foreign competition, so that the low Swedish duties of 1931 no longer reflected the full scope of Swedish agrarian protection. In the year 1930 a compulsory milling regulation was introduced for rye and wheat (quotas until 1931: 60–85%), and by monopolizing the corn trade Swedish rye and wheat prices were successfully kept far above the world market level. Moreover, in 1931 Sweden established a sugar monopoly, which was designed to stimulate Swedish beet-cultivation and Swedish sugar-production.[1] Thus since the world economic crisis, even in Sweden in two important spheres of agriculture duties became a secondary expedient of commercial policy.

2. FINLAND
(Comp. Table A1 for Finland in Appendix)

Despite the overwhelming agrarian character of its population Finland, too, was dependent upon substantial imports, especially for its corn-consumption, while the dairy industry of its peasants yielded a considerable export surplus and imports of animal foodstuffs were unimportant; fruit and vegetables in 1927 represented about 2·2% and in 1931 about 3·2% of the total imports.[2] Finnish cereal imports, on the other hand, were very considerable, as Table A shows.

TABLE A: FINNISH CORN IMPORTS, 1913–1931
(In Mill. Finmk. and %)

Group	1913 Mill. Fmk.	1913 % of T.I.	1927 Mill. Fmk.	1927 % of T.I.	1931 Mill. Fmk.	1931 % of T.I.
Total Imports . .	495	100·0	6400	100·0	3465	100·0
Of which:						
Corn and corn products	100	20·0	650	10·2	265	7·6

T.I. = Total Imports.
See *Finlands Handel på Ryssland och utrikes Oster*, 1913, also *I A Ulkomaankauppa*, 1927, and *Utrikes Handel*, 1931.

Although Finland, before the War, was united with Russia, and possessed its own customs tariff, yet the most important cereals and many goods of classes AII–IV were free of duty and were mostly imported from Russia. The Finnish agrarian tariff of 1913 was therefore of small importance. Its very high general level was the result of a few high duties on cheese,

[1] Comp. *Trade Barriers*, pp. 492–498.
[2] Comp. *Memor. u. Statistiques*, I.

fruit, vegetables (partly fiscal duties), sugar, alcohol, and tobacco, whilst the duty-free items had no weight. A closer analysis was therefore useless.

Although the agrarian import structure of Finland was not altered after the country gained political independence, in 1917, Finnish agrarian tariff policy in post-War times assumed from the start a decidedly protectionist character, which was reflected even in 1927 in the very high general agrarian tariff level of 57–58% (this time, however, in contrast to 1913 a higher average from numerous high duties). For the fiscal freedom of 1913, as regards the most important agrarian products, disappeared after the War with two exceptions (wheat and potatoes). While the new corn duties were still very moderate, the flour duties were fixed very high, in order to assist the development and protection of a Finnish milling industry [1] (comp. Table B, below). The duties upon certain kinds of vegetables and fruit were prohibitive, bringing the level of this class up to 124%. For the high level of class Av amounting to 86–87% the sugar and cocoa duties were mainly responsible.

TABLE B: DUTIES ON IMPORTANT AGRARIAN
COMMODITIES IN FINLAND, 1913–1931
(*In % of Prices*)

Goods	1913	1927	1931
Wheat . . .	Duty free	Duty free	Duty free
Rye . .	,,	23·2	162·0
Rye flour . .	,,	25·6–37·6	152·0–233·0
Wheat flour . .	,,	42·7–72·0	120·0–200·0
Oranges . .	165·0	37·0	95·0
Raw sugar . .	197·0	117·0	350·0
Cocoa powder .	43·0	195·0	285·0
Wine in casks .	76·0	160·0–240·0	165·0–247·0

Finnish agrarian protectionism was considerably stiffened by the world economic crisis. Increases in the duties on

[1] Comp. *Trade Barriers*, p. 367.

corn, flour, meat, potatoes, fruit, sugar, and tobacco in the years 1930–31 brought up the Finnish general agrarian tariff level to a height of 95–109% (excluding Avi). In sharp contrast to 1927 the rye and barley duties now were very high too.

Despite this drastic protection, in the year 1931, Finland also introduced a compulsory milling regulation in order to shelter its rye and oats production (quota 30% for rye, 70% for oats) while wheat-milling remained free, owing to the insignificant Finnish wheat cultivation.[1]

3. POLAND (1913: RUSSIA)
(Comp. Table A1 for Poland in Appendix)

Poland is the first of those above-mentioned European countries with high agrarian exports (see p. 85) respecting which the exposition of agrarian tariff policy and agrarian tariff levels could be confined to a summary of their principles and some characteristic details, because the agrarian difficulties of these states consisted much less in checking agrarian imports by duties, and other means, than in diverting their agrarian exports to the markets of other nations. In this connection agrarian protection in those countries could be most readily discerned where certain branches of their agrarian production showed a partial deficit, for which reason these classes of goods merited special attention.

As the greater part of Poland belonged to Russia in 1913, the duties of the Russian tariff in force in 1913 were utilized for the calculation of those agrarian duties which would have been applied to the importation of goods in the year 1913 in that area that is now Poland.

Pre-War Russia admitted all cereals and most dairy produce duty free, as she was Europe's leading export country. Only flour was subjected to a considerable duty. On the other hand, Russia imposed on vegetables, fruit, sugar, chocolate, and cocoa,

[1] Comp. *Trade Barriers*, pp. 367–368.

as well as wine and tobacco, such heavy duties as were found nowhere else in Europe in 1913 (comp. Table B, p. 92). Therefore classes AIV and V reached tariff levels of 80% and 132% respectively. Accordingly the Russian general agrarian tariff level showed the exceptional height of 69·5% without and 77·5–82% with the duties of class AVI. Here, as in all other spheres, the extreme Russian tariff reached by far the highest European pre-War figures.

Although the new Poland in general remained a country of corn exports, the trend of Polish corn and flour imports and exports from 1927 to 1931 showed great fluctuations. In times of bad harvests, in fact, Polish corn production was not sufficient to cover the corn requirements of the country,[1] so that in the year 1927 not less than 9·4% of the total imports consisted of corn and corn products, whereas in 1931 it was only 0·6% [2] (comp. Table A).

TABLE A: POLISH AGRARIAN IMPORTS, 1927–31
(*In Mill. Zlotys and %*)

Group	1927 Mill. Zl.	1927 % of T.I.	1931 Mill. Zl.	1931 % of T.I.
Total Imports . .	2890	100·0	1470	100·0
Of which :				
Cereals . . .	280	9·7	33	2·2
Flour . . .	52	1·8	3	0·2
Animal fats . .	50	1·7	1	0·07
Fish . . .	47	1·6	29	2·0

T.I. = Total Imports.
Vgl. *Annuaire du commerce extérieur de la Republique Pol.*, 1926–27, 1931.

The Polish tariff of 1924, which, with considerable alterations remained in force until the new Polish tariff of 1932–33 came into operation, admitted all kinds of corn free in 1927, like the Russian of 1913. Flour only was taxed, heavily in

[1] Comp. *Enquête*, I, pp. 123–128.
[2] Comp. *Memorandum and Statistiques*, II.

the case of wheat flour and lightly in the case of rye meal (comp. Table B, below). In view of Polish exports no great importance could be attached to the duties on live-stock and dairy produce. On the other hand, the duties on vegetables, fruit, and Southern fruit, which were of unusual height and recalled the Russian pre-War tariff, needed special mention.

The tariff level of this class in 1927 reached the prohibitive height of 213–242%, and thus exceeded the Russian one of 1913 by 170–200%. Thanks to high sugar duties, designed to protect the Polish sugar industries, and very high duties on chocolate and cocoa, class Av reached a tariff level of 61% in 1927, while much heavier duties on alcoholic beverages and tobacco brought that of class Avi up to 142%. In 1927 Poland's general agrarian tariff level amounted to 68–75%, and thus corresponded to the extreme protectionism which had been the policy of Poland since her foundation.[1]

TABLE B: DUTIES ON IMPORTANT AGRARIAN COMMODITIES IN POLAND, 1927–31
(1913: RUSSIAN DUTIES)
(*In % of Prices*)

Goods	1913	1927	1931
Wheat . . .	Duty free	Duty free	100·0
Rye	,,	,,	97·5
Wheat flour . . .	26·0	39·0	132·0
Rye flour . . .	35·0	8·8	116·0
Oranges . . .	205·0	105·0	270·0
Cauliflower . . .	37·0	316·0	560·0
Raw sugar . . .	290·0	74·0	370·0
Cocoa powder . .	86·0	113·0	165·0
Raw tobacco . .	400·0	415·0	314·0

From the end of 1928, and with growing intensity since the beginning of the world economic crisis, Poland continued this protectionist agrarian tariff policy, in spite of increasing exports of corn, live-stock, dairy products, in spite of granting

[1] Comp. *Trade Barriers*, p. 455.

export premiums, import certificates, and other measures calculated to increase her agrarian exports.[1] In 1928–29 heavy duties were imposed upon the cereals hitherto admitted free; in 1930–31 there were fresh increases in the duties on flour and sugar and further increases in the corn duties. Consequently, the tariff level of class AI (corn and flour) in 1931 rose to 97·5%, while that for class Av rose to 160%, especially on account of the increased duty on raw sugar. In 1931 Poland's general agrarian tariff level reached 102–118%, and was thus 75–100% higher than the Russian one of 1913.

At the commencement of 1932 Poland embarked upon a still more drastic policy with regard to agrarian imports by a temporary but total prohibition of all imports of some important agrarian products, such as corn, flour, hops, vegetables, fats, fruit, etc., while the permitted imports were dependent upon quotas and the granting of licences.[2]

In this case also, tariffs fell into the background as an instrument of commercial policy.

4. ROUMANIA
(Comp. Table AI for Roumania in Appendix)

Roumania's agrarian tariff policy interested us only in the case of a few classes of goods, because the country yielded a great export surplus of corn, live-stock, and animal foodstuffs and had only introduced for sugar a monopolistic organisation of its production and distribution.[3]

Post-War agrarian reforms benefited the peasantry, who favoured the cultivation of barley and maize. The immediate consequence of such reforms was a sharp decline in the wheat exports of the large estates, compared with the pre-War level.[4] In the years 1927–29 a small importation of wheat even became necessary, but generally speaking, Roumania produced more

---

[1] *Trade Barriers*, pp. 458–464.
[2] Ibid., p. 457.
[3] Ibid., pp. 471–472, 476.
[4] Comp. *Enquête*, I, pp. 74–75.

cereals than she needed for her own requirements. Her traditional protectionist tariff policy manifested itself in the sphere of agrarian consumption by duties on such industrialized foodstuffs as flour, margarine, chocolate, etc., as well as on vegetables, fruit, sugar, and wine, commodities which in most cases were imported. The general agrarian tariff level of 1913 reached 34–35%, excluding duties on alcoholic drinks, or, 40–41·5% including them.

In the post-War period some of the tariff rates of 1927 were much increased, such increases being fivefold in the case of fruit and vegetables, with the result that for all the thirty-eight goods of group A the rates on an average represented 300–330% of the 1913 rates.

The Roumanian tariff level of 1927 remained considerably below this increase, because of the raised agrarian price level; with a height of 43·5–47·5% it was 28–30% higher than that of 1913 (excluding Avi).

The new Roumanian tariff of 1929, which did not change many duty rates, reduced the wine duties and increased the rates of duty on vegetables to 670–690% of the 1913 position.

As, however, the agrarian price level fell sharply up to 1931, the agrarian tariff level rose correspondingly. With a height of 85–90% it represented 250–255% of the 1913 level.

TABLE A: DUTIES ON IMPORTANT AGRARIAN COMMODITIES IN ROUMANIA, 1913–31
(In % of Prices)

Goods	1913	1927	1931
Oranges . . .	4·1	30·0	80·0
Raw sugar . .	100·0	67·0	195·0
Margarine . .	84·0	77·0	157·0
Cocoa . . .	26·0	90·0–135·0	160·0
Wine in casks . .	160·0	92·0	174·0

Even in an agrarian-surplus country such as Roumania, only eleven, out of thirty-seven goods examined, were subjected to duties below 30% in 1931, while fourteen had to pay duties between 30% and 100% and in the case of twelve the duty was over 100%. Table A throws some light upon a number of these duties so far as they represented imported products, or, like sugar, were products of artificially restricted supply in the home market.

5. HUNGARY

(Comp. Table A1 for Hungary in Appendix)

To a still greater degree than Roumania, Hungary is a country of mainly agrarian exports of corn, live-stock, animal foodstuffs, fruit, tobacco, and wine. The discussion, therefore, of its agrarian tariff policy is of little value, and may be confined to a few explanations.

The Hungarian tariff of 1924 raised the rates of duty, compared with the Austro-Hungarian tariff of 1906, in all classes of goods, with the exception of the corn duties, so that the year 1927 showed on the average an increase of Hungarian duty rates of 50–80% compared with the Austro-Hungarian rates of 1913. As, however, the sharp upward trend of the agrarian price level counteracted these increases to a considerable extent, the Hungarian agrarian general tariff level of 1927, with a height of 28·5–34·5%, was no more than 5–10% above that of the Dual Monarchy of 1913.

Up to the end of the year 1931 Hungarian agrarian tariff policy remained very stable. Its only noticeable feature was a sharp increase in the sugar duty, already much higher than in pre-War time, which was carried through in 1931 (comp. Table A).

The Hungarian general tariff level of 1931, increased to 56–64%, was, therefore, with the exception of the sugar duty, *almost entirely the consequence of the sharp fall in agricultural prices.*

Since 1930 Hungary sought to deal with its surplus production by a comprehensive monopolistic organisation of the whole corn trade, the granting of export premiums, the conclusion of preferential commercial treaties, the restriction of imports by a licence system, and other commercial methods outside the sphere of tariff policy. Duties were important only in the case of sugar, owing to the monopoly which Hungarian producers exercised over the home market.[1]

TABLE A: DUTIES ON IMPORTANT AGRARIAN
COMMODITIES IN HUNGARY, 1927–1931
(1913: AUSTRO-HUNGARIAN DUTIES)
(*In % of Prices*)

Goods	1913	1927	1931
Wheat flour . .	57·0	47·0	84·0
Raw sugar . .	21·0	70·0	266·0
Margarine . .	22·0	64·0	84·0
Cocoa powder . .	90·0	94·0–110·0	137·0–160·0

6. YUGOSLAVIA (1913: SERBIA)
(*Comp. Table A1 for Yugoslavia in Appendix*)

The discussion of the agrarian tariff policy of Yugoslavia (1913: Serbia) can be confined to a few remarks, because this country also yielded a considerable export surplus of corn, live-stock, animal foodstuffs, fruit, and tobacco. Before the War the Serbian general agrarian tariff level reached a height of 28·5–34·5%. The duties on the goods in class Av, mainly industrialized foodstuffs and sugar, were high, whilst the (mostly nominal) duties on other products were moderate (comp. Table A).

While the new Yugoslav tariff of 1925 diminished by 45% the rates of duty on corn and flour, those of the other classes were raised so sharply that the year 1927 showed on the average an increase in the rates of duty of 120–210% compared with 1913. The general agrarian tariff level did not rise so much, by reason of the sharp upward trend in agrarian prices. With a height of 41·5–46% it was 33–45% above that of 1913.

[1] *Trade Barriers*, pp. 400–410.

Duties on meat and alcohol were increased, while the tariff level of class AI (corn and flour) declined from 25·7% in 1913 to 9·2% in the year 1927.

TABLE A: DUTIES ON IMPORTANT AGRARIAN COMMODITIES IN YUGOSLAVIA, 1927–31

(1913: SERBIAN DUTIES)

(*In % of Prices*)

Goods	1913	1927	1931
Wheat . . .	27·6	9·0	69·0
Maize . . .	21·0	7·5	74·0
Wheat flour . .	23·0	13·7	98·0
Raw sugar . .	79·0	51·0	140·0
Margarine . .	150·0	115·0	153·0
Wine in casks .	36·0–50·0	55·0–123·0	56·0–126·0

Yugoslavia's reactions to the world economic crisis were different from those of Roumania and Hungary, which have a similar economic structure to Yugoslavia. Although, like them a corn-exporting country, she replied to the collapse in world corn prices by a sharp increase of duties, shown in Table A, which brought the level of the corn and flour duties to a height of 80%, equal to 310% of the position of 1913. In view of Yugoslavia's high grain surplus this corn tariff policy was only in some degree comprehensible when it is borne in mind that in 1930 the whole of the imports and exports of wheat, and in 1931 the total imports and exports of grain, were brought under state monopoly. Prices above the world-market level were guaranteed to the producers, in consequence of which a protective tariff for the maintenance of the artificial prices formed the necessary complement to this policy.[1] The sugar duties were also raised sharply. In 1931 Yugoslavia's general agrarian tariff level reached 70–80% (230–245% of 1913).

[1] Comp. *Trade Barriers*, pp. 533–537.

G

7. BULGARIA
(Comp. Table A1 for Bulgaria in Appendix)

Bulgaria's export structure was characterized by a high surplus production of tobaccos, corn, live-stock, and some animal foodstuffs; its import structure by very small agrarian imports. Consequently, here, too, the details of tariff policy were of small importance for the appraisement of Bulgarian agrarian policy. The pre-War agrarian tariff level was 23–26% in 1913 (excluding Av1). Very heavy duties on sugar, margarine, and cocoa powder brought the tariff level of class Av up to 55–56% even in 1913, whereas most of the other goods were subjected to moderate duties (compare Table A, p. 99).

With the new tariff of 1922, and its revision by the reform of 1926 (a very comprehensive raising of the 1922 rates in respect of over 200 items, sometimes by as much as 50%), Bulgaria erected tariff walls *of a height that existed in no other country of Europe,* not merely for industrial products, but even for most of her agrarian exports commodities. Compared with 1913 the duty rates for all the thirty-eight goods of group A were raised on an average by 330–390%, and, excluding duties on alcohol and tobacco, the general agrarian tariff level reached 71–86%, or 106–135% (equal to 300–330% of the position of 1913), if we include them. Of thirty-eight articles seventeen were potentially taxed between 1% and 50%, three between 50% and 100%, and eighteen over 100%.

Bulgaria reacted to the world economic crisis in a manner similar to that of Jugoslavia. Since 1931 a monopoly has been established for buying and selling corn, in order to keep the Bulgarian prices above the world-market level, and the low corn duties were raised until their rates were equal to 380% of their height in 1913 [1] (comp. Table A).

Thus the tariff level of class A1 (cereals and flour) rose from 9·7% in 1913 to 66·7% in 1931. For the remaining classes the

[1] Comp. *Trade Barriers,* pp. 318–321, 327.

prohibitive duties of 1927 remained in force, but, owing to the lower agrarian price level, they signified much higher potential tariff levels.   The general tariff level of all goods in group A (without alcohol and tobacco duties) reached in 1931 123–144%, equal to 530–550% of the tariff level of 1913!   In 1931 the raw-sugar duty reached 350%;   it was accompanied by the prohibition of imports so long as the home production remained unconsumed.[1]

TABLE A: DUTIES ON IMPORTANT AGRARIAN COMMODITIES IN BULGARIA, 1913–1931
(In % of Prices)

Goods	1913	1927	1931
Wheat . . .	2·8	5·4	42·7
Rye . . .	2·8	5·3	59·0
Wheat flour . .	18·0	41·0	74·0
Oranges . .	12·5	110·0	183·0
Raw sugar . .	100·0	127·0	350·0
Margarine . .	60·0	155·0	200·0
Wine in casks .	60·0–150·0	310·0–680·0	310·0–680·0

8. SPAIN
(Comp. Table A1 for Spain in Appendix)

In spite of her predominantly agrarian character, in spite of large exports of fruit, wine, vegetables, and rice, Spain was temporarily dependent upon foreign supplies for some agrarian products.   This was the case particularly with wheat and maize, owing to great fluctuations in her corn-production; and in a lesser degree the same held good with meat, fish, and cattle.[2]   Consequently, Spanish tariff policy, as regards these goods, proves interesting for this study.   Table A shows the proportions of total agrarian imports and imports of corn and fish to the total imports of Spain.

With a height of 32% the tariff level of class A1 (cereals and flour) before the War corresponded nearly with that of the great

---

[1] Comp. *Trade Barriers*, p. 326.
[2] Comp. Ibid., p. 481.

European industrial countries. Already in 1913 the duty on wheat flour was particularly high (comp. Table B, p. 101). Among the other class tariff levels that of class Av was especially high.

TABLE A: SPANISH AGRARIAN IMPORTS, 1913–31
(*In Mill. Pesetas and %*)

Group	1913 Mill. Pes.	1913 % of T.I.	1927 Mill. Pes.	1927 % of T.I.	1931 Mill. Pes.	1931 % of T.I.
Total Imports . .	1305	100·0	2575	100·0	1175	100·0
Agrarian Imports .	270	20·6	420	16·3	170	14·5
Of which:						
Cereals and products of cereals . .	135	10·3	71	2·8	19	1·6
Fish . . .	42	3·2	85	3·3	34	2·9

T.I. = Total Imports.
Comp. *Estadistica General*, 1913, 1927, 1931.

In the post-War period Spain increased protection in all spheres, including agriculture, by the new tariff of 1922 and its revisions during the succeeding five years. A 70% increase in the duty rates of 1913 brought the tariff level of class AI up to a height of 41%, which was 30% above the pre-War level, maize and wheat flour being subjected to particularly heavy duties. In the endeavour to make Spain as independent as possible of foreign corn imports, however, Spanish agrarian policy of the post-War period resorted to much more drastic methods. Since 1926 the importation of foreign wheat was generally prohibited, quotas being admitted only by special decree "in such quantities as were calculated to maintain a fair internal price."[1] Compulsory milling regulation, price-fixing, strict regulations regarding flour and bread selling, supplemented this policy. Owing to the danger of a shortage of wheat, the import prohibition was lifted, first in 1928 and

[1] Comp. *The Spanish Wheat Import Prohibition in H.-A.*, 1926, p. 1507.

then in 1931, when the duties were abated for a quota of 20,000 dz.[1] Spain pursued the same policy with regard to maize imports.[2] Consequently, Spain's corn duties since 1926 had only a limited practical value for judging her corn-import policy, and the large decreases of her corn imports in post-War times (comp. Table A). With regard to the other classes, the raising of the duty rates (by an average of 90–110% compared with 1913) exerted only a moderate effect, in view of the sharp upward trend in the agrarian price level. The general Spanish agrarian tariff level in 1927, being 42–48%, was only about 10% above the level of 1913 (excluding class AVI).

TABLE B: DUTIES ON IMPORTANT AGRARIAN
COMMODITIES IN SPAIN, 1913–31
(*In % of Prices*)

Goods	1913	1927	1931
Wheat	29·2	19·6	71·0
Maize	19·0	60·0	103·0
Wheat flour	50·0	59·0	130·0
Lard	46·0	40·0	66·0
Butter	28·0	35·0	50·0
Raw sugar	312·0	153·0–216·0	420·0
Cocoa powder	87·0	188·0	270·0
Margarine	35·0	154·0	202·0

By denouncing most of her conventional rates in the years 1927–28, and by the coming into full force about the year 1929 [3] of her autonomous tariff of 1922, Spain's rates of duty, especially upon corn and flour, were considerably increased (to about 190% of their pre-War level). This, combined with the sharp fall in corn and flour prices since 1929, brought the tariff level of class AI for the year 1931 up to almost 100%—i.e. three times the level of 1913. As for the remaining classes the

[1] Comp. *Trade Barriers*, pp. 482–484.
[2] Comp. *H.-A.*, 1929, p. 1149; 1930, pp. 1081–1082.
[3] Comp. Ibid., 1927, p. 1925; 1929, p. 2502.

sharp rise of their tariff levels was almost wholly caused by the fall in prices. Spain's general agrarian tariff level reached in 1931 78–83%, being almost double that of 1913.

At the end of the year 1931 Spain fundamentally changed her commercial policy. She fixed quotas for her most important agricultural and industrial imports. So here, too, tariffs ceased to be the most important expedient of commercial policy for the regulation of imports.[1]

C. GENERAL TENDENCIES IN THE AGRARIAN TARIFF POLICY OF POST-WAR EUROPE COMPARED WITH 1913
(Comp. Table IVA, and Graph A of Appendix)

The foregoing short analysis of the development of agrarian tariff policy and potential agrarian tariff levels of thirteen pre-War and fifteen post-War European states enables us to detect characteristic resemblances and dissimilarities in the development of the policy of individual states or groups of states, while the choice of the last normal pre-War year as a basis of comparison rendered us valuable service.

Europe's general agrarian tariff levels for the years 1913, 1927, and 1931 (without the duties on alcohol and tobacco) have been marked on graph A in such a way that from the two figures of the agrarian tariff level of every country in each of the three years the arithmetical means have been ascertained. Then, by employing the same scale for all countries, these averages have been recorded so as to show the trend of the potential agrarian tariff level in each country in the three test years, as well as to facilitate comparisons among all the countries of Europe.

These figures will be found in Table IVA of the Appendix, in addition to the relative changes as well in the general agrarian tariff levels as in the height of the rates of duty (ascertained in the same way) in comparison with 1913.

---

[1] Comp. Decree of the Spanish Government of December 23, 1931, in *H.-A.*, 1932, p. 1292, and *Trade Barriers*, p. 485.

Before the War a European tariff level above 30% was an exception. Only Finland, Roumania, Serbia, and Spain, to an extreme degree Russia, exceeded this figure in 1913.[1] These were not countries that imported considerable quantities of agricultural goods, but, with the exception of Finland, showed great agrarian exports.

The extensive reduction in the general volume of European production during the War, especially of European agrarian output, led in nearly all importing countries to a comprehensive suspension of many important agrarian duties. For the first post-War years these duties remained suspended, or were substantially lowered, owing to the slow revival of European agricultural production, which was impeded by demobilizations, inflations, and the creation of new states. These first post-War years were in particular marked by an enormous increase in cereal cultivation in North and South America, as well as in Australia, which compensated for the European shortage.

In contrast to these conditions, in the sphere of industrial production there existed tariffs and other import-reducing barriers of a rigour hitherto unknown in Europe,[2] which were explained partly by the over-capacity of the European War industries. These were compelled to return to the production of goods used in peace time, and encountered great difficulties in selling their products in impoverished markets.

About the year 1925, the period of Europe's slow economic recovery closed. This year European wheat production (excluding Russia) reached the pre-War level for the first time.[3] Most of the European currencies were legally, or *de facto*,

[1] In the case of Italy and Sweden the exceptional height of one class tariff level caused this figure to be exceeded. Therefore the figures of their general agrarian tariff levels calculated *without* the tariff levels of these special classes being *lower* than 30%, have been used in Table IVA. Comp. pp. 70–71 and 86 of this book.

[2] Comp. the study of the Geneva Economic Committee of 1935: *Considerations of the present evolution of agricultural protectionism*, p. 15, hereafter cited as *Considerations*, further, *Trade Barriers*, pp. 40–41.

[3] *Considerations*, pp. 16 and 27.

stabilized in 1925 or 1926–27. Germany regained her commercial liberty, and the reparations problem was solved for some time by the Dawes Plan.

The desire to re-create in Europe "normal" conditions, corresponding to the freedom of exchange in pre-War times, found particular expression in the numerous commercial treaties of the years 1926–27, in which attempts were made to lower the high level of industrial tariffs. The World Economic Conference of 1927, and the commercial policy of the years 1927 and 1928 which was influenced thereby, formed the culminating point of these tendencies. Characteristic of the conditions then prevailing in European tariff policy was the comment in the League study on Tariff Levels that "in most countries the duties on manufactured articles have been increased much more than those on agricultural products. Indeed, in a number of cases, even when the general level of the tariff has been raised, agricultural duties have been lowered."[1]

The simultaneous inquiry of the Vienna Chamber of Commerce stated that "the duties on semi and wholly manufactured industrial goods were the chief factors determining the tariff levels of European countries."[2]

If we compare the height of agrarian duty *rates* of the year 1927 with that of 1913 (see Table IVA) it can be seen that with the exception of two small industrial countries (Belgium and Austria) and one raw material country (Sweden), all the nations had raised their agrarian duty rates.

A few of the countries of industrial Europe which were most important markets of agrarian products, like Germany and Switzerland, had done this very considerably. Italy and Czechoslovakia substantially; France very little. It should, however, be remembered that precisely those rates on the most important agrarian import products, such as cereals, showed in 1927 the smallest increases over 1913, and often none at all, so that the

---

[1] Comp. *Tariff Levels*, p. 17.
[2] Comp. *Vienna Study*, p. ix.

height of duties on corn and flour in 1927 were less than in 1913 in all the deficit countries of Europe.

The rates of duty were much more raised in the countries of agrarian Europe, but owing to the high degree of their agrarian self-sufficiency, and in view of the fact that the increases were chiefly introduced for such articles of refined consumption as fruit, vegetables, colonial produce, and highly industrialized foodstuffs, these increases signified little.

Another result is disclosed by comparing the agrarian tariff *levels* of 1927 and 1913 in Table IVA. The sharp rise in nearly all agrarian prices compared with the year 1913,[1] which amounted to 49% [2] according to the world agrarian index of the Kiel Inquiry (which also included colonial produce), while according to the index of this study it reached an average of about 30%, caused the agrarian tariff levels to fall below the figures of 1913 not only in Belgium, Austria, and Sweden, which imposed lower or the same *rates* of duty, but also in Italy and France, which imposed higher duties.

In the remaining three countries of industrial Europe, in Germany, Switzerland, and Czechoslovakia, on the other hand, the tariff levels for agrarian products already in 1927 were considerably higher than in 1913 (by about 25–46%); in agrarian Europe, with the exception of Sweden, they were everywhere above the position of 1913; in the case of Poland, Hungary, and Spain very little (3–9%), in the case of Finland, Roumania, Yugoslavia more considerable (17–38%), in the case of Bulgaria a unique increase of 220%.

This was a certain indication that very soon after the partial restoration of pre-War agricultural production in some of the deficit countries of industrial Europe (Germany, Italy, Czechoslovakia, and Switzerland) agrarian protectionist tendencies could be discerned, from about 1925, while the rise in the agrarian tariff level in agrarian Europe must be judged more

[1] See Index List of A-prices in Appendix.
[2] See *Enquête*, I, p. 259.

as a manifestation of fiscal purposes or of efforts to impede imports, in order to rectify the balance of payments.[1]

The outbreak of the world economic crisis in the autumn of 1929, in conjunction with the peculiar post-War difficulties of world economy (international debts and reparations problems) which were by no means overcome in 1929, gave a strong impetus to all agrarian protectionist tendencies in Europe. The increases of agrarian duties, which were decreed with particular severity during the three years, 1929, 1930, and 1931, by the leading import countries of industrial Europe, and the fall in agrarian prices produced a complete revolution in agrarian tariff levels for the year 1931, in comparison with those of 1913 and 1927.

Tariff levels reached unprecedented heights.[2] *If a tariff level over* 30% *was an exception in the Europe of* 1913, *in* 1931 *such an exception was a tariff level under* 30% *or even* 40%, which of all the countries investigated was maintained only by Belgium, Sweden, and Switzerland. All the other countries of industrial Europe reached general agrarian tariff levels of over 50%. Of special significance was the enormous increase in the tariff levels of the three greatest agrarian import markets (besides Great Britain), Germany, France, and Italy, of which German agrarian protection with a general tariff level of 82·5% took by far the lead.

With the exception of Sweden, all the general agrarian tariff levels of agrarian Europe rose over 60%, Bulgaria, Poland, and Finland exceeding the 100% mark.

Whereas the 1927 upward trend in rates of duty was fully or substantially counteracted by considerable increases in prices, in 1931 there were big increases in some of the general agrarian tariff levels with *rates of duty remaining unchanged,* caused by an average decline in the price level (of the goods investigated) of 31·5%.[3] This showed instructively the de-

---

[1] See *Considerations,* pp. 16–17, and *Trade Barriers,* p. 46.

[2] See *Trade Barriers,* p. 46.

[3] Or 21·7% if we include class Avi. See in the Appendix the A-list. The Kiel Agrarian Index showed an average fall of 11% compared with 1913. See *Enquête,* I, p. 259.

velopment of the agrarian tariff levels in agrarian Europe. With the exception of increased corn duties in Finland, Poland, Bulgaria, Spain, and Yugoslavia, rates of duties upon agrarian products in the countries of *Border* Europe remained practically unchanged in 1931 compared with 1927, whereas all their general agrarian tariff levels in 1931 were far higher than those of 1927 (see Table IVA and graph A).

Consequently, *increases* of duty rates were bound to express themselves in ever-sharper rises in the tariff level, and this mainly affected imports of cereals, live-stock, meat, and sugar.

The enormous increase in the duties on these goods up to 1931 has caused, above all, the raising of agrarian tariff levels in industrial Europe. It is characteristic that an industrial country so important for agrarian imports as Germany, with a traditionally moderate tariff policy, reached a higher agrarian tariff level in 1931 than high protectionist countries like Hungary, Yugoslavia, and Spain, or that the corn, live-stock, and meat duties in the countries of industrial Europe surpassed the corresponding duties in most of the high protectionist countries of agrarian Europe.

The most important result of this European agrarian tariff policy between 1929 and 1931 was an extensive reduction of export and import relations in the sphere of the corn trade. The great deficit countries of industrial Europe—Germany, France, and Italy—as well as the chief deficit countries of agrarian Europe, like Sweden, Finland, and Spain, stimulated their own grain production at prices kept far above the world level (see Table A, p. 108), thus tending to become self-sufficient and thereby accelerating the rapid fall of world prices and the diminution of the areas under cultivation in those parts of the earth where local conditions most favoured the raising of crops. Whereas the areas under wheat-cultivation overseas shrunk between 1929 and 1932, they expanded in the deficit countries of Europe during the same period from 51·7 Mill. to 56·1 Mill. acres.[1]

[1] See *Trade Barriers*, p. 157.

Up to 1931 European sugar duties destroyed imports in the same way as the grain duties. Deficit countries of both industrial Europe (France, Italy, Austria, and since 1919 also Great Britain) and agrarian Europe (Sweden, Roumania, Yugoslavia, Bulgaria, and Spain) distinguished themselves in competition with the European sugar export countries (Germany, Czechoslovakia, Poland, Hungary, and Belgium) by such extreme protection, combined in a number of countries, like Germany, Sweden, Roumania, Hungary, Bulgaria, and Yugoslavia, with other measures for the entire regulation of production that countries which were once big importers of sugar tended more and more to supply their own needs. What happened in the case of grain also happened here. The sugar production of countries producing at a price far above the world-market level increased, while that of the countries by nature most favourably situated, like Java and Cuba, declined, and the growing tendency towards self-sufficiency had to be paid for by the consumer at prices which were 300–400%, or even higher, above world-market prices.[1]

TABLE A: WHEAT PRICES IN THE WORLD MARKET AND IN EUROPE (LONDON, GERMANY, FRANCE, ITALY)

(Per bushel in dollar cents)

Place	1929–30		1931–32	
	cents per bushel	London =100	cents per bushel	London =100
London . .	131	100	59	100
Berlin . .	162	123	152	258
Paris . .	145	110	174	294
Milan . .	188	143	148	250

Comp. *Trade Barriers*, p. 158.

Compared with the extensive degree of disintegration of export and import countries, which extreme European corn and sugar protection had brought about by 1931, the effects of

[1] See *Trade Barriers*, pp. 279–282.

the duties upon the imports of the remaining important classes of agrarian goods up till this year were still relatively mild. They were most severe in connection with the lowering of Germany's and Italy's meat and live-stock imports by the duties of this year, which were very high in the case of Germany.[1] The worst for the great group of dairy produce and for all other agrarian imports not yet affected by duties, was yet to happen.

This was not long delayed. About the middle of 1931 the world economic crisis took a sudden turn for the worse through the outbreak of a credit crisis in Europe and the collapse of the political and commercial debt system, followed by England's departure from the Gold Standard. All those agrarian prices which hitherto had fallen relatively little, such as those of dairy produce, followed the collapse of grain and sugar prices, and about the turn of the year 1931 all European countries resorted to that new commercial policy which surpassed the previous drastic agrarian tariff policy by pushing duties into the background, the chief expedients of which were quotas, import licences, currency restrictions, and partial monopolies. They no longer evinced agrarian protectionist tendencies only, but in many countries showed in equal measure intentions to protect the balance of trade or policies of a purely political nature. This new trade policy compelled the traditional free-trade countries like England, Belgium, and Holland, Denmark and Norway to adopt retaliatory measures. Its first effort was directed mainly against the imports of meat and dairy produce into industrial Europe, which were very quickly reduced in a similar manner to the grain and sugar imports by 1931, in this case, too, at the cost of excessive dearness of the articles in question in the countries where their importation was barred.[2]

As in this more recent period of European agrarian policy only a secondary part has been assigned to tariffs in connection

[1] See *Considerations*, pp. 29–30.
[2] See Ibid., pp. 18–21, 26–30.

with the reduction of imports, no useful purpose would be served in carrying the calculations of tariff levels beyond the year 1931. Nevertheless, the inquiries of Part III, which investigate the *individual* effects of the agrarian tariff policy here described upon the export situation of the various countries of Europe, will indicate the further devastations which must be laid to its account, by giving short summaries of the trend of foreign trade relations during these years (1932–34).

The trade conditions first produced by high agrarian duties and then accentuated by more drastic measures have been concisely described by the American Senate Inquiry of 1933, which stated that "the restrictions to international trade upsurged in this period have been carried beyond any point ever before attained in modern peace times." [1]

[1] *Trade Barriers*, p. 40.

OUTLINES OF EUROPEAN INDUSTRIAL TARIFF POLICY AND DEVELOPMENT OF POTENTIAL INDUSTRIAL TARIFF LEVELS BETWEEN 1913 AND 1931

PRELIMINARY REMARK: *Industrial and Agrarian Countries of Europe as Markets for Industrial Products*

IN connection with the following inquiry into the potential tariff levels of forty-four semi-manufactured goods of group B, and sixty-two manufactured goods of group C, of the A-list, and the changes in European industrial tariff policy during the period between 1913 and 1931, which will be carried out in the same way and in respect of the same countries as our inquiry into agrarian tariff policy, we must in the first place emphasize the special difficulties which the great complexity of industrial production presents to any tolerably representative exposition of the industrial tariff level of a country, even if the inquiry embraces only the more important products of the most important industrial classes of goods.[1] We shall therefore find it more difficult to compare changes in the imports of particular industrial goods with simultaneous important changes in the industrial tariff policy of the importing country than in the case of the imports of great agrarian standard products. Owing to the minute subdivision of industrial imports into many items, the changes of magnitude involved were so numerous that only special inquiries could take them into account and carry through useful comparisons of the effects of individual industrial duties with changes in imports.

The tables in the text showing the magnitudes of the industrial imports of the countries are intended only to indicate the degree and the nature of their industrial import requirements,

[1] See pp. 52–53 of this book.

as well as the importance of the countries as markets for industrial products. Wherever industrial imports were not evenly distributed among the different classes of goods, but were concentrated upon a few large items, this has been duly emphasized.

In our analysis of agrarian tariff policy and agrarian tariff levels we were primarily concerned with the development of the agrarian imports of the great industrial countries. The expectation that we shall be primarily concerned with agrarian Europe in analysing industrial tariff policy will not be fulfilled. For, contrary to the conditions of European agrarian foreign trade, the same weight did not attach to the import of industrial goods by agrarian Border Europe as *to the reciprocal exchange of industrial products by the industrial countries of Central Europe themselves.*

Of total exports of industrial Europe averaging 32·2 Md. Mk. in 1909–13, 16·4 Md. (51%) constituted an exchange of goods among the countries of Central Europe, and only 3 Md. (9·3%) were taken by Border Europe. Of the post-War average 1925–28 of total Central European exports of 48·7 Md. Rm. the share of the industrial countries amounted to 21·2 Md. (43·5%), and that of Border Europe to 7·3 Md. (14·9%). It should be added that in post-War times the share of Border Europe considerably increased statistically owing to the changes of frontiers.

Very similar conditions were to be found in connection with the secondary importance of Border European agrarian countries as buyers of wholly manufactured goods of Central European industrial countries. Of total exports of these commodities by industrial Europe, amounting to 18 Md. M. in the year 1913, Border Europe took only 1·63 Md. M. (9%). Of a total of 27·8 Md. Rm. in 1928 the proportion was only 3·8 Md. (14%), while the exchange among the countries of industrial Europe amounted in 1913 to 6·52 Md. M. (36%) and in 1928 to 8·8 Md. Rm. (32%).[1]

The industrial countries of Europe, therefore, both before and after the War, were much better customers to each other

---

[1] See for above figure, *Gaedicke*, op. cit., pp. 55–62.

than the agrarian countries of Border Europe. The investigations of *Gaedicke* and *von Eynern* have clearly demonstrated this important fact in the economic integration of industrial Europe.

If, nevertheless, great importance must be attached to the analysis of the industrial tariff policy and the potential tariff levels of the countries of agrarian Europe, this is due less to their *actual* purchasing power for the industrial products of Central Europe than to future developments. It is the question so vigorously discussed in all the industrial countries of the world, of the industrialization of the hitherto agrarian countries as a cause of growing and lasting difficulties of finding markets for the industrial exports of the old industrial countries and the great part which the industrial tariff policy of agrarian states is called upon to play in this connection.

In view therefore of the high degree of the integration of industrial production among the countries of Central Europe, their industrial tariff policy between 1913 and 1931 remained of such great importance that in the following investigations we have first of all described the conditions of industrial Europe, country by country, and then dealt with agrarian Europe.

A. INDUSTRIAL (CENTRAL) EUROPE

1. GERMANY [1]

(See Table AI and AII in Appendix)

Although, after Great Britain, Germany was Europe's greatest exporter of semi- and wholly-manufactured goods, she was at the same time, between 1913 and 1931, a very important customer for industrial products, particularly semi-manufactured goods. Table A shows the most important items of these industrial imports.

The paramount position of semi-manufactured goods among Germany's industrial imports is clearly shown by the table.

---

[1] Comp. outline of German industrial commercial policy by Prof. *Röpke*, loc. cit., pp. 24–39.

TABLE A: GERMAN INDUSTRIAL IMPORTS, 1913–31
(*In Mill. M., Rm. and* %)

Group	1913 Mill. M.	% of I.I.	1927 Mill. Rm.	% of I.I.	1931 Mill. Rm.	% of I.I.
Total Imports .	10770	—	14230	—	6730	—
Of which:						
Finished goods .	1370	100·0	2525	100·0	1225	100·0
Of which:						
Yarns . . .	323	23·5	880	34·9	264	21·6
Chemicals . .	201	14·7	160	6·4	112	9·1
Semi-manufactured iron goods .	49	3·6	258	10·2	113	9·2
Machinery . .	86	6·3	144	5·7	59	4·8
Vehicles . .	47	3·4	114	4·5	22·4	1·8
Tissues . .	169	12·4	316	12·5	161	13·1
Clothing . .	167	12·2	253	10·0	98	8·0

I.I. = Industrial Imports ("Fertigwareneinfuhr" of German Statistics).

For figures for 1913 and 1927 see *Enquête*, II, p. 91; for 1931 see *Stat. Jahrbuch für d. dt. Reich*, 1932, pp. 176, 178.

Finished goods, *in the strict sense of the term*, on the other hand occupied a more modest position.[1] Raw materials and semi-manufactured goods comprised 63·5% of Germany's total

---

[1] The discussion of this table of German industrial imports provides an opportunity to draw attention to a difficulty which applies to all the following tables of a similar kind. The trade statistics of the various countries, from which the informative surveys of their industrial imports have been taken, follow the division of the *Brussels International Goods List* of 1913, which does not separate so sharply semi-finished from finished goods as we have done in our A-list. By "semi-finished" goods we mean goods that have to undergo a further industrial process before they are fit for consumption or reproductive use. Consequently, the heading "finished goods" in most of the tables comprises such semi-finished goods as yarn, partly woven fabrics, etc., in addition to finished goods in the precise meaning of the term, such as dresses, tools, motor-cars, etc. For an understanding of the import structure and the tariff policy of a country it is of great importance to separate these two groups as sharply as possible, for which reason Gaedicke rightly attempts a more precise division into raw materials, semi-manufactured, and

imports in 1913—raw materials, of course, accounting for the major portion. Imports of finished goods in the exact sense were only 7·7%. For 1928, the corresponding figures were 59·5% and 9·6%.[1]

This situation was distinctly indicated in the German industrial tariff of 1902, so far as it remained valid in 1913. The duties on highly manufactured goods were on the whole very low; in the case of semi-manufactured goods not so low as in that of finished goods, where Germany's superiority was greatest. In 1913 the potential tariff level of semi-manufactured goods amounted to 13–17·5%, and thus approximated to the height of duties upon semi-manufactured goods of the metal and chemical industries; whereas the semi-manufactured goods of the wood and paper industries and the mineral oils were taxed higher and the great classes of semi-manufactured textiles were taxed lower. Various goods in each class were taxed considerably higher, others lower, than the class averages indicated (see Table B, p. 118). The duties on cotton tissues, cellulose, rolled iron, wrought-iron tubes and cast iron reached a considerable height. Among the chemicals numerous fertilizers and dyes were on the free list. The potential tariff level of industrial finished goods in 1913 was 8·5–11·7%, and therefore very low. The tariff levels of the classes of textiles, glass, metal-ware, and machinery were somewhat higher, those of the classes of vehicles, apparatus, toys, and rubber tires somewhat lower than this general figure. Here, too, the duties on various goods in a number of classes exceeded the average figures very considerably (see Table C, p. 118).

The post-War industrial tariff policy of Germany was

manufactured goods (see *Gaedicke, Vol. of Tables*, p. v), so that his figures for 1913, 1925, and 1928 differ from those of the Trade Statistics. Unfortunately, equally accurate figures were not available for 1927 and 1931, and we must perforce be content with figures relating to goods far too summarily described as "finished goods." For this reason Gaedicke's figures for 1913 and 1928 are often added in the text.

[1] *Gaedicke, Vol. of Tables*, p. 19.

influenced by events which happened in the first post-War years. While almost all the important agrarian duties had been removed during the War and the years which followed, up to 1925, the duty rates (fixed in paper Marks) of numerous industrial items were raised by a series of tariff revisions and decrees, chiefly during the years 1922–23, in order to adjust tariff revenue and tariff protection to the falling value of the paper Mark. Out of 946 items of the German tariff, 277 were wholly or partially raised up to the end of 1923, and this number included only 46 agrarian (chiefly colonial produce and goods of refined consumption) against 231 industrial products.[1] When the Mark was stabilized at its pre-War value in 1924, these rates were not substantially reduced. Thus Germany, since 1925, possessed again not only an agrarian tariff but also an industrial tariff of a strongly protectionist character with regard to many goods, the new rates of which were considered by Dr. *Harms* as often directly prohibitive. But these increases of duties, discreetly carried out, did not attract the attention they deserved in Germany, where public opinion was concentrated upon the struggle over the reintroduction of the agrarian duties that was raging at the time.[2]

The tariff increases were generally moderate in the case of semi-finished goods. Tissues were particularly hard hit. Duties on fabrics, velvet, and plush were raised between 200–500%. The rates on semi-manufactured textiles were raised on an average by 60%, while chemical duties were increased between 100–200%. For the whole of group B there was an average increase in duty rates during 1927 of between 20–50% compared with 1913. Yet, not only was Germany's potential tariff level for semi-finished goods, with 10·5–18·6%, very little above that of 1913 (about 5%), but also those of the different classes, and only the height of the duties on mineral oils was far above the level of 1913.

This is explained by the sharp upward trend in the prices

[1] *Harms*, op. cit., pp. 72–75, and Appendices I and II.
[2] Ibid., op. cit., pp. 72–77.

of semi-finished goods, which amounted to an average of 42%
for the forty-four semi-finished articles. The prices of
textiles, chemicals, wood, and paper materials had risen above,
while those of metal goods were somewhat below this figure,
prices of mineral oils being below even the level of 1913.[1]

In the tariff of 1925 the taking over of the inflation rates of
duties exerted a much sharper effect among the finished goods.
Most heavily hit of all were the textiles, as the average increase
in their duty rates, compared with 1913, amounted to 350–
400%. Various increases within this class far exceeded this
figure, and reached as much as 800%. Notable, also, were the
increases in the rates for glass and ceramics and for the vehicle
class, in which one observes a 300–400% increase in automobile duties. Very steep was the rise in the duty on watches,
which represented 400–650% of the rates of 1913.[2] The
average increase in the rates of duties upon finished goods in
group C amounted to 100–145%, and thus represented between
two and two and a half times the pre-War rates.

Here, too, we can perceive the retardative effects upon the
growth of the tariff level exerted by the upward trend of the
prices of industrial finished goods, which amounted to an
average of 21% compared with 1913; although the price level
of the class of machinery was 60–76%, that of the class of paper
goods and metal-wares 28–38% above the pre-War position,
while that of the vehicles was 34% below it.

Anyhow, the potential tariff level of group C rose in 1927
to a height of 15·5–22·7%, and was thus 80–95% higher than
in 1913 in one of the leading industrial countries, while the
agrarian tariff level was only 15–35% higher. Moreover, the
classes most heavily hit by duty increases showed a greater rise
than this average figure. Thus, the tariff level of the textile
class reached 21–43%, which was equivalent to a growth of
110–200% compared with 1913, and that of the vehicles class,
with 24–40%, reached 390–625% of the position of 1913.

[1] See Index List of Prices of A-list in Appendix.
[2] See examples of increases quoted by *Harms*, op. cit., App. VI.

TABLE B: DUTIES ON SEMI-MANUFACTURED GOODS IN GERMANY, 1913–31
(*In % of Prices*)

Goods	1913	1927	1931
Cotton yarn, raw, up to No. 50 .	1·8–5·4	3·4–9·3	11·0–14·0
Raw worsted	1·5	2·4	3·6
Bleached cotton piece-goods .	20·0–49·0	9·9–49·5	13·0–65·0
Cellulose	34·4	24·0–36·4	19·0–33·0
Wooden planks unplaned, soft wood	13·3	12·5–16·7	17·2–23·0
Cast iron	16·4	13·2	17·3
Rolled iron not further manu-factured	25·0–50·0	26·0–78·0	27·2–81·6
Crude iron sheets . . .	18·7–28·0	17·0–28·7	22·8–34·0
Aluminium sheets . . .	7·4	5·9	24·0
Nitrogen	26·0	13·3	110·0
Petrol	8·7–13·0	35·8	163·0

TABLE C: DUTIES ON MANUFACTURED GOODS IN GERMANY, 1913–31
(*In % of Prices*)

Goods	1913	1927	1931
Leather shoes	6·1–9·1	7·5–16·0	10·3–51·0
Hosiery (cotton) . . .	22·4–56·0	28·2–100·0	26·2–94·0
Woollen clothing . . .	6·7–20·0	4·9–18·7	6·2–25·2
Artificial silk stockings . .	16·6	57·0–64·0	82·0–91·0
Cotton suits	9·6–24·0	32·3–116·0	21·7–73·0
Printing paper . . .	22·4	18·0	24·0
Polished sheet glass . . .	39·0	93·0	68·0
Combustion engines . .	3·2–67·0	1·9–54·0	2·0–59·0
Private cars	2·0–5·5	30·0–50·0	9·7–27·2
Simple pocket watches . .	9·4	39·0	44·0
Motor-tires	6·7	21·0–26·2	24·6–30·8

Whereas the industrial tariff level rose sharply up to 1927, in contrast to the agrarian tariff level, which had been increased only slightly compared with pre-War times, between 1927 and 1931 German industrial tariff policy pursued an equally contrary course to German agrarian tariff policy, but in an opposite sense. Compared with the agrarian duties, which showed sharp increases from 1929 onward, industrial duties, which were much more tied by commercial treaties, persisted up to 1931 in a state of great stability. Of noteworthy increases of duty between 1927 and 1931 those relating to mineral oils, shoes, raw aluminium sheets, and nitrogen were all that need be mentioned, so that the changes which took place in the height of duties of 1931 compared with 1927 resulted mainly from falling prices.

In 1931 the potential tariff level of group B rose to 19–27·8%, equivalent to 145–160% of 1913. The unprecedented height of duties on mineral oils (265–450%) was the result of a sharp fall in prices combined with enormous increases in rates of duty.[1]

The group of manufactured goods showed no appreciable change compared with 1927. The tariff level of the vehicle class fell from 24–40% in 1927 to 8·8–22% in 1931, a consequence of the progressive fall in German motor-car duties since 1927. With a potential tariff level of 15–21·6% in 1931, group C remained practically unchanged compared with 1927.

Surveying German industrial tariff policy in the post-War period as a whole, it must be called decidedly protectionist up to 1925, in view of the retention of the inflation duties on luxury articles, and particularly in the sphere of manufactured goods. Only a fraction of the group of goods affected by the increases deserved the description of "luxuries," while semi-manufactured goods, like cotton and woollen fabrics, rolled iron, aluminium wire, or finished goods like woven garments, clothing, shoes, porcelain, watches, motor-cars, etc., were of great importance for supplying the needs of a much larger section of the population than that of the wealthy class.

Such increased protective duties were bound to raise the general price level of industrial products in Germany, and as the German industry produced the protected goods in large quantities, it must be assumed that protectionist intentions were decisive [2] in retaining this tariff policy in 1924, which was

[1] Comp. *Röpke*, loc. cit., pp. 36–37, 59.
[2] See *Harms*, op. cit., pp. 77–78.

directed mainly against competitive foreign industries working with cheaper labour.[1] From 1925 onward, however, the course of German industrial tariff policy was decidedly moderate, and remained so, even after the outbreak of the world economic crisis, up till 1931.[2] The large proportions of exports to total output of nearly all German industries and Germany's character as a leading exporter of manufactured goods, intent on avoiding any protectionist retaliation by foreign countries, explained this tariff policy.

2. FRANCE
(See Table A1 for France in Appendix)

Although, both before and after the War, and by virtue of the extent of her exports and imports of semi and wholly manufactured goods, France represented the second great industrial country of the European continent, she was dependent for the supply of her industrial requirements upon an incomparably greater percentage of industrial imports than Germany, especially for supplying the requirements of finished goods. This fact shows the fundamentally agrarian character of this country before 1914.[3] In 1913 not less than 16·6% of her total imports comprised industrial finished goods (more than double the German figure); among the 61·3% of the total imports which comprised industrial raw materials and semi-manufactured goods were considerable quantities of the latter, although raw materials were the main constituents of this class, as in every industrial country.

After the War, industry expanded in France to a far greater extent than in any other industrial country of Europe, with the result that the structure of French economy was profoundly changed and the composition of French imports was considerably altered.

[1] See *Enquête*, II, p. 324.
[2] Comp. *Röpke*, loc. cit., p. 33.
[3] See *Enquête*, II, p. 95.

TABLE A: FRENCH INDUSTRIAL IMPORTS, 1913–31
(*In Mill. Frs. and %*)

Group	1913 Mill. Frs.	1913 % of I.I.	1927 Mill. Frs.	1927 % of I.I.	1931 Mill. Frs.	1931 % of I.I.
Total Imports	8420	—	53000	—	42200	—
Of which:						
Manufactured goods	1660	100·0	5750	100·0	9170	100·0
Of which:						
Machinery and instruments	320	19·3	1030	18·0	1900	20·6
Paper articles	94	5·7	450	7·8	560	6·1
Tools, metal	88	5·3	380	6·6	740	8·1
Chemicals	n.i.	n.i.	780	13·6	680	7·4
Ready-made furs	88	5·3	280	4·9	320	3·5

I.I. = Industrial Imports.
n.i. = no information.
See *Tableau général*, 1913, 1927, 1931.

There was, in fact, a decline in the imports of industrial finished goods, owing to growing self-sufficiency, so that in 1928 they dropped to 11·9% of the total imports (a reduction of almost 30% compared with 1913), whereas the proportion of raw materials and semi-manufactured goods rose to 64·2% of the total imports, thanks to the demand of an expanding industry;[1] and the increased percentage of imports of industrial finished goods in 1931 is to be ascribed to temporary favourable conditions.[2] Table A shows the amounts of some important groups of imports: in particular the sharp rise in the imports of machinery and metal-ware between 1913 and 1931, which reflects the post-War industrialization of France.

Prior to the War, France possessed the highest industrial tariff level of Central Europe. This old and firmly rooted protectionist feature of French economic policy was clearly manifested in the duties on semi-manufactured goods. The average of duties upon semi-manufactured textiles in 1913 (between 13–62%) was exceptional. The wide margin

[1] These figures are taken from *Gaedicke, Vol. of Tables*, p. 19.
[2] Cf. p. 69 of this book.

between the minimum and maximum figures is explained by the unusually differentiated structure of the French tariff, "the most complicated in the world." [1] Moreover, the duties on cotton yarn and fabrics were even far in excess of these figures (see Table B, p. 124). A high degree of protection was also granted to semi-manufactured metal goods, particularly to the heavy iron industry. The tariff level of class BIII fluctuated between 27·5% and 41%, many of its duties being in excess of the latter figure. By way of contrast, the average figures for paper and wood manufactures and chemicals (with the exception of the very high aniline-dye duty) were low. The tariff level of the whole group B in 1913 reached the unusual height of 16·5–34·3%. Entirely outside this category were the revenue duties on mineral oils, with an average of 138–194%.

French tariff policy before the War in respect of industrial finished goods was very moderate. In 1913 the potential tariff level of group C reached 13–20%. From this, however, the protective duties on textiles deviated considerably (tariff level of class CI: 21–34%). Cotton hosiery and clothes were taxed still higher. On the other hand, the remaining classes of group C, with the exception of paper goods and metal-ware, were below this level. The duties on dynamos were notably heavy (see Table C, p. 124).

As a result of the War, France experienced a great expansion of her heavy-iron industry, through the incorporation of Alsace-Lorraine, the strengthening of her cotton-spinning and her chemical industries, and, stimulated by the post-War evolution of French currency and capital market conditions (inflation and reparations), a lively development of her general industry, which was particularly marked in a number of typical post-War industries, such as the artificial-silk, the motor-car, the motor-tire, the paper, and the chemical industries.[2]

It was the intention of French economic policy, after the

[1] See *Eichhorn, Zolltarif für Frankreich*, p. 2.
[2] See *Die Wirtschaft des Auslandes*, pp. 65–80, hereafter cited as *W.d.A.*, also *Enquête*, II, pp. 95–97.

stabilization of the franc in 1926–27, to replace the old tariff of 1910, which was awkwardly adapted to post-War conditions by the method of additional co-efficients, by a tariff framed to correspond to the post-War price level; the new duties were designed in particular to afford French industry more effective protection against the feared *concurrence allemande* than the pre-War tariff. This new tariff, however, remained in the drafting stage, and its place was taken by the tariff stipulations of the commercial treaties of 1927–28 (with Germany, Belgium, Italy, and Switzerland).

Between 1927 and 1931 they formed France's actual industrial tariff. No less than 1700 industrial items were affected by them, mostly by increases upon pre-War rates, although not to the extent intended by the French draft tariff.[1]

This trend can clearly be seen in the figures of potential tariff levels, and is still more sharply outlined by a comparison of the absolute height of France's pre-War and post-War rates upon semi and wholly manufactured articles. The rates of duty of group B were on the average 10–40% higher, for chemicals and metals up to 50%, while the tariff level of group B, owing to the upward trend of prices, was only about 10% higher. In spite of the general increase in rates, the tariff levels of the classes of textiles, wood, paper, and chemical goods in group B were even slightly below their figures of 1913; only semi-manufactured metal goods, with 18–58%, showed in 1927 an increase of 40% compared with 1913. Various commodities again were marked by duties far in excess of the average figures. The complete reverse was the case with mineral oils, the duties of which declined to 38–63%—i.e. to merely 30% of the level of 1913—in consequence of extensive reductions of their rates.

The post-War increase in duties on industrial products was more visible in the picture of the virtual French tariff level of finished goods. The level of group C rose to 21·5–30%, and was thus 50–70% higher than in 1913, whilst rates of duty on

---

[1] See *Proix*, op. cit., p. 4, and *W.d.A.*, p. 68.

finished goods in 1927 were on an average 80–140% higher than in 1913. The differences between the rates of the minimum and the maximum tariff of all classes were smaller in 1927 than they were in 1913. Moreover, the tariff level of each class was raised very much. Particularly sharp increases may be noted in a number of cases. The duties on vehicles rose to 230–350% of their 1913 level, metal goods to 250%, machinery to 200%, and only textile duties, in spite of heavy increases in rates, were somewhat lower than in 1913, owing to a still greater increase in prices.

TABLE B: DUTIES ON SEMI-MANUFACTURED GOODS IN FRANCE, 1913–31

(In % of Prices)

Goods	1913	1927	1931
Raw cotton yarn up to No. 50	3·7–83·0	4·9–130·0	6·9–185·0
Raw linen yarn . . .	4·7–37·0	8·5–67·0	9·7–80·0
Bleached cotton fabrics . .	17·3–173·0	13·0–115·0	17·0–180·0
Pig iron	18·3	10·2–25·5	12·0–25·0
Iron sheets not worked . .	23·4–40·0	9·5–30·0	9·0–29·0
Iron tubes not worked . .	28·0–43·0	25·0–39·0	22·0–34·5
Iron wire	49·0–175·0	50·0–450·0	52·0–460·0
Aniline dyes . . .	20·5–36·5	1·8–6·0	2·2–7·0
Cellulose	11·1–22·2	11·0–22·0	11·0–22·0

TABLE C: DUTIES ON IMPORTANT FINISHED GOODS IN FRANCE, 1913–31

(In % of Prices)

Goods	1913	1927	1931
Cotton hosiery . . .	45·0–90·0	47·0	43·0
Silk and artificial silk stockings	10·8–21·6	31·0–62·0	44·0–88·0
Silk ribbons	6·7–9·9	39·5–55·0	49·5–68·5
Printing paper . . .	28·3	34·0	45·0
Coloured porcelain . .	13·4	49·5	49·3
Knitting machines . . .	7·8–13·0	16·6–82·0	15·5–79·0
Dynamos	8·4–71·0	12·5–168·0	10·3–160·0
Tool machinery . . .	7·4–11·0	5·0–26·2	5·2–27·0
Motor-cars	5·5–11·0	45·0	44·0–86·0
Telephone apparatus . .	5·4–9·9	18·0	18·0
Toys	26·5	39·0–78·0	45·0–90·0

In 1927 the French tariff levels of several classes of group C were much higher than those in 1913 and the respective German figures in 1927.

	French Tariff Level	German Tariff Level
	%	%
Paper . . .	33·0	12·1
Metal goods . .	17·5–22·7	0·5–15·0
Machinery . . .	12·0–37·0	3·7–15·0
Toys and tires . .	23·0–43·3	14·5–17·0

In connection with these significant increases, it is noteworthy that the duties to protect French industries of capital goods were disproportionately raised—industries, the expansion of which was especially marked after the War (heavy industries, engineering, motor-car, rubber tires, and printing-paper industries).

Between 1927 and 1931 French industrial tariff policy remained stable because it was tied by commercial treaties with regard to about 70% of all rates. (The Franco-German commercial treaty of 1927 did not expire until 1935.[1])

The increases recorded among nearly all classes of groups B and C were, as in the case of Germany, almost entirely the result of the downward trend in the prices of industrial goods, which assumed greater dimensions in 1931 owing to the world economic crisis.

The tariff level for semi-manufactured goods rose in 1931 to 16·2–47·5% (=100–140% of 1913); that for industrial finished goods to 23·6–34·4% (=175–185% of 1913).

The year 1931 was the last in which duties were the chief instrument for regulating imports. The impossibility of raising the tied rates on the one hand, and on the other the firm determination to cut down drastically not only agrarian but also industrial imports, prompted the introduction of quotas even for industrial imports at the beginning of 1932 in order to rectify the balance of trade and to protect French

[1] See *Jones*, op. cit., pp. 141 and 143.

industries. By July of that year over 1100 industrial products were subjected to quotas.[1] French industrial protectionism, already strongly marked in the height of industrial tariffs, had found in 1932 a new method by erecting barriers insurmountable to the import of industrial goods.

3. ITALY

(See Tables AI and AII for Italy in Appendix)

Pre-War Italy even more than France was mainly agricultural; yet it had an extensive foreign trade in industrial goods which made it the third greatest Continental market for and supplier of industrial raw materials and commodities. Its increasing industrialization provided a substantial surplus of industrial imports over exports. 23·4% of Italy's total imports comprised industrial finished goods, while 19·1% comprised semi-manufactured goods. After the War Fascism pursued a policy of intensive industrialization.

By 1927 the import of industrial finished goods had fallen to 16% of the total imports, i.e. it had declined by 30% compared with 1913. Although finished goods in 1931 were again 20·8% of the total imports they failed to reach the pre-War proportion (see Table A).[2]

Italy's pre-War duties on semi and wholly manufactured goods generally represented a moderate tariff, which exhibited definitely protectionist tendencies for a few industries only. They were most marked in the heavy iron industries, as well as in certain branches of the paper, textile, and glass industries.[3]

In 1913 the tariff level for group B reached 21–28%, textiles and chemicals, however, showing lower figures; only semi-manufactured goods of the metal industries with a level of

[1] See account of French quota policy since 1931–32 in *Jones*, op. cit., pp. 141–146.

[2] Italian trade statistics separate raw materials, semi and wholly manufactured goods very carefully, which enables us to select only the important figures.

[3] See *W.d.A.*, p. 175.

TABLE A: ITALIAN INDUSTRIAL IMPORTS, 1913–31

(In Mill. Lire and %)

Group	1913 Mill. L.	1913 % of T.I.	1927 Mill. L.	1927 % of T.I.	1931 Mill. L.	1931 % of T.I.
Total imports	3645	100·0	20375	100·0	11645	100·0
Of which:						
(a) Semi-manufactured						
goods .	700	19·1	4230	20·7	2465	20·4
(b) Manufactured goods	852	23·4	3265	16·0	2410	20·8
I.I. (=a+b)	1552	42·5	7495	36·7	4875	41·2

I.I. = Industrial imports without industrial raw materials.
T.I. = Total Imports.
See *Movimento Commerciale*, 1913, 1927, 1931.

28–34%, and with even higher duties on single semi-manufactured iron goods exceeded the average (see Table B, p. 128). The fiscal duties on mineral oils were also exceptionally high.

The potential tariff level for finished goods being 12·6–16·7%, was much lower than that for semi-manufactured goods. Thanks to heavier duties on hosiery, on cotton and wool, and particularly on silk and artificial silk goods (see Table C, p. 128), the tariff level of the class of textiles, with 15·5–19·5%, exceeded this average. It was surpassed still more by that of class CII (paper goods); most of all by the duties on glass and ceramic goods.

On the other hand, the duties on metal goods were below the tariff level of group C; those of machinery and vehicles considerably below it.

Very soon after coming into power, the Fascist Government applied itself to the comprehensive industrialization of Italy with the same energy that it directed to the intensive development of Italian agriculture. In contrast to the agrarian policy, tariffs played a decisive part in the furtherance of these aims, although the many other means at the disposal of Fascism for penetrating Italian economy were not neglected.

In respect of all the classes in groups B and C rates had been raised by the year 1927, in some instances so drastically as to bring about a sensational change in Italy's industrial tariff level of 1927, compared with 1913. The strongest degree of protection was afforded to the great industries of capital goods: the chemical industry, the heavy metal industries, the engineering industries, as well as the automobile, paper, glass, and rubber industries. Of industries engaged in producing consumer's goods, silk and artificial silk production was strongly protected.

TABLE B: DUTIES ON IMPORTANT SEMI-MANUFACTURED GOODS IN ITALY, 1913-31
(In % of Prices)

Goods	1913	1927	1931
Raw cotton yarn up to No. 50 .	4·4–15·0	3·3–34·0	5·3–54·0
Raw artificial silk yarn . .	Duty free	21·0	30·0
Pig iron	13·2	28·0–41·0	33·0–48·0
Iron sheets not worked . .	29·5–40·0	31·6–61·0	30·0–58·0
Aluminium sheets not worked .	25·0	24·0–40·0	60·0–92·0
Nitrogen	Duty free	11·0	56·0
Sulphurated ammonia . .	16·5	19·5	108·0
Aniline dyes	Duty free	12·0–45·0	14·4–54·0
Petrol	57·0	115·0	360·0

TABLE C: DUTIES ON IMPORTANT FINISHED GOODS IN ITALY, 1913-31
(In % of Prices)

Goods	1913	1927	1931
Leather shoes . . .	8·2	7·7–27·0	10·7–37·5
Cotton hosiery . . .	23·0–32·0	16·3–23·0	19·5–39·0
Artificial silk stockings .	20·0–24·0	46·5–70·0	?
Printing paper . . .	35·5	20·5	27·0
Sheet glass	35·0–56·0	20·0–85·0	18·5–80·0
Wood-working machinery .	6·9–12·2	24·5–72·0	23·5–69·0
Dynamos	10·4–16·4	21·0–43·0	20·0–41·0
Motor cars	1·8–5·4	45·0–55·0	137·0
Radio apparatus . . .	?	11·4	102·0–125·0
Motor-tires	6·0	21·0	40·0

? = the respective duties could not be ascertained.

On an average, rates for group B were raised by more than 50–110% compared with 1913, in addition to which numerous goods, still on the free list in 1913, notably chemicals, became liable to new high duties (e.g. aniline dyes). Duty increases among the chemical group were higher still,[1] while some articles showed rises which were fourfold the rates of 1913. Taking 1913 as 100, the rates for leather amounted to 300–600%, for pig iron to 280–440%, etc. In spite of the rising prices of industrial products, such a strengthening of protective barriers was bound to express itself in a higher tariff level so that, with a tariff level of 22–35% for semi-manufactured goods Italy had reached a figure 5–25% above that of 1913.

The great group of semi-manufactured metal goods rose to a much greater extent than is indicated by this average figure. Their duties reached the unprecedented average of 38–63% (equal to 235–285% of 1913). Further, the tariff level of chemicals rose to between two and three times that of 1913, while the rise was least of all in the case of semi-manufactured textiles.

Protected by these high tariff walls, certain industries of capital goods developed rapidly.[2]

The tariff levels of finished goods also rose strongly. With an average increase of rates of 115–185% for all goods of group C its tariff level rose to 22·2–34·5%. In other words, it increased by 75–100% compared with 1913. Within this large group, however, the tariff levels of the single classes developed quite differently. Vehicles rose to 43–53% (equal to 800–840% of 1913), machinery to 11·5–21·3% (180–285% of 1913). Steam engines, dynamos, etc., were taxed very heavily (see Table C, p. 128). Among textiles, sharp increases of duties on silk and artificial silk goods effected a rise in the class tariff level of 24–50% compared with 1913, while the level of metal goods rose by 44–100%.

---

[1] For reasons of principle, statistical indications of the average increase in rates are often impossible owing to the goods free of duty in 1913. See pp. 35–36 of this study.   [2] See *W.d.A.*, pp. 174, 185.

Some of the protected branches of the industries of finished goods also expanded much, such as the automobile, the machinery, and the artificial silk industries. In 1927 the output of the machine-producing industry reached 240% of the output of 1913, while the production of artificial silk expanded by 100% between 1926 and 1929.[1] Average Italian imports of finished goods had declined by 32% between 1910–14 and 1927.[2]

In contrast to the stability of German and French industrial tariff policies, which were more fixed by treaties between 1927 and 1931, Fascism continued to use high tariffs as a method of protection even after 1927. At the end of 1929 duties were raised afresh, especially on semi- and wholly-manufactured goods of the linen, cotton, wool, chemical, and engineering trades. In 1930 there was a drastic increase in the motor-car duties, in 1931 fresh increases in the duties on products of the aluminium, nitrogen, radio, and telephone industries. In consequence of the English currency depreciation in September 1931, a general 15% *ad valorem* duty was imposed upon all articles the rates of which were not tied or exempted by special decree. The result of all these measures, combined with the sharp fall in prices of industrial products in 1930–31, was a further raising of Italy's industrial tariff walls in the year 1931. The tariff level of group B reached 40–59% (=190–205% of 1913) and all class levels likewise rose sharply.

The most striking of them were the figures for semi-manufactured metal goods, rising to 45–85% (=160–255% of 1913), and for chemicals, rising to 44·5–59·5% (=485–585% of 1913).

The new increases in the duties on semi-manufactured aluminium goods, on nitrogen and sulphurated ammonia, were plainly revealed here, in conjunction with the other duties which were already high.

The tariff level of group C amounted to 34–50% (=300% of 1913). The figures of some classes reached higher figures.

[1] See *Enquête*, II, pp. 107–108.
[2] *W.d.A.*, p. 174.

At their head were *vehicles*, with a tariff level of 93–111% (=1680–1820% of 1913), among which the sharply increased motor-car duties indicated the retaliatory policy provoked by the very high new American Tariff of 1930.[1]   The tariff levels of glass and ceramic with 42·5–61%, and toys and rubber tires with 33·5–58% likewise surpassed, although not in such marked degree, the already high general figure of group C, while metal goods just reached it.   The rest of the classes, on the other hand, remained considerably below it.   Of 62 manufactured articles, 38 were liable in 1931 to duties between 1–30%, 13 to duties between 30–50%, and 11 to duties over 50% (some over 100%).

This tariff policy had already placed Italy in 1927 at the head of industrial protectionism among the great industrial countries of Europe.   The increases imposed up to 1931, however, were so great that in this year Italy exceeded *all* industrial countries of Europe in the height of her tariff walls.

4. GREAT BRITAIN

The introduction of duties on a whole series of industrial articles by England in War time and the immediate post-War period made it necessary, in our analysis of Europe's potential industrial tariff levels up to 1931, to devote some attention also to Great Britain, but, owing to the majority of the groups of semi- and wholly-manufactured goods remaining on the free list, it was impossible to compile tables of potential tariff levels similar to those for the other European countries.

As the duties were usually *ad valorem* duties and remained stable, a short summary without comparisons between the various groups and years was sufficient.[2]

Before the War Great Britain imposed no duties on industrial goods. In 1915 financial reasons and considerations of the balance of trade prompted Mr *Reginald McKenna*, then

---

[1] Comp. *Jones*, loc. cit., pp. 76–83.
[2] Comp. *H. Williams*: *Through Tariffs to Prosperity*, especially Chaps. II and III.

Chancellor of the Exchequer, to introduce *ad valorem* duties of 33·3% upon motor-cars, cycles, watches, musical instruments, and films. At the end of the War these duties were retained by various Conservative Cabinets, which were becoming more and more susceptible to the idea of a moderate tariff and the encouragement of Empire trade by means of preferential duties.

With regard to a second group of goods, England's dependence upon German supplies, which was painfully felt during the War, prompted the levying of *ad valorem* duties of $33\frac{1}{3}$% upon such articles. In the case of optical glasses and photographic apparatus the rate was even 50%. By this protection, it was intended to develop native industries.

These duties were to protect the key industries, so called because their products were declared to be vital for the industrial process as a whole and especially for England's readiness in case of war. All synthetic chemicals, scientific and electrical instruments and apparatus were affected. The import of dyes was prohibited for a period of ten years commencing from 1921 and only permitted in an emergency by licence.

The third great group of goods, upon which the Conservative Party demanded tariffs during the years 1923–25, were articles for which a Board of Trade Inquiry had established the existence of unfair competition or dumping. These duties were vigorously opposed by the Liberal and Labour Opposition after the Conservative victory of 1924, but in the years 1925–28 they were introduced for a whole series of industries. In 1925 duties of 33·3% were imposed on silk and artificial silk stockings, on lace and embroidery, on gloves and cutlery, and also specific duties on silk and artificial silk yarns and tissues; [1] in 1926 on packing paper (16·7%), in 1927 on ceramic goods (specific duties), in 1928 on enamel-ware and metal household goods (25%). The Dominions received a preference amount-

---

[1] Duties on silk yarn in 1927 reached about 30%, on artificial silk 78% of the value; those on silk and artificial silk fabrics about 34–41%. In 1931 the duties on silk yarn were about 50%, on artificial silk 100%, tissues 54–76%.

ing to 33·3% of these rates.   The introduction of duties on iron and steel was refused by Mr. *Baldwin*, in spite of the growing agitation of the trades concerned.

The Labour Party, which came to power in 1929 under *J. Ramsay MacDonald*, announced the removal of these anti-dumping duties, but by 1931 owing to great budgetary difficulties, they had only abolished the duties on gloves, lace, and cutlery; for the revenue produced by the duties was urgently required.   The extent of the trades protected in post-War times by these duties is very considerable; they employed about 500,000 workers.[1]

In contrast to the heavy permanent depression which hung over England's unprotected basic industries (textiles, coal, iron and steel, engineering, and shipbuilding), these trades were among her most thriving industries between 1919 and 1931.   The tariffs, by cutting imports, had secured them a far greater share of the home market than fell to the lot of the staple industries.[2]   This fact, together with the rising movement of industrial protection in Europe and in the United States of America, certainly contributed greatly to the victory of those forces in England in November 1931 which had been turning away from Free Trade since the beginning of the century (*Chamberlain*) and looking in the direction of closer Empire union by demanding the imposition of a moderate tariff.   Finally, during the crisis of 1931, simultaneously with the departure from the Gold Standard, they achieved the introduction of protectionism, and at Ottawa in 1932 effected a marked fiscal severance of the Empire from the rest of the world.

5. BELGIUM
(*See Table A1 for Belgium in Appendix*)

Among the small countries of industrial Europe Belgium before and after the War was the greatest customer for industrial raw materials and semi-manufactured goods.   With a

[1] *Williams*, op. cit., p. 155.
[2] *W.d.A.*, pp. 6, 23, 30–32.

high degree of industrialization, still increasing after the War, and possessing important semi-manufacturing industries, which depended on exports, Belgium yet imported large quantities of industrial manufactured articles of every kind. Of the total imports of 1913 raw materials and semi-manufactured goods accounted for 64·5%, finished articles for 11%. In 1928 the proportions were 60·5% and 18%; in 1931 they were even 29·4% and 46%, according to Belgian trade statistics which included a number of semi-finished goods in the category of "finished goods." Belgium's supplementary industrial requirements have therefore tended to increase since the War, although comparisons were rendered difficult by Belgium's Customs Union with Luxembourg. Table A shows the magnitudes of Belgian industrial imports, without going into details.

TABLE A: BELGIAN INDUSTRIAL IMPORTS, 1913–31 *
(*In Mill. Frs. and* %)

Group	1913 Mill. Frs.	1913 % of T.I.	1927 Mill. Frs.	1927 % of T.I.	1931 Mill. Frs.	1931 % of T.I.
Total Imports . Viz.:	4635	100·0	29040	100·0	24000	100·0
(a) Raw materials, semi-finished	2665	57·0	15280	52·7	11000	46·0
(b) Finished goods	870	18·8	6600	23·8	7060	29·4
I.I. = (a + b) .	3535	75·8	21880	75·5	18060	75·4

I.I. = Industrial Imports.
T.I. = Total Imports.
See *Tableau général du commerce de la Belgique*, 1913, 1927, 1931.

* Owing to the importance of transit trade, the 1913 figures can not be compared with 1927 and 1931 (see p. 73 of this book). "Finished goods" of the Table are not identical with Gaedicke's classification.

As in the case of agriculture, Belgium before the War pursued a definitely free-trade policy, with very low duties, even in the case of industrial articles. With numerous articles in all classes of group B on the free list, its tariff level in 1913 reached a height of 6·5–8·7%, at which level, and frequently below it, most articles were taxed. An exception to this rule was cotton tissues, which were heavily taxed (see Table B, below). The tariff level for finished goods was somewhat higher, being 8·7–10·2%, but the duties on machinery, apparatus, and vehicles were considerably lower than this figure would indicate.

TABLE B: DUTIES ON IMPORTANT INDUSTRIAL
SEMI-FINISHED GOODS IN BELGIUM, 1913–31
(*In % of Prices*)

Goods	1913	1927	1931
Raw cotton yarn, up to No. 50	1·2–4·8	0·7–3·0	0·6–2·2
Raw artificial silk yarn . .	Tax free	15·0–18·0	18·8–22·5
Cotton tissues . . .	9·4–40·0	6·9–20·0	9·0–26·0
Pig iron	2·4	1·0–1·5	1·2–1·7
Sulphurated ammonia . .	Tax free	60·0	110·0

Even in the post-War period Belgium adhered to a moderate industrial tariff policy, although a number of characteristic exceptions deserve to be mentioned. The new tariff of 1924 only moderately increased the duties on semi-manufactured goods compared with 1913,[1] so that the general tariff level of group B in 1927 rose only to 9·7–11%, while textiles and semi-finished metal goods even fell below their pre-War levels.

The changes in the duties on finished goods were more considerable. Their general tariff level rose by about 40% to 8·3–14%. Within group C, however, a few classes were more strongly protected, and the goods in question were the products of industries which played a big part in Belgian

---

[1] Figures showing the raising of industrial duty rates in 1927 and 1931 compared with 1913 could not be given owing to the large number of goods on the free list in 1913, which was much reduced in 1924, et seq.

economy, so that even in this free-trade country there were symptoms of post-War industrial protection.

The duties on machinery, for example, were raised by 180–650% compared with 1913, so that the tariff level of their class rose to 7·4–15·3% (=180–530% of 1913). In the case of metal goods the change from 13% *ad valorem* duties to specific duties after the War resulted in the class level rising to 9·6–17·7% (=160% of 1913). Leather, silk, and artificial silk goods, as well as some machines, were taxed above the average (see Table C).

TABLE C: DUTIES ON IMPORTANT INDUSTRIAL FINISHED GOODS IN BELGIUM, 1913–31
(*In % of Prices*)

Goods	1913	1927	1931
Leather shoes . . .	10·0	5·5–21·0	7·7–31·0
Cotton hosiery . . .	15·0	18·0–30·0	16·0–27·0
Artificial silk stockings . .	15·0	25·0	25·0
Motors	1·4–8·4	4·0–32·0	3·5–24·5
Dynamos	0·8–4·8	5·3–24·7	5·1–24·0
Private motor-cars . ·.	3·3–8·8	7·8–17·4	12·8–28·4

Between 1927 and 1931 Belgian industrial tariff policy remained fairly stable. The rise in the tariff levels of groups B and C was almost entirely due to the general fall in prices. Only the rise in the tariff level of mineral oils was to be explained by increased fiscal duties combined with a heavy fall in the prices of the articles. But even with the 1931 figures (tariff level of group B, 15–16·1%; tariff level of group C, 9·2–16·5%) Belgium showed striking moderation compared with the industrial tariff levels of other countries.

6. SWITZERLAND
(*See Tables A1 and A11 for Switzerland in Appendix*)

In spite of the high development of some of her export industries and the vital importance of industry to the general economic structure, Switzerland is dependent in many spheres of industrial production upon supplementary imports, and forms consequently an important industrial market. In 1913 39% of the total imports consisted of industrial raw materials and semi-finished goods, 28·2% of finished goods. In 1928 the corresponding figures were 41·1% and 30·6%.[1] Owing to the great prosperity of the population and the concentration of Swiss industrial production upon a few very important trades dependent on exports, the proportion of imports of finished goods, distributed over many different branches of production, was particularly high for an industrial country, and the absolute amounts, as Table A shows, were very large in view of a population of 4·1 millions.

TABLE A: SWISS INDUSTRIAL IMPORTS, 1913–31
(In Mill. Frs. and %)

Group	1913 Mill. Frs.	1913 % of T.I.	1927 Mill. Frs.	1927 % of T.I.	1931 Mill. Frs.	1931 % of T.I.
Total Imports .	1920	100·0	2565	100·0	2250	100·0
Viz.:						
(a) Raw materials .	685	35·3	893	34·8	680	30·2
(b) Manufactures .	635	33·0	974	37·8	983	43·5
I.I. = (a + b) . .	1320	68·3	1867	72·5	1663	74·0

T.I. = Total Imports.
I.I. = Industrial Imports.
See *Statistik des Warenverkehrs der Schweiz*, 1913, 1927, 1931.

The Swiss industrial tariff policy of pre-War times took account of this large supplementary requirement of industrial consumption by fixing very moderate rates of duty. The tariff level of group B amounted in 1913 to 6·4–8·3%. Only cellulose, iron wire, and perfumes were taxed more heavily than these figures indicate (see Table B, p. 138).

Industrial finished goods likewise showed a low general tariff level, 7·6–11·1% in 1913. A striking exception, however, even in 1913, were the duties on paper, glass, and ceramic,

[1] See *Gaedicke, Vol. of Tables*, p. 19.

which raised the tariff levels of their classes to 17·2–19% and 12·4–23%. The figures of nearly all the other class tariff levels were below the general average. In only a few cases, e.g. upon paper, sheet glass, and iron domestic utensils, duties were levied in 1913 which considerably exceeded the average (see Table C, below).

TABLE B: DUTIES ON IMPORTANT INDUSTRIAL SEMI-FINISHED GOODS IN SWITZERLAND, 1913–31
(In % of Prices)

Goods	1913	1927	1931
Raw cotton yarn, up to No. 50	1·7–5·0	6·3–7·5	9·0–10·8
Bleached cotton tissues .	12·8	15·0	21·8–30·8
Cellulose	33·4	60·0	53·5
Crude aluminium . .	1·0	1·9	30·0
Aluminium plate . .	5·0	10·0	44·0
Perfumes	10·6–21·2	14·0–28·0	11·3–20·6

TABLE C: DUTIES ON IMPORTANT INDUSTRIAL FINISHED GOODS IN SWITZERLAND, 1913–31
(In % of Prices)

Goods	1913	1927	1931
Leather shoes . . .	3·7–6·5	8·6–17·2	11·7–49·0
Cotton hosiery . . .	10·5	18·3	17·0
Artificial silk stockings .	6·7	20·1	29·0
Printing paper . . .	22·6	51·0	67·0
Cement	24·2	36·6	38·6
Sheet glass . . .	21·6–35·0	26·7	31·0
Iron household utensils .	4·2–21·0	8·4–33·0	10·0–40·0
Private cars . . .	4·4	10·0–27·6	27·2–46·5

The new Swiss tariff of 1921 increased on the average the rates of duty on semi-manufactured goods by 110–140%. Consequently, the tariff level of all the goods in group B rose, and reached 9·8–13·1% in 1927 being 155–160% of the position in 1913.

Considerably greater even than in the case of semi-finished goods was the rise in the Swiss post-War tariff level for industrial finished goods. With duty rates increased by 150–200% it rose to 15·3–20%, a doubling of the pre-War position. Printing paper, cement, plate-glass, and motor-cars were taxed far above the average (see Table C, p. 138).

Swiss industrial tariff policy, limited in its freedom by trade agreements, met the world economic crisis by raising duties considerably in a number of cases where Swiss industries competed with foreign products. This, combined with the general fall in prices during 1931, substantially raised the Swiss industrial tariff level. (Tariff level of group B in 1931: 12·6–17·8% = 95–215% of the level of 1913.)

With regard to finished goods most duty rates remained unchanged between 1927 and 1931; their general potential tariff level rose to 20·3–24% (=215–270% of 1913). Very high were the duties on paper goods with a class tariff level of 56% (=295–320% of 1913) which assumed prohibitive proportions.[1] This was also true of vehicles and metal goods. The other class tariff levels remained below the general average and did not appreciably change.

Although figures of the tariff level in Switzerland both in 1927 and in 1931 showed high increases compared with 1913, they still remained relatively low in view of the very low starting-point of the pre-War level and in view of the industrial tariff levels of most other states in Europe in 1931. From Table A it will be seen that the import of manufactures in 1931 was higher than in 1927, so that the previous duty increases seem to have had very little effect. As, however, Switzerland in the year 1931 was affected more and more by the world economic crisis, in consequence of the worsening of the situation in middle Europe, especially in Germany and Austria, and was exposed to more severe competition, particularly from German industry, while the chief markets of Switzerland in Europe and overseas were gradually closed, thanks to stringent tariff or other protectionist measures, at the beginning of 1932 she proceeded to fix quotas for agrarian

[1] See *Reichlin*, op. cit., p. 44.

and industrial imports, which by 1932 embraced about 200 commodities.[1] Thus Switzerland also made a fundamental change in her trade policy, which compels the student to devote his attention in the first place to the new methods of import restrictions.

7. AUSTRIA (1913: AUSTRIA-HUNGARY)
(*See Table A1 for Austria in Appendix*)

The dismemberment of the Austro-Hungarian Monarchy in 1919 added two states to pre-War industrial Europe. One of them, viz. Austria, by virtue of the great industries of finished goods in Vienna and the important semi-manufacturing metal, wood, and paper industries, based upon the ore deposits of Styria and the timber wealth of the country, became an industrial country to a very large extent. On the other hand, by the new frontiers Austria lost important industries in Bohemia and Galicia (formerly parts of the Dual Monarchy) for supplying her industrial requirements.

TABLE A: AUSTRIAN INDUSTRIAL IMPORTS, 1927–31
(*In Mill. Schill. and %*)

Group	1927 Mill. Sch.	1927 % of T.I.	1931 Mill. Sch.	1931 % of T.I.
Total Imports . . .	3190	100·0	2210	100·0
Viz.:				
Finished goods . . .	1125	39·0	854	38·6

T.I. = Total Imports.
See *Statistik des auswärtigen Handels Oesterreichs*, 1927, 1931.

Whereas only 23·4% of Austria-Hungary's imports (including the Monarchy's great agrarian areas) in 1913 were industrial finished goods, this percentage had grown to 31·4% in the highly industrialized Austria of 1928.[2] These large industrial requirements, combined with the great export dependence of

[1] See *Jones*, op. cit., pp. 135–136.
[2] *Gaedicke, Vol. of Tables*, p. 19.

Austrian industries induced the Austrian Government to follow a very moderate industrial tariff policy, in contrast to the protectionist course of the Dual Monarchy. This policy became more protectionist after 1926 in reaction to protectionist tendencies of the neighbouring countries.[1] The moderate tariff of 1924 was, between 1926 and 1931, brought to a slowly rising level by five tariff supplements with considerably higher duty rates, but these increases had only been partially put into force by 1929.

The tariff level of group B in 1927 was 13·4–17%, or about 20–30% below the Austro-Hungarian level of 1913, and only in the case of the chemical duties exceeded the pre-War level by about 10%. The highest duties were imposed on the products of the heavy metal industries (tariff level of their class: 29·5%). Printed cotton tissues, a number of semi-finished iron goods, petrol, and perfumes were taxed very high (see Table B).

TABLE B: DUTIES ON IMPORTANT SEMI-FINISHED
GOODS IN AUSTRIA, 1927–31
(1913: AUSTRO-HUNGARIAN DUTIES)
(*In % of Prices*)

Goods	1913	1927	1931
Raw cotton yarn, up to No. 50	3·6–8·5	3·7–8·7	5·2–12·0
Printed cotton tissues . .	31·0–80·0	24·8–53·5	35·5–60·0
Tinned sheets . . .	51·0–60·0	Tax free	32·0–41·0
Iron plates, not worked . .	32·6–42·0	2·8–16·8	16·6–26·0
Perfumes	45·0	59·0	47·5
Petrol	45·0	51·0	97·0–138·0

The general tariff level for finished goods was the same as in 1913, but contained considerable differences in respect of some class levels. The rates of duties on textiles were increased by 35–50% compared with 1913, and the tariff level of their class rose by 20–35%. A similar increase in duty rates had a

[1] Comp. *W.d.A.*, pp. 243–244.

greater effect in the case of the tariff level of the finished metal goods, which reached a height of 25·6–43% (=150% of 1913). The duties on the goods of the remaining classes were lower than in 1913.

TABLE C: DUTIES ON IMPORTANT FINISHED GOODS IN AUSTRIA, 1927–31
(In % of Prices)

Goods	1913	1927	1931
Leather shoes . . .	6·0–9·1	6·0–19·0	8·2–31·0
Cotton hosiery . . .	35·0–49·0	55·0–74·5	76·5–118·0
Cotton garments . . .	13·6–35·0	12·3–55·0	8·3–66·0
Artificial silk stockings . .	18·4	54·0	46·0
Iron household utensils . .	25·6–35·0	28·3	36·0
Steam-engines . . .	10·0–32·0	8·6–13·0	5·9–60·0
Private motor-cars . .	7·7–17·5	40·0	36·4–74·0
Watches	12·0	20·0	25·6
Toys	5·6–46·4	4·0–38·6	4·6–38·6

Austrian trade policy reacted to the world economic crisis by putting into force many of the duty increases specified in the Supplemental Tariffs of 16th July 1930 and 14th July 1931.

With regard to semi-manufactured goods this had led by 1931 to an appreciable raising of the tariff level to 18–23·2%, which was now well 5% above the height of 1913. Noteworthy was the rise in the tariff level of semi-finished metal goods to 30·5–37%.

With regard to finished goods, the classes of the textiles, machinery, and vehicles were hard hit by new duties, so that, e.g., the tariff level of the class of finished textiles rose to 22·2–36·6% (=140–150% of 1913).

The general tariff level of group C reached 21·5–34·2% in 1931 and was thus 45% higher than the Austro-Hungarian level of 1913. With these changes between 1927 and 1931 Austria too entered the ranks of the industrial protectionist countries of Europe as regards important industrial classes, contrary to her former policy, and contrary to the policy of other small industrial countries like Belgium and Switzerland.

8. CZECHOSLOVAKIA
(See Table A1 for Czechoslovakia in Appendix)

The second industrial state which emerged from the Dual Monarchy in 1919, Czechoslovakia, inherited her industrial regions containing large deposits of raw materials, in addition to important agricultural areas. Consequently, the industrial supplemental requirements of semi- and wholly-manufactured goods were lower than in the case of Austria, but the proportion of raw materials (less the proportion of semi-manufactured goods classed under the same heading) required chiefly for the great Czech textile industries was much higher. In 1928 finished goods in the more exact sense of the term accounted for 19·8% and raw materials and semi-manufactured goods for 58·2% of the total imports.[1] Imports of semi- and wholly-manufactured goods were distributed over numerous items, without any special class achieving prominence, or any characteristic changes taking place between 1927 and 1931.

TABLE A: CZECH INDUSTRIAL IMPORTS, 1927–31
(In Mill. Crowns and %)

Group	1927 Mill. Cr.	1927 % of T.I.	1931 Mill. Cr.	1931 % of T.I.
Total Imports . . . . . Viz.:	18000	100·0	11800	100·0
(a) Raw materials, semi-finished goods	8540	47·4	5000	42·2
(b) Finished goods . . .	4940	27·4	4000	35·0
I.I. = (a + b) . . . . Viz.:	13480	74·8	9000	77·2
Cotton	2200	12·2	800	6·8
Wool	1620	9·0	580	4·9

T.I. = Total Imports.
I.I. = Industrial Imports.
See *Aussenhandel der Cz. Republik*, 1927–31. Figures of industrial imports taken from *Memorandum und Statistiques*, II, in which important semi-manufactured goods are included under the heading "Finished goods."

[1] *Gaedicke, Vol. of Tables*, p. 19.

In spite of the advanced stage of Czech industry, in spite of the importance of exports for her largest branches, Czechoslovakia, in sharp contrast to Austria, pursued an industrial protectionist tariff policy from the outset. In 1927 the duty rates on semi-manufactured goods of group B were 60–70% higher on an average than the Austro-Hungarian of 1913. In 1927 this was reflected in a still moderate growth in most of the Czech tariff levels for manufactured goods compared with the already high Austro-Hungarian levels of 1913. On the other hand, semi-finished wood and paper goods and mineral oils were taxed about 10–50% lower than in 1913; the general tariff level of group B amounted to 20–23·5% (about 5–10% higher than in 1913). Different goods in almost every class were taxed far in excess of the average figures (tissues, cellulose, and most semi-finished iron goods) (see Table B).

TABLE B: CZECH DUTIES ON IMPORTANT SEMI-MANUFACTURED GOODS, 1927–31
(1913: Austro-Hungarian Duties)
(*In % of Prices*)

Goods	1913	1927	1931
Raw cotton yarn . . .	3·6–8·5	4·9–11·6	6·9–16·2
Raw artificial silk yarn .	Tax free	14·8	22·5
Bleached cotton tissues, up to 500 gr.	7·1–24·7	10·5–42·0	14·0–56·0
Woollen tissues . . .	18·0–26·0	17·6–33·0	17·1–30·0
Cellulose	35·0	39·0	35·0
Cast iron	19·2	16·0	17·0
Rolled iron . . .	51·0	46·5	53·0
Iron sheets, not worked .	51·0–60·0	46·0–46·5	54·5–67·0
Sulphurated ammonia . .	Tax free	13·0	80·0
Ammonia sulphur . .	11·0	13·1	68·0

The protectionist tendency of Czech industrial tariff policy was more marked in the sphere of finished goods. Duty rates were increased by 95–145% compared with 1913. In the case of metal goods, apparatus, and instruments the rise was as much as 160%.

Consequently the potential tariff level of group C rose more than that of group B, viz. by 75–90% to a height of 25·5–46%. The class levels of metal goods, vehicles, toys, and tires considerably exceeded this general figure, while the rise in the case of the remaining classes kept pace with them or lagged behind. The tariff level of the class of machinery (19·4–30%) rose least of all compared with the pre-War duties (about 23–38%).

TABLE C: CZECH DUTIES ON IMPORTANT INDUSTRIAL FINISHED GOODS, 1927–31
(1913: Austro-Hungarian Duties)
(*In % of Prices*)

Goods	1913	1927	1931
Cotton stockings	16·5–26·0	21·4–41·5	26·0–51·0
Cotton garments	13·6–35·0	18·0–80·0	18·1–55·0
Woollen stockings	17·3–25·0	31·0–39·4	37·0–47·0
Artificial silk stockings	18·4	90·0	128·0
Printing paper	27·0–36·0	34·0	43·5
Sheet glass	45·0–135·0	21·8–72·0	20·4–67·0
Sewing machines	5·4	35·0	36·0
Metal-working machines	16·3–20·0	51·0	52·0
Private motor-cars	17·7	47·0–67·0	43·0
Radio apparatus	17·2–28·5	57·0	70·5
Motor-tires	10·0	20·7–27·6	20·0–44·5

Protected by such high tariff walls the industrial tariff policy of Czechoslovakia, whose duties on industrial goods were frequently tied by trade agreements, underwent little change in 1922-29 and in the first two years of the economic crisis up to 1931. Noteworthy only were the increases in duties on the goods of the chemical and heavy metal industries. There were even a few abatements in the industry of finished silk goods and in the motor-car industry. The rise in the industrial tariff level of 1931 was chiefly to be attributed to the fall in the industrial price level. (Tariff level of group B in 1931: 26·8–32·2% = 145% of 1913.)

With regard to industrial finished goods, with the exception of reduced duties on a number of textiles and motor-cars, there was practically no change. The tariff level of group C rose to 29–44% (185–200% of 1913), nearly all class levels moving upward to the same extent.

With these figures Czechoslovakia in 1931 exceeded all the industrial countries of Europe, with the exception of Italy. As, however, since the end of 1931 Czechoslovakia also practised a strict system of exchange control and import licences, not only for agrarian but also for industrial imports,[1] even the high figures of her tariff levels did not give the full measure of her protective policy.

B. AGRARIAN (BORDER) EUROPE

PRELIMINARY REMARK: *Differences in the Industrial Receptivity of the Agrarian Countries of Europe*

Of the eight foodstuff and raw material countries of Border Europe, whose industrial tariff policy and industrial tariff levels we have to consider, only three—Sweden, Spain, and Poland—imported annually semi- and wholly-manufactured goods and industrial raw materials to a value between fifty and one-hundred million pounds both before and after the War. The remaining five—Finland, Roumania, Hungary, Yugoslavia, and Bulgaria—never imported more than fifty million pounds worth.

Although the proportion of industrial imports to the total imports of these countries, according to their agrarian character, was usually much greater than was the case with the countries of industrial Europe, owing to the considerably smaller *absolute* amounts of imports, their importance as actual import markets was small.

Consequently, it was sufficient, when dealing with the smaller industrial markets of Europe, to indicate the development of trade in general and to emphasize characteristic features of their industrial tariff policy, especially as the tables AI in the Appendix have been calculated for them with equal complete-

---

[1] See *Greiff*, op. cit., pp. 49, 57–59.

ness for the great markets and contain data which are not mentioned in the text. First the conditions of Sweden, Finland, and Poland, then those of the south-east countries of Europe, and finally those of Spain have been discussed.

1. SWEDEN
(See Table A1 for Sweden in Appendix)

In spite of a number of highly developed and important export industries (metal, wood, and paper industries, engineering and electrical industries), based upon the wealth of ore and timber, pre-War Sweden was dependent upon considerable imports of semi- and wholly-manufactured articles. Of the total imports for 1913 raw materials and semi-manufactured goods accounted for 53·2%, while industrial finished goods constituted 24·8%. The great rise of Swedish prosperity, during and after the War, was responsible for the rise of the imports of industrial finished goods, so that in 1928 they comprised as much as 34% of the total imports, while raw materials and semi-manufacturing goods comprised only 41·3% of imports. In view of a population of only 6·14 millions (1930) these imports were very large, distributed over all branches of industrial production (see Table A, p. 148).

In consequence of the necessity of their high industrial imports Swedish tariff policy before and after the War was very liberal. Notable exceptions were to be found in only a few branches of industry.

The duties on industrial semi-manufactured goods were generally very low. Semi-finished wood and paper goods, as well as mineral oils, were on the free list. Semi-finished textiles were seldom taxed more than 4–10%, and only cotton tissues had to pay duties far above the average (see Table B, p. 148). Important too were the considerably higher duties (17–32%) on almost all goods belonging to the industry of semi-finished iron goods which forms one of Sweden's important industries. This indicated some protectionist tendencies. The tariff level of group B in 1913 was fairly high, being 22–28·6%, but was calculated from the duties upon only twenty-three of its commodities, while twenty-one were on the free list.

TABLE A: SWEDISH INDUSTRIAL IMPORTS, 1913–31
(*In Mill. Crowns and %*)

Group	1913		1927		1931	
	Mill. Cr.	% of T.I.	Mill. Cr.	% of T.I.	Mill. Cr.	% of T.I.
Total Imports . .	1070	100·0	1599	100·0	1431	100·0
Viz.:						
(a) Raw materials, semi-manufactured articles	566	53·0	529	33·1	432	30·2
(b) Wholly manufactured articles . . .	264	24·5	665	41·6	711	49·7
I.I. =(a + b) . . .	830	77·5	1194	74·7	1143	79·9

T.I. = Total Imports.
I.I. = Industrial Imports, including raw materials.

As Swedish trade statistics did not divide goods into semi- and wholly-manufactured goods, the figures for 1913 were taken from *Gaedicke, Vol. of Tables*, p. 19, and for 1927 and 1931 from *Statistiques*, I and III.

TABLE B: IMPORTANT DUTIES ON SEMI-FINISHED GOODS IN SWEDEN, 1913–31
(*In % of Prices*)

Goods	1913	1927	1931
Raw cotton yarn, up to No. 50	4·0–6·7	4·2–7·0	5·9–9·9
Bleached cotton tissues . .	29·0–36·7	16·6–22·5	22·0–34·0
Cast iron	Tax free	Tax free	Tax free
Rolled iron	12·7–70·0	11·2–60·0	15·2–38·0
Iron sheets, not worked .	25·0–41·5	23·0–38·4	27·0–45·0
Perfumes	98·0	58·0	31·3–47·0

Finished goods were generally liable to moderate duties, although the general tariff level of group C, amounting to 22·5–26·5%, was by no means low for pre-War conditions. The tariff levels of the most important classes, however, such as machinery, vehicles, textiles, and paper goods, were below this level, while those of the remaining classes of the metal goods

(16·6–31·6%), toys and motor tires (45%), were considerably above it. A few high duties were above the average figures (see Table C).

TABLE C: IMPORTANT DUTIES ON FINISHED GOODS, 1913–31
(*In % of Prices*)

Goods	1913	1927	1931
Leather shoes . . .	17·0–22·7	13·4–37·2	11·4–45·6
Cotton garments . . .	18·0–31·3	36·0–63·0	20·4–38·0
Woollen garments . .	22·4–26·1	7·8–9·1	7·9–12·9
Sheet glass	40·0–60·0	21·5–31·0	29·0–36·4
Tool machines . . .	5·1–20·4	3·0–12·0	3·1–5·6
Dynamos	13·4–49·0	8·5–31·0	8·1–30·0
Radio apparatus . . .	29·0	14·1	17·3
Private motor-cars . .	15·0	15·0	15·0

In the post-War period Sweden, in contrast to the industrial tariff policy of *all* European states, maintained nearly all her pre-War rates of duties, which, in view of the trend of prices, signified a considerable lowering of her tariff walls. Only in the year 1921 was there a notable increase in the duties on luxuries, which was strongly reflected in the tariff level of finished textiles, as well as in the watch duties.

The general tariff level of group B fell to 14·8–21·4% in 1927, which was 67–75% of the position in 1913.

The general level of group C fell to 18·7–23%, which was 83–86% of 1913.

The new Swedish Tariff of 1930 increased a number of duties on semi-finished industrial goods as well as on textiles and also imposed new duties on commodities hitherto on the free list (silk and artificial silk yarn, mineral oils, and ammonia), while it reduced duties on a number of important semi-finished iron goods but otherwise left duty rates unaltered. The tariff level of group B, amounting to 17·2–18·7% in 1931, was even lower than in 1927, in spite of the fall in prices. This was a remarkable instance of liberal trade policy in the Europe of 1931.

As regards finished goods the new Swedish Tariff raised duties sharply in the case of only a few metal goods, increasing the tariff level of their class to 13·3–33·7%. The remaining classes showed fairly uniform rises in their tariff levels, due to the fall in prices. The tariff level of group C rose in 1931 to 21–26% and thus approximated to the level of 1913. Compared with the trend of events in the rest of Europe, Sweden displayed unusual stability and moderation in her tariff policy, even after the onset of the world economic crisis. A stronger industrial tariff protection did not gather force in Sweden until she left the gold standard in 1931, a step which operated as a new general *ad valorem* tariff against the gold countries; simultaneously, she raised the duties on numerous industrial products in the beginning of 1932, at the same time instituting exchange control for luxury imports.[1]

2. FINLAND
(See Table A1 for Finland in Appendix)

Finland, like Sweden, possesses vast forests and has a number of industries which use wood and paper as their raw materials. Owing to the high percentage of the population engaged in agriculture and forestry (1920: 65%)[2] and the absence of other important industries, Finland is largely dependent upon imports of manufactured goods. In 1913 industrial finished goods accounted for 29·3% of the total imports: 33·3% represented raw materials and semi-manufactured goods. In 1928 the percentage of finished goods was as high as 38·8%, while raw materials and semi-manufactured articles were 35·2%.[3] In Table A some of the most important groups of industrial imports are shown.

Before the War, extensive import freedom existed for Russia, the chief supplier; therefore the industrial duties of 1913, some of which were very high, were only of interest as comparative figures.

[1] Comp. *Greiff*, op. cit., p. 48. [2] *W.d.A.*, p. 343.
[3] *Gaedicke, Vol. of Tables*, p. 19.

TABLE A: FINNISH INDUSTRIAL IMPORTS, 1913–31
(*In Mill. Finnish Mk. and %*)

Group	1913 Mill. Fmk.	1913 % of T.I.	1927 Mill. Fmk.	1927 % of T.I.	1931 Mill. Fmk.	1931 % of T.I.
Total Imports . . .	495	100·0	6390	100·0	3465	100·0
Of which:						
Semi and wholly manufac-						
tured metal goods .	37	7·5	747	11·7	393	11·4
Machinery, apparatus, tools	33	6·7	520	8·1	255	7·9
Fabrics	26	5·2	407	6·4	212	6·1
Vehicles	?	—	385	6·0	96	2·8

T.I. = Total Imports.
See *Finnish Trade Statistics*, 1913, 1927, 1931. No classification into raw materials, semi and wholly manufactured goods is given.

Finland's post-War industrial tariff policy was characterized by heavy duties on luxury goods and those of certain industries. With regard to others considerable reductions of pre-War duties were made.

Within the group of semi-manufactured goods, with a tariff level of 19·4–21% in 1927, textile and metal goods and chemicals were taxed lightly, while semi-manufactured wood and paper goods were admitted free. An exception were the duties on cotton and woollen tissues and heavy duties on iron goods (see Table B).

TABLE B: DUTIES ON IMPORTANT SEMI-MANUFACTURED GOODS IN FINLAND, 1913–31
(*In % of Prices*)

Goods	1913	1927	1931
Upper leather . . .	3·3	3·0–3·9	9·6–23·0
Raw cotton yarn, up to No. 50	11·0	5·8–8·0	9·3–13·0
Raw artificial silk yarn .	5·7	85·0 .	113·0
Bleached cotton tissues .	47·0	9·6–38·0	16·0–112·0
Woollen tissues, weighing up to 500 gr. . . .	53·4–80·0	8·9–19·8	21·6–46·0
Rolled iron . . .	25·0	21·2–82·2	21·6–82·8
Perfumes	94·0	130·0–195·0	103·0–154·0
Iron sheets, not worked .	28·0–35·0	17·0–41·0	20·0–48·0

For finished goods, with a tariff level of 15·5–20·1%, protection was strongest among the textile class (26·4–38%); leather goods and particularly the products of the silk and artificial silk industries, also of the glass and porcelain industries, had very high duties too. The tariff levels of the remaining classes, on the other hand, were very low.

TABLE C: DUTIES ON IMPORTANT INDUSTRIAL FINISHED GOODS IN FINLAND, 1913–31
(In % of Prices)

Goods	1913	1927	1931
Leather shoes . . .	23·2	7·6–45·0	35·0–87·0
Cotton clothes . . .	24·0–50·0	62·0–190·0	64·0–152·0
Artificial silk stockings .	22·0	46·0	80·0
Sheet glass . . .	204·0	26·0–46·0	27·0–43·0
Dynamos	9·5–40·0	16·0–30·0	7·5–30·0
Motor-cars . . .	0·5–2·5	8·7	14·0–28·0
Pianos	13·0	25·7	38·4
Toys	52·0	360·0	410·0

The Finnish industrial tariff, which was revised annually and accorded rebates from the rates of duty to Finland's customers as provided in the commercial treaties, but did not fix the absolute height of rates, changed mainly by numerous increases in textile duties. The duties were also raised in respect of a number of other industries. The tariff level of semi-manufactured goods rose but slightly in 1931 to 19·7–23·5%, although that of semi-manufactured textiles changed much more than the general level, rising to 21·8–29·4%, and exceeding the pre-War level by 15–25%.

The tariff level of the goods in group C in 1931 was 19·1–26·3% (=40–50% of the pre-War level). The rise in the levels of all classes compared with 1927 was caused by the fall in prices, with one important exception: on textile goods Finland raised almost every duty in 1931, which made them 85–105% higher than the already heavy duties of 1913. Consequently, the tariff level of this class rose from 26·4–38% in 1927 to 39–58% in 1931 (nearly 200% of 1913).

The figures of most other classes of group C remained quite moderate in 1931, and the character of Finland's industrial tariff underwent no fundamental change through the modifications effected up to 1931.

3. POLAND (1913: RUSSIA)
(See Table A1 for Poland in Appendix)

Poland, the largest of the post-War states of Eastern Europe, remained faithful during the whole post-War period, to the exceptionally high Russian industrial tariff protection of pre-War times, within the shadow of which in the first line the Russian iron and metal industries, had developed quickly.[1] In spite of the large proportion of her population engaged in agriculture and forestry (1921: 64% of the total population, against only 15% engaged in industry and handicraft),[2] Poland aimed deliberately at industrialization and the reduction of industrial imports. From Russian times she had inherited some big industries, while great natural resources are within her boundaries (timber, ore, mineral oil, and coal deposits). This protectionist policy has been partly successful (see Table B, p. 154), although, as Table A shows, the imports of industrial finished goods remained high in relation to total imports.

The Polish Tariff of 1924 (revisions included up to 1927), with its more than 2500 items and sub-items, formed one of the most complicated post-War tariffs. Although its rates were lower than the very high Russian pre-War rates, yet *Polish industrial duties were among the highest in Europe.* Some industries were protected by especially high duties, compared with which those of other branches of production remained comparatively low.

With a tariff level of group B of 28% excluding, and 35·5–43·5% including, the mineral oil duties, it was mainly the

---

[1] *Enquête*, II, p. 110.
[2] *W.d.A.*, p. 426.

industries of semi-manufactured textile, metal, and chemical goods that received the strongest protection.[1]

TABLE A: POLISH INDUSTRIAL IMPORTS, 1927–31
(*In Mill. Zlotys and %*)

	1927		1931	
Group	Mill. Zl.	% of T.I.	Mill. Zl.	% of T.I.
Total Imports . . .	2690	100·0	1470	100·0
Of which:				
(a) Raw materials, semi-manufactured goods . .	1140	39·4	590	40·0
(b) Manufactured goods . .	1130	39·0	684	46·5
I.I. = (a + b)	2270	78·4	1273	86·5

T.I. = Total Imports.
I.I. = Industrial Imports.
See *Annuaire du commerce extérieur*, 1927, 1931; (b) also includes a number of semi-manufactured goods.

TABLE B: IMPORTS OF SOME GROUPS OF INDUSTRIAL GOODS INTO POLAND, 1927–31
(*In Mill. Zlotys*)

Group	1927	1931
Yarns	107·0	58·0
Made-up textile goods	25·2	11·0
Semi and wholly manufactured metal goods .	186·0	109·0
Machinery	206·0	85·0
Electric machinery	91·0	65·0

See *Polish Trade Statistics and Commerce Yearbook*, 1928, p. 525; 1932, p. 205.

Already in 1927 the high tariff level of semi-manufactured goods was supplemented by a much higher tariff level of

[1] It should be borne in mind that these heavy protectionist duties on semi-manufactured goods might also be abated for protectionist purposes. As soon as it was apparent that semi-manufactured goods were intended to be imported in order to be manufactured into finished export goods, the Polish tariff granted abatements from the rates in force. This is a typical example of the post-War industrial

finished goods.   This amounted to 41·7–69·5%, and was
lower than the Russian level of 1913 only by 15%.   Here, too,
the heavy duties upon the goods of a few industries explained
its height.   First the duties on textile finished goods (see
Table D, p. 156) which brought the class level up to 78–96%,
or 82–105% *above* the Russian level, and further the duties on
metal and glass goods.   Very high, too, in fact, the highest in
Europe, were the duties on apparatus and instruments, with a
class tariff level of 60–67%, and on machinery, with 20·4–
46·6%.   The duty on toys, amounting to 970–1290% defied
comparison so completely that we had to ignore it in calculating
the average.

TABLE C: DUTIES UPON IMPORTANT SEMI-
MANUFACTURED GOODS IN POLAND, 1927–31
(1913: RUSSIAN DUTIES)
(*In % of Prices*)

Goods	1913	1927	1931
Raw cotton yarn, up to No. 50	32·6–44·0	19·0–23·4	22·5–28·0
Raw artificial silk yarn . .	64·0	115·0	146·0
Bleached cotton tissues . .	43·0–165·0	22·3–100·0	29·0–133·0
Bleached woollen tissues .	47·0–63·0	35·0–60·0	42·0–71·0
Foundry iron . . .	90·0	86·0	103·0
Raw aluminium . . .	52·5	77·0	90·0
Refined petroleum * . .	376·0	120·0	870·0
Sulphurated ammonia . .	44·0	37·0	105·0

* In view of the importance of the Polish oil industry, oil duties too
in Poland have a protectionist character.

Of 62 finished goods in group C not less than 21 had to
pay duties of more than 50%.   From 1924–27 this drastic
tariff policy had reduced the proportion of finished goods to

protectionism of the agrarian countries of Europe, which employed
all means to promote industrialization and even *before* the world
economic crisis resorted to fresh methods which cannot be discovered
merely by an inquiry into tariff levels.   See, e.g., Polish Order on
abatement of duties on glass bars and hoop iron in *H.A.*, 1931,
pp. 788–789.

the total imports from 51% to 39%.[1]   Under the shelter of the extreme watch duties, an entirely new watch-making industry developed in Poland, which became a serious competitor to Switzerland.   Duties on tissues favoured the development of Polish weaving and supplanted the German supplier.[2]

TABLE D: DUTIES ON IMPORTANT MANUFACTURED GOODS IN POLAND, 1927–31
(1913: RUSSIAN DUTIES)
(In % of Prices)

Goods	1913	1927	1931
Leather shoes	41·0	13·0–78·0	17·7–67·0
Cotton stockings	22·0	37·0	43·0
Cotton clothes	95·0	110·0	102·0
Woollen hosiery	47·0	53·0	64·0
Artificial silk stockings	25·0	210·0	300·0
Iron, etc., household articles	17·0–47·7	13·5–67·5	16·5–82·5
Looms	29·0–114·0	25·0–47·0	26·0–47·5
Internal combustion engines	38·0	12·8–71·0	17·6–71·0
Motor-cars	2·4–5·3	18·2–46·5	31·0–78·0
Radio apparatus	20·0	73·5	91·0
Inexpensive watches	82·0	150·0	194·0
Toys	103·0	970·0–1290·0	1100·0–1470·0

Between 1927 and 1931, and especially since the beginning of the world economic crisis, Poland further raised the autonomous duties upon many industrial products, although tariff conventions prevented the majority of these increases from becoming effective until 1931; therefore the further rise in the Polish tariff level during 1931 was rather due to the fall in prices.   The tariff level of group B rose in 1931 to 34–46% (excluding duties on petroleum).   Because of the high starting-point of 1927, all the rises in the tariff levels, even when specific duties remained unchanged, were bound to be high as soon as prices began to fall.

The same applied to the duties upon finished goods in 1931.

[1] See *W.d.A.*, pp. 435, 437.
[2] See *Jones*, op. cit., pp. 127–128, and *Enquête*, II, pp. 211, 218.

Although the general tariff level here, compared with 1927, fell to 43–61·5%, this was only due to the much reduced duties upon glass and ceramic wares.   The tariff levels of all the other classes, on the other hand, rose in 1931 according to the magnitude of the fall in prices of their goods (with exception of the machinery class).

Tables A and B clearly show the extent of the decline of Polish imports in 1931.   Nevertheless, at the commencement of the year 1932, Poland resorted to a much more rigorous policy.   The import of more than two hundred commodities (both agrarian and industrial) was prohibited.[1]   This measure limits the practical value of any analysis of Polish tariff policy during the period of prohibition.

4. ROUMANIA
(See Table A1 for Roumania in Appendix)

With the discussion of Roumanian industrial tariff policy we start our description of those agrarian countries of South-Eastern Europe which even before the War pursued a policy of strong industrial protection, although they had an almost completely agrarian structure and depended on large imports to cover their industrial requirements.   By virtue of her great natural resources in mineral oils, ore, timber and other raw materials, and the important industries based upon the exploitation of these resources, Roumania was the most industrialized of this group of countries.   Special caution, however, should be observed in any comparison between pre-War and post-War Roumania, as the Peace Treaties of 1919 in reality formed a new State bearing an old name.   This can be inferred from the one fact that Roumania had 7·2 million inhabitants in 1912, but 17·7 million inhabitants in 1927.[2]

In 1913 no less than 67·1% of the total imports were finished goods, 24·6% being raw materials and semi-manufactured

[1] See *Greiff*, op. cit., p. 84.
[2] *Commerce Yearbook*, 1928, p. 535.

goods, while in 1928 the corresponding figures were 65·7% and 24·9%.[1] It was noteworthy that even if the League of Nations Statistics were used, which were wide enough to include a number of semi-manufactured goods under the heading "finished goods," the proportion of finished goods to Roumanian total imports in 1931 fell to 60·7%, while raw materials and semi-manufactured articles rose to 28·8%.[2]

TABLE A: ROUMANIAN INDUSTRIAL IMPORTS, 1913–31 †
(*In Mill. Lei and %*)

Group	1913 Mill. L.	1913 % of T.I.	1927 Mill. L.	1927 % of T.I.	1931 Mill. L.	1931 % of T.I.
Total Imports	590	100·0	33900	100·0	15800	100·0
Of which:						
Semi and wholly manufactured metal products	173	29·3	5800	17·1	3100	19·6
Textiles *	98	16·5	13700	40·0	5553	35·0
Machinery	59	10·0	3200	9·4	1650	10·4
Paper, paper goods	7·4	1·2	540	1·6	370	2·3

T.I. = Total Imports.

* Both textile raw materials and semi and wholly manufactured articles.

† See *Comertul âl Romaniei*, 1913, 1927, 1931. No classification into raw materials, semi and wholly manufactured goods.

With a tariff level of 26·6–33·6% for group B before the War, Roumanian protection was concentrated less upon all semi-manufacturing industries than upon certain important branches. Among the generally moderate duties on semi-manufactured textile goods it was chiefly tissues; among the very high-class tariff level of semi-manufactured wood and paper goods it was cellulose which was most heavily taxed. The tariff level of class BIII was also low; iron sheets and wire, however, were subjected to high duties.

[1] *Gaedicke, Vol. of Tables*, p. 19.   [2] *Statistiques*, III.

TABLE B: DUTIES ON IMPORTANT SEMI-MANUFACTURED GOODS IN ROUMANIA, 1913-31
(*In % of Prices*)

Goods	1913	1927	1931
Raw cotton yarn, up to No. 50	1·2	1·3	1·7
Raw artificial silk yarn . .	24·2	22·8	81·0
Upper leather . . .	8·9	13·6–22·5	15·3–56·5
Bleached cotton tissues . .	12·3–26·0	20·4–98·0	17·2–173·0
Wood pulp	110·0	43·0–298·0	38·0
Cellulose	27·6–35·0	43·0–62·0	67·0–96·0
Rolled iron	8·1	57·0	23·5–88·0
T-U-X iron . . .	22·0	66·0	87·0
Perfumes	27·0	54·0–175·0	70·0–350·0

The tariff level of industrial finished goods in 1913 was lower than that of semi-manufactured articles; it amounted to 22·5–28·5%. The classes of machinery, of apparatus and vehicles were generally taxed more lightly than this general average, but even in 1913 the protection accorded to the paper industry, as well as to glass goods and cement, was notably strong, while among textiles the products of the industry of made-up articles and silk and artificial silk products were taxed far above the average figure (see Table C).

TABLE C: DUTIES ON IMPORTANT MANUFACTURED GOODS IN ROUMANIA, 1913-31
(*In % of Prices*)

Goods	1913	1927	1931
Leather shoes . . .	41·0–64·0	32·5–129·0	45·0–180·0
Cotton clothes . . .	12·8–58·0	69·0–565·0	87·0–925·0
Artificial silk stockings . .	41·0	52·0	610·0
Printing paper . . .	85·0	54·0–64·0	82·0–125·0
Cement	48·0	180·0	110·0
Common household utensils .	9·1–43·0	9·9–86·0	14·8–95·0
Tool machines . . .	4·4–8·8	2·6–6·1	2·4–12·0
Radio apparatus . . .	11·0	192·0	84·0–135·0
Locomotives . . .	48·0–56·0	31·2–36·4	41·0–47·0

Roumania's post-War policy is characterized by industrial protection of the most drastic kind, designed to stimulate the development of systematically selected industries, and by a rise of *all* rates, sometimes only for fiscal reasons. Upon semi-manufactured articles the tariff of 1927 imposed rates on an average 60–110% higher than in 1913, resulting in a general tariff level 25% higher than 1913, which amounted to 20·8–44·5% including petroleum duties.[1] The cotton and woollen weaving trades, the leather production, the paper and iron semi-manufacturing trades were hardest hit by the new duties.

The increase in Roumanian duties on finished goods was very remarkable in comparison with 1913. The tariff level, with average increases of the rates between 270 and 360%, rose to 165–210% of the pre-War level, reaching an average of 36·8–60·3%. The figures of the classes of machinery and vehicles, however, remained practically unchanged, while those of the paper goods fell from their high level of 1913 to 46–53%, but all the rest of the classes were heavily taxed, the duties in a number of cases being prohibitive, as, for example, the textile class with a tariff level of 70–163%, equal to 475–600% of 1913. It was chiefly the finer textile goods (silk and artificial silk and linen), liable to duties often over 100%, which contributed to the attainment of this figure, *with the consequence that Roumania had the highest textile duties in Europe.*

Further, the duties on cement, glass and metal finished goods and electrical apparatus showed huge increases. In some trades this tariff policy led to the expansion of home production at very high prices, as in the paper and textile trades, also in the semi-manufacturing metal trades.[2] In Roumania, too, duties formed only a part of a system of industrial protection, which ever since the "Act to encourage the home industry"

---

[1] In view of Roumania's important oil industry, petroleum duties must, as in the case of Poland, be taken into account in analysing Roumania's industrial protection.

[2] See *W.d.A.*, pp. 310–311.

passed in 1912 stimulated the development of Roumanian industry by the use of many different methods (tax reliefs for new enterprises up to twenty and thirty years, lower railway rates, etc.). Big rebates were allowed from excessive duties whenever it was required to import goods for the purpose of starting industries not already existing in Roumania.[1]

In 1929 Roumania introduced a new tariff, which came into force in 1930, and, with its more than 1800 items, may rank, like the Polish, among the most complicated in Europe. As regards the semi-manufactured goods there were *fresh increases* in the duties on practically every article. Owing to the downward trend of prices, such increases raised the tariff level of group B considerably and brought it up to 37–53·5% in 1931, which was equal to 140–165% of 1913.

In contrast to this tendency the new tariff lowered the rates on most manufactured articles, which was, however, counteracted by the fall in prices to such an extent that the tariff level of group C still rose somewhat compared with 1927, viz. to 40·4–69·5%. Among textiles new increases of the duties upon the classes of cotton, woollen, silk and artificial silk goods, in contrast to sharp reductions in the classes of glass and ceramic goods, machinery and apparatus, resulted in raising the class tariff level to the unprecedented height of 110–232%, an important part being played by the exceptional duties on silk and artificial silk. It was therefore not surprising that the import of textile manufactures declined from 27·1% of the total imports in 1927 to 12·7% in 1931.[2]

Thus the policy of drastic agrarian protection pursued by European industrial countries since the outbreak of the world economic crisis encountered in 1931 prohibitive tariffs on a number of groups of manufactures in the biggest agrarian and raw material country of South-Eastern Europe.

[1] Text of law in *H.A.*, 1913, pp. 257–265; 1927, p. 1660; and *W.d.A.*, p. 306.

[2] Comp. *Memor. and Statist.*, II.

5. HUNGARY

(See Table A1 for Hungary in Appendix)

Hungary, the third of the Danubian Succession States, constituted by the Treaty of Trianon in 1919, was a preponderantly agrarian country with a large grain surplus. Although without any important industrial raw materials, she possessed some important industries in her capital of Budapest, and her few other big cities: food manufacturing, metal industries, engineering. These industries, which existed already in pre-War times, were organized to serve a much larger economic area than the restricted territory of the new State of 1919. In order to maintain these industries, and even to establish new ones, despite the limited home market, Hungarian economic policy during the whole post-War period has been of a definitely protectionist character so far as industry is concerned, and tariffs have been ruthlessly employed for this purpose as well as many other devices. From Table A it will be seen that this policy of industrialization, so far as it aimed at restricting foreign imports, has been remarkably successful in some cases, although with the consequence of very high prices of the protected articles.

The Hungarian Tariff of 1924, which followed in many lines the Austro-Hungarian Tariff of 1906, exceeded the latter's industrial duties, most of which were very high for pre-War times, in practically all groups; yet a number of industries could be clearly discerned as the main objects of protection. In the production of semi-finished goods it was the textile and iron trades, while wood and paper goods were on the free list, and the high tariff level of chemicals was due solely to the fiscal duties on perfumes. Among textiles there were increases in the duties on yarn, heavier increases still in the duties on tissues, the home production of which was practically started after the War,[1] with the result that, rates being increased on an average by 70–165%, the Hungarian tariff level for semi-

[1] See *Enquête*, II, pp. 211, 219.

textile goods was 10–47% higher than the Austro-Hungarian of 1913. The rise in the tariff level of semi-manufactured metal goods to 35–38·6% was the consequence of particularly heavy increases in the duties on the most important products of the heavy iron industry (see Table B, p. 164). The tariff level of group B in 1927, with 21–32%, was 15–45% higher than in 1913.

TABLE A: HUNGARIAN INDUSTRIAL IMPORTS,
1927–31
(*In Mill. Pengö and %*)

Group	1927 Mill. P.	1927 % of T.I.	1931 Mill. P.	1931 % of T.I.
Total Imports	1180	100·0	540	100·0
Of which:				
(*a*) Raw materials and semi-manu-				
factured goods . . .	440	37·2	245	45·5
(*b*) Finished goods . . .	657	55·6	237	43·9
I.I. =(*a*+*b*)	1097	92·8	482	89·4
Of which:				
Cotton and woollen tissues . .	153	12·9	30	5·5
Cotton and woollen yarns . .	65	5·7	18	3·4
Semi and wholly manufactured				
iron and steel goods . .	37	3·1	12	2·3
Machinery and apparatus . .	56	4·8	19	3·5

T.I. = Total Imports.
I.I. = Industrial Imports.
See *Commerce extérieur de la Hongrie*, 1927, 1931, and *Commerce Yearbook*, 1928, p. 325; 1932, p. 135.
"Finished goods" includes important semi-manufactured articles.

Much sharper was the rise of the tariff level of finished goods, which reached 22·7–41%, equal to 155–170% of 1913. Numerous increases of duties on finished textile goods (see Table C, p. 165), brought the group tariff level up to 25–44%, equal to 157–210% of 1913. Similar sharp increases in the duties on metal goods raised their class tariff level to 55–61%, which had an almost prohibitive effect and was equal to 220–320% of

1913. Duties on paper goods were also raised considerably, while the strengthening of the tariff protection afforded to machinery was not so apparent in 1927 owing to the sharp upward trend in prices, although the Hungarian tariff level of 14·5–31% was considerably high in comparison with most other machinery tariff levels. Even stronger protectionist tendencies were shown in fixing the duties on apparatus and instruments, particularly on electrical goods. Rates were 100–140% higher than in 1913, the tariff level was 35–65% higher than in 1913.

TABLE B: DUTIES ON IMPORTANT SEMI-MANUFACTURED ARTICLES IN HUNGARY, 1927–31
(1913: Austro-Hungarian Duties)
(In % of Prices)

Goods	1913	1927	1931
Raw cotton yarn, up to No. 50	3·6–8·5	8·0–22·0	14·3–30·0
Printed cotton tissues .	31·0–80·0	33·4–110·0	37·4–125·0
Rolled iron	51·0	57·0	65·0
Iron sheets, not worked	32·6–42·0	52·0–93·0	61·0–110·0
Perfumes .	45·0	110·0–206·0	89·0–166·0

This tariff protection was accompanied by an extensive system of other protectionist measures. As in the case of Roumania or Poland, the tariff granted freedom of duties or rebates between 10 and 50% from the autonomous rates for certain imports of semi-manufactured goods subjected to quota restrictions. The imports of these goods were supposed to be necessary for the development of Hungarian industry, or to be manufactured into finished goods inside the country.

Other quite typical measures of European post-War protectionism, besides duties, such as preference in obtaining public orders, came within the limits of the present inquiry only to remind us again that even before the world economic crisis tariffs in a number of countries were obviously insufficient to enable us to judge of the full extent of protection in such countries.

TABLE C: DUTIES ON IMPORTANT FINISHED
GOODS IN HUNGARY, 1927–31

(*In % of Prices*)

Goods	1913	1927	1931
Cotton linen . . .	35·0–49·0	34·6	32·0
Cotton clothes . . .	13·6–35·0	27·0–153·0	17·6–103·0
Artificial silk stockings .	18·4	68·0	96·5
Silk ribbons . . .	10·0–16·4	115·0	143·0
Printing paper . . .	27·0–36·0	17·0–60·0	21·2–74·0
Cast-iron lamps . .	18·4–36·8	206·0–274·0	232·0–310·0
Sewing machines, without stand	5·4	1·6	39·4
Internal combustion engines	46·0–126·0	16·2–37·0	17·5–118·0
Dynamos	8·2–20·5	23·7–52·0	41·0–82·0
Motor-cars . . .	7·7–17·5	16·0–28·0	28·5–52·5
Radio apparatus . .	17·2–28·5	28·6	70·0

From 1924 to 1927 Hungarian industrial policy had reduced the proportion of imported manufactured textile goods to total imports from 25·1% to 19·7%, raised the output of steel by about 50%; the number of textile workers had risen from 16,000 in pre-War time to 40,000 persons in 1927 in spite of the immense reduction in the area of the Hungarian kingdom [1] (compared with 1913).

Between 1927 and 1931 Hungarian industrial tariff policy remained relatively stable. In July 1931 duties were raised on a number of industrial goods, but owing to commercial treaties these increases could not yet exert their full effect, so that the sharp rises in the tariff levels of all industrial groups were due more to the fall in prices. The tariff level of group B

---

[1] For Hungary's exceptional regulations for the import of certain products see *H.A.*, 1925, pp. 570, et seq., 1926, pp. 718 et seq., 1928, p. 1787, and for the development of industry *W.d.A.*, pp. 283, 286, 293.

reached 24·4–40·6%, duties on textiles and semi-metal goods rising sharply. The tariff level of group C, with 29·7–55·6%, rose much more than that of group B. Special attention ought to be given to the development of the duties upon machines. Owing to heavy increases in the duties on power and sewing machines, the tariff level of this class rose to 24–50·5% (=170–210% of 1913), and thus represented the highest machinery tariff level in Europe during the year 1931.

In the year 1931 Hungary adopted new and still more drastic measures to regulate her imports. Currency restrictions, clearing agreements, licences, and import prohibitions were introduced for reasons of monetary policy.[1] So here, tariffs too lost after 1931 the primary position which they had occupied in the system of protection.

6. YUGOSLAVIA (1913: SERBIA)
(See Table A1 for Yugoslavia in Appendix)

The changes which the end of the War brought to Yugoslavia were so great that actually a new state emerged, whose population rose from 4·8 millions in 1913 to about 13 millions in 1927. In spite of the existence of great forests and ore deposits, Yugoslavia was even more of an agricultural country than Roumania and Hungary; industry was still in its infancy. This was reflected in the high proportion which industrial products bore to the total imports.

In 1913 raw materials and semi-manufactured goods accounted for 37·5% and finished goods comprised 53·5%. In 1928 the proportions were practically unchanged.[2]

Serbia's industrial tariff was generally moderate. With a tariff level for group B of 15·2–19·2%, which reflected the figures of nearly all classes, duties more than the average were only imposed on the products of the cotton-weaving industry and the heavy industries, as well as on part of the chemical industry (see Table B, p. 167).

[1] *Greiff*, op. cit., pp. 52–53, 56–57, 60.
[2] See *Gaedicke, Vol. of Tables*, p. 19.

TABLE A: YUGOSLAVIAN INDUSTRIAL IMPORTS,
1927-31
(In Mill. Dinar and %)

Group	1927 Mill. D.	1927 % of T.I.	1931 Mill. D.	1931 % of T.I.
Total Imports . . .	7300	100·0	4800	100·0
Of which:				
Cotton and woollen tissues .	1422	19·5	739	15·3
Cotton yarns	452	6·2	229	4·8
Iron goods	300	4·1	267	5·6
Machinery and apparatus .	347	4·8	296	6·2

T.I. = Total Imports.

See *Statistique du commerce extérieur du royaume de Yugoslavie*, 1927, 1931. For 1913 no Serbian statistics were available, but such would have been of little worth in view of the completely changed post-War conditions. Only since 1931 imports have been classified into raw materials, semi and wholly manufactured goods.

TABLE B: DUTIES ON IMPORTANT SEMI-MANUFACTURED GOODS IN YUGOSLAVIA, 1927-31
(1913: Serbian Duties)
(In % of Prices)

Goods	1913	1927	1931
Raw cotton yarn . .	10·4–16·8	5·5–8·3	7·1–10·6
Bleached cotton tissues .	21·2–67·0	16·5–41·4	21·0–42·0
Woollen tissues . . .	11·0–23·6	18·5–36·4	23·4–45·5
Raw steel	13·8	41·4	48·0
Cast iron	Duty free	33·0	35·0
Sulphurated ammonia .	Duty free	40·0	61·0
Nitrogen	17·8	48·0	56·0

The tariff level of finished goods, being 15–21·5%, might also be called moderate. Nearly all kinds of machines were on the free list; vehicles, apparatus, and instruments were below the general average; metal, paper, and glass goods were taxed higher; ready-made goods, paper for newspapers, cement, etc., were subjected to duties considerably higher than the average (see Table C, p. 168).

TABLE C: DUTIES ON IMPORTANT MANUFACTURED GOODS IN YUGOSLAVIA, 1927–31

(In % of Prices)

Goods	1913	1927	1931
Leather goods	22·2–37·0	10·8–32·4	14·9–45·7
Cotton hosiery	22·6	68·0	35·0–70·0
Cotton clothes	12·4–39·0	32·4–110·0	22·0–64·0
Artificial silk stockings	21·0–26·0	36·0	51·0
Printing paper	31·0	15·4–42·0	48·0
Portland cement	61·0	98·0	110·0
Internal combustion engines	Duty free	6·6	7·1
Pocket watches	4·8	55·0–90·0	71·0–120·0

In a number of trades Yugoslavia's post-War industrial tariff policy manifested decidedly protectionist tendencies, although it remained moderate in comparison with the tariff policy of the other south-eastern agrarian countries, and showed little trace of the feverish industrialization tendencies operating in Hungary, Roumania, or Bulgaria. The tariff level of group B, with rates increased between 90 and 125% compared with 1913, rose by about 35% to 19·2–23·2%, while the level of semi-textile goods fell by 15–20% compared with the pre-War level. On the other hand, there was an unmistakable tendency to strengthen the protection afforded to the semi-manufacturing metal trades, as well as the industry of fertilizers.

Protectionist tendencies were also clearly discernible in the post-War period among a number of trades producing finished goods. The tariff level of group C rose to 23–33%, equal to 150% of 1913. While the levels of the classes of machinery, vehicles, and apparatus were raised by heavy increases in duties from their very low level in the year 1913 to a height between 10 and 24%, in 1927 the tariff levels of the classes of textiles, metal, glass, and ceramic wares reached a respectable height even in Yugoslavia, and only the class of paper goods fell slightly below its level of 1913. Duties on ready-made textile articles, artificial silk fabrics, cement, watches, etc., reached prohibitive dimensions.

Although Yugoslavia's industry did not make very great progress up till 1931, this partial protectionist tariff policy undoubtedly reduced the foreigner's share in covering the textile deficit, in favour of a slowly developing home industry [1] (comp. Table A, p. 167).

Between 1925 and 1931 Yugoslavia's industrial tariff policy remained substantially the same. There were a number of increases in duties upon the semi-manufactured textiles and metal goods, but in the finishing textile trades there were even appreciable reductions in duties, so that the rise in the tariff level was almost entirely due to the fall in prices. The tariff level of group B reached 29–32·5% in 1931, the tariff level of group C 27·2–38·5%, which brought it up to 180% of the pre-War level. Only the changes in the tariff level of the class of the metal goods to 31·2–63% and of paper goods to 37% ought to be mentioned.

7. BULGARIA
(See Table A1 for Bulgaria in Appendix)

With small resources in coal and ore deposits, both before and after the War, Bulgaria was a predominantly agrarian country. Consequently, the proportion of industrial imports, especially of industrial finished goods, was very large. In 1913 finished goods accounted for 45%, raw materials and semi-manufactured goods for 27%, of the total imports. In 1928 the figures were 49% and 45·7%.[2] The total amounts of these imports are shown in Table A, p. 170.

Efforts to industrialize the country date in Bulgaria from long before the War. A law for the encouragement of industry was passed as early as 1894 and was revised in 1905 and 1909. Nevertheless, the industrial tariff of 1914, although containing

---

[1] Comp. *Commerce Yearbook* 1927, p. 670, and *W.d.A.*, p. 300.

[2] See *Gaedicke, Vol. of Tables*, p. 19. The strikingly small proportion of raw materials and semi-manufactured goods is explained by the abnormal conditions of this year (Balkan War).

a number of very high rates of duty, was on the whole moderate. The tariff level of group B amounted to 21·2–27·2% and the tariff levels of the classes of textile, paper, wood, and metal semi-manufactured goods were even below it.

TABLE A: BULGARIAN INDUSTRIAL IMPORTS, 1913–31
(*In Mill. Lewa and %*)

Group	1913 Mill. L.	1913 % of T.I.	1927 Mill. L.	1927 % of T.I.	1931 Mill. L.	1931 % of T.I.
Total Imports . .	189	100·0	6200	100·0	4700	100·0
Of which:						
(a) Raw materials, semi-manufactured goods	29	15·5	1280	20·6	990	21·1
(b) Finished goods .	126	66·5	4630	74·5	3500	74·5
I.I. = (a + b) . .	155	82·0	5910	95·1	4490	95·6

T.I. = Total Imports.
I.I. = Industrial Imports.
See *Statistique du commerce du royaume de Bulgarie*, 1913, 1929. For 1931 the official Bulgarian figures were not at my disposal, and therefore were taken from *Statistiques*, III, and *Commerce Yearbook*, 1932, p. 27.

With a general tariff level of group C of 18·7–20·3%, finished goods were liable only to moderate duties in 1913; the classes of machinery, apparatus, and vehicles were taxed no higher than 4–12%, while the most important machines were on the free list; only luxury articles had to pay higher duties (e.g. expensive watches).

Finished textile, glass, and ceramic goods were taxed somewhat more heavily, while paper goods were liable to comparatively high duties.

With the new tariff of 1922 and the numerous increases in duties on the most important agrarian and industrial items imposed in 1926, Bulgaria completely abandoned her pre-War tariff policy and proceeded to introduce such heavy duties on the products of nearly all industries *that her tariff levels for*

*groups B and C were higher than all the other corresponding tariff
levels in Europe, both in* 1927 *and in* 1931, including the high
tariff walls of Poland and Roumania. Within these enor-
mously raised general tariff levels protection was plainly
directed to certain industries, while others were liable to
relatively or absolutely light taxation. With rates which
represented about 250–300% of 1913, the tariff level of group
B rose in 1927 to more than double the level of the last pre-
War year, i.e. to 44–55%. By far the hardest hit were the
semi-manufactured textile goods, so that their tariff level, with
rates sevenfold higher than in 1913, reached a height of 76–
99%. The increases in chemical duties were also great.

TABLE B: DUTIES ON IMPORTANT SEMI-MANUFACTURED GOODS IN BULGARIA, 1913–31
(In % of Prices)

Goods	1913	1927	1931
Raw cotton yarn up to No. 50	16·6–33·2	27·4–44·0	34·0–69·0
Artificial silk yarn	49·0	350·0	440·0
Bleached cotton tissues	13·0	48·0–90·0	63·0–120·0
Cellulose	22·0	42·0	38·0
Rolled iron	16·0	31·0–54·0	36·0–62·0
Iron tubes, not worked	24·6	46·0–80·0	41·0–71·0

TABLE C: DUTIES ON IMPORTANT MANUFACTURED GOODS IN BULGARIA, 1913–31
(In % of Prices)

Goods	1913	1927	1931
Leather shoes	21·0–42·0	53·0–110·0	61·0–125·0
Cotton linen	34·0	137·0	127·0
Cotton clothes	17·0–26·0	47·0–312·0	35·0–230·0
Woollen stockings	22·5	77·0	93·0
Printing paper	28·0	26·0–65·0	34·0–85·0
Portland cement	30·0	73·0	83·0
Iron household utensils	8·4–42·0	24·0–60·0	29·0–72·0
Pocket watches	29·0	80·0	100·0
Radio apparatus	11·0	54·0	67·0
Toys	80·0	240·0–544·0	275·0–660·0

The rise in the tariff level of finished goods left that of the semi-manufactured goods far behind. With rates increased by 400–575% compared with 1913, the tariff level of group C rose to 56–94%. Machinery and vehicles, however, remained at low levels, so that the enormous increase had to be borne by the remaining six classes. Rates on finished textile goods were raised by 840–1000%, and their class level rose to 121–126%, which was equal to 630–750% of 1913. Very high, too, were the tariff levels of the classes of the glass and ceramic goods, metal and paper goods, apparatus, and instruments. The rise of their rates and tariff levels compared with 1913 was between 200 % and 400%. Of the 62 articles in group C only a third, viz. 20, were liable to duties under 30%, 25 to duties over 50%, the rest to duties between 30 % and 50%.

Such prohibitive tariff levels evinced Bulgaria's determination to industrialize the country, although, according to the provisions of the 1928 version of the law for the encouragement of industry (as with Poland, Roumania, and Hungary), all duties on raw materials and semi-manufactured goods might be abated or completely remitted, if the goods in question could not be produced in Bulgaria in sufficient quantities or at all, or if they were designed to be worked up into finished goods in factories promoted by the law and controlled by the Government.[1]

As the number of these factories was very great,[2] a considerable fraction of Bulgarian imports might have escaped the high Bulgarian duties. One must not, therefore, draw too far-reaching conclusions from the rates of the Bulgarian tariff on semi-manufactured articles as to the extent of tariff protection accorded to Bulgarian industry. In fact, one must also take account of the regulations which permit the free admission of *semi*-manufactured goods in certain instances in order to

[1] See text of law in *H.-A.*, 1928, pp. 2784–2790. List of possible exemptions on pp. 2176–2190. The law contains also other provisions for encouraging Bulgarian industrial production and lowering industrial imports.

[2] Comp. *W.d.A.*, p. 323.

understand tendencies of industrialization in Bulgaria, because they throw light upon the extent of industrial protection for certain *finished* goods trades.   Up to the year 1931 there were no substantial changes in Bulgarian rates, so that any rises in her tariff levels were explicable from the fall in prices.   The tariff level of group B reached in 1931 57·5–72·5%.   Only twenty-two of its forty-four articles were liable to duties below 50%.

The potential tariff level of group C rose to 70–110%.   In this case of 62 articles, 21 were taxed below 30%, while 33 were taxed above 50%.   Although these duties put Bulgaria in the forefront of European tariff protection, owing to the absence of other essential conditions for industrialization (large home markets, large capital resources, etc.), this policy achieved success in only a few spheres, the chief of which was self-sufficiency in sugar and coal.[1]   Agriculture still plays the dominant part in Bulgarian economic life.

8. SPAIN
*(See Table A*I *in Appendix)*

Spain, which has extensive ore and coal deposits, was, even before the War, a country of high industrial protectionism which was more or less checked only by the influence of Spanish agriculture.   This was dependent upon export trade and inclined towards free-trade.[2]   As, however, only certain special industries of the country, chiefly the mining, textile, and metal industries, in addition to the exporting cork industry, had grown to considerable dimensions before the War, the proportion of semi and wholly manufactured articles to the total imports was high and remained so even after the War.   In 1913 raw materials and semi-manufactured goods accounted for 46·1%, industrial finished goods comprised 31·1%; in 1928 the proportions were 48·4% and 36·6%.[3]

[1] See *W.d.A.*, pp. 322–323, 331.
[2] See *Jones*, op. cit., pp. 245–246.
[3] *Gaedicke, Vol. of Tables*, p. 19.

Table A shows the absolute magnitudes of the total Spanish imports and the industrial imports, which were distributed among numerous groups for 1913–31.

TABLE A: SPANISH INDUSTRIAL IMPORTS, 1913–31
(*In Mill. Pesetas and %*)

Group	1913		1927		1931	
	Mill. P.	% of T.I.	Mill. P.	% of T.I.	Mill. P.	% of T.I.
Total Imports .	1306	100·0	2576	100·0	1175	100·0
Of which:						
(*a*) Raw materials .	521	40·0	936	36·4	442	37·8
(*b*) Manufactures .	483	37·0	1193	46·0	560	48·0
I.I. = (*a* + *b*) . .	1004	77·0	2029	82·4	1002	85·8

T.I. = Total Imports.
I.I. = Industrial Imports.
See *Estadistica general*, 1913, 1927, 1931.
"Manufactures" also included semi-manufactured goods.

Before the War Spanish industrial duties were the highest in Europe with the exception of the Russian. Semi-manufactured articles had to pay duties of 20·3–32·0% on an average, although semi-wood and paper articles were liable to very low duties, while prohibitive duties were imposed on semi-manufactured textiles and duties on tissues were much higher than the average (see Table B, p. 175). The most important products of the Spanish iron industry were also highly taxed, their class tariff level being 32–36·6%.

Among industrial finished goods, which reached a potential tariff level of 35·7–49·4%, it was again the textile trades that were surrounded by a very high protectionist wall. Heavier still were the duties on paper, glass, and ceramic goods, but lower, although still prohibitive, were the duties on metal goods (see Table C).

For Spanish conditions the level of machinery duties was moderate, although here very important machines, such as internal combustion engines, dynamos, steam engines, were taxed far higher than the average.

TABLE B: DUTIES ON IMPORTANT SEMI-MANUFACTURED GOODS IN SPAIN, 1913-31
(In % of Prices)

Goods	1913	1927	1931
Upper leather . .	10·6–21·2	27·0	40·0
Raw cotton yarn up to No. 50 . . .	12·0–22·0	24·6–57·4	32·0–74·0
Raw worsted . .	44·0–53·0	60·0–76·0	80·0–100·0
Bleached cotton tissues .	41·0–200·0	39·4–140·0	52·0–186·0
Foundry iron . .	17·0	38·0	54·0
Raw steel . . .	9·0	36·0	35·0
Iron sheets, not worked .	36·4–45·0	93·0–126·0	140·0–190·0
Copper wire . .	12·7–13·6	26·2–52·0	35·4–70·0
Aniline dyes . .	31·2	21·0–42·0	20·5–41·0
Sulphurated ammonia .	0·3	39·0	72·0

TABLE C: DUTIES ON IMPORTANT MANUFACTURED GOODS IN SPAIN, 1913-31
(In % of Prices)

Goods	1913	1927	1931
Leather shoes . .	66·0	58·0	66·0
Cotton linen . .	125·0	69·0–183·0	64·0–170·0
Cotton clothes . .	18·0–136·0	39·0–480·0	260·0–320·0
Printing paper . .	25·0–100·0	50·0–114·0	68·0–153·0
Sheet glass . . .	35·0–195·0	27·0–117·0	25·0–103·0
Iron household utensils	7·0–21·0	25·0–72·0	30·0–87·0
Looms . . .	20·4	46·0	65·0
Internal combustion engines . . .	29·0	8·9–78·0	8·6–115·0
Steam engines . .	21·3	12·0–45·0	11·0–41·0
Locomotives . .	16·0–28·0	44·0–65·0	64·0–83·0
Motor-cars . . .	?	16·0–39·0	22·0–56·0
Motor-tires . . .	37·5	33·4–89·5	44·0–122·0
Toys	133·0	96·9–256·0	110·0–294·0

In the post-War period, especially since Primo di Rivera, Spain attempted to consolidate and even to extend her industries

which had rapidly developed in war-time; this was carried
through by combining heavy tariff protection with an elaborate
neo-mercantilist system for the active encouragement of
industry.

Consequently, the rates of the new tariff of 1922, combined
with the additional rates of 1926, set in force in 1927, raised
Spanish tariff walls, already high in 1913, to an extraordinary
level. Duties on semi-manufactured articles rose on an average
to 220–260% of the 1913 level, those on metal goods even to
360–390%. The potential tariff level of semi-manufactured
articles rose to 33–45%, although the figures of the tariff levels
of the classes of semi-manufactured textile, wood, and paper
goods were little changed compared with 1913. As only dyes
and fertilizers were more heavily taxed among chemicals, semi-
manufactured metal goods with a class level of 70–86% (=235%
of 1913) were mainly responsible for the rise in the tariff level
of the whole group.

The same marked rise was exhibited by the duties on finished
goods, the level of which in 1927 reached 44·4–81%. Apart
from apparatus and instruments, the levels of all the classes in
group C were heavily increased. In this connection we have
to mention the sharp increases in Spain's post-War machinery
duties, which brought the tariff level of this class up to 21–
36% and represented an average increase between 55 and 160%
compared with 1913.

Of 62 industrial finished goods only 23 were liable to duties
below 30% in 1927, while 27 were liable to duties above 50%.

By the "Law for the Encouragement of Spanish Industry," [1]
of the 30th April 1924, Spain established besides these industrial duties, only exceeded or equalled in Europe by Bulgaria
and Poland, an ingenious system for the active encouragement
of industry, which must be taken into account in any inquiry
into her scheme of protection. This law permitted newly

[1] See text of law in *H.-A.*, 1924, pp. 1091–1095; 1930, pp. 1651–
1655. Numerous other advantages were granted the undertakings in
question in addition to tariff concessions.

established industrial undertakings engaged in producing goods hitherto unknown or scarce in Spain, to import raw materials and semi-manufactured articles *duty free* up to a period of five years. Consequently, the high duties on the semi-manufactured products of the textile and metal trades were only valid for Spanish industries already existing. A law passed in 1926 also temporarily suspended the dye duties and replaced them by the much more drastic expedients of import prohibitions and import licences, in order to develop a Spanish dye industry,[1] while the duties on coal, semi- and wholly-manufactured metal goods, motor-cars, and machinery were reinforced in their import-lowering effect by compelling all concession holders and public authorities to buy Spanish products.[2]

The output of Spain's textile, metal, and chemical industries rose considerably under the protection of this industrial policy, while coal import requirements fell from 40% of Spanish consumption in 1914 to 20% in 1924; the textile industry was capable of supplying the greater part of Spanish requirements, but all this, of course, was accompanied by very high prices of the protected goods of Spanish production and a rise in the general cost of living.[3]

The level of Spain's industrial duties was considerably raised by 1931, on the one hand by the fall in prices of industrial commodities which had set in since 1930, on the other by the extensive denunciation in 1927 and 1928 of all those commercial treaties in which Spain had fixed rates below the level of the minimum tariff of 1925 (*duanas consolidadas*); further by increases in the duties on aluminium products in 1928, but particularly through a series of duty increases in 1930, which, in addition to semi-manufactured silk and artificial silk goods, mainly affected machinery, motor-cars, apparatus, films and rubber tires; these drastic reinforcements of tariff protection,

[1] See *H.-A.*, 1926, pp. 642–643.
[2] Text of these regulations, *H.-A.*, 1926, pp. 1508–1509, 1716; 1927, pp. 2112, 2246–2247.
[3] See for above figures and remarks *Enquête*, II, pp. 107–108; *W.d.A.*, pp. 216–227; *Commerce Year Book*, 1928, p. 570.

which increased some of the rates in force by as much as 700%, were chiefly Spain's answer to the American Tariff of 1930. Thus the potential tariff level of group B rose to 42–57%, metal goods with 87·5–98% reaching the highest class level, followed by textiles with 40–88%, and then by semi-manufactured wood and paper goods at a great distance. Of 44 articles in group B, 24 were liable to duties above 50%. The tariff level of finished goods rose to 55–96%. The figures of most classes were increased only by the fall in prices. Of 62 articles in group C, 30 were liable to duties above 50%.

With the quota restrictions imposed on Spanish imports at the end of December 1931,[1] a new and much more drastic device for the regulation of imports appeared in Spanish commercial policy, which from 1932 onwards deprived the analysis of her tariff policy for the duration of the quotas of much of its practical value for appraising the protectionist tendencies of Spain.

C: GENERAL TENDENCIES OF EUROPEAN INDUSTRIAL TARIFF POLICY BEFORE AND AFTER THE WAR
(See Table IVA, graph B.C. in Appendix)

The first important conclusion to be drawn from the comparison of Europe's industrial pre- and post-War tariff levels (see Table IVA of Appendix) is that a rise in post-War rates had occurred almost without exception in industrial as well as agrarian Europe, both for semi and wholly manufactured articles.

In respect of semi-manufactured goods only two European countries—Sweden and Poland—and in respect of wholly-manufactured goods only one—Finland—had on the average lower rates in 1927 than in 1913. The increase of duties was generally considerably greater for finished goods than for semi-manufactured articles both in industrial and agrarian Europe.

[1] Comp. p. 102 of this book.

With regard to semi-manufactured goods, Switzerland, Italy, and Czechoslovakia and the same countries and Germany with regard to manufactured goods were conspicuous in raising their rates. In agrarian Europe, Bulgaria, Spain, and Roumania left all other Powers behind in raising rates, while Poland could show decreases only in comparison with the abnormally high Russian pre-War level, and occupied a front-rank position among protectionist countries.

The sharp rise in prices of semi-manufactured goods, amounting on an average to 42·2% in 1927 compared with 1913 in respect of 44 commodities in List A, prevented a sharp rise (above 50%) in the general tariff levels of semi-manufactured goods both in industrial and in agrarian Europe in 1927 (with the exception of Switzerland, Bulgaria, and Spain).

With an average increase of 20·8% in the prices of 62 goods in group C in 1927, the tariff levels of manufactured goods rose more sharply in industrial Europe, particularly in Germany, Italy, and Czechoslovakia, and in agrarian Europe everywhere (with the exception of Sweden, Poland, and Finland); in Bulgaria, Spain, and Roumania they rose to unprecedented heights.

In 1931, when the general price level of the semi-manufactured goods of the A-list was 2·4% and that of the wholly manufactured goods of the A-list 5·5% below that of pre-War time, all European countries stood well above their pre-War tariff levels, only Sweden and Finland being rare exceptions, together with Poland, despite her extremely high tariff level. Throughout the agrarian east and south-east of Europe as well as in Spain, and in industrial Europe in Italy and Czechoslovakia, levels reached often prohibitive heights.

In this almost universal raising of the industrial tariff walls of Europe we find already in 1927, even in countries with moderate tariffs, a number of industries which were the favoured objects of European post-War tariff policy. Among the semi-manufactured goods heavy increases in duties could be found on tissues, artificial silk yarns and chemicals throughout Europe, on iron and steel goods in Italy, France, Czechoslovakia, and throughout agrarian Europe. Equivalent increases of duties on the goods of the cotton-spinning and wool-combing industries, of the leather trade and the semi-manufacturing wood and paper trades, were much more infrequent. The extent of increase of rates and consequently of the rise in tariff levels was generally much more considerable in the case of the duties on the goods of the weaving and semi-manufacturing metal trades imposed by the countries of agrarian Europe. Only Italy with her duties on heavy metal goods approached the extreme tariff levels of the agrarian countries of the east and south-east and of Spain. With regard to chemicals almost every country in Europe reached very high tariff levels.[1]

In view of the importance of the semi-manufactured products of the metal and chemical industries for modern industry the accentuation of European post-War protection in this sphere had special significance. It meant for the countries concerned a rise in the general cost of living, and must inevitably extend to the protection of all those numerous industries whose costs of production were influenced by the rising prices of the protected semi-manufactured articles.

When the question of raising the iron and steel duties was being discussed in Germany in 1925, an expert like Professor *Harms* regarded the consequences as so serious for the whole German price level that he felt forced to utter an urgent warning against such a tariff policy.[2]

In comparing the tariff level figures of semi- and wholly-manufactured goods, therefore, it must always be borne in mind that high duties upon semi-manufactured articles involved compensating high protection for the industries of wholly manufactured goods.

[1] The raising of chemical duties in almost the whole of Europe does not sufficiently appear from the figures in Tables AI, because a much more comprehensive selection of goods would have been necessary for that purpose, which would necessitate a special inquiry. See the figures of the world's chemical tariff levels cited in *Enquête*, II, p. 199.   [2] See *Harms*, op. cit., pp. 367–368.

This explained partly the prevailing tendency almost throughout Europe towards heavy increases in the duties on finished goods in post-War tariffs. Within this general movement of the tariff levels of finished goods the most important result was a universal rise in the tariff levels of the textile trades throughout Europe. On the other hand, a raising of tariff barriers to protect the motor-car industry was common only to industrial Europe.

Increases in the duties on the products of the paper, toy, watch-making and rubber industries out of proportion to the general increases were widespread in industrial Europe. The territorial and also, in most cases, numerical extent of duty increases in respect of the remaining industries was distinctly less. Notably heavy increases in machinery duties in France and Italy were exceptions in industrial Europe.

In most of the countries of agrarian Europe the classes of machinery, vehicles, apparatus and instruments were far behind the products of other industries as regards the rise in tariff levels. Only Poland, Hungary, and Spain imposed unusually high duties on machinery and vehicles; only Poland and Bulgaria had high tariff levels for apparatus and instruments (watches).

On the other hand, the duties on the finished products of the paper, glass, ceramic, metal, toy-making and rubber trades reached prohibitive proportions in many cases during the post-War period in the agrarian countries of the east and south-east, as also in Spain. Omitting the exceptional tariff levels of class VIII (toy-making and rubber-tire industries), largely due in 1931 to an unusual decline in the prices of these goods, not only to extreme duties, the tariff levels of the class of the finished textile goods were still far the highest in all the countries of agrarian Europe, with the exception of Spain, Hungary, and Yugoslavia. In these three countries they were exceeded by the duties on finished metal goods.

With regard to the location of industries, the industries of labour and consumption orientation [1] were subjected to specially heavy duties throughout agrarian Europe, and consumer's goods industries were taxed more heavily than capital goods industries.

This preponderance of protection for industries of consumer's goods showed the extent to which this tariff policy was the means of promoting the industrialization of these countries. For not only theoretically but also historically it was just those industries (especially the textile trades) with which the industrialization of capitalist countries began. [2]   And it was above all the industries of consumption and labour-orientation of dense agrarian populations to which, according to Schlier's investigations into modern Europe, favourable opportunities for expansion must be accorded. [3]

In the old industrial countries of Central Europe, the centre of tariff protection was also to be found rather in the industries of finished goods than in those of semi-manufactured commodities, rather in the industries of consumer's goods than in those of capital goods.   From the point of location the industries of labour and consumption orientation were generally more protected than those of the transportation orientation.   But the industries of capital goods, owing to the great importance of protection for the motor-car industry, occupied a greater place within the framework of industrial protection in industrial Europe than in that of agrarian Europe.   Further, within the industries of labour and consumption orientation the marked growth of industrial Europe's tariffs was definitely limited to the trades of the quantitative labour orientation. [4] (Especially semi and wholly manufacturing textile trades.)

Dr. *Schlier's* inquiries into the location of European post-War

---

[1] With regard to these terms comp. the translation of Alfred Weber's *Standorts - Theorie* by *F. Friedrich*, "The Location of Industry," New York, 1928. For the classification of industries according to location, see *Schlier*, op. cit., p. 47.

[2] Comp. *Enquête*, II, pp. 8–9.   [3] See *Schlier*, op. cit., pp. 30–31.

[4] See Schlier's interpretation of this new term of the theory of location of industries, introduced with the consent of Alfred Weber. *Schlier*, op. cit., pp. 32–33.

industry have shown that [1] the industries of the old European industrial countries are seriously threatened not in the first place by the organization of new European industries of quantitative labour orientation in agrarian Europe, but mainly by the rapid development of the great Far Eastern textile industries, and the great export losses of the European countries on non-European textile markets which caused a keener competition in Europe. This was one important reason for the striking post-War increases, chiefly in the duties on textile finished goods, in the tariffs of most of the old European industrial countries.

Although the same industries were often selected for protection, a stronger *defensive* character was imparted to the industrial tariff protection of Central Europe compared with the *offensive* industrial tariff protection of agrarian Europe, intent on the development of certain new industries. The main purpose of this defensive protection was to preserve the old and threatened industries hitherto dependent on world markets and to reserve them their home markets.[2]

If we compare the increase of the duties on industrial goods with that on agrarian goods from 1913 to 1927, the much greater rise of industrial tariff levels of industrial Europe than that of her agrarian levels is apparent, while in agrarian Europe industrial and agrarian tariffs rose substantially, but the former more than the latter. Since most of these countries naturally did not import agrarian goods to any amount compared with their industrial imports, the rise of duties on this class of goods was of far greater importance for the curtailment of their imports than the rise of agrarian duties. Consequently, industrial exports were more severely checked throughout

[1] Comp. *Schlier*, op. cit., pp. 33, 37, 41.

[2] This does generally not apply to chemical protection in Europe's industrial countries, whose purpose is not the defensive maintenance of existing, but the organization of new home industries (military reasons). Nor does it apply to the industrial tariff policy of Italy, which is rather to be considered a "young" industrial country. See *Enquête*, II, p. 104.

Europe in 1927 by tariffs than in 1913. It was for this reason that the World Economic Conference of 1927 devoted special attention to the tariff problem, and in the first place to industrial tariffs. In the report of that conference it was stated "that the raising of tariff barriers in most countries is almost entirely due to the raising of industrial tariffs." [1]

The extensive fixing of industrial duties by the commercial treaties of the years 1927–29, mostly remaining in force until 1931, and the agrarian protectionist movement in Europe between 1929 and 1931, which the world economic crisis of 1929 provoked and lashed until it assumed incredible dimensions, produced between 1929 and 1931 a complete reversal of these conditions. In industrial Europe agrarian tariff levels rose from the mostly low levels of 1927 to enormous heights; in agrarian Europe they rose as well but more slowly. Industrial tariff levels in industrial Europe, on the other hand, ascended only slowly, more as a result of the fall in prices than through increases in duties, from their position in 1927. The industrial tariff levels of agrarian Europe, already high in 1927, grew stronger corresponding to their higher starting figures of 1927, although here too the fall in price was more responsible than increases of duties.

While agrarian imports were threatened with destruction by the heavy duties combined, by 1931, with the extensive adoption of new import-lowering methods, industrial imports in 1931 were nowhere showing such signs of devastation as agrarian imports, and it was not until 1932, until the general appearance of quotas, currency restrictions, etc., that also the industrial exports of the industrial countries shrank to unexampled dimensions.

Nevertheless, even before 1929 the protectionist industrial tariff policy of countries not yet or but feebly industrialized in a number of typical spheres of European and world-wide industrial post-War protectionism, exerted perceptible effects upon the industrial exports of the old industrial countries,

---

[1] See "Conférence économique int.," *Rapport définitif*, p. 30.

especially of those of the industries of the quantitative labour-orientation. The Kieler investigations into world exports of industrial products between 1913 and 1928 revealed for 1928 a quantitative decline in the yarn exports of England, Germany, and the U.S.A., of 34% compared with 1913, in exports of tissues of 12%. The exports of consumer's goods of these three states declined from 57% to 53% of their total exports. The figures of the rise in the value of the world exports of important industries in Table A, show that the figures for the products of the toy-making, textile, and semi-manufacturing iron trades remained below those of the great export groups to which they belong, cotton yarn most of all, then toys and ready made clothes, and semi-manufactured iron goods least of all.

TABLE A: WORLD EXPORTS OF IMPORTANT
INDUSTRIAL GOODS, 1913–28 [1]

1913 = 100, *value of world exports of :*

Group	1928
I. Consumer's goods total	166
II. Capital goods total	179
III. "Means of Transport" *	293
Of which:	
1. Semi-manufactured textiles	160
2. Wholly manufactured textiles	163
Out of which:	
a. Cotton tissues	159
b. Cotton yarn	135
c. Ready-made clothes	137
d. Toys	137
e. Semi-manufactured iron goods	175
f. Machinery	199

* By "Means of Transport," the Kieler investigation lumped together the production of the vehicle, apparatus, paper, and motor-tire industries, which are branches of typical post-War demands.

[1] See *Enquête*, II, pp. 140–145.

These figures confirmed the conclusions of *Schlier*, who found in the countries of industrial Europe striking differences between the growth of the total industry and the development of the textile industry in the post-War period (see Table B).

TABLE B: DEVELOPMENT OF GENERAL INDUSTRY AND OF THE TEXTILE INDUSTRY IN CENTRAL EUROPE[1]

(Showing growth (+) or decline (−) in numbers of employed in %)

Country	Period	General Ind.	Textile Ind.
		%	%
Germany . . .	1907–25	+29	+16
Great Britain . .	1907–24	+14	+ 0
France	1906–21	+ 9	−21
Switzerland . .	1911–29	+24	−10
Czechoslovakia . .	1913–24	+ 8	−11

If these data of some diminishing industries and shrinking exports of the *old* industrial countries are compared with the figures of growing production of similar, strongly protected, industries in the *agrarian* or the *new industrial* countries [2] (such as Italy), and if we add to these facts the disproportional rise in machinery exports shown in Table A, p. 185, a partial industrialization of countries that were industrially insignificant before the War, can clearly be seen. In this process European tariff policy before and after the outbreak of the World Economic Crisis has played an important part.

[1] See *Schlier*, op. cit., pp. 33–34.
[2] Comp. pp. 374–376 of this book.

PART III

ACTUAL TARIFF LEVELS IN EUROPE 1913-31
(See Tables B1–IV of Appendix)

I

DETAILS OF THE METHODS OF CALCULATING ACTUAL TARIFF LEVELS

THE main differences between potential and actual tariff levels to which attention has been already drawn in Part I [1] with other details concerning the methods employed to calculate actual tariff levels may be summarized as follows:—

1. The commodities taken into account were only the most important of the actual exports of the countries in question. The exports of these goods must amount to a certain minimum export value. These minima stated in exact details in the following sections of Part III were usually between 1–3% of the total exports. The greater part of such articles must have been exported to Europe.

2. Consequently there did not exist a general list of goods with uniform "normal" prices for the calculation of all the actual tariff levels, comparable to the A-list of goods for the inquiries of Part II. There were only the varying individual export prices of the exporting countries which had to be compared with the rates of duty of the countries into which these goods were imported.

3. As only the larger or a few smaller countries with high purchasing power constituted large import markets for European goods, there were only limited possibilities for compiling tables of their actual tariff levels in Tables B of the Appendix, not only regarding the number of countries, but also with regard to the classes or groups of goods.

Such calculations have been made only of those countries to which at least three commodities in each of at least three classes of one of the three main groups of the A-list have been

---

[1] Comp. pp. 28 et seq. of this study.

actually exported.[1]   Very often incomplete tariff levels of only one or two groups of goods could be calculated.[2]

4. Since one country imported different goods from various European countries, different averages of the duties imposed by its tariff on these goods resulted.   They have been called the "national indices" of the tariff level of a country for the various countries exporting goods to it.   Or we could speak of these averages as the actual tariff levels of country A (importer) for countries B, C, D, etc. (exporters).

Each Table D of the sections of this part shows such actual tariff levels, viz. the tariff levels of the chief markets to which the exports of the country concerned were directed.   Only such customers were included to which at least three goods of at least two classes of a group of goods were exported from the country in question.   As in Part II, the height of duties upon important commodities has often been stated, especially in cases where averages of the tariff levels of groups or classes of goods could not be estimated.

5. The figures of the potential and the actual tariff levels in Tables AI and B of the Appendix show considerable differences.   These are explained by the different prices and goods with the help of which the figures were arrived at.   It will be noticed that in a number of cases in which figures were available, both for the potential and for the actual tariff levels of the same country, the figures of the actual tariff levels are lower than those of the potential.   This is explained by the fact that the higher the average figure of all the duties of a group or class of goods owing to high duties on certain of their articles, the greater will be the tendency for actual imports to be confined to goods that are more lightly taxed.   This phenomenon

---

[1] The classification of goods of this list has been applied also for the inquiries of Part III.

[2] Tables of actual tariff levels could be calculated for Germany, France, Italy, Great Britain, Belgium, Switzerland, Austria, Czechoslovakia, Poland, Roumania, Yugoslavia, Spain, Sweden, Denmark. Only those for Germany, Italy, Switzerland, and Spain are published as examples.

appeared particularly in the case of countries with high tariff levels.[1]

6. The political and geographical changes which the peace treaties of 1919 effected in Europe rendered impossible comparisons between the pre-War and post-War situation in connection with inquiries into the actual tariff levels and their effects upon the export movements in all those cases where new countries emerged from the War. For the analysis of the height of duties upon the actual exports of the Baltic States and Poland, of the Danubian Succession States and Yugoslavia, no comparison whatever with 1913 were possible. In the case of Russia, on the other hand, her exclusion from all the references in this book to the post-War period prompted us to refrain from describing her pre-War conditions.

[1] Compare the figures of actual and potential tariff levels, for example, in the case of Italy and Spain, which are highly protected countries, with the figures, exhibiting much slighter differences, of Switzerland.

In the case of countries of moderate tariff policy, on the other hand, actual tariff levels sometimes surpass the potential tariff levels. This occurred if only the higher taxed goods of a group or a class of goods were actually imported; then the average of the duties imposed on them must be higher than the average of all goods of the respective group or class which had to be calculated for their potential tariff level.

II

OUTLINES OF THE ECONOMIC INTEGRATION
OF EUROPE

(According to Gaedicke and von Eynern)
(See Table III in Appendix)

THE system of European export relations in pre-War and post-War Europe is very complicated. The investigations of *Gaedicke* and *von Eynern* into the economic integration of Europe have greatly facilitated the understanding of this kind of foreign trade relationships. These analyses, therefore, were a valuable aid for the following inquiries, as they could be used for the classification of the important export markets of each country. In the exposition of potential tariff levels, *Alfred Weber's* conception of an industrial Central and an agrarian Border Europe, which is also the basis of *Gaedicke* and *von Eynern's* book, has already been employed. As, however, in that part of the study the actual export structures of the single countries had not to be considered, details of the book of Drs. *Gaedicke* and *von Eynern* were of no interest.

Now it is necessary, however, to elucidate in somewhat greater detail this picture of the economic integration of Europe before the War and up to the outbreak of the World Economic Crisis in 1929, in order to compare it with the development of the duties on the actual exports of the various European countries to their most important European markets. Only thus will it be possible to discuss the question if and to what extent European post-War tariff policy, especially between 1929 and 1931, was a serious menace to the economic integration of Europe.

The most important result of the post-War tendencies of inter-European foreign trade was a restoration of the pre-War conditions of European integration,[1] which was effected with surprising success between 1925 and 1929 at a time when Europe's share of world trade was visibly shrinking.[2] The most important data for the relationships here discussed are set forth (after Gaedicke and von Eynern) in Tables A and B (Table B, p. 194).

TABLE A: FOREIGN TRADE OF TOTAL, CENTRAL, AND BORDER EUROPE, 1913 AND 1929

(In Mill. M., Rm., and %)

Group	1913 Mill. M.	%	1929 Mill. Rm.	%
AI. Europe's Total Imports . .	53518	100·0	82875	100·0
Of European origin . .	32331	60·4	46948	56·6
II. Central Europe's Total Imports	44665	100·0	65841	100·0
Of European origin . .	25094	56·2	34291	52·0
III. Border Europe's Total Imports	5885	100·0	15131	100·0
Of European origin . .	4892	83·3	11730	77·0
BI. Europe's Total Exports . .	44748	100·0	67347	100·0
Of European destination .	30389	67·9	44023	65·9
II. Central Europe's Total Exports	36845	100·0	52454	100·0
Of European destination .	23435	64·0	31497	60·0
III. Border Europe's Total Exports	4619	100·0	12897	100·0
Of European destination .	3937	85·2	10993	85·0

See *Gaedicke, Vol. of Text*, pp. 18, 59, 70.

Tables A and B plainly reveal Europe's extraordinary importance as the supplier of and customer for her own products, which in pre-War and post-War times was so great that taking a yearly average between 1909 and 1913 the European share of the total foreign trade failed to reach 50% only in the case of a single country, viz. Great Britain. Between 1925

[1] Making due allowance for changes in the price level when calculating the values of imports and exports.

[2] Comp. *Gaedicke*, op. cit., pp. 6–9, 31–32, 125.

N

and 1930 only two countries, Great Britain and France, imported less than 50% from Europe, and again only Great Britain sent less than 50% of her total exports to Europe (see Table III of Appendix). With this exception it may be said that "the European internal market for European countries was more important than the rest of the world at the time." [1]

TABLE B: THE FOREIGN TRADE OF CENTRAL AND BORDER EUROPE, 1913 AND 1929
(*In Mill. M., Rm., and %*)

Group	1913 Mill. M.	%	1929 Mill. Rm.	%
A: *Imports*				
I. Central Europe's Total Imports	44665	100·0	65841	100·0
Imported from:				
Central Europe	17847	40·0	23417	35·5
Border Europe	7246	16·4	10874	16·5
Outside Europe	19571	43·6	31550	48·0
II. Border Europe's Total Imports	5885	100·0	15131	100·0
Imported from:				
Border Europe	1043	17·7	2247	14·8
Central Europe	3849	65·3	9483	63·0
Outside Europe	993	17·0	3401	22·2
B: *Exports*				
I. Central Europe's Total Exports	36845	100·0	52454	100·0
Exported to:				
Central Europe	18362	50·0	22614	43·2
Border Europe	5074	13·8	8882	17·0
Outside Europe	13410	36·4	20957	39·8
II. Border Europe's Total Exports	4619	100·0	12897	100·0
Exported to:				
Border Europe	737	16·0	2111	16·3
Central Europe	3201	69·5	8882	69·0
Outside Europe	682	14·5	1904	14·7

See *Gaedicke, Vol. of Text*, pp. 59, 70.

[1] See *Gaedicke, Vol. of Text*, pp. 59, 70.

Generally speaking, Europe was more important as a customer than as a supplier. In post-War times the decline in Europe's share in the total European import requirements in favour of imports from outside Europe is a characteristic European aspect of the frequently discussed problem of the "de-Europeanizing" of world trade, an index also of the penetration chiefly of overseas agrarian and North American industrial exports to Europe.[1]

If we consider the conditions separately for the two great European groups, for Central industrial and Border agrarian Europe,[2] very important differences appeared. Owing to the fact that nearly all the great countries of Europe (Russia being the exception) belong to Central Europe, the proportions of Central European imports and exports to the total European imports and exports, and also to internal European foreign trade, were overwhelmingly great, even in the post-War period. The relative growth of Border Europe's export and import figures in 1929, which was so much greater than that of Central Europe, was largely nothing else than the result of the establishment of new states, expressed in these connections in the transformation of pre-War internal into post-War external trade movements, so that all the figures of Border Europe in 1929 were too high compared with 1913 and not strictly comparable.[3]

If we consider the degree of foreign trade connection of the countries with Europe in the two groups, we find, both with regard to imports and still more so with regard to exports, that Border Europe was integrated with Europe to a far greater extent than Central Europe.[4] The great powers of Central

[1] *Gaedicke, Vol. of Text*, pp. 9, 37, 56–57, 68.

[2] It should here be mentioned that in the above figures of Gaedicke and von Eynern for industrial Europe, Holland is also included in this part of Europe, which is justified by the extraordinary industrialization of this country since the War, and the preponderance of the industrial population, although, according to our other principle of classification (see pp. 47, 48 of this book), Holland should be included in agrarian Europe.   [3] Comp. *Gaedicke, Vol. of Text*, pp. 29–30.

[4] See *Gaedicke*, pp. 49, 68.

Europe, were generally as regards imports integrated with Europe below the average, and (with exception of Germany) the same held good with regard to their exports. England, France, Italy, Belgium, and Switzerland have been de-Europeanized to an increasing degree in the post-War period, England and France owing to a deliberate empire policy.[1]

The trend of European tariff policy in post-War times was therefore of much greater importance for the countries of Border Europe than for a number of the countries of Central Europe.

If, finally, we inquire into the composition of European exports and imports of Border and Central Europe according to their origin or destination from or to these two zones of European economy, we encounter the problem of *Europe's spheres of integration* [2] ("Verbundenheitssphären").

We find that European imports, and to a still greater extent the European exports of *Central* Europe, came mainly from Central Europe itself or went there; consequently, Border Europe was less important as supplier to and customer of Central Europe than was Central Europe itself. In the post-War period this exchange of goods between the countries of industrial Europe diminished in favour of trade with overseas countries, without thereby increasing the share of Border Europe. Central Europe formed the *first great sphere of European integration*, and for this reason the trend of tariff policy in the Central European industrial countries was usually more important for the latter than the development of tariffs in Border Europe, in connection with which only the analyses of the conditions of the individual countries can reveal the very varying degrees in which the industrial countries of Europe were interested in exports to Central Europe.

The integration of Border Europe with Central Europe represented *a second great sphere of European integration*, which, from the export standpoint, was mainly concerned with

---

[1] See *Gaedicke*, pp. 37, 56–57, 99, 110.
[2] Ibid., op. cit., p. 123.

raw material and agrarian exports from the Border countries to Central Europe, and from the import point of view with the supply of manufactures to these countries by industrial Europe.[1]

The figures in Table B on p. 194 indicate plainly the vital importance of these relationships for the export trade of the Border countries. Consequently, the development of Central European tariff policy concerned them very closely, whereas, in view of the lesser exchange of goods among themselves, their own tariff policy was mostly a question of secondary importance.

Within this integration of Border and Central Europe three narrower spheres may be distinguished. First, the exports of the Border countries of north and north-eastern Europe —of the Scandinavian and Baltic countries—were up to 1931 attracted chiefly by England and only in the second place by Germany and Western Europe; their imports came mainly from Germany, and only in the second place from Great Britain.[2]

The eastern and south-eastern Border countries of Europe and three Central European industrial powers (Germany, Austria, and Czechoslovakia) formed a second sphere of integration.

In the first place, tendencies towards a reconstitution of the old Austro-Hungarian economic area were distinctly perceptible in spite of the new frontiers. Further, Germany, as an agrarian import market for eastern and south-eastern exports, and as exporter of manufactured goods, represented one of their most important customers and suppliers, while Austria and Czechoslovakia were closely connected with Germany by the well-known process of integration of industrial countries.[3]

Lastly, a close bond united the three most distant countries

[1] Comp. *Gaedicke, Vol. of Text*, pp. 68–71.
[2] Ibid., pp. 72–75.
[3] Ibid., pp. 76–79.

of Border Europe, Greece, Spain, and Portugal, with Great Britain and France; their relations with Germany were looser. They exported chiefly agrarian products and raw materials to Central Europe, and imported raw materials and manufactures.[1]

Such were the principal features of the "economic integration of Europe" which Gaedicke and von Eynern have drawn, with much detail not mentioned here relating to the composition, the values, and the regional distribution of Europe's external trade movements. It is important to keep these ramifications continuously in mind now that we are about to analyse the duties on the actual exports of the various European countries to their most important markets. First, we shall deal with the countries of industrial Europe (Central Europe) in the order observed in the foregoing part, and afterwards the countries of agrarian Europe (Border Europe) will be discussed in the following order:—

(*a*) Denmark and Holland.
(*b*) The countries of North-Eastern Europe: Sweden, Norway, and Finland.
(*c*) The Baltic countries: Esthonia, Lettland, and Lithuania.
(*d*) Poland.
(*e*) The South-Eastern countries: Roumania, Hungary, Yugoslavia, and Bulgaria.
(*f*) The Mediterranean countries: Greece, Spain, and Portugal.

With a survey of the effects of tariff policy upon the reciprocal integration of the various countries up to the year 1931, the statistical inquiries will conclude.

[1] Comp. *Gaedicke*, pp. 79–80.

III

LIMITS OF THE TEXTUAL ANALYSIS OF THE ACTUAL TARIFF LEVELS

IN order to calculate the figures of actual tariff levels the official trade statistics of twenty-four European countries have been checked with regard to prices, quantities, and total values of their most important export goods, and the height of duties upon them in the most important export markets has been computed. The extensive material upon which these calculations were based could not be published for reasons of space, any more than the corresponding material relating to Part II of this book.

We could do no more than indicate the number of export goods found to be important for each country investigated; further, the share which their export value bore to the total exports of the country.

In this connection, it should be borne in mind that the groups of raw materials on the free list, frequently very large, and also the goods mainly shipped outside Europe, were not taken into account. In the case of any country, therefore, of which the exports largely consisted of these goods or whose exports went much to overseas, the proportion of the selected goods to the total exports must be small.

Finally, it should be pointed out that 1929, and not 1927, has been chosen as the first post-War year for the tables in the text which elucidate the structures of exports, because it was not until this year that most European countries reached their maximum exports before the crisis, so that the effects of the crisis up to 1931 could be better inferred in comparison with the figures of 1929. This deviation from the year 1927, which was always chosen for the calculation of the tariff levels, was permissible, as calculations (unpublished) showed that with respect to the tariff levels, the year 1929 offered no appreciable differences whatever compared with 1927. As far as possible, we have included figures relating to the trend of exports up to 1933 or 1934, in order to indicate more recent developments after 1931.[1]

[1] For the tables in the text, our most important sources after the trade statistics were: (1) The *Stat. Germ. Jahrbuch*, 1913, 1914, 1931–35, which in its *Intern. Übersichten*, contains much material relating to this question. (2) The League of Nations statistics *Statistiques*, I and III (for exact title see bibliography). These sources will not be otherwise quoted in detail.

IV

ACTUAL TARIFF LEVELS FOR THE EXPORTS OF INDUSTRIAL EUROPE

1. *Germany and the Tariffs in Europe*

(a) *Composition and Value of German Exports*

EVEN before the War, but to a still greater extent in the post-War period, the chief constituents of German exports were industrial raw materials, semi- and wholly-manufactured goods (comp. Table A, p. 202). Among the great industrial Powers of Europe only Great Britain's exports showed a greater percentage of manufactured goods (see Table II in Appendix). Nevertheless, before the War, the absolute figures of German agrarian exports (rye, oats, wheat, flour, sugar) were very considerable, and it was not until the post-War period that there was a great shrinkage in this portion of German exports, partly due to new duties in the chief markets, partly due to other causes as changes in the consumption of rye and wheat, decline in agrarian production, etc., so that in 1931 exports of agrarian products only formed 4·2% of the total exports, while those of finished goods alone accounted for about 75%.

All the great manufacturing trades were represented in the very differentiated German exports of finished goods. In addition there was a very substantial export of raw materials and semi-manufactured goods, especially of the coal, metal, chemical, and leather trades.

Germany's highly developed industrial organisation reveals a preponderance of industries of capital goods over industries of consumer's goods. The former employed 55% of the workers (semi-manufacturing trades 26%, all others 29%).[1] This great importance of the industries of capital goods was

[1] See *Schlier*, op. cit., pp. 44, 53, and *Enquête*, II, p. 9.

reflected in German post-War industrial exports by a characteristic increase, relative as well as absolute, in the exports

TABLE A: CHIEF GROUPS OF GERMAN
EXPORTS, 1913–31

(*In Mill. M., Rm. and % of Total Exports*)

Group	1913 Mill. M.	%	1929 Mill. Rm.	%	1931 Mill. Rm.	%
Total Exports (without precious metals)	10100	100·0	13480	100·0	9600	100·0
Comprising:						
A. Livestock, foodstuffs	1043	10·4	724	5·3	406	4·2
B. Raw materials, semi-manufactured goods	2600	26·3	2930	21·7	1810	18·9
C. Finished goods	6400	63·3	9830	73·0	7380	76·9
Including:						
Fuel	723	7·2	861	6·4	609	6·3
Chemicals	776	7·8	1226	9·1	844	8·7
Textiles 1	1235	12·2	1500	11·1	993	10·3
Textiles 2	663	6·6	967	6·5	655	6·8
Iron, iron goods	1340	13·3	1910	14·2	1375	14·3
Capital goods	1131	11·2	1890	14·1	1796	18·7
Toys, etc.	446	4·5	548	5·3	512	3·3

Textiles 1 = Silk, woollen, and cotton goods.
Textiles 2 = Ready-made clothes, leather, leather goods, and fur goods.
Capital goods = Machinery, electrical appliances, and vehicles.
Chemicals = Chemical basic materials, dyes, pharmaceutica.
Toys = Toys, musical instruments, glass, pottery.

See *Auswärtige Handel Deutschlands*, 1913, 1; 1927, 11; and *Monatliche Nachw. ü. d. ausw. Handel Dtschds.*, December number, 1931.

of a number of the great industries of capital goods. In 1913 the exports of the chemical, machinery, vehicles, electrical, and paper industries amounted to 21·6%, but in 1931 the proportion was 31%; and even if Germany's great exports of capital goods in 1931 were taken into account, mainly in response to the Russian demand (about 750 Mill. Rm.), this tendency was plain enough throughout the post-War period,[1] while the export trends of the great industries of consumer's goods lagged perceptibly behind.

The percentage of exports to total production differed materially from branch to branch in German industry. In some cases it reached very high permanent figures, and after 1929 assumed a dangerous character, so that the (relatively) well-maintained figures of German industrial exports in 1931 represented to a considerable extent exports at a loss occasioned by the credit crisis of this year. Table B shows the export percentages of a number of important German industries.

TABLE B: EXPORT QUOTAS OF GERMAN INDUSTRIES, 1913, 1928

In % of their total production the exports of the following industries amounted to:

Industry	1913	1928
Rolling works, cast iron	26·6	27·3
Electrical industry	25·5	19·1
Cotton industry	21·6	10·4
Iron and steel goods industries	33·2	31·0
Machinery	26·4	29·2
Chemical industry	35·5	31·3
Paper industry	43·3	37·5
Toys	73·5	55·9

See *Enquête*, II, p. 85.

Of Germany's total output of finished goods in 1913 about 29·9% were exported, while in 1928 the proportion was 24·4%. Particularly characteristic among the figures of Table B was the rapid fall in the export share of the cotton industry, which furnished a distinct parallel to the lag in the growth of the German textile trades compared with other industries (see Table B, p. 186 of this book).[2] This is a typical example of the decline in the textile exports of an old industrial country, which will also be met with in other old industrial States.

[1] See *Gaedicke*, p. 94.   [2] See *Schlier*, op. cit., pp. 26–33.

In the years of the crisis, 1930 and 1931, internal German purchasing power fell to such an extent that, in 1931, not less than 40% of the whole of German industrial production had to find an outlet abroad. In the toy trades the export share rose to 90%, in the machinery trades to 63%, and in the china trades to 45–60%.[1]

The list of goods, comprising 108 industrial products and only 15 agrarian products, which was framed in order to test the duties on Germany's actual exports, reflects the predominant position of industrial over agrarian exports.

Table B2 shows the export values of the goods it comprises, and their proportions to the total German export groups concerned. We have included all those goods in German export statistics, which in 1913 or 1927 or 1931 reached an export value of over 20 Mill. Rm. and were mainly exported to European countries.

TABLE B2: PROPORTION OF GERMAN LIST OF GOODS TO TOTAL GERMAN EXPORTS
(In Mill. M., Rm. and %)

Group	1913 Mill. M.	= % of	1927 Mill. Rm.	= % of	1931 Mill. Rm.	= % of
Total List . .	5720	56·6 of T.E.	6000	55·5 of T.E.	5270	55·0 of T.E.
15 agrarian products .	820	78·5 of A.E.	309	65·6 of A.E.	227	55·7 of A.E.
108 industrial products	4900	54·0 of I.E.	5691	42·7 of I.E.	5043	54·6 of I.E.

A.E. = Agrarian Exports.
I.E. = Industrial Exports.
T.E. = Total Exports.

If the list excluded a great part of German industrial exports, it should be borne in mind that in the first place most of the industrial raw materials on the free list were excluded, which, like textile raw materials, ore, hides, stones, clay, etc. figure among the exports of nearly every industrial country (to some extent, in reality, transit goods), further, that the German export statistics contained numerous goods whose values were

[1] See *Weltwirtschaft*, 1932, pp. 32–36; *Maschinenbau*, 1932, vol. xi, p. 24, and *Wirtschaftsdienst*, March 1932, pp. 326–330.

below the minimum limit of 20 Mill. Mk. owing to the high degree of specialization among manufactured goods. Finally, the analysis of the territorial distribution of exports will show to what extent their extra-European integration has led to an exclusion of exports from the list.

(b) *Geographical Distribution of German Exports*

In pre-War as in post-War days Europe was more important as a market to Germany than for any other great European industrial country. Both in 1913 and in 1927 Europe bought about 75% of German exports, while in 1931 this share rose to 81%. For Germany's best customers, like Great Britain, France, Holland, the Scandinavian countries, and Switzerland, belonged, in 1931, to those countries where the destruction of purchasing power still lagged far behind that in the centre, the east, and south-east of Europe, as well as in the agrarian raw material countries overseas; and this favourable territorial distribution of German exports was reinforced by their composition, inasmuch as the prices of industrial products fell more slowly than those of agrarian products and raw materials.

Both before and after the War the states of Central Europe (including Holland) took the greatest part of German exports to Europe, in 1913 72%, in 1929–31 nearly 66%.[1] In detail, however, noticeable changes could be revealed. In Central Europe, Great Britain, which was Germany's best customer in 1913, had a much smaller share of Germany's total exports;[2] the same although to a lesser degree was the case with Belgium, while the shares of France and Holland increased considerably. In Border Europe the most important change compared with pre-War times was the increased export, both absolute and relative, to the Scandinavian markets, while the eastern and south-eastern countries of Border Europe at the most

[1] See *Gaedicke, Vol. of Text*, pp. 152–153.
[2] Ibid., p. 89.

retained their pre-War importance as customers for German goods. Probably by 1931 the percentages taken by these countries had somewhat diminished (so far as comparisons are possible).[1]

TABLE C: GERMANY'S PRINCIPAL MARKETS, 1913–31

In Mill. M. and % of total German exports, goods were exported to:

Country	1913 Mill. M.	%	1929 Mill. Rm.	%	1931 Mill. Rm.	%
Total Exports . .	10100	100·0	13500	100·0	9600	100·0
Of which to:						
Total Europe . .	7680	76·0	9920	73·7	7780	81·0
Comprising:						
Great Britain . .	1440	14·2	1330	9·7	1147	11·8
Austria-Hungary * .	1100	10·9	(1400)	(10·6)	(878)	(9·2)
Czechoslovakia . .	—	—	658	4·9	424	4·4
Austria . . .	—	—	441	3·3	275	2·9
Russia . . .	880	8·7	354	2·6	762	7·9
Poland-Danzig . .	—	—	425	3·1	188	2·0
France (without Saar)	790	7·8	935	6·9	834	8·7
Netherlands . .	694	6·9	1355	10·1	955	9·9
Belgium . . .	551	5·4	609	4·5	463	4·8
Switzerland . .	536	5·3	627	4·7	542	5·6
Italy . . .	393	3·9	602	4·5	341	3·6
Scandinavian States .	774	7·7	1374	10·2	1048	10·9
South-East † . .	189(?)	—	508	3·7	286	3·1

* Austria-Hungary, 1929–31 = Total of exports to Austria, Czechoslovakia, Hungary, and Yugoslavia (not strictly comparable with 1913).

† South-East = 1913: Exports to Roumania, Serbia, and Bulgaria; 1929–31: exports to Roumania, Hungary, Yugoslavia, and Bulgaria; comparison with 1913 very doubtful.

How far these changes were connected with the most important modifications of the tariff policy of these vital German markets sketched in the second part of this book will be shown by the following detailed analysis of Germany's export relationships.

[1] See *Gaedicke, Vol. of Text,* pp. 87–88.

(c) *Actual Tariff Levels of the chief Markets of Germany*

I. *Germany and Industrial Europe*

(aa) *Germany and Great Britain*

German exports to England, which reached almost $1\frac{1}{2}$ milliard M. in 1913, consisted for the greater part of expensive manufactures of all kinds, besides a very large item of semi-manufactured iron and chemical goods. Finally, in 1913 England bought about 75% of Germany's sugar exports, to the value of about 190 million M. and was also a good customer for a number of other agrarian products (oats, hops, etc.). Apart from a light fiscal duty on sugar, all German exports to England were admitted free (in 1913).

The very important decline in England's relative share in German post-War exports, which long before 1931 had even led to an absolute decrease in the export figures compared with 1913, may be traced with great certainty to English post-War tariff policy. In fact, the particular German exports to England which declined considerably in 1929 and 1931 in comparison with other goods, exhibiting in some cases absolute decreases and in others preserving only the same proportions as in 1913 (which meant a quantitative reduction in view of the post-War upward trend in industrial prices up to 1931),[1] were chiefly sugar, chemicals, silk goods, cotton lace, motor-cars, apparatus, and instruments, and all these were goods liable to new English duties mostly of $33\frac{1}{3}$%. In the case of a number of articles the English tariff reached a considerably higher level. Sugar, which was taxed about 6–15% in 1913, was subjected in 1927 to a duty between 34% and 70%, in 1931 between 73% and 189%. Silk trimmings were liable in 1927 to duties between 25% and 123%, optical glasses to a duty of 50%. England's actual tariff level for Germany, calculated upon the export of respectively 14 and 16 finished goods,

---

[1] Comp. *Gaedicke, Vol. of Text*, pp. 87–88.

amounted in 1927 to 32·7–35%, in 1931 to 31·5–39% (see Table D, p. 226).

The decline in the export of the articles concerned was remarkable in some cases. We will mention two examples. Between 1913 and 1931 German sugar exports were reduced from 190 million M. to 15 million Rm., the exports of dye stuffs from 45 million to 28 million.

The example of Anglo-German export relationships shows how effective the English industrial (and sugar) duties were even before 1932. In speaking of England as the only great European "free-trade" country up to the crisis of 1931, especially as regards States whose exports to this country were largely manufactured goods, this description must therefore be taken *cum grano salis*.

What, however, was at stake for Germany when England adopted general protection did not transpire until after 1931. Tariffs and the depreciation of the Pound led between 1931 and 1934 to a great shrinkage of German exports to England, which fell to 383 million in 1934—that is, by 66% compared with 1931 (by 81% compared with 1929). This can only be described as an extensive destruction of the once so flourishing Anglo-German export relationships.

(bb) *Germany and France*

To a yet greater extent than in the case of England, Germany's exports to France consisted of industrial raw materials, semi- and wholly-manufactured goods. Of agrarian products only wheat and rye flour were exported to France in any quantity in 1913 (about 70 million M.). After the War, especially after the conclusion of the commercial treaty of 1927, the importance of France as a market for German goods continually increased until 1931. In this year France bought 9·8% of the total German exports. In this connection reparation payments in kind played a great part—in 1929 France received reparation deliveries of 486 million Rm. and in 1931 of 265 million Rm.,[1] and the encouragement given to these reparation imports by the French Government imposes caution in judging the Franco-German exchange of goods and the influence of French tariff policy upon German post-War imports. Heavy increases in French duties, which in normal circumstances might have led to a reduction in imports, could in this case be counteracted.

If in fact we survey the development of duties on German imports to France, we find that in 1927 they were lower both for agrarian and for semi-manufactured products, but even in this year were higher for finished goods than in 1913. In 1931 they rose steeply in respect of agrarian products, more moderately in respect of manufactured goods; in respect of semi-manufactured goods even in 1931 they remained below pre-War level (see the figures in Table D, p. 226).

Particularly impressive were the French increases in duties on German metal goods and machines (actual French tariff level for metal goods 20% in 1913, 50–60% in 1927–31, of machinery 10% in 1913, 20% in 1927–31), and yet it was here that German exports to France notably increased. Only the financing of these exports on reparations account, together with the intensive post-War industrialization of France, can explain such a contrary movement of duties and imports.

With the belated outbreak of the crisis in France in 1931, with the ending of reparations by the Hoover moratorium, the ascending curve of German exports to France reached its highest point in the year 1931. By France's adoption of quota restrictions, in isolated cases in 1931, but extensively in the following year, not only agrarian but also industrial imports of German goods by France were sharply cut. By 1934 German exports to France had fallen to 282 million Rm.— that is, to 34% of the 1931 figure; nor has any reversal of this rapid downward trend been apparent up to the present (1936).

[1] *Stat. Jahrbuch*, 1932, p. 213.

O

(cc) *Germany and Italy*

Similarly, as with France, German exports to Italy were largely increased by reparation deliveries in the post-War period, so that in 1929 Italy bought a higher share of the total German exports than in 1913. But here, by 1931, the extent of German exports had shrunk not only absolutely but also relatively. Before the War it was mainly semi-manufactured products of the iron, steel, and chemical trades, and further numerous finished goods that Germany exported to Italy. After the War reparation coal and coke were added and largely contributed to the increase of German exports compared with 1913. Nevertheless, the effect of very drastic industrial duties on German exports was more obvious in the case of Italy than in France. Whereas before the War the actual Italian tariff level of fourteen German semi-manufactured articles of group B amounted to 13–17%, in 1927 and 1931, thanks to heavy increases in the Italian duties on semi-manufactured metal and chemical products, the actual tariff levels of these two classes rose to 19–39 and 27–55% respectively, and such increases could not fail to have a marked effect upon the imports of the goods in question. In 1927, and still more so in 1931, very considerable reductions in German exports were apparent as regards such highly protected goods as pig iron and numerous chemical products.

The Italian tariff level of finished goods also rose steeply in the post-War period. For forty-two German manufactured articles it amounted in 1913 to 12·7–14·4% and in 1927 and 1931 to 22–31 or 29·5–45%.

The increases in the Italian duties on metal goods, vehicles, apparatus, and machinery were particularly heavy. In all these classes German exports to Italy showed by 1927 lessened or unchanged figures and in 1931 substantial reductions. Italy's protectionist industrial tariff policy therefore decisively checked German industrial exports, although, even in 1927 and 1929, these reductions were compensated by increased reparation deliveries. The diminution, both absolute and relative, in German exports to Italy, visible in 1931, persisted up to 1933. The small increase which appeared in 1934 compared with 1933 only brought German exports to Italy up to 246 million Rm., which, although representing an increase over 1931, was still below the position of 1913.

(dd) *Germany and Belgium*

As Belgium adhered even in the post-War period until 1931 to a free-trade commercial policy, her actual tariff level (numerous articles being on the free list) for German exports changed very little compared with 1913, and in some cases was even lower (between 5 and 14% for semi-manufactured goods) than in that year.

As regards German manufactured articles, however, even in Belgium a slight protectionist raising of duties was perceptible, the Belgian actual tariff level for twenty-seven German export manufactures rising from 7–8% in the pre-War period to 8–16% in the post-War epoch (metal goods as much as to 22%). Consequently, German exports remained at a very high level up to 1931. The more drastic quota and tariff policy provoked by the crisis adopted by Belgium since 1932 substantially reduced German exports to Belgium, which in 1934 were valued at 236 million Rm., being 54% of the amount of 1931.

(ee) *Germany and Switzerland*

The unmistakable protectionist tendency of Swiss post-War tariff policy, analysed in the second part of this book, up to 1931 little disturbed the closely woven general texture of German-Swiss export relationships, nor did it prevent Switzerland in 1931 from taking even more German exports than in 1913, although in particular spheres German exports had been appreciably reduced by this time. German exports to Switzerland consisted in the first place of highly specialized semi-finished goods, in respect of which the Swiss actual tariff level for twenty-three German products in 1913 amounted to about 2·6–5% and in 1927–31 to about 2·6–7·7%.

Germany also exported all kinds of highly specialized manufactures. For forty-six of them the Swiss actual tariff level reached 8–10% in 1913 and 14–20% in 1927 and 1931. (But there were duties on metal goods up to 24%, on vehicles after the War up to 52%, on paper goods after the War up to 31%.)

For German agrarian exports (flour and sugar) the Swiss actual tariff level was raised from about 20% in 1913 to 40% in 1929 and 130% in 1931. The heavily increased duties caused corresponding declines of exports in a number of cases. The export of flour was completely destroyed by 1931.

In general, however, the purchasing power of Switzerland sustained quite well the duty increases, which in spite of their extent, usually remained within moderate limits, starting from a low pre-War basis. Only when Switzerland adopted stringent quota restrictions in 1932, as defence against the effects of the crisis which had been spreading in Switzerland since 1931, there occurred an unprecedented shrinkage of mutual trade relationships, which caused German exports to drop in 1934 to 295 million (54% of 1931), a tendency which has shown no appreciable signs of reversal up to the present time (1935–36).

(ff) Germany and Austria

Before the War Austria-Hungary was Germany's second best export market. From the figures set out in Table C, p. 206, showing German exports to the Austrian Succession States, it will be seen that German marketing possibilities in the former Austro-Hungarian economic area were constantly diminishing, to such an extent that German exports to England, Scandinavia, and Holland in 1931 were more important than to the four Succession States. The majority of these exports was industrial finished goods, although a few textile and chemical semi-manufactured articles, as well as coal and coke, were important. Austria-Hungary's actual tariff level for twelve semi-manufactured German goods amounted in 1913 to 8·3–9·8%, for thirty-four finished goods to 16–25%.

The chief finished goods exported were metal goods, machinery, apparatus, and vehicles.

The destruction of the Danubian Monarchy did not essentially alter the composition of German exports to Austria, or her tariff level for semi-manufactured goods coming from Germany, although the tariff level for finished German goods rose to about 23–43%, which was largely due to the increased duties on metal goods and vehicles.. These were (1913) on the average 17·4–28·5% (1927–31, 23–51%).

It was impossible to classify the 1913 exports of Germany in terms of the territory of the present Succession States. This fact prevented comparisons of the post-War export movements with 1913. The sharp decrease in German exports in 1931 compared with 1929 was, however, due more to the severe effects of the crisis which were felt in Austria during this year than to a drastic Austrian tariff policy. Owing to the particular severity of the crisis in Austria since 1932, to Austrian import and currency restrictions, and probably also to the aggravation of political tension after 1933, the absolute and relative decline in the Austrian share of German exports, which set in during 1931, has continued ever since that date. In 1934 the Austrian share of German exports, amounting to 107 million Rm., represented no more than 39% of the 1931 figures.

(gg) Germany and Czechoslovakia

The importation of German goods to Czechoslovakia was very similar to that of German exports to Austria except that Germany's export of semi-manufactured goods were somewhat more specialized and those of finished goods somewhat less than in the case with Austria.

The much stronger Czech protectionism was expressed in correspondingly higher actual tariff levels for Germany. For twelve German semi-manufactured articles the Czech tariff level amounted in 1927 to 10·3–12·6%, in 1931 to 13·8–17% (as much as 28%, however, in the case of semi-manufactured metal goods). Compared with the Austrian tariff of 1913, the Czech duties on finished goods were more increased by 1927 than the Austrian ones. For thirty-four finished articles (especially metal goods, apparatus, machinery, and vehicles), the Czech actual tariff level in 1927 and 1931 was about 28–55%. In the case of some articles Czech duties had reached prohibitive heights by 1927, still more so by 1931 (e.g. radio apparatus 46–52%, tool machines 52%, motor-cars 34–55%). As regards the latter goods sharp decreases in German exports to Czechoslovakia can be found between 1927 and 1931, to such an extent that, in spite of the general decline, they are plainly due much more to high duties than to the diminished purchasing power of 1931.

In 1932 Czech import policy became more drastic, employing the new devices of quotas, exchange restrictions, and licences, and after 1931 German exports to Czechoslovakia declined both absolutely and relatively so rapidly that in 1934 they amounted to no more than 148 million Rm. and only represented 38% of the 1931 figures.

II. Germany and Agrarian Europe

PRELIMINARY REMARK: Grouping of European Border States

The States of Border Europe as markets for Germany were of varying importance. Some of them were so unimportant that no useful purpose would be served by analysing their duties on German exports, while others were of high significance. In the following sections we have classified the sixteen States concerned in groups, and only dealt with few of the larger States individually. The order was:

1. Netherlands; 2. Scandinavia (Denmark, Sweden, Norway, and Finland); 3. Baltic States (Esthonia, Lettland, Lithuania); 4. Poland; 5. South-Eastern Europe (Roumania, Hungary, Yugoslavia, Bulgaria); 6. The Mediterranean States (Greece, Portugal, Spain).

(aa) *Germany and the Netherlands*

In no other country in Europe did German post-War exports increase so much when compared with 1913 as in the case of the Netherlands. Holland was Germany's fifth best customer before the War, and climbed to first place in 1929, and even in 1931 still occupied the second place. All groups of goods were represented, finished goods being most prominent. This peculiar development was rendered possible only by the consistent Dutch free-trade policy, even in post-War Europe. All goods were admitted practically free or taxed by fiscal duties of 5–8% at the most. In 1931 German exports to Holland, valued at 955 million Rm., were 38% above the value of 1913, an improvement which was only exceeded by German exports to Sweden. And it was not until 1932 that Holland resorted to sharp import-restricting quotas, because the duties and other import-restricting measures of her most important markets (especially Germany and England) reached unprecedented proportions. Since then Germany's flourishing export trade with Holland has been much reduced. From 1931–34 it declined continuously and fell to 482 millions, which represented only 50·5% of the value of 1931 and not much more than 33·3% of that in 1929.

(bb) *Germany and the Scandinavian States*

The four North European States became very important German markets during the post-War period, and in the aggregate they constituted Germany's second-best European customers in 1929 and 1931. Denmark and Sweden took by far the largest share (1913, 65%; 1927, 70%; 1931, 76% of German exports to Scandinavia). The chief exports were highly specialized semi- and wholly-manufactured goods, coal, and coke. Also cereals (rye and oats), flour, and sugar were exported, especially to Denmark, Norway, and Finland. This favourable development was reinforced in the case of Denmark and Norway by a strong free-trade policy, which admitted numerous semi- and wholly-manufactured articles and nearly all agrarian products free of duty and imposed very moderate duties on the rest. In Sweden it was the retention of nearly all the pre-War rates in spite of the higher post-War price level which gave German exports a great impetus. Although Finland pursued a pronounced protectionist policy in connection with various industries, the separation of the Finnish market from Russian pre-War imports and the supply of Finland's industrial requirements by Central and Western Europe stimulated German trade.

There is no need to elucidate the changes of the Scandinavian tariff levels for German exports in view of extensive free trade or a few low fiscal duties in the case of Denmark and Norway, while in the case of Finland the volume of her industrial imports from Germany was so slight as to render it hardly worth while.[1] From 1913 to 1931 the Swedish tariff level for German semi-finished goods fell from 24–32% to 10–18%, while nineteen German finished articles were liable to duties on the average of 16–24% in 1913, and 11–22% in 1927 and 1931.

In one direction only Sweden and Norway joined general European protectionism after the outbreak of the world economic crisis. Since 1929 they increased the corn and sugar duties, especially Finland. (Rye duty in Sweden, 1913, 29%; 1931, 50·5%; rye-flour duty and wheat-flour duty in Finland, 1913, 0 (free); 1931, 190% and 110%).

[1] So far as the actual tariff levels of these countries for Germany could be calculated, they may be gathered from Table D, p. 226.

By 1931 German agrarian exports to Scandinavia were much reduced by these duties, and German flour exports to Finland in 1931 were as good as destroyed, while exports of manufactures to all these countries were well maintained even in 1931.

The departure from the Gold Standard by all four Scandinavian countries at the end of 1931, the adoption of retaliatory measures against the drastic restriction of imports of live-stock and dairy produce into Germany, quotas and duty increases in Sweden, and currency restrictions in Denmark since 1932 all inflicted heavy losses upon the highly developed trade relationships between Germany and these countries. The result was that German exports to Scandinavia, which were valued at 538 million Rm. in 1932, shrank to 461 million in 1934, which represented only 51 and 44% respectively of the 1931 figures.

(cc) *Germany and the Baltic States*

Measured by the total value of German exports the importance of the three Baltic States, Esthonia, Lettland, and Lithuania, was, of course, very small. In 1929 all three countries together bought German goods to the value of 192 million Rm. and in 1931 the value of German exports was 112 million Rm. These imports consisted of numerous small items of German semi- and wholly-manufactured articles, the latter predominating in consequence of the slight industrial development of these countries, although Esthonia and Lettland have successfully attempted to start textile industries. Compared with the high Russian pre-War tariff level the tariffs of these States in most cases signified a lowering of tariff barrier for German exports. But the Lettish tariff of 1928 produced such a rise in the industrial tariff level, compared with the previous tariff, that in 1931 the Lettish duties on German semi-manufactured textile goods, with an average height of 29–33%, considerably exceeded the Russian of 1913. Combed yarn was liable to a duty of 40–45%. The production of finished textile goods was sheltered by high protectionist duties in all three States even in 1927, and still more so in 1931, which reduced German textile exports.[1] (Lettish duty on German cotton stockings, 1927, 28·5%; 1931, 46·7%.) Calculations of the actual Baltic tariff levels for German exports have been omitted. The heavy increase in textile duties was the essential factor in judging their industrial tariff policy.

(dd) *Germany and Poland*

In spite of her excessive tariff levels the Russia of 1913 was a very important market for Germany's semi- and wholly-manufactured goods. These exports consisted mainly of semi-manufactured metal and chemical goods, as well as of the finished products of the chemical, metal, machinery, apparatus, and vehicle industries. Textile goods were of less importance, as Russia was rapidly developing her own textile trades under the shelter of a protective tariff. In 1913 the Russian actual tariff level for German semi-manufactured goods was 41–46%, and for twenty-eight wholly-manufactured goods 46–48%.

Owing to its much smaller extent and to general impoverishment, Poland could never have offered Germany a substitute for the lost Russian market during the period when a completely transformed Russia withdrew as a buyer of German goods (up till about 1925). Whereas, however, from this time forth Russia increasingly figured as a buyer, chiefly of German capital goods, the political and economical tension between Germany and Poland effected quite unusual conditions in German-Polish trade. Between 1925 and 1931 both countries applied their autonomous duties—which was an exceptional case in European post-War commercial policy during this period—and thereby erected tariff walls of unexampled height between each other. The consequence was an extensive destruction of German exports to Poland and vice versa long

---

[1] See *Enquête*, II, pp. 218–219 and 285–287.

before the outbreak of the world economic crisis. The Polish actual tariff level of 1927 for German semi-manufactured goods, amounting to 13·4–20·8%, meant a sharp fall compared with the Russian pre-War level, but the introduction of *additions* to the autonomous duties in the year 1928, affecting chiefly Germany, drove the Polish actual tariff level up to 37–52% in 1931. (Semi-manufactured metal goods, 1927, 20·5–39%; 1931, 60–113%.) With regard to finished goods the Polish actual tariff level for twenty-eight German articles (mainly machinery, apparatus, and metal goods), amounting to 35·5–52%, already in 1927, exceeded the Russian level of 1913, and continued to rise until in 1931 it reached 67–115%. In individual cases still higher duties could be found.

In view of such barriers, it is not surprising that German exports fell year by year, textiles being affected most of all, while machinery and apparatus, urgently required by Poland, were affected least. Between 1927 and 1931 among all classes of goods the export of some articles was diminished by one-half, by two-thirds, and even more. The inquiries of the Kiel Enquête respecting the period 1924 and 1929, which were the best years of European post-War economy, show a decline in German exports of tissues to Poland from 67 million to 24 million Rm., of German ready-made clothes from 55 to 11 million Rm.[1]

No other important European State showed such a marked decline in its relative share of the total German exports between 1929 and 1931 as did Poland (reduction 35%). Poland's resort to stringent import prohibitions and quotas in the year 1932, conjoined with the severe pressure of the crisis upon her, a country highly dependent upon exports and very poor, much accentuated the devastating effects of the German-Polish tariff war. In 1932 German exports did not exceed 93 million Rm. Although the policy of *Adolf Hitler* has effected a fundamental change in German-Polish relationships, in the sense of peaceful political co-operation, since December

[1] *Enquête*, II, pp. 279–281.

1933, the German exports to Poland continued on the down-grade. In 1934 German exports failed to rise above the value of 55 million Rm. and were no less than 71% below the already very small figure of 1931. If the new German-Polish friend-ship is to effect a transformation in German-Polish economic relations, it will have to restore the integration of production between Germany and her largest eastern neighbour, once so flourishing in pre-War times, but systematically ruined during the post-War period up to the present time (1935).

(ee) *Germany and the European South-East*

German pre-War exports to the Balkan States—Roumania, Serbia, and Bulgaria—amounting to 189 million M. in 1913 were of slight importance. The great increase in the total German exports to the four States of south-eastern Europe—Roumania, Hungary, Yugoslavia, and Bulgaria—to 507 million in 1929 was the result of the incorporation into Roumania and Yugoslavia of portions of former Austro-Hungarian terri-tory, as well as of the re-shaping of Hungary, and is therefore useless for comparison with 1913. It may, however, be stated (see pp. 205–206 of this book) that the receptivity of the Balkan States for German industrial exports has by no means improved in the post-War period.[1] Before the War only Roumania, which bought 140 million M. of German exports, was a substantial market, while Bulgaria and Serbia together only bought goods to the value of 49 million M. Also after the War Bulgaria remained too small a market for Germany, owing to general impoverishment and excessive tariffs, to justify calculations of actual tariff levels for German exports. In

---

[1] This is also shown by the fact that the value of Germany's export figures for approximately the same territory in 1913 and 1927, viz.: for Austria-Hungary, Roumania, Serbia, and Bulgaria in 1913, and for Austria-Hungary, Czechoslovakia, Roumania, Yugoslavia, and Bulgaria in 1929–31 show diminishing percentages to total exports. 1913, 12·8%; 1929, 11·9%; 1931, 10·4%. See *Gaedicke, Vol. of Text*, pp. 89, 91, 92.

spite of the population more than doubling, German exports to Roumania only increased to 169 million Rm. in the year 1929. Hungary and Yugoslavia respectively bought 145 and 153 million Rm. of German goods in 1929. In 1931 German exports to all four states were below 100 million Rm.

Finished goods predominated among the German exports. The chief semi-manufactured articles were yarns, metal goods, and chemicals. Among finished goods, the machine-making, apparatus, and metal industries took a leading place, while textile exports appreciably diminished. In the case of Roumania and Yugoslavia a certain amount of machinery was exported on reparations account.

Roumanian duties on semi-manufactured German goods reached an average of 19–50% in 1913, of 22·5–54% in 1927, and 35–77% in 1931. For thirteen German finished articles (chiefly metal goods and machines) the Roumanian actual tariff level was in 1913, 18–21%, while in the post-War period it was 18–50%. These figures give an idea of the rising tariff barriers which German exports had to surmount in Roumania after the War. Some duties were even much higher. Duties on cotton and woollen tissues were as much as 95%.

German exports of semi-manufactured goods to Hungary were too small to provide actual tariff levels. For ten German finished goods the tariff level in 1927 was 34–54%, which rose to 42·5–61% in 1931. (It was 16–25% in Austria-Hungary in 1913.) Metal goods and machines had to pay very high duties (machines up to 47% in 1931, metal goods up to more than 120%). Only highly specialized manufactures urgently required could overcome duties like these, and yet even here the shrinkage of German exports between 1927 and 1931 was often great.

Yugoslavian industrial protectionism remained far behind that of Hungary or Roumania, not to mention the high tariff walls of Bulgaria. The actual tariff level for seven German finished goods (metal goods and machines) worked out at 16·4–24% in 1927 and 1931.

Yet in respect of all these States, although least in the case of Yugoslavia, it must be emphasized that a great part of their high duties could not be comprehended in the calculation of *actual* tariff levels, owing to their effect in excluding imports altogether, so that the analysis of their *potential tariff levels* was more necessary in their case than in that of less extreme protectionist countries, in order to judge their tariff policy.

Between 1925 and 1929 particularly, the import of textile manufactures by these countries diminished, and the amount of wholly-manufactured imports generally was below the pre-War level.[1] The effects of the world economic crisis were severe in these agrarian countries, so that their share of the total German exports in 1931 only amounted to 3·1%. Further heavy falls in the prices of their export products, involving a fresh diminution of purchasing power; quota and currency restrictions, as well as the prohibition of certain imports in 1931 and 1932, reduced very much German exports to these four south-eastern States, which (1934) only amounted to 141 million Rm. and were 61% below the already low figures of 1931.

(ff) *Germany and the Mediterranean States*

Among the three Mediterranean States, Greece, Portugal, and Spain, only Spain was a sufficiently important customer to justify the provision of figures of actual tariff levels, whilst German exports to Portugal and Greece were limited to a very small volume.[2] In 1913, the three countries together bought 219 million M. worth of German goods. The figures for 1929 and 1931 being 359 million and 236 million Rm. respectively, and Spain's share being 143, 218, and 132 million M. respectively. By far the greater part of the goods exported were German finished articles, although Spain bought a certain amount of semi-manufactured chemical and metal

[1] See *Enquête*, II, pp. 218–219, 267–268, 274–275.

[2] As regards Greece, post-War exports were stimulated to some extent by the increased population and temporary reparation deliveries.

goods. Machinery, apparatus, vehicles, and metal goods constituted the main export groups.

The Spanish tariff level for semi-manufactured German goods was no more than 2·2–4·4% in 1913 and 1927, and rose to only 12–12·5% in 1931. The high Spanish post-War duties on the most important semi-manufactured products of the metal and chemical trades had the effect of excluding imports of these trades, therefore for the purpose of our calculation they remained mostly potential duties.

For German exports of finished goods the Spanish tariff level in 1913 was 28–41% and rose to 49–106% in the post-War period. If despite such duties a considerable quantity of German machines, metal goods and vehicles found their way to Spain, it was because they were mainly highly specialized products which were needed in connection with the Spanish industrialization, and were admitted in a number of cases at specially low duties.[1] Moreover, in the case of numerous goods these duties were responsible for sharp declines in exports between 1927 and 1931 or even in comparison with the figures of 1913.[2]

The fluctuations of the Peseta, the revolutionary unrest since 1931, the severe pressure of the world economic crisis upon Spain, and her adoption of quota restrictions since 1932 much reduced German exports after 1931. In 1934 German exports fell to a value of 87·5 million Rm., being 63% of 1913, but only 40% of 1929.

(d) General Trend of German Exports, 1913–34
(See Table D, p. 226)

If we contemplate the general trend of German exports between 1913 and 1931, we find that after the stabilization of

[1] See Part II, pp. 176–177 of this book.

[2] Only one example need be mentioned. With a duty of 20% in 1913, Germany exported locomotives to Spain to the value of 10 million Mark; with a duty of 53% in 1927 to the value of 6 million Rm.; with a duty of 73% in 1931 German exports were extinguished.

the Mark in 1924, they showed a steady rise in values and volume up to the culminating point of the year 1929; then Germany's exports had practically regained the volume of 1913, even after allowance is made for price changes. Their composition, however, had distinctly changed in favour of export of capital goods, while their geographical distribution revealed far-reaching pre-War tendencies. The set-back of 1931 remained less in extent of import shrinkage of almost all the other European States (see Table I of Appendix). It seemed as if Germany's unparalleled agrarian protection since 1929, the ever rising tariff walls in Europe, and the profound changes in European and world economy caused by the War, would not provoke structural changes in German exports. But the circumstances which made this apparently favourable development in 1931 possible were quite special and transitory. Owing to the increasing displacement of consumer's goods by capital goods in the total of her exports, Germany was less severely hit by European and world industrial protection, which imposed permanent high duties on consumer's goods, especially on textile articles. The non-recurring requirements of Russian industrialization and the 400 million Rm. reparations exports helped also to maintain Germany's export. Moreover, Germany enjoyed the benefit of the contrasting movement of agrarian and industrial prices which operated so much to the detriment of agrarian and raw material countries in the first years of the crisis. In 1931 the world agrarian export index of the Kiel Enquête was 89, the index of German finished goods 115 (1913 = 100).[1]

These non-recurring assets of German exports were reinforced by the equally transitory advantages of their geographical distribution. Germany was very fortunate in 1931 in that she was most closely connected with countries that in the main pursued a liberal tariff policy (Holland, Scandinavia, Great Britain, Switzerland, and Belgium), so that these States

[1] See *Enquête*, I, p. 254.

alone took 32·8% of her exports in 1931, whereas the fortresses of European protection, Poland, the south-eastern States, Spain, and Italy played a lesser part, although Germany's exports suffered severely in this quarter in 1931.

When the free-trade States in 1931 and 1932 adopted retaliatory measures against the ever-increasing German agrarian protection, when the countries in the Sterling area departed from the Gold Standard, when quota restrictions were introduced all over Europe, when reparations were extinguished and exports to Russia dwindled, Germany's exports fell rapidly. A very heavy shrinking process started in 1932 and reached figures in the following years which would have been deemed hardly possible in 1931. In 1932 German exports were reduced to 5·74 milliard Rm., in 1934 to 4·17 milliard Rm., and were therefore in this year only 43·5% of the 1931 and 30·8% of the 1929 figures. Such a level as this is in the long run fatal to an industrial country like Germany, not only for the discharge of her private debts, but also for supplying her vital needs in agricultural produce and raw materials.

TABLE D: IMPORTANT ACTUAL TARIFF LEVELS FOR GERMAN EXPORTS, 1913–31

Country	A			B			C		
	1913	1927	1931	1913	1927	1931	1913	1927	1931
England	—	—	—	—	—	—	Duty free	(14) 32·7–35·0	(16) 31·5–39·0
France	(7) 49·5–56·0	23·3–27·7	121–132·0	(10) 16·3–24·6	8·7–14·5	9·0–15·5	(47) 12·0–18·2	20·6–42·0	22·5–50·0
Italy	—	—	—	(14) 12·8–17·3	18·9–39·0	26·8–55·0	(42) 12·7–14·4	22·2–31·0	29·5–45·0
Belgium	—	—	—	—	(16) —	—	(27) 6·9–8·5	8·1–14·4	8·5–16·0
Switzerland	—	—	—	(23) 2·6–5·0	3·0–5·7	4·0–7·7	(46) 8·3–10·5	14·0–19·0	16·2–20·4
Austria					(6) 3·1–11·5	11·0–19·0	—	(37) 27·7–43·5	23·0–41·0
Czechoslovakia				—	(12) 10·3–12·6	13·8–17·0	—	(34) 27·7–49·0	29·0–55·0
Denmark				—			(17) 12·2–17·2	12·0–12·0	12·1–13·1
Sweden				(13) 24·5–32·5	10·5–18·0	11·0–18·3	(19) 16·4–24·0	11·2–21·3	11·6–22·0
Norway							(6) 15·7–16·6	11·2–19·0	12·6–23·2
Finland							(11) 11·2–20·0	11·3–17·0	14·0–19·8
Poland				(9) 18·8–50·0	(10) 13·4–20·8	37·0–57·0	—	(28) 35·5–52·0	67·0–115·0
Roumania					22·5–54·0	35·0–77·0	(13) 17·7–20·8	17·7–50·0	8·3–44·0
Hungary							—	(10) 34·0–54·0	42·5–61·0
Yugoslavia							—	(7) 16·4–24·0	24·0–25·4
Spain				(7) 2·2–4·4	2·5–3·2	12·0–12·5	(32) 28·0–41·0	49·0–106	51·0–105·0

Whenever a year has not been filled in, it is because a calculation was impossible. (For method of calculation see p. 190.) The small figures printed as indices to the figures of the Tariff Levels indicate the number of articles actually exported, from the duties on which the figures have been calculated. Figures have only been given for the three groups of the agrarian products (Group A), semi-manufactured articles (Group B), and finished goods (Group C).

2. *Great Britain and the Tariffs in Europe*

(a) *Composition of English Exports*

English exports are chiefly industrial. In 1913 and 1927 finished goods comprised 80%, and in 1931, 75% of the total English exports, while the export of raw materials and semi-manufactured articles fluctuated between 11 and 13% (see Table A).

TABLE A: MAIN GROUPS OF ENGLISH EXPORTS,
1913–31
(*Figures without re-exports and precious metals*)
(*In Mill. £ and % of Total Exports*)

Group	1913 Mill. £	%	1929 Mill. £	%	1931 Mill. £	%
Total Exports . .	525	100·0	729	100·0	390	100·0
Of which:						
Agrarian exports .	32·6	6·2	55·7	7·3	35·5	9·1
Raw materials and semi-manufactured goods . .	70	13·3	79	10·7	47·0	12·0
Finished goods .	411	78·5	574	79·5	292	75·0
Comprising:						
Coal, coke . .	53·7	10·2	52·8	7·7	37·6	9·6
Tissues ⌠Cotton .	127·0	24·2	135·0	18·5	56·6	14·5
and ⌡Wool .	37·7	7·2	53·0	7·3	25·1	6·4
Yarns ⌊Other * .	15·0	2·8	27·0	3·7	14·0	3·6
Iron and steel † .	62·0	11·8	77·0	10·5	35·7	9·1
Machines & vehicles ‡	59·4	11·2	89·7	12·4	62·7	16·0

* Comprises yarns and tissues from other textile raw materials except silk and artificial silk, also ready-made clothes.
† Comprises semi- and wholly-manufactured articles.
‡ Comprises machines, vehicles, and ships.
See *Annual Statement of the Trade of the United Kingdom*, 1914, 1931.

The export of textile goods and its development occupied a central position in British foreign trade. With over 38% in 1913, 33% in 1929, but only about 28% of the total exports in 1931, they have formed the main problem of English post-War exports. Next in importance came the exports of iron and steel, the engineering, vehicle and coal industries. The exports of these five groups constituted over 70% in 1913, and between 63 and 65% in post-War times of the total English exports.

Exports were vital for many of these trades, as may be seen from the unusually high proportion of export to their total output. In the case of the tinned sheet industry the export share was 97%, in the cotton industry 87%, in the engineering industry about 50%, and about 40% in the iron and steel industry.[1]

In contrast to the high specialization of German exports, the bulk of English industrial exports consisted of the products of a few great industrial groups (highly specialized among themselves), and, owing to the paramount position of textiles and the preponderance of finished goods among iron and steel exports, no such marked displacement of consumer's goods by capital goods was to be found here as in the case of Germany, so that 48·8% of the total exports in 1913 consisted of consumer's goods and 48·3% in 1928, compared with 37·8% and 41·5% respectively in the case of Germany.[2]

These facts are reflected by the composition of the export list for calculating the actual tariff levels for English exports. Excluding all goods below £1,000,000 in value, it comprises four English agrarian and twenty-nine English semi- and wholly-manufactured products (see Table B).

From the figures in Table B it is obvious that as regards both industrial and agrarian exports, more than half are not included in the list, and this feature is still more marked in· the post-War period. Even by taking into account that the exports of raw materials which were duty free represented a considerable part of the goods not included (great coal exports) in view of the above composition of English

[1] Comp. *W.d.A.*, pp. 20–29. Figures from 1924.
[2] Comp. *Gaedicke, Vol. of Tables*, p. 19.

exports, this is not a satisfactory explanation. That is only likely to be forthcoming from an analysis of the geographical distribution of the English exports.

TABLE B: PERCENTAGES OF ENGLISH LIST OF GOODS TO TOTAL ENGLISH EXPORTS
(*In Mill. £ and %*)

Group	1913		1927		1931	
	Mill. £	= % of	Mill. £	= % of	Mill. £	= % of
Total List . .	227·4	43·2 of T.E.	261	36·8 of T.E.	133	34·0 of T.E.
4 agrarian products .	11·9	37·0 of A.E.	16·3	31·2 of A.E.	11·4	32·0 of A.E.
29 industrial products	214	44·5 of I.E.	232	36·5 of I.E.	121	36·0 of I.E.

T.E. = Total Exports.
A.E. = Agrarian Exports.
I.E. = Industrial Exports.

(b) *Geographical Distribution of English Exports*

No single European State was, even in 1913, so little integrated with Europe as England, both in respect of exports and imports (see Table C, p. 230).

This development steadily continued after the World War, long before the Ottawa Agreements of 1932. In 1913 Europe's share in the total English exports only amounted to 35·8%. In 1929 it was 30·5%. In 1931, owing to the later outbreak of the crisis in England's best European markets, the share rose to 43%, but it dropped to 39% in 1933 [1] (34% excl. Irish Free State).

This relatively slight export connection of England with Europe was the main reason why a list of only thirty-three articles could be compiled for the calculation of actual European tariff levels for England's exports. Moreover, Europe happened to be an important market for just those goods which played a less important part in the total of English exports. In 1913 and 1928 the raw materials and semi-manufactured goods

[1] See *Gaedicke, Vol. of Tables*, p. 3, and *Stat. Jahrbuch*, 1934, p. 126.

(coal, yarns, semi-finished metal goods) exported to Europe comprised more than 50% of the English total exports of these classes of goods, which were the less important part of total British exports, and also more than 50% of English exports to Europe, whereas English finished goods sent to Europe represented only about 20% of British manufacturing exports, and 40% of English total exports to Europe.[1] Consequently,

TABLE C: ENGLAND'S PRINCIPAL MARKETS,
1913–31

*In Mill. Pounds and % of total English export goods
were exported to:*

Country	1913		1929		1931	
	Mill. £	%	Mill. £	%	Mill. £	%
Total Exports . .	525	100·0	729	100·0	390	100·0
Of which to:						
Empire . . .	195	37·0	324	44·5	171	44·0
Foreign countries .	330	63·0	405	55·5	220	56·0
Europe . . .	188	35·8	252	34·6*	167	43·0*
Comprising:						
Germany . .	40·7	7·7	37·0	5·1	18·4	4·7
France . . .	28·9	5·5	31·7	4·3	22·6	5·8
Netherlands . .	15·4	2·9	21·8	3·0	13·7	3·5
Denmark, Sweden .	14·0	2·7	21·2	2·9	16·3	4·2
Italy . . .	14·6	2·8	16·0	2·2	9·9	2·6
Belgium . .	13·2	2·5	19·4	2·7	10·0	2·6
Scandinavia † .	22·5	4·3	35·1	4·8	25·5	6·5

* Without exports to Irish Free State 30·5% (1929), 35·2% (1931).
† Scandinavia = Denmark, Sweden, Norway, and Finland.

many articles which were very important for English extra-European markets had to be excluded from the list, owing to their small exports to Europe. Table C, above, shows that few countries in Europe were of striking importance to English total exports: in Central Europe, Germany, France, Italy, and Belgium; in Border Europe, Holland and the Scandinavian countries, as well as Spain. (English exports to Spain

[1] See *Gaedicke, Vol. of Text,* pp. 114–117.

in pre-War and post-War periods amounted to between 8 and 12 Mill. £, in 1931 only 5·3 Mill. £.)

To England's close integration with the Scandinavian States was due the fact that she was less closely integrated with Central Europe than other European countries, and more closely integrated with Border Europe, so that in 1927 England sent 46% of her European exports to Border Europe and as much as 49% in 1930.[1] The purpose of the following analysis is to show how far European tariff policy is responsible for the very considerable shrinkage in English exports between 1913 and 1931.

(c) *Actual Tariff Levels of the Chief Markets of England*

I. *England and Industrial Europe*

(aa) *England and Germany*

Before the War Germany was England's best European customer and remained so until 1929. In 1931 France occupied this position. English exports consisted chiefly of coal, yarns, tissues, and semi-manufactured metal goods, in addition to a number of industrial finished goods spread over a series of smaller items. The actual German tariff level for English exports of semi-manufactured goods reached 12–17% in 1913, and was not substantially altered in the post-War period. (Textiles, however, were liable to duties up to 26%, cotton tissues up to 60%, in 1931 even up to 80%.) Both before and after the War, the German duties on the largest group of English textile exports, viz. cotton and woollen yarns, remained at a low level (2–12%). It might be expected, therefore, that during the post-War period the German duties would exert an unfavourable influence only upon English exports of cotton tissues, which in fact showed a striking decrease in 1927 compared with 1913. For the heavy fall which all the remaining classes of important English exports

[1] *Gaedicke, Vol. of Text*, pp. 152–153.

to Germany exhibited in 1931 (the total exports fell by 50% between 1929 and 1931), no satisfactory explanation can be found in a drastic German tariff policy. So far as Germany was concerned, it was rather due to the severe effects of the crisis upon German purchasing power, but we shall have to add some other reasons when we come to consider the general trend of English exports (see p. 237).

(bb) *England and France*

England's exports to France were concentrated within similar classes of goods as the Anglo-German exports, except that woollen yarns and tissues were the chief constituents of textile exports, instead of cotton yarns as with Germany, and that exports of coal and machinery occupied a larger place. The French tariff level for ten English semi-manufactured articles was 12–32·4% and showed no appreciable change in the post-War period. (Duties on English textiles, however, were 11–70% in 1913 and 8–83% in the post-War era.[1]) Very high were the French duties on cotton tissues, which amounted to 200% in 1913, and on yarns rising to 120% in 1931. Among finished goods, the sharp rise in the French duties on machinery in the post-War period was noticeable (textile machinery was liable to 6–15% in 1913 and to 25–38% in the post-War period).

As with Germany so with France, we could not find that the duties had any marked effect on the general development of English exports to France. Those English export groups which declined sharply in 1927 compared with 1913 (iron and steel goods, semi-manufactured woollen goods) were not particularly hard hit by the French post-War duties; only the reduction in England's exports of cotton yarns and machinery in 1927 compared with 1913 could be successfully traced to this cause. In 1931 English exports as a whole suffered

---

[1] French duties on yarns and tissues are very differentiated, hence the wide limits between minimum and maximum duties.

considerable reduction, due to the beginning of the crisis in France, but, owing to the more favourable economic conditions there, the reduction was kept within more moderate limits than in the case of Germany, so that France became Great Britain's best European customer.

(cc) *England and Italy*

Both before and after the War coal constituted about 50% of England's exports to Italy. The balance was distributed over classes of goods too small for the calculation of actual Italian tariff levels. Nevertheless, it is obvious that tariff policy has here played a great part in connection with the decline in English post-War exports. Where England suffered the greatest losses, in exports of iron, steel, and woollen tissues to Italy, heavy Italian duty increases particularly impeded English trade. (Woollen tissues in 1913, 9·5–14%, in post-War period up to 30%; pig iron, 1913, 12·6%, 1927–31, 24–43%. Tinned sheets, 1913, 38–50%, post-War period up to 60%.) Even in the decline of coal exports, from 6·2 Mill. £ in 1913 to 5·2 Mill. £ in 1931, the 10% duty on coal imposed in the latter year probably played some part, in conjunction with reduced Italian demand, caused by the development of water power and general reduction in purchasing power in this third year of the economic crisis.

(dd) *England and Belgium*

In the post-War period up to 1929 England's exports to Belgium showed an unusual improvement, but in 1931 suffered an almost 50% set-back compared with the figure of 1929. Even less than in the case of the States hitherto discussed could this set-back be attributed to the very moderate Belgian tariff policy. For the actual Belgian tariff level for English semi-manufactured articles before and after the War reached only 3–8% (only cotton tissues were taxed 9–28% in 1913 and 1927–31).

II. *England and Agrarian Europe*

PRELIMINARY REMARK : *The Grouping of the European Border States*

We have already stated that only the Scandinavian States, Holland, and Spain were of any great importance to England so far as her export markets in the Border States of agrarian Europe were concerned. Consequently, we can dismiss with a few remarks English exports to Poland, the south-eastern States, Greece, and Portugal, owing to their small value.

(aa) *England and the Netherlands*

Like the exports to Belgium, British exports to Holland were developing very favourably in 1929. In the year 1931 there was a set-back, not quite so severe, but sufficiently serious, which again in view of Holland's free-trade policy, could not be attributed to the effects of tariffs.

(bb) *England and the North European Countries*

England's exports to Northern Europe (Denmark, Sweden, Norway, and Finland), like post-War exports of Germany to Scandinavia, developed very well. English exports to no other European country expanded so much, compared with 1913, as to Denmark. Even the set-back of exports during the crisis year of 1931 was not so severe with regard to these countries as to Great Britain's other European markets. As with Belgium and Holland, this intensification of British exports was favoured by the very moderate tariff policy of the Scandinavian countries. As exceptions, the Norwegian and Swedish duties on printed cotton tissue deserve mention. In Norway before the War they amounted to 19–45% and remained at about this height in the post-War period. In Sweden they reached 32–49% in 1913, but fell to 30% in the post-War period. Since 1932 England and the Scandinavian States have drawn still closer together. In 1933 English exports, valued at 27·4 million £, reached 107% of their value in 1913.

(cc) *England and Spain*

Up to 1929 English exports to Spain expanded in an encouraging way compared with pre-War conditions, so that this year Spain, by taking 12 Mill. £ worth of English goods, was England's best customer in Border Europe after Holland. In 1931, however, English exports to Spain suffered a very severe set-back, which more than halved the export values of 1929. This was due as much to the raising of Spanish duties as to the effects of the crisis. Coal and coke had played a prominent part in English exports, and it was just in this field that Spain, intent on promoting self-sufficiency, had pursued a strong protectionist policy.[1] The coke duty was raised from 17% in 1913 to 33–39% in the post-War period, the coal duty of 21% remained unchanged, but even at this height it considerably stimulated Spanish output in view of the heavy transport costs of this commodity. Consequently, English coal exports persistently declined in the post-War period. Further, Spain made drastic increases in the post-War duties on all semi- and wholly-manufactured goods produced by the metal and machine industries. (1913, tinned sheets, 38%; 1927–31, 70%; spinning jennies, 1913, 17%; 1931, 32%, etc.) These increases were reflected in large reductions in English exports of iron, steel, and machinery during 1931. For English textile goods the Spanish tariff level was so high as to exclude any appreciable volume of imports, and therefore only remained potential. Consequently, England's exports to Spain were more and more restricted to urgently needed special articles, as in the case of German exports.

(dd) *England and Poland*

In spite of her extreme protective system, pre-War Russia was an important market for English semi-manufactured textile and metal goods, as well as machinery (1913, the actual

[1] See p. 177 of this study.

Russian tariff level for English clothes amounted to 44–89%).
Poland has been of only small importance as an English market,
in spite of the lowering of her duties compared with the Russian
level. (Polish tariff level, 1927–31, for English semi-manufactured textile goods 14–27%.) Up to 1931 English exports
to Poland had fallen considerably, a decline mainly due to the
bad economic situation, but probably in part also attributable
to the excessive duties on the chief English exports being too
high in relation to the reduced purchasing power of Poland's
population. (For cotton yarns, 15–35%, for textile machinery
between 13% and 40%.)

(ee) *England and the South-Eastern States*

Both before and after the War the south-eastern States of
Europe were very small markets for English goods, so that,
like Spain and Poland, no actual tariff levels for England could
be formed. Without doubt, however, the development of
English exports of tissues was considerably checked by the
drastic tariff policy of these States, chiefly of the duties of
Roumania, Bulgaria, and Hungary. (E.g. English cotton
tissues were taxed 14–64% in Roumania in 1913 and 22–72%
in 1927–31.) A characteristic instance of this check to textile
exports was the decline in England's exports of yarns and
tissues (between 1926 and 1929) to the four south-eastern
States from 144 to 100 Mill. Rm., while the other classes of
English manufactures exported to the south-east also showed
a backward tendency, as the total English exports of finished
goods to these countries between 1925 and 1929 fell from
225 Mill. to 194 Mill. Rm.[1] Up to 1931 this shrinkage continued to such an extent that, even after taking into account
the difficult economic situation in 1931, we must admit that
tariff protection had a great influence upon the persistently
unfavourable development of English exports.

[1] See *Enquête*, II, p. 275.

(ff) *England and the Mediterranean States (Greece and Portugal)*

Although of all the industrial States of Europe Great Britain was Portugal's and Greece's most important supplier, the purchases of these two small countries were not large enough and much too confined to certain commodities (chiefly semi-manufactured textile goods) for computing actual tariff levels. Before the War Greek duties on five English semi-finished textile articles amounted on an average to 19–27%, after the War to 31% (but Greek duties on cotton tissues in 1913, 19·5%; in post-War times 26–79%; on woollen tissues, 1913, 18%; post-War up to 36%). In particular the raising of the Greek duties on English tissues resulted in sharp declines of their export up to 1931.

Similar things happened in Portugal. The average of Portuguese duties on three English semi-finished textile articles rose from 18–38% in 1913 to 20–120% in 1931. This enormous increase was the result of drastic increases in Portuguese duties on bleached and printed cotton tissues and on jute yarn. The consequences were sharp reductions of English exports of these goods. (From 1913 to 1931 cotton tissues exports declined from 0·33 Mill. £ to 0·13 Mill. £.)

As with Italy, Spain, and the south-eastern States, so as regards Greece and Portugal, English post-War exports encountered great difficulties in the shape of rising tariff walls, which, independently of diminutions in purchasing power caused by the crisis, were bound to have a disintegrating effect upon the imports of the States concerned, from Great Britain.

(d) *General Trend of English Exports*, 1913–34
(See Table D, p. 238)

A comparison of the figures of the total English exports between 1913 and 1931 (see Table A, p. 227) with the figures of the rest of the European countries (see Table I of the

Appendix) shows that the most striking difference between Great Britain and the rest of Europe was the particularly heavy shrinkage in English exports recorded in 1931 in comparison with 1913 and 1929. With a loss of 46% compared with 1929, only Spain showed a larger decline than England.[1] If we consider the development of actual tariff levels of England's most important European markets between 1913 and 1931 (see Table D), and inquire whether their tariff policy was largely responsible for this decline of exports, the answer must be in the negative, so far as it relates to European tariff levels, even in 1931. For England's European exports were largely shipped to the free-trade States, or consisted of products which, like yarns or machinery, were usually subjected to low duties.

TABLE D: IMPORTANT ACTUAL TARIFF LEVELS FOR ENGLISH EXPORTS, 1913–31
(Only tariff levels for Group B = semi-finished goods.)

Country	1913	1927	1931
Belgium	[8] 4·6–8·3	[11] 2·6–5·2	3·4–6·9
Germany	[16] 12·0–16·7	, 9·0–15·0	11·1–19·0
France	[10] 12·3–32·4	[11] 8·8–27·3	10·2–36·4

Two other important factors have been of much greater importance for the very unfavourable development of the post-War English exports. As these factors have gained ever greater influence upon the course of English commercial

---

[1] Moreover, the English development compared with 1913 was even more unfavourable than the post-War figures indicate, if it be borne in mind that these include English exports to *Ireland*, which in 1913 was part of the home market. In 1931 these exports amounted to 30·5 Mill. £. Assuming that the 1931 price level was approximately that of 1913 (according to the world trade index of the *Stat. Jahrbuch* of 1934, p. 121, it was 100·8, 1913 equal 100) and deducing, for purposes of comparison with 1913, the full value of England's Irish exports from the 1931 exports, the latter would only amount to 360 million Pounds in that year, i.e. they reached only 49·5% of 1929, and therefore, suffered a loss of 50·5%. This unfavourable position was unique in Europe in 1931.

policy both before and after 1931, some reference to them is necessary for an understanding of European tariff policy in the post-War period. The first factor was an extra-European phenomenon, which is clearly shown in the statistics of English exports. Whereas English exports to Europe declined between 1929 and 1931 by 85 Mill. £, exports to countries outside Europe fell three times as much (253 Mill. £), of which 153 Mill. £ related to the Empire and 100 Mill. £ to foreign countries outside Europe. It was these losses in extra-European exports which constituted England's chief post-War problems, and the shrinkage of European exports was but a feeble reflexion of them.

When the Balfour Committee [1] investigated England's position in 1925, in its analysis of the actual tariff levels of England's eighteen largest European and extra-European markets in 1914 and 1924, it came to the conclusion that "generally speaking the tariff levels for English exports had not been substantially raised compared with 1914," [2] as the duty increases had been neutralized by the rise in prices. If, however, we study these figures, we find that even in 1924 there were characteristic exceptions, which in some degree indicated what was to happen to English exports outside Europe up to 1931. The Indian tariff level in 1924 was 300% higher than in 1914, although it was still low (10·5%), and the tariff level of the U.S.A. grew from 19·5% in 1914 to 32% in 1924, after the introduction of the protectionist Fordney McCumber tariff of 1922. [3] Moreover, India, the United States, and China had raised their duties on cotton tissues much more than these average figures indicated; [4] and cotton tissues were England's most important export goods. Protected by these tariffs and favoured by a very low level of wages, the cotton industry developed so quickly in India, China, and Japan that between 1929 and 1931 alone English exports of cotton yarns and tissues fell from 135 Mill. £ to 56 Mill. £. If therefore we

---

[1] See *Balfour Report*, pp. 538–585.
[2] Ibid., p. 541.
[3] Ibid., p. 545.
[4] Ibid., pp. 574–576.

seek to ascertain the part played by tariffs in the severe crisis of English post-War exports, we must look at extra-European tariffs and not at the tariff policy of countries which constituted such small markets for England as Italy, Spain, Greece, Portugal, and the south-eastern States, where drastic textile protection had likewise developed in the post-War period.

Consequently, when the *Macmillan Committee* investigated England's economic position in 1931, in analysing the causes of the reduction of English exports and the permanent unemployment in England's great export industries, the Report mentioned the duties, "especially on textiles," [1] but it laid much greater stress upon a second factor, which had facilitated the expansion, gradually spreading from the textile to other trades, of chiefly Asiatic competition in England's best extra-European markets (Empire as well as non-Empire States).

Since 1925 the general English price level was higher than that of the other great countries on the Gold Standard. The Gold Standard connected England closely with the price systems of the other Gold Standard countries, the levels of which in 1925 and onwards would have made necessary a sharp deflation of the whole English price system even between 1925 and 1929, much more after the beginning of the world economic crisis, if English competitive power were to be maintained. Up to 1931 English wage and salary earners, politically organized in the Labour Party, which held office between 1929 and 1931, managed to ward off the heavy social and political sacrifices and convulsions which such deflation would have involved. [2]

By abandoning the Gold Standard in September 1931 and introducing a general protective tariff, followed in 1932 by the Empire Preference arrangements of Ottawa, England displayed great energy in changing the direction of her general economic policy, with results which are still (beginning of

---

[1] Comp. *Report on Finance and Industry,* §§ 111, 122, hereafter quoted: *Macmillan Report.*

[2] Comp. *Macmillan Report,* § 123.

1936) incalculable for world economy. This change of policy, however, has largely removed the two main causes of the crisis in English foreign trade, as the fall in the English price level (expressed in gold currencies) not only gave a fresh impetus to English exports, but, in conjunction with the tariff, protected the huge home and Empire markets from foreign competition in a way hitherto unexampled. Without any great interference by the State, England and the Empire surmounted the crisis of 1929–31 as did no other capitalist economy in the world. This is already shown by the 1934 statistics of European exports. If England was almost at the bottom in 1931, with a falling off of 46% of her export compared with 1929, her 1934 exports, showing a reduction of "only" 45·5% compared with 1929, represented by far the best results of all the States of Central Europe (see Table I in Appendix). The only question was whether, and if so, for which of the States of Europe this very extensive currency and commercial isolation of England and the Empire since 1931 could be maintained without the most serious economic consequences for other countries. The following inquiries will assist in clarifying this question, as they will show distinctly how important the English market was for numerous European States up to 1931.

3. France and the Tariffs in Europe

(a) Composition of French Exports

The great changes in the French post-War economic structure in the direction of a "far-reaching industrialization, perhaps the most intensive among all the great industrial countries of Europe,"[1] and particularly the large expansion of the industries of capital goods within the general framework of French industry, are plainly reflected in the French post-War export statistics, although already in 1913 the proportion

[1] Comp. Enquête, II, p. 295.

of industrial products to the total French exports (88%) was unusually large for a country with such a substantial agrarian population, and did not change appreciably in the post-War period. But before the War French exports consisted for the most part of consumer's goods. It was rather the displacements of the groups of goods within the total exports, as well as their big absolute increases in post-War time, compared with 1913, which indicated the modifications of French economy (see Table A).

TABLE A: MAIN GROUPS OF FRENCH EXPORTS,
1913–31
(*In Mill. Frs. and % of Total Exports*)

Group	1913 Mill. Frs.	%	1929 Mill. Frs.	%	1931 Mill. Frs.	%
Total Exports	6880	100·0	50100	100·0	30400	100·0
Viz.:						
A. Agrarian exports	839	12·2	6080	12·1	4300	14·1
B. Raw materials, semi-manufactured goods	1858	27·0	12570	25·0	7180	23·6
C. Finished goods	4183	60·8	31500	62·9	18950	62·3
Including:						
Tissues, made up clothes	1244	20·9	9625	18·1	4920	16·1
Iron and steel	84	1·2	2630	5·2	1930	6·4
Machinery	123	1·8	2190	4·4	1550	5·1
Metal goods	121	1·8	1850	3·7	1250	4·1
Motor-cars	227	3·3	1610	3·2	837	2·8
Chemicals	213	3·1	169	2·5	1310	4·3

While the relative proportions of only the most important groups of consumer's goods (textiles, luxury goods, perfumes, drugs) steadily fell during the post-War years from 24·7% of the total exports in 1913 to 19·7% in 1931, the proportion of the groups of iron, steel, metal goods, machinery, chemical, and motor-cars to total exports rose from 10·4% in 1913 to 22·7% in 1931, and while, analogous to the development in most of the old industrial countries of Europe, the French textile industry declined by 21% between 1906 and 1921 (number of workers), French industry as a whole increased by 9% during the same period. The output of the heavy iron industry, however, increased by 29%, and of the engineering industry by 61%.[1] Taking the average value of French exports during 1910–14 as 100, in 1927 iron and steel exports amounted to 660, motor-car exports to 487, machinery exports to 305, while textile exports mostly fluctuated about the figure of 150. By 1925 the motor-car industry had grown to be the most important European car-exporting industry, while the heavy iron industry exported 25–33·3% of its output.[2] With the end of French inflation in 1927 the enormous growth in French exports reached its culminating point, so that by 1929 French export figures already declined. This, however, did not affect in principle the relation between the main classes of commodities in the French pre-War and post-War export; on the contrary, in the considerably reduced French exports of 1931, the relative share of capital goods was even strengthened at the expense of consumer's goods. Agrarian exports (wine, vegetables, fruit, etc.), forming 12–14% of the total exports in pre-War and post-War times, suffered no appreciable change.

To test the actual tariff levels of the French main European markets, a list of those seventy-eight French export goods was compiled, of which the export value in 1913 reached at least 20 Mill. Francs, and in 1927–31 at least 100 Mill. Francs. Table B, p. 244, shows how the values of these goods stood in relation to the total exports of the years in question.

As in the case of Great Britain, the high percentage of goods not included in the list is surprising. As duty-free raw materials represented an insignificant part of the total French exports, the explanation of this will have to be sought in the analysis of the geographical distribution of French exports.

[1] *Schlier*, op. cit., pp. 27–28, 33, 35.
[2] *W.d.A.*, pp. 75–80.

TABLE B: PROPORTION OF FRENCH EXPORT LIST
TO TOTAL FRENCH EXPORTS

(*In Mill. Frs. and %*)

Group	1913 Mill. Frs. = % of		1927 Mill. Frs. = % of		1931 Mill. Frs = % of	
Total List	2567	37·4 of T.E.	25775	46·5 of T.E.	14266	46·6 of T.E.
16 agrarian goods	504	60·0 of A.E.	3330	60·0 of A.E.	2790	65·0 of A.E.
62 industrial goods	2063	34·0 of I.E.	22445	45·0 of I.E.	11466	44·0 of I.E.

T.E. = Total Exports.
A.E. = Agrarian Exports.
I.E. = Industrial Exports.

(b) *Geographical Distribution of French Exports*

In fact, the geographical distribution of French exports was similar in nature to the English, in the sense that even before the War, and still more after 1919, France had broken away from Europe to a striking extent, as regards both imports and exports (see Table C). Central Europe was so much in the foreground as a market for French exports that in Border Europe only Spain deserved to be mentioned at all. No less than 90% of France's European exports went to Central Europe both before and after the War.[1]

The most important structural change in French post-War exports was the ever-increasing importance of the Colonies as French markets. Up to 1929 the whole colonial empire bought on an average 15%, in 1930, 21%, and in 1933 over 27% of French exports,[2] a distinct parallel to the development of British trade with the Empire. Thus, even before the War, Europe was less important for France than for Germany, and became still less important after 1919. This was, however, the case in varying degrees for the different groups of goods, more so for wholly than for semi-finished articles, which even after 1919 were almost entirely (95%) sold to Europe, whereas

[1] *Gaedicke, Vol. of Text*, p. 101.
[2] Ibid., p. 99, and *Statistiques*, III.

finished products in the shape of capital goods were exported
thither, amounting to 75% of the whole in 1913 and only 60%
in 1928. Finished products in the shape of consumer's goods
exported to Europe amounted to 51·5% of the whole in 1913
and in 1928 only to 40·4%.[1] The conditions existing in
France's principal European markets were again very diverse.
Light will be thrown on this matter by the following detailed
analysis of French export relationships, which will also show
the part played by tariff policy in the trend of French exports
up to 1931.

TABLE C: CHIEF FRENCH MARKETS, 1913–31

*In Mill. Frs. and % of French Total Exports, French goods were
exported to:*

Country	1913 Mill. Frs.	%	1929 Mill. Frs.	%	1931 Mill. Frs.	%
Total Exports .	6880	100·0	50100	100·0	30400	100·0
of which to:						
Total Europe .	4800	69·7	31000	61·9	18700	62·0
Including:						
Great Britain . .	1454	21·0	7625	15·1	5090	16·7
Belgium .	1108	16·0	7220	14·3	3580	11·8
Germany .	867	12·0	4740	9·4	2750	9·0
Switzerland .	406	5·9	3380	6·7	2310	7·6
Italy . .	306	4·4	2210	4·4	992	3·2
Algiers, Tunis .	653	9·4	5510	11·0	4780	15·6
U.S.A. . .	423	6·1	3335	6·6	1540	5·0

(c) *Actual Tariff Levels of the Chief Markets of France*

I. *France and Industrial Europe*

(aa) *France and Great Britain*

Before the War Great Britain was France's best market in
the world, and remained so as far as Europe was concerned up
to 1931, although her relative share of the total French exports
persistently remained considerably below the pre-War position.

[1] *Gaedicke*, pp. 102–103.

French exports to England were in the first place consumer's goods [1] (textiles, fashionable luxury goods, motor-cars, etc.). In addition there was a considerable export of wines, and after the War an appreciable growth in the export of semi-finished iron products. Before 1914 only wine exports were liable to English fiscal duties, which even at that time were high (average 62–75%). After the War these duties were considerably increased, so that their average height reached 103–184% in 1927 and 117–215% in 1931. In spite of the high purchasing power of the English market, these duties obviously injured French exports, which in volume and value had by 1929 fallen below the 1913 figures, while the decline was still more marked in 1931.

After the War the new English duties on certain textiles (silk and artificial silk goods, gloves, lace of all kinds), as well as on chemicals and motor-cars, were bound to hit French exports. For silk and artificial silk products some of the English duties reached a very considerable height (1927, 56%; 1931, 71%).

Up to 1927 the low prices resulting from French inflation neutralized the obstacles to exports which arose from tariff barriers. In 1929, on the other hand, and still more so in 1931, it was in these particular classes of goods that French exports sustained the heaviest losses.

In spite of these duties England was France's best European customer even in 1931, as numerous French finished goods were still on the free list. A decisive reversal, assisted by the depreciation of Sterling, came in 1932, when England resorted to protection. Within two years French exports fell from a value of 5·1 Milld. Frs. to 1·6 Milld. Frs., so that instead of 16·7% England bought only 9·1% of French exports (being merely 23% of what she had bought from France in 1913) and fell behind Belgium and Germany in the list of France's European markets. This can only be described as an extensive destruction of the Anglo-French economic integration since 1931, faint signs of which were perceptible as far back as

[1] *Gaedicke*, pp. 106–107.

the end of the War, but which did not assume great importance until the introduction of general tariff protection in England.

(bb) *France and Belgium*

Both before and after the War relations between France and Belgium were so close that this little country was France's second best European market prior to 1914 and remained so up to 1931. The greater part of French exports consisted in raw materials and semi-finished industrial products (wool, ore, semi-manufactured metal goods, yarns, chemicals). In addition there was a brisk export trade in various kinds of finished articles, both consumer's and capital goods. In particular, French exports of machinery, tools, and metal goods to Belgium received a great stimulus after the War. Up to 1931 the moderate Belgian tariff policy was no obstacle worth mentioning to this integration. We had therefore to do no more than to indicate the Belgian actual tariff levels for French exports in 1913, 1927, and 1931. In the case of semi-finished articles it amounted in these three years to 7–14%, in the case of finished goods to 9–20·3% (see details in Table D, p. 253). Among the Belgian duties on finished goods those on metal goods were raised most; they reached a height of 20%, i.e. nearly three times that of 1913. Motor-car duties were also considerably raised, viz. from 7·5% in 1913 to about 30% after the War. Until recent times (1935) Belgium has not only retained her importance as a market for France, but has even enhanced it. In 1933 Belgium took 11·6% of the total French exports and moved into the first place in the list of France's European markets.

(cc) *France and Germany*

More than in exports to England and Belgium, semi-finished articles were prominent among French exports to Germany. This was particularly the case in the post-War period,[1] after

[1] *Gaedicke*, pp. 107–109.

Germany had lost her ore deposits in Lorraine and an important part of her cotton-spinning industry in Alsace. Ore, yarns, leather, and semi-finished metal goods became such important classes among French exports to Germany that French exports of finished goods and agrarian products (textiles, motor-cars, luxury articles, wine, vegetables, fruit, etc.), although by no means insignificant, declined in comparison.

Here, too, apart from individual cases, it may be said that up to 1931 German duties were no considerable obstacle to French exports. The great losses which they sustained in 1931 compared with previous years were due in the first place to the shrinkage in the purchasing power of German customers.

For ten French agrarian products the German actual tariff level between 1913 and 1931 remained fairly uniform at about 30%; for twenty-five French semi-manufactured articles between 1913 and 1931 at about 11–27%.

Lastly, for French exports of finished goods the German actual tariff level in 1913 was about 8%, in the post-War period between 20 and 34%. This sharp rise was caused by German post-War increases in the duties on finished goods, some of which were very considerable indeed, especially on textiles and motor-cars. But they did not hit Franco-German exports as a whole very severely, because the latter were increasingly restricted to semi-finished articles. As the total French exports between 1931 and 1933 dwindled to an extraordinary degree, Germany not only maintained her position as France's third European market, in spite of a 40% drop in her orders from France compared with 1931, but, owing to the more accentuated decline in French exports to England, became France's second-best market during the year 1933.

(dd) *France and Switzerland*

Just as for Germany, so for France, Switzerland became an ever improving market in the post-War period. Although she raised her duties considerably in 1921 and since 1929 favoured strong agrarian protectionism, no one could complain, generally speaking, about the height of Swiss tariff barriers which French exports had to surmount up to 1931, although in some cases heavy increases in the Swiss duties led to sharp falls in French exports. For French agrarian exports the Swiss actual tariff level in 1913 amounted to 12–19·4%, in post-War times to about 14–30%.

For French exports of semi-finished goods the Swiss tariff level remained at 15–18% between the years 1913 and 1931; for French finished goods it remained stable between 6–22% during the same period, and therefore at moderate figures.

Between 1931 and 1933 French exports to Switzerland dropped by more than 40%, and in 1933 had only reached a value of 1·33 Milld. Frs., equal to 7·2% of the total French exports, a consequence of the much more drastic commercial policy which Switzerland had pursued, chiefly through quota restrictions and duty increases, since 1932. This shrinkage, however, did not affect the position of Switzerland as France's fourth-best European market.

(ee) *France and Italy*

In spite of her large population, Italy was France's least important market in Central Europe. The small Italian purchasing power, the similar surplus production of the most important industries of consumer's goods (textile trades) of the two countries, and, further, the high Italian post-War duties on finished goods, destroyed any great export chances for French industries of consumer's goods in Italy. Consequently, French exports to Italy consisted largely of duty-free raw materials (wool, etc.). Also the enlarged French heavy iron industry of the post-War period was able to increase considerably its exports to Italy up to 1927, although Italian duties were much higher after 1919 than in 1913. (Actual Italian tariff level for French semi-manufactured iron goods: 1913, 29–38%; 1927, 56–120%.) By 1929 exports of these as of nearly all the other classes of goods declined, and dropped up to 1931 by more than 50% compared with 1927. The Italian duties had certainly contributed to this drastic reduction, besides the general falling off of purchasing power. Up to 1933 the importance of Italy as a market of France continued to decline, as in that year she bought only 492 Mill. Frs. worth of goods, equal to no more than 2·7% of French exports. Thus, she became a country in recent years insignificant for French exports.

II. *France and Agrarian Europe*

(aa) *France and Spain*

In spite of the unusually high Spanish pre-War tariff level and its rising to an excessive height after 1919, France was able to increase her exports to Spain up to 1929 to such an extent that during this year she exported to that country 3·2% of her total exports against only 2·2% in 1913 (French exports to Spain: 1913, 151 Mill.; 1929, 1590 Mill.; 1931, 685 Mill. Frs. = 2·2, 3·2, 2·2% of total exports). As in the case of Germany and England, this is largely explained by the export of goods which Spain could not yet produce herself (e.g. machines, motor-cars, certain tools and chemicals), or by the export of luxury goods, whose Spanish purchasers were not deterred even by very high duties. Between 1929 and 1931, however, owing to the economic crisis, political unrest and the heavier burdens which these occurrences imposed on the Spanish consumer, French exports to Spain were reduced to such an extent that by 1931 Spain was only taking the same relative share of French exports as in 1913. In 1933 Spain bought French goods to the value of 377 Mill. Frs., which represented only 2% of the total exports. It was not possible to calculate an actual tariff level for any class because the exports were distributed over many small items. But we may quote a few examples to show what tariff barriers some French exports to Spain had to surmount, and what a devastating effect was caused by these duties. Let us take the duties on and the export volume of copper-wire and superphosphate in the years 1913, 1927, and 1931. These were the products of two industries which Spain had tried to develop by every available means. In respect of copper-wire the Spanish duty rose from 13–14% to 24–47%, and then to 26–51%; the volume exported from France fell from 29,000 tons to 1300, and then rose to 1500. In respect of superphosphates the duty rose from 0% (duty free) to 21%; the volume exported fell from 1,050,000 (1927) to 50,000 quintals (= 100 kilo). With such duties it was not surprising that, in spite of great geographical advances and many possibilities of economic co-operation between the two countries, economic integration has been achieved only to the slight extent indicated by the trend of French exports to Spain between 1913 and 1933.

(bb) *France and the Remainder of Border Europe*

The whole of the remaining States of Border Europe were so unimportant as markets for French exports that it was not worth while analysing the French exports to them. Only, one thing should be borne in mind with regard to exports to the States of South-Eastern Europe. Like German and English exports of finished goods, French exports were so impeded by heavy duties on these articles, especially textiles, that even before the crisis (between 1925 and 1929) they fell from 112 Mill. to 106 Mill. Rm. French textile exports were particularly hard hit, as they declined during the same period from 45 Mill. to 29 Mill. Rm., which no doubt expressed a development of a *structural kind*.[1]

(d) *General Trend of French Exports*, 1913–34
(See Table D, p. 253)

The trend of French exports between 1913 and 1931 and the actual tariff levels of the principal French markets in Europe

[1] See *Enquête*, II, p. 275.

may be summarized as follows. Up to 1927 French exports increased rapidly: they suffered a slight set-back in 1929 and showed a marked decline in 1931. The development of important actual European tariff levels up to 1931 could not be held mainly responsible for this set-back nor for the increasing French commercial disintegration from Europe (see Table D, p. 253), although without any doubt the introduction of the English post-War duties hit particularly the exports of French consumer's goods between 1927 and 1931.[1] It was rather the destruction of the purchasing power of France's foreign customers brought about by the political and economic crisis of 1931, on the one hand, and on the other the disparity between French export prices and the trend of prices outside France in 1931, which were largely responsible, as in the case of England, for the huge drop in French exports during 1931.[2]

The very unfavourable position of French exports after 1931 up to recent times, however (in 1934 French exports were only 59% of their value in 1931 and 35·5% of their value in 1929), is largely due to the tariff policy and other defensive measures adopted by France's European customers and the U.S.A., especially to Britain's tariff policy since 1932. Perhaps a still greater part was played by the devaluation of the Dollar and the Pound, in comparison with which the French price level has remained too high up to the present time (1935). This disquieting development has accelerated the strong post-War tendency of French exports to seek outlets outside Europe. It should be borne in mind that in 1934 only 55% of French exports were received by Europe, which indicates that the time may not be far distant when, following the example of Great Britain, France too will rely more upon markets outside than inside Europe.

[1] On the other hand, the high American tariff of 1930 lowered the highly developed French exports of consumer's goods outside Europe very hard, so that France's exports to the U.S.A. were more than halved between 1929 and 1931.

[2] Comp. *Proix*, op. cit., pp. 27, 29 and 36.

TABLE D: IMPORTANT ACTUAL TARIFF LEVELS FOR FRENCH EXPORTS, 1913-31

Country	A (Foodstuffs)			B (Semi-manufactured goods)			C (Finished goods)		
	1913	1927	1931	1913	1927	1931	1913	1927	1931
Belgium .	—	—	—	[25] 7·2–8·3	[27] 9·9–13·1	[21] 9·1–14·0	[21] 9·1–10·4	12·6–19·2	12·6–20·3
Germany .	[10] 31·0–35·0	[12] 26·0–35·3	30·3–34·3	[25] 11·2–22·0	12·0–24·1	13·4–26·6	—	—	—
Great Britain .	—	—	—	Duty free	[7] 33·3	33·3	Duty free	[9] 42·3	52·0
Switzerland .	[10] 12·1–19·4	[12] 14·3–24·7	19·3–30·0	[22] 5·2–10·2	6·4–15·5	8·4–18·0	[11] 5·9–16·7	[13] 12·7–21·1	12·8–22·0

4. *Italy and the Tariffs in Europe*

(a) *Composition of Italian Exports*

When discussing the industrial tariff policy of Fascist Italy in the preceding part,[1] attention was called to the very intensive post-War industrialization of this country. This is also shown by the most important figures of export statistics, as well as by the growth of industrial exports from 56% of the total exports of 1913 to about 65% in 1929 and 1931. Finished goods were responsible for this rise in industrial exports (see Table A). As the table shows, apart from exports of yarns and motor-cars, it was chiefly textile finished goods that were exported, while the highly developed Italian industries of capital goods concentrated upon supplying an increasing proportion of the rapidly growing home demand.

TABLE A: MAIN GROUPS OF ITALIAN EXPORTS,
1913–31
(*In Mill. Lire and % of Total Exports*)

Group	1913 Mill. L.	%	1929 Mill. L.	%	1931 Mill. L.	%
Total Exports .	2512	100·0	14880	100·0	10210	100·0
Viz.:						
A. Agrarian exports	762	30·0	3585	24·6	2960	29·2
B. Industrial semi-finished goods .	605	24·0	3280	21·8	2040	20·0
C. Industrial finished goods . .	805	32·0	6400	43·0	44400	43·0
Including:						
Agrarian products * .	467	18·5	2375	15·9	1900	18·6
Raw silk . .	359	14·3	1275	8·5	597	5·9
Yarns † . . .	41	1·6	828	5·5	663	6·5
Tissues ‡ . .	386	15·4	3450	23·1	1456	14·3
Motor-cars . .	32	1·3	356	2·4	154	1·5

* Agrarian products =fruit, wine, cheese, eggs, olive oil.
† Yarns =cotton and artificial silk yarns.
‡ Tissues =linen, cotton, woollen, silk, and artificial silk tissues.

[1] See pp. 127–130 of this book.

For the same reasons as in the case of France (inflation and currency fluctuations were not ended until 1927) the high-water mark of Italian exports was reached before 1929, so that the export figures of 15·6 Milld. Lire for 1927 were somewhat higher than those of 1929. The development of particular industries and the export share of their output was very unequal. Before the War the silk industry occupied the first place as an exporting trade among the textile industries. The artificial silk industry developed very favourably in the post-War period and Italy was in 1929 the greatest European producer, but Japanese competition inflicted such heavy losses in the Italian raw silk industry in the post-War period that the cotton trade became the most important post-War export industry. In the woollen industry, too, the export of tissues increased very greatly. The rise of the Italian motor-car industry was decisively based upon export, which increased in value from 32 Mill. Goldlire in 1913 to about 160 Mill. Goldlire in 1927, from which figure it then fell considerably, but remained above the pre-War level. Until the economic crisis the average export share of the output of this industry amounted to about 60–75%, that of the silk industry, 1913, by 26%; 1927, only to 9·7%. In 1929 Italy exported about 21% of her total output of finished goods.[1]

The favourable development of post-War Italian industrial exports did not, however, alter the fact that even after 1919 agrarian exports remained of far greater importance for Italy than for all the other industrial States of Europe. Until 1930 the proportion of agrarian exports to total exports fell, but in 1931 agrarian exports regained their pre-War position because textile exports were reduced very greatly under the influence of the heavy duties on textile exports.

In compiling the Italian list of exports, we had therefore to take into account the importance of agrarian exports. We have selected eighteen agrarian and twenty-two industrial products of Italy and have included all Italian goods the export

[1] *W.d.A.*, pp. 173–206, *Enquête*, II, pp. 106–107.

of which attained at least 10 Mill. Lire in 1913 or 40 Mill. Lire in 1927–31 (see Table B).

TABLE B: PROPORTION OF ITALIAN EXPORT LIST TO TOTAL EXPORTS
(In Mill. Lire and %)

Group	1913 Mill. L. = % of		1927 Mill. L. = % of		1931 Mill. L. = % of	
Total List	1090	43·5 of T.E.	8000	51·4 of T.E.	4665	45·6 of T.E.
18 agrarian products	510	66·5 of A.E.	2980	75·5 of A.E.	2085	70·0 of A.E.
22 industrial products	580	43·0 of I.E.	5020	43·0 of I.E.	2580	35·4 of I.E.

T.E. = Total Exports.
A.E. = Agrarian Exports.
I.E. = Industrial Exports.

In view of the fact that duty-free raw materials (marble, sulphur, hides, etc.) comprised only about 9–14% of Italy's total exports, a considerable part of the total exports has been excluded from the list of essential European export goods, which prompts the reflection that Italy must have sought outlets outside Europe for her exports to a large extent. This will be shown in the following section.

(b) *Geographical Distribution of Italian Exports*

Between 1909–13, Italy exported on the average 66·6% of her total exports to Europe, so that even before the War Italy was more loosely integrated with Europe than any other industrial State on the Continent (see Table III of Appendix). This tendency was accentuated after the War, when the export trade with North and South America, with Asia and Africa, increased in importance to such an extent that Europe took only 59·2% on an average of Italy's total exports in the period 1925–30. After the outbreak of the world economic crisis, Europe's share again increased to 64·5% in 1931; this was a return to the position of 1913. Among European markets those of Central Europe were the most important, as the following table shows.

TABLE C: ITALY'S PRINCIPAL MARKETS, 1913–31

In Mill. Lire and % of Total Italian Exports were sent to:

Country	1913 Mill. L.	%	1929 Mill. L.	%	1931 Mill. L.	%
Total Exports .	2512	100·0	24880	100·0	10210	100·0
Total Europe .	1587	63·2	8542	57·5	6580	64·5
Germany . .	343	13·7	1777	11·9	1090	10·7
Great Britain . .	260	10·3	1477	9·9	1200	11·0
Switzerland . .	249	9·9	1050	7·0	770	7·5
France . . .	231	9·2	1304	8·7	1120	11·0
Austria-Hungary * .	221	8·8	973	6·5	763	7·5
Austria . . .	—	—	427	2·8	378	3·8
U.S.A. . . .	268	10·7	1717	11·5	1046	10·2
Argentine . .	186	7·4	984	6·6	829	8·1

* Austria-Hungary, 1927–31 = the total exports to Austria, Czecho-slovakia, Hungary, Yugoslavia.

Italian exports to Border Europe went chiefly to the south-eastern countries and to Greece and Spain. These States together bought Italian goods to the value of 1050 Mill. Lire in 1929 and 637 Mill. Lire in 1931 (=7% and 6·2% of Italy's European exports). The values of exports to the different countries were so small that a special analysis of Italian exports was only worth while in the case of Italy's most important markets in industrial Europe, that is, Germany, Great Britain, Switzerland, and Austria-Hungary (1927–31, Austria). Relationships with other countries have been summarized.

(c) *Actual Tariff Levels of the Chief Markets of Italy*

I. *Italy and Industrial Europe*

(aa) *Italy and Germany*

Before and after the War and until the beginning of the world economic crisis, Germany was Italy's best European customer; but in 1931 yielded this place to Great Britain.

R

Italian exports to Germany consisted largely of agrarian products (fruit, vegetables, eggs) as well as of a few large items of industrial raw materials (marble, sulphur, raw silk). Semi- and wholly-finished articles (yarns, motor-cars, hats, etc.) played a subordinate part. This type of exports, only a few of which had to compete with German protected in- dustrial products, encountered very moderate duties both in pre-War and post-War times. (German actual agrarian tariff level for Italy, 1913, 5–7·5%; post-War time, 5–18%.) Of Italian industrial products motor-cars and motor-tires were affected by German post-War protection of finished goods. Thus the German duties on motor-cars were 24–40% in 1927, still 12–31% in 1931, and those upon motor-tires, in 1913 not more than 5%, reached 16–32% in post-War times. Here exports declined distinctly between 1913 and 1927. The severe set-back to Italian exports in 1931, however, was definitely due to the crisis in Germany and the fall in agrarian export prices, not to the German duties. Up to 1933, Italian exports to Germany, compared with the trend elsewhere, fell little (782 Mill. Lire), so that during this year Germany received 12·2% of Italy's total exports and became again Italy's best customer in Europe. Consequently, Italian exports have been relatively little affected by the German import policy, which has been much more stringent since 1932–33.

(bb) *Italy and Great Britain*

Italian exports to Great Britain consisted of a large pro- portion of industrial finished goods, especially of silk tissues and other textiles, although agrarian exports occupied an important place. In 1913 all these exports were duty free, but after 1919 they had to contend with duties of 33⅓% in the case of motor-cars, lace and gloves, and with even much higher duties in the case of silk and artificial silk products (English actual tariff level for Italian mixed silk tissues, 1927, 23–58%; 1931, over 130%). The exports of silk tissues and artificial silk yarn fell considerably between 1925 and 1929, although exports to England as a whole were well maintained up to 1931. The establishment of a general English tariff, the extension of Empire Preferences after 1932 and the depreciation of the Pound injured Italian exports so severely that in 1933 they fell to 682 Mill. Lire, that is, less than 50% of the value of 1929.

(cc) *Italy and Switzerland*

Italy's exports to Switzerland were in the main agrarian products and raw materials. In 1913 the Swiss actual tariff level for Italian agrarian exports was about 23–33%. After the War they encountered much higher tariff walls, so that by 1927 Switzerland's tariff level for Italy's agrarian exports rose to 19–42%, and in 1931 even to 40–78%. Increases of duties were particularly heavy for live-stock, flour, fruit and wine, products which could also be produced in Switzerland, and by 1927 these duties had almost destroyed Italian exports of cattle and wheat flour, while severe losses had been inflicted on wine exports before 1931.

On the other hand, with the exception of the duties on motor-cars, Swiss duties upon Italian industrial exports remained low (between 3–12%, motor-cars between 24–53%). After 1931, Switzerland increased her percentage of imports from Italy in spite of her more drastic quota and tariff policy, and in 1933 bought 485 Mill. Lire worth of Italian exports, being 8·1% of the total Italian export.

(dd) *Italy and France*

The composition of Italian exports to France was similar to that of Italy's exports to Germany and Switzerland. Up to 1931 they encountered no severe impediments in the form of French duties, and in the post-War period, with the growth of French purchasing power, they developed steadily, so that in 1931 France nearly rivalled England in being Italy's best

European customer, whereas in 1913 she had occupied only the fourth place. For the most important Italian agrarian exports to France, the French duties were very low (2–10%). An exception was wine, the duty upon which was 37·5% in 1913, and, after the increase of French wine duties, 1929–30, rose to 63–126% in the year 1931, without so far doing much damage to Italian exports.

The structure of the principal Italian export industries (textile) and of the French market gave slight impetus to the export of industrial finished goods to France. Only the motor-car export enjoyed a boom up to 1927, in spite of the large French production, but in 1929, and much more in 1931, motor-car exports decreased. No doubt the excessive increases in the French motor-car duties contributed to this result. Italian motor-car exports had to surmount a duty of 45% in 1927, of 53–105% by 1931; during the same period, Italian exports declined from 41 Mill. Lire to 8·4 Mill. Lire. The extensive quota restrictions enforced by France since 1932 affected Italy so adversely that in 1933 Italian exports to France, with a value of 458 Mill. Lire, attained only a good third of the figure of 1929.

(ee) *Italy and Austria-Hungary* (1927–31, *Austria and Czechoslovakia*)

In 1913 the Austro-Hungarian Monarchy was an important Italian market, mainly for fruits and, to a minor degree, for manufactures. The majority of Italy's agrarian products were on the free list, or liable to low duties (5–9%). Even the export of manufactures was not greatly impeded by duties, which reached only 9–18%.

After the War the former Austro-Hungarian territory probably lost some of its receptivity for Italian goods (see Table C, p. 257). So far as the Central European residue of this territory, comprising Austria and Czechoslovakia, was concerned, the actual tariff levels for Italian agrarian exports in 1927 and 1931 rose only moderately (Austria, 8–20·8%; Czechoslovakia, including heavy increases in the duties on southern fruit, 1927, 17–23%; 1931, 27–38%). On the other hand, Austria raised the duties on yarn, textile goods, and motor-car tires considerably compared with 1913, notably in 1931 (21–60%). As, however, Italy's industrial exports to Austria, as well as to Czechoslovakia, were of small extent, these rises meant little. In spite of the close political connection between Austria and Italy, and numerous attempts at economic co-operation, Italian exports to Austria were still falling in 1933, when they were valued at 132 Mill. Lire, which was not even one-third of the 1929 figures. In the following chapter some details will be given as to the trend of Italian exports to the remaining agrarian territory of the old Habsburg Empire, viz. to Hungary and Yugoslavia.

II. *Italy and Agrarian Europe*

(aa) *Italy and the South-Eastern States*

Whereas Italy's exports to the countries of industrial Europe were restricted chiefly to agrarian products and industrial raw materials, her main exports to the States of agrarian Europe consisted in semi and wholly finished textile goods. South-Eastern Europe and the Balkan States were the chief markets for these Italian textile exports in the post-War period.[1]

During the whole of the post-War period exports of Italian finished textile goods to Roumania and Yugoslavia had to contend with the high protectionist textile duties of these States, especially on tissues, and to surmount actual tariff levels which showed great rises compared with 1913, while Bulgarian textile duties for Italy (as well as for all other States) were so excessive as to remain for the most part potential; Hungary, in view of her own well-developed industry and

[1] Only Italian silk goods sought an outlet in the markets of Western Europe with their greater purchasing power.

high duties, bought only small quantities. From 1913–27 and then to 1931 Roumania's actual tariff level for Italy's most important textile exports (cotton tissues) changed from 20–57% to 17–34% and then to 39–68·5%, and in the case of Yugo-slavia from 11–20% to 16–42·4% and then to 23–48·3%. Like German, English, and French exports of finished textile goods, also Italian exports to South-Eastern Europe declined between 1925 and 1929, from 490 to 385 Mill. Lire.[1] In the following two years they sustained further heavy losses. Since then Italy's exports to these States, although on a very much lower scale, have developed more favourably than her exports to Central and Western Europe, so that in 1933 they reached 5·2% of the total Italian exports, compared with only 3·8% in the year 1931.

(bb) Italy and Greece

Among the Mediterranean States of Border Europe, Greece deserved to be mentioned as a customer for Italian textiles, especially in connection with the tariff problem; a heavy rise in the actual Greek tariff level has to be recorded here. Whereas Italian cotton and woollen tissues were on the average liable to duties of 14–32% in 1913, they had to pay duties of 21–47% by 1927, and of 29·5–65·2% in 1931. Exports declined between 1927 and 1931 from 100 Mill. Lire to 26 Mill. Lire.

(d) General Trend of Italian Exports, 1913–34

If we survey the trend of Italian exports and the develop-ment of the actual tariff levels of their important European markets between 1913 and 1931,[2] a clear distinction must be drawn between conditions in Central and Border Europe: the considerable shrinkage in Italian exports, which was

[1] See Enquête, II, p. 275.

[2] Owing to the distribution of her exports among a few agrarian and industrial products, we must refrain from compiling a Table D of actual tariff levels for Italy, as these few articles would not suffice for the calculation of figures for classes or groups. This applies to all sections in the following pages where Table D is missing.

particularly obvious in 1931 compared with 1929, could not be ascribed to heavy duty increases, as regards Italy's vital markets in Central Europe. The low Italian exports to Central Europe during this year were due largely to the fall in the prices of Italy's agrarian products and the reduced purchasing power in Central Europe. The losses sustained by Italian exports to Border Europe, on the other hand, which largely represented finished textile exports, were pre-eminently due to the protective policy of these States, and only incidentally to the reduced purchasing power caused by the crisis. An event which happened outside Europe was bound to exert also an unfavourable influence upon the trend of Italian exports. The high American Tariff of 1930 hit most severely the considerable Italian industrial exports to the U.S.A.[1]

Since 1931 Italy's exports have fallen again very much. In 1934 they were valued at 5120 Mill. Lire, which was only 50% of those of 1931, and no more than 34·4% of 1929. The numerous currency depreciations and restrictions, import quotas, etc., of all important European and overseas markets of Italy were no doubt more responsible for this decline than fresh increases in duty, especially as Italy remained on the Gold Standard after 1931. The severe permanent depression of Italian economy since 1929 (a recovery did not begin until the preparation for the Abyssinian adventure at the beginning of 1935) and the starting of an African War in the autumn of 1935, avowedly based on the need for economic expansion, plainly indicated that such an export level for a densely populated country like Italy is in the long run intolerable and bound to lead to grave economic and political complications.

5. Belgium and the Tariffs in Europe

(a) Composition of Belgian Exports

Belgium, which since 1922 forms a single economic area with Luxemburg, has passed through a phase of intensive

[1] Comp. *Jones*, op. cit., pp. 76–83.

industrialization in the post-War period. This is clearly shown in Table A by the striking relative growth of the exports of finished goods from 39% of total exports in 1913 to 56% in 1931, as well as by the absolute rises in the main groups of Belgian industrial exports.[1]

TABLE A: CHIEF GROUPS OF BELGIAN EXPORTS, 1913–31

(*In Mill. Frs. and % of Total Exports*)

Group	1913 Mill. Frs.	%	1929 Mill. Frs.	%	1931 Mill. Frs.	%
Total Exports . .	3716	100·0	31900	100·0	23200	100·0
Viz.:						
A. Agrarian exports .	372	10·0	2680	8·4	2160	9·3
B. Raw materials, semi-manufactured .	1826	49·1	10200	32·0	7900	34·0
C. Finished goods * .	1436	38·7	18900	59·0	13000	56·0
Comprising:						
Iron, steel † . .	243	6·6	4300	13·5	3800	15·9
Tissues . . .	123	3·3	2300	7·2	1760	7·6
Yarns . . .	244	6·6	1440	4·5	950	4·1
Chemicals, machinery .	156	4·2	2020	6·3	2040	8·7

* "Finished goods" also including a few semi-manufactured articles.

† Also manufactures, made by iron and steel.

The iron and steel trades, as well as the textile trades, and also the glass, cement, chemical, and paper trades progressed favourably up to 1929. The most important export industries were the coal, metal, glass, and textile industries. In 1929 more than 50% of the total output of finished goods were exported, in the rolling-mill industry the export reached on

[1] Great caution is necessary when comparing figures of Belgian exports in pre-War and post-War times. In the first place the figures after 1922 contain the exports of Luxemburg, the pre-War values of which contained in the German statistics are unknown. Moreover, the 1913 Belgian statistics, owing to the inclusion of transit trade, are incomparable with post-War figures. After 1919 other statistical methods excluding transit figures were adopted.

an average 59% of the output, and in the sheet-glass industry 95%.[1] In a memorandum for the second Economic Conference of 1930 in Geneva, the Belgian Government stated that 50% of the agrarian and industrial production was exported, and that a loss of export markets would shake the foundations of Belgium's economy.[2]

In order to ascertain the actual tariff levels of Belgium's most important European markets a list was compiled of fifty-two export goods, which reached values of at least 10 Mill. Frs. in 1913 or at least 100 Mill. post-War Frs. in 1927–31 (see Table B).

TABLE B: PROPORTIONS OF BELGIAN EXPORT
LIST TO TOTAL EXPORTS
(*In Mill. Frs. and %*)

Group	1913		1927		1931	
	Mill. Frs.	= % of	Mill. Frs.	= % of	Mill. Frs.	= % of
Total List . . .	1310	36·0 of T.E.	12170	45·7 of T.E.	10165	43·7 of T.E.
5 agrarian commodities .	95	39·2 of A.E.	940	41·4 of A.E.	785	36·2 of A.E.
47 industrial commodities	1215	37·0 of I.E.	11230	45·7 of I.E.	9380	45·0 of I.E.

T.E. = Total Exports.
A.E. = Agrarian Exports.
I.E. = Industrial Exports.

The exclusion of so large a portion of Belgian exports from the list is due not so much to the preponderance of extra-European exports as to the high proportion of transit goods to total exports in 1913, on the one hand, and of raw materials, which mostly enter duty free (coal, hides, etc.), on the other.

(b) *Geographical Distribution of Belgian Exports*

Taking 80·2% of the total exports on an average between 1909 and 1913 and 70·5% on an average between 1925 and 1930, Europe was by far Belgium's most important market,

[1] See *Enquête*, II, pp. 106–108, and *W.d.A.*, pp. 103–114.
[2] See answer of the Belgian Government to the Economic Committee of the League of Nations in *Proceedings of the Second International Conference with a view to concerted Economic Action*, pp. 126–131, hereafter cited as *Proc.*, II.

although in post-War times it yielded some of its importance to overseas markets (U.S.A. and the Congo). From Table C it will be seen that Central Europe was of vital importance to Belgium.

TABLE C: BELGIUM'S PRINCIPAL MARKETS,
1913–31

In Mill. Frs. and % of the Total Exports, Goods were sent to :

Country	1913 Mill. Frs.	%	1929 Mill. Frs.	%	1931 Mill. Frs.	%
Total Exports .	3716	100·0	31900	100·0	23200	100·0
Viz.:						
Germany . .	940	25·2	3800	12·0	2400	10·3
France . .	762	20·0	4020	12·6	4070	17·6
Great Britain .	512	13·8	5800	18·2	4920	21·2
Netherlands .	321	8·9	4040	12·7	2970	12·8
U.S.A. . .	106	2·9	2150	6·7	1150	5·0

The following sections dealing with the trend of Belgian export and the actual tariff levels important to Belgium could be confined to Germany, France, England, and Holland, as these countries formed Belgium's vital markets before and after the War, while the remainder of Belgian exports to Europe were distributed over numerous smaller items.

(c) *Actual Tariff Levels of the Chief Markets of Belgium*

I. *Belgium and Industrial Europe*

(aa) *Belgium and Germany*

Before the War Germany received 25% of Belgium's exports and was her most important market. This figure, however, exaggerated Germany's importance as a market for Belgian agrarian and industrial products, as it included a considerable volume of transit goods. Consequently, Germany's importance for Belgium in post-War times did not decline to the extent that might be assumed from the 1929 figure (in Table C) of 12% of total Belgian exports, although Belgian post-War exports were concentrated so much more upon other markets that Germany occupied only the fourth place in the list of Belgian customers. Germany was chiefly important as a buyer of Belgian agrarian products (horses, potatoes, eggs), further, of yarns and semi-finished metal goods, least as a buyer of finished goods. In 1913 the German actual tariff level for agrarian products was 8–10%, in 1927 it reached 14–39%. In post-War times the heavy increases in the German duties on horses destroyed the Belgian export of horses which was very important in 1913. For Belgian semi-finished textile goods the German duties remained low (5–10%), but were considerably higher in the case of semi-finished metal goods (12–18% before and 14–36% after the War). Belgium's great losses in 1931 in her export trade with Germany were due more to the crisis than to German tariffs. By 1933 Belgium's exports to Germany had fallen to 1450 Mill. Frs.

(bb) *Belgium and France*

Already before the War Belgium's integration with France was very intense. In the post-War period the importance of France as a buyer of Belgian goods increased steadily. In addition to a number of agrarian products the chief Belgian exports were coal, industrial raw materials and metals; much less important were the exports of semi and finished textile goods, and of other finished goods. This aggregate of Belgian exports encountered very low French actual tariff levels. (For agrarian products the average in 1913 was 6–12%, in post-War period 6–15%; for semi-manufactured articles 7–23%.) Belgian exports expanded during the whole time, with the result that in 1931 they were greater than in 1929. By 1933 they had dropped to 2970 Mill. Frs. which was a very favourable sum compared with Belgian exports to other countries, so that this year France, in buying 20% of the total exports, was by far the best customer of Belgium.

(cc) *Belgium and Great Britain*

To a much larger extent than in the case of Germany and France, Belgium's exports to England, both before and after the War, consisted of semi and wholly finished articles. England was not only the best European market for Belgian finished goods, but also for the great industries of semi-finished metal goods. All commodities could be exported to England free of duty, except sugar, which was liable to a duty of 6–14%.

No doubt the fact that even after the War until 1931, the great English market remained duty free for nearly all of Belgian important export products, was a decisive factor in the very favourable development of post-War exports. In 1929 and in 1931 England was Belgium's best market. On the other hand, after 1919 the English sugar duties of 30–76% had by 1927 seriously injured, and by 1931 completely destroyed, exports. The introduction of the English Tariff in 1932, and the depreciation of the Pound, had a disastrous influence upon Belgian exports. By 1933 they had fallen to 1·7 Md. Frs., i.e. by 63·6% compared with 1931; this was a reduction of exports within two years such as Belgium experienced in the case of no other of her important European customers.

II. *Belgium and Agrarian Europe*

Belgium and the Netherlands

The Netherlands, which took 8·9% of Belgian exports in 1913, became an expanding market for Belgium in the post-War period, owing to the Dutch free-trade policy; the exports to Holland comprised all classes of goods. Although exports fell to 1·77 Md. between 1931 and 1933, owing to the crisis and the Dutch quota policy, Holland still retained her place as Belgium's third-best customer, which she had occupied since 1927.

(d) *General Trend of Belgian Exports*, 1913–34

Up to 1929 Belgian exports continually increased, which was due partly to their composition (many duty-free or lightly taxed products) but chiefly to Belgium's growing integration with two countries pursuing a liberal trade policy (England and Holland). The set-back in 1931, therefore, could not in any way be imputed to the raising of duties by Belgium's chief European customers, whereas the American Tariff of 1930 was no doubt mainly responsible for the halving of Belgian exports to the U.S.A. From 1931 to 1934 Belgian exports suffered a severe shrinkage, as in 1934 they were valued at 13·6 Md. Frs., which was only 41% of the value of 1929 and 58·5% of the amount of 1931. For this marked decline the new English tariff policy, in conjunction with the depreciation of the Pound, and the retention of the old gold parity by Belgium were mainly responsible, but in the case of other markets, the introduction of quota restrictions and exchange controls, etc., were more important factors than duty increases. By a devaluation of the Belgian franc in the spring of 1935, Belgium sought by monetary means to improve her economic position, which between 1930 and 1934 as foretold in the memorandum of 1930 grew very serious in consequence of the far-reaching destruction of her foreign trade.

6. *Switzerland and the Tariffs in Europe*

(a) *Composition of Swiss Exports*

In spite of lacking any deposits of industrial raw materials, long before the World War Switzerland had built up a very important industry, which was to a great extent dependent upon exports. The exports consisted first of all of textiles, machinery, apparatus, and chemicals, but the surplus milk was also exported in the form of cheese, condensed milk, and chocolate (see Table A, p. 270).

TABLE A: MAIN GROUPS OF SWISS EXPORTS,
1913–31
(In Mill. Frs. and % of Total Exports)

Group	1913 Mill. Frs.	%	1929 Mill. Frs.	%	1931 Mill. Frs.	%
Total Exports	1376	100·0	2104	100·0	1348	100·0
Viz.:						
A. Agrarian Exports	200	14·6	212	15·4	150	11·2
B. Raw materials, semi-manufactured	153	11·1	219	10·4	148	11·0
C. Finished goods	1023	74·3	1673	79·5	1050	77·8
Including:						
Foodstuffs *	176	12·8	177	8·4	122	9·1
Cotton goods	261	19·0	235	11·2	135	10·0
Silk goods	271	19·7	298	14·2	193	14·2
Watches and parts	183	13·2	277	13·2	143	10·6
Machinery and apparatus	115	8·4	309	14·7	200	14·7
Chemicals	67	4·8	175	8·3	149	11·0

* Foodstuffs = dairy produce and chocolate.

After the War the importance of industry for Swiss total economy increased. Between 1911 and 1929 Swiss industry as a whole grew by 29%, but the engineering industry expanded by 61% (number of workers), and the value of exports of finished goods increased between 1913 and 1929 by 78%.[1] In view of the small home market the great Swiss industries were highly dependent on export. In some branches, like the great watch-making industry, 90–95% of the output was exported. In 1929 29% of the total production of finished goods was exported.[2]

In order to ascertain the actual tariff levels which were important to Switzerland, thirty-six Swiss export products were selected, the export of which reached at least 10 Mill. Frs. in 1913, 1927, or 1931.

A considerable part, especially of Swiss industrial exports,

[1] See *Schlier*, op. cit., pp. 33, 35, and *Enquête*, I, pp. 106–108.
[2] See *Enquête*, II, p. 106, and *Jones*, op. cit., p. 105.

could not be included in the list, because of the preponderance of highly specialized manufactures the various items of which did not reach a value of 10 Mill. Frs., and, secondly, because of the geographical distribution of Swiss exports.

TABLE B: PROPORTIONS OF SWISS EXPORT LIST TO TOTAL SWISS EXPORT
(In Mill. Frs. and %)

Group	1913 Mill. Frs. = % of		1927 Mill. Frs. = % of		1931 Mill. Frs. = % of	
Total List	768	55·6 of T.E.	994	49·0 of T.E.	648	48·0 of T.E.
3 agrarian products	169	84·0 of A.E.	186	85·0 of A.E.	120	79·0 of A.E.
33 industrial products	599	51·0 of I.E.	808	47·5 of I.E.	528	44·0 of I.E.

A.E. = Agrarian Exports.
I.E. = Industrial Exports.
T.E. = Total Exports.

(b) Geographical Distribution of Swiss Exports

Between 1909 and 1913 Switzerland was largely dependent on Europe as a market for her exports, as the average proportion sent to European countries was 75% of the total

TABLE C: SWITZERLAND'S PRINCIPAL MARKETS,
1913–31
In Mill. Frs. and % of Total Swiss Exports goods were exported to:

Country	1913 Mill. Frs.	%	1929 Mill. Frs.	%	1931 Mill. Frs.	%
Total Exports	1376	100·0	2104	100·0	1348	100·0
Of which to:						
Germany	306	22·2	355	16·9	198	14·7
Great Britain	236	17·2	288	13·7	236	17·5
France	141	10·2	182	8·6	156	11·6
Italy	89	6·5	158	7·5	94	7·0
Austria-Hungary *	78	5·7	152	7·2	105	7·9
Austria	—	—	68	3·2	45	3·3
U.S.A.	136	9·9	207	10·5	92	6·8

* Austria-Hungary 1929–31 = total of exports to Austria, Czechoslovakia, Hungary, and Yugoslavia.

exports, but this figure fell to an average of 68·6% between 1925 and 1930. As Table C shows, the U.S.A. were a very important market for Switzerland both before and after the War.

Both before and after the War, it was the great industrial States of Central Europe which were of vital importance for Switzerland's European exports, the remainder of which were distributed among numerous European countries. Consequently, we have confined the following details of actual tariff levels for Swiss exports to the above-mentioned States, while conditions in agrarian Europe could be discussed shortly.

(c) *Actual Tariff Levels of the Chief Markets of Switzerland*

I. *Switzerland and Industrial Europe*

(aa) *Switzerland and Germany*

Before the War Germany was by far Switzerland's most important customer and retained this position in the post-War period until 1929, although her relative share had appreciably declined. In 1931, however, this place had to be yielded to England. Cheese, chocolate, raw silk, cotton and silk tissues, watches, and machinery were the most important goods among Swiss exports to Germany. Relative and even absolute declines in the export of particular articles were visible long before 1929, for which German duties were largely responsible. (E.g. in the case of chocolate, the duty on which rose from a pre-War level of 18% to about 40–42% between 1927 and 1931, also in the case of silk tissues and watches.) For Swiss exports of finished textile goods Germany's actual tariff level rose from 10·4% in 1913 to about 33–40% in the post-War period; in the case of watches the German duties reached a height of 50% between 1927 and 1931, while the duty on parts of watches rose to 20% at the most. Consequently, Switzerland turned more and more to the export of such parts, as otherwise the export of her watch industry would have suffered still more severely.

For Swiss semi-finished textiles and machinery, on the other hand, German tariff policy worked out favourably, as the duties imposed did not exceed 17%. The very severe general set-back which Swiss exports to Germany suffered in 1931 compared with 1929 was, in spite of the above-mentioned heavy increases in some German duties, due, on the whole, more to the effects of the crisis than to German tariff policy, as the actual German tariff level for Swiss finished goods compared with 1913 showed no excessive height (1913, 5–7%; 1927–31, 18–25%).

By 1933 Swiss exports to Germany had dropped to 130 Mill. Frs., and even in more recent years (1935) were hit less by duty increases than by other German import-reducing measures dictated by the crisis.

(bb) *Switzerland and Great Britain*

Duties were primarily responsible for a very unfavourable development of Swiss post-War exports to Great Britain. Absolute decreases in the export figures of a number of commodities compared with 1913 occurred long before the world economic crisis. For the great proportion of silk tissues, embroidery, and watches among the exports to Great Britain had rendered them particularly susceptible to the English post-War duties even before 1931. For nine important Swiss finished articles, which in 1913 were exported to England free of duty, the English actual tariff level in the post-War period was 43%, silk ribbons were even subject to duties of 91–115%. By 1929 the exports of silk ribbons, plain embroidery, and watches were reduced remarkably. Much more serious were the consequences of the introduction of a general English tariff in 1932 for the development of Swiss exports. In 1933 Swiss exports to England, valued at 88 Mill. Frs., were only 37·5% of the export in 1931 and 1913. In taking only 10·3% of Swiss exports England became in this year (1933) Switzerland's third-best customer.

(cc) *Switzerland and France*

Before the War and still more after the War, France was an excellent market for Swiss industries (machinery, chemicals, apparatus). In spite of the considerably higher French post-War duties on machinery (1913, 6–24%; 1927–31, 7–37%), the rapid post-War industrialization of France favoured this section of Swiss export, so that up to 1931 it developed more than exports to Germany and Great Britain. Although Swiss exports to France decreased a little between 1931 and 1933, yet in the latter year they amounted to 142 Mill. Frs., which showed a loss of only 8% compared with 1931. No doubt the composition of these exports, and France's maintenance of the Gold Standard, contributed to this result. France became the most important European market for Switzerland in 1933.

(dd) *Switzerland and Italy*

Swiss exports to Italy were very similar in character to those to France, and up till 1929 developed steadily, with an increasing volume of machines, chemicals, and agrarian products, so that even in 1931, in spite of a heavy absolute drop caused by the crisis, Italy still took a larger relative share from Switzerland than in 1913. Contrary to the trend of events in the German and English markets, the export of watches was well maintained, favoured by very moderate Italian duties (5–8%). Even after 1931 the export developed favourably, as in the case of France; in 1933 Switzerland exported 80 Mill. Frs. worth of goods to Italy, a result which was not far below the figures of 1931.

(ee) *Switzerland and Austria-Hungary* (1927–31, *Austria, Czechoslovakia*)

Before the War Austria-Hungary was of some importance as a market for Swiss goods, especially for yarns and unworked tissues, chemicals, machinery, and watches; the Austria-

Hungarian duties were moderate (6–15%). After 1919 this relationship with Austria and Czechoslovakia proved so stable that these two countries alone in 1929 and 1931 bought as much as the whole Dual Monarchy in 1913. Austrian duties on semi-manufactured goods, like the Czech duties, remained at about the level of the equivalent Austro-Hungarian duties of 1913, but the actual tariff levels for finished goods rose above the pre-War position: in Austria to about 8–13%, in Czecho-slovakia to 13–20·5%. The development of tariff levels, therefore, was favourable to Swiss exports. By 1933 the share of both countries in Swiss exports declined; they bought 46 Mill. Frs. worth of Swiss goods in 1933, which was only 5·4% of the total Swiss exports—that is, less than Austria-Hungary bought in 1913.

II. *General Remark on the Duties on Swiss Exports Imposed by the States of Agrarian Europe*

The great part played by quality and highly developed specialization of a number of Switzerland's most important exports, such as watches and machinery, created a world market for these goods. This explains the great geographical dispersion of Swiss exports besides those to the countries of Central Europe or to the U.S.A. Numerous overseas States and States of Border Europe participated in the absorption of this residue. Without giving details, the position of these Swiss exports to Border Europe in the post-War period may be summarized as follows: As far as machinery or dye-stuffs were concerned, Switzerland had only to overcome moderate duties (Spain and Poland being exceptions with duties on machinery between 20–85%). The export of watches, however, encountered very high duties in many States of Border Europe, and the same applied in an even greater degree to the exports of chocolate and finished textile goods.

(d) *General Trend of Swiss Exports, 1913–34*
(See Table D)

The composition of Swiss exports, among which consumer's goods were prominent (textiles, watches, and chocolate), made it inevitable that in the post-War period they would be affected by duty increases of Switzerland's principal European customers much more than the exports of the great industrial countries or of Belgium.

TABLE D: ACTUAL TARIFF LEVELS FOR
SWITZERLAND
Actual Tariff Levels for Group C (finished articles)
(*In % of Prices*)

Country	1913	1927	1931
Germany . . .	[17] 5·6–7·3	18·2–24·2	19·6–25·0
France . . .	[9] 5·9–12·9	13·9–39·5	15·1–41·0
Great Britain .	[9] Duty free	43·0	47·0
Italy . . .	[9] 8·3–12·3	9·3–17·3	9·8–18·3
Austria-Hungary (1927–31, Czechoslovakia) .	[8] 7·0–10·3	12·9–20·2	12·6–20·5

Up to 1929 the serious decline in exports of cotton and silk goods, chocolate, and ready-made watches was more than offset by the rise in machine and chemical exports, or the extensive reorganization of the Swiss watch industry before referred to.[1]   But when the crisis broke out in 1929, severely curtailing the purchasing power of Switzerland's most important customers during the next two years, and when the U.S.A., Switzerland's most important overseas customer, introduced a new tariff in 1930, which taxed Swiss watches between 100 and 266% and was prohibitive in its effect, Swiss exports entered upon a sharp downward course. By 1934 they had fallen to a value of 820 Mill. Frs., which was only 39·5% of the value of 1929 and 61·5% of 1931. So far as

---
[1] See *Jones*, op. cit., pp. 108, 121–122 and 127–131, for conditions of Swiss watch exports.

tariffs came into the question, this huge descent was due to the introduction of the English Tariff in 1932, although the currency depreciations probably exerted a still greater influence in the case of the exports of Switzerland and the other gold-block countries. Without any integration with colonies and without possibilities of a colonial export trade, it is until now (1935) not clear how Switzerland will manage to raise this low export level which in the long run will prove intolerable for her highly developed industrial structure and her great industrial population.

7. Austria and the Tariffs in Europe

(a) Composition of Austrian Exports

The exports of the little succession State of Austria consisted so largely of industrial goods that we could leave out of account the small agrarian exports, consisting of live-stock and dairy produce. As will be seen from Table A, p. 278, nearly three-quarters of the total exports consisted of highly specialized finished goods, in addition to which there was a substantial export of industrial raw materials (timber, ore) and semi-finished articles (yarns, semi-metal and paper articles).

The industries of Austria were nearly all dependent upon export to a very large extent. In 1929, 37% of the whole output of finished goods were exported.[1] In order to ascertain the most important actual tariff levels, the duties on thirty-seven Austrian manufactures, of which at least 10 Mill. Schillings worth were exported in 1927 or 1931, were selected. Their total value (1107 Mill. in 1927, 625 Mill. Schillings in 1931) comprised 56% or 50·5% respectively of Austrian industrial exports. The remainder (not included in the list) is largely explained by the export of duty-free raw materials and the splitting up of the export statistics among more than 1400 items, many of which were under the 10 Mill. limit.

[1] *Enquête*, II, p. 106, and *W.d.A.*, pp. 248–249.

TABLE A: PRINCIPAL GROUPS OF AUSTRIAN EXPORTS, 1927–31

(In Mill. Schillings and % of Total Exports)

Group	1927 Mill. Sch.	%	1931 Mill. Sch.	%
Total Exports	2100	100·0	1327	100·0
Viz.:				
B. Raw materials and semi-finished articles	477	23·4	269	20·3
C. Finished goods . . .	1492	71·0	966	72·8
Including:				
Timber	217	10·6	102	7·9
Finished textile goods * . . .	348	17·0	246	19·0
Leather and yarn	260	12·7	198	9·9
Semi- and wholly-manufactured metal goods	250	12·2	158	12·2
Machinery, apparatus, motor-cars .	140	6·9	100	7·7
Paper and paper goods . . .	127	6·2	109	8·4

* Finished textile goods = cotton, woollen, silk, leather and furrier's goods, ready-made clothes.

(b) Geographical Distribution of Austrian Exports

Europe bought on the average nearly 88% of Austrian exports in the period 1925–30, and this overwhelming European orientation was just what would be expected in view of Austria's geographical position and her earlier connection with the political and economic history of the Dual Monarchy.

It would also be expected that the South-Eastern European States (Hungary, Roumania, Yugoslavia), former markets of Austrian industry, would form the leading centres of attraction for its exports. Table B, however, shows that in 1927 the Central European countries were much larger customers for Austrian goods, while the south-eastern Border States diminished their shares of the total Austrian exports between 1927 and 1931, and this perpetuated a tendency which dated from about 1925. In this year Austria exported 43%, in 1930 only 33·5% of her European exports to Border

Europe.[1] The balance was distributed in small items over the rest of Europe and overseas. The detailed analyses will show that tariffs were the main cause of the increasing disintegration of Austria and her old south-eastern markets.[2]

TABLE B: PRINCIPAL MARKETS OF AUSTRIA, 1927–31

In Mill. Schillings and % of Total Exports, goods were exported to:

Country	1927		1931	
	Mill. Sch.	%	Mill. Sch.	%
Total Exports . . .	2100	100·0	1327	100·0
Viz. to:				
Germany	381	18·1	214	16·2
Czechoslovakia . . .	241	11·5	156	11·8
Italy	168	8·0	109	8·2
Switzerland	114	5·4	95	7·2
Hungary	203	9·7	93	7·0
Yugoslavia	157	7·5	100	7·5
Roumania	128	6·1	45	3·4
Poland	106	5·0	57	4·3

(c) *Actual Tariff Levels of the chief Markets of Austria*

I. *Austria and Industrial Europe*

(aa) *Austria and Germany*

In the post-War period up to 1931 Germany remained Austria's best customer by far. Among the goods exported to that country timber played the greatest part. Austria also exported leather, yarns, semi-finished iron goods (actual German tariff level for these goods, 9–14%). The great reduction of nearly all exports in 1931, and especially of timber exports, must be attributed to the crisis, and not to high German duties. Among exports of finished goods, high-class woollen and silk textiles, leather goods, metal goods, machinery,

---

[1] See *Gaedicke, Vol. of Text*, p. 153.
[2] See *Layton-Rist Report*, part I, pp. 26, 29; part II, pp. 88–89.

and motor-cars occupied the most important place (actual German tariff level, 1927, 19–22%; 1931, 24·5–35%). Here, too, not high German duties were the cause of the sharp fall in exports during 1931. By 1933 exports to Germany had dropped to 117 Mill. Schillings (=55% of 1931, 30·7% of 1929). Although even in this year Germany was still Austria's best customer, the absolute value of the goods exported was reduced so much as to suggest an extensive reduction of Austria's once so flourishing export trade with Germany.

(bb) *Austria and Czechoslovakia*

Austria's second-best market was a territory which was a part of Austria-Hungary before the War, viz. Czechoslovakia. In the post-War period textile exports played a part which was particularly important and was determined by the separation of the two economic areas which had been united in pre-War times. Before the War Vienna was pre-eminently the seat of a great spinning and clothing industry, while Bohemia was the seat of a flourishing weaving industry. Consequently, Austrian post-War textile exports to Czechoslovakia, next to yarns, consisted largely of tissues, which were first imported from that region, then worked up in Vienna, and then re-exported to numerous neighbouring countries, including Czechoslovakia.[1] Austria's exports of semi- and wholly-finished metal goods, machinery, and motor-cars were also appreciable. The Czech actual tariff level for semi-finished goods worked out at 20–27%; for finished goods at 22–34%. In the case of motor-cars and telephone apparatus Czech duties were so high (motor-cars 40–50%, telephone apparatus 100–175%) that exports were nearly destroyed. Nevertheless, the reduction of nearly 50% in the 1931 exports of Austria to Czechoslovakia compared with 1929 was only partly due to the high Czech duties, and more attributable to the diminution of purchasing power. After 1931 Austrian exports took

[1] See *W.d.A.*, p. 248.

a decided turn for the worse. In 1933 they amounted to a value of 60 Mill. Schillings, which was only 38·4% of the value of 1931 and 20% of the value of 1929. The policy of exchange control and import licences pursued by Czechoslovakia had obviously inflicted severe injury.

(cc) *Austria and Italy*

Italy was Austria's third-important customer in Central Europe. The backbone of exports to that country consisted of timber and semi-finished paper goods, which were very lightly taxed in Italy, in addition to leather and semi-finished metal goods, paper, and a few finished articles. Here Austria had to contend with very high actual tariff levels (between 28 and 57%), and the export of leather and iron bars declined sharply in 1931. It was mainly due to the great proportion of semi-finished wood and paper goods, as well as to the close political connection of Austria with Italy, which had been drawn much tighter since 1933, that exports after 1931 developed much better than in the case of Germany and Czechoslovakia, and, at a figure of 87 Mill., only represented a loss of 21% compared with 1931, so that in 1933 Italy became Austria's second-best market.

(dd) *Austria and Switzerland*

Switzerland is the last Central European market which possesses some importance for Austria. Chiefly for semi-finished wood and metal goods, but also for a number of smaller items of finished goods, Switzerland was a good customer of Austria, although in 1931 Swiss duties were considerably raised in order to protect Swiss production of wood and aluminium, so that the Swiss actual tariff level for Austria's semi-finished articles rose from 5% in 1927 to 20% in 1931, while the duties on finished goods remained moderate (6–14·5%). By 1933 Switzerland had increased her relative share of Austrian exports to 8·2% (63 Mill. Schillings), and thus became Austria's fourth largest market.

II. *Austria and Agrarian Europe*

PRELIMINARY REMARK: *Austria's relations to Border Europe were mainly confined to Hungary, Poland, Roumania, and Yugoslavia, of which Hungary had belonged entirely to the Austro-Hungarian economic area in 1913, while considerable portions of the other States had also belonged to it. Although it was not possible to compare the pre-War and post-War exchange of commodities between these territories, the causes for the reduction of their mutual post-War trade can be shown*

(aa) *Austria and Hungary*

Up to 1931 Hungary was Austria's most important customer in Border Europe, but in that year yielded this place temporarily to Yugoslavia. Yarns, tissues, clothing, in addition to paper goods and timber, were the most important exports. Since 1919 Hungary imposed very high duties upon these exports in order to develop her own industries. The Hungarian actual tariff level for Austrian finished goods reached 26–37% in 1927 and 33–47% in 1931, while the actual tariff level for Austrian semi-finished textile goods fluctuated between 9% and 28%. By 1929 these duties had caused a considerable decline in Austrian exports to Hungary (from 203 to 169 Mill. Schillings); during the same period exports of yarns and tissues dropped from 36·2 to 18·7 Mill. After the outbreak of the world economic crisis, the high tariff level and the decrease of purchasing power in Hungary affected Austrian exports so badly that in 1931 they showed a loss of 55% compared with 1929. Since then, under the influence of the "Triangular Treaties" between Italy, Austria, and Hungary, the process seems to have been reversed, as in 1933 the exports reached a value of 77 Mill. Schillings, representing a loss of 17% compared with 1931, and comprising 10% of the total Austrian exports, which made Hungary the third-best market for Austrian goods, instead of fifth-best as in 1931.

(bb) *Austria and Yugoslavia*

Metal goods and machinery, next to semi and wholly finished textile and paper goods, were more prominent among exports to Yugoslavia than to Hungary. Between 1927 and 1931 exports developed more favourably than in the case of Hungary, because industrialization and protectionism had not made such progress in Yugoslavia as in Hungary. For semi-finished textile goods the actual Yugoslav tariff level was about 8–30%, but semi-finished metal goods were taxed heavily (45–60%). Among the finished goods only paper articles encountered high duties (30–40%). The exports of the remaining goods had to surmount tariff levels of about 12–25%. In 1933 the exports dropped to 56 millions, although Yugoslavia's relative share of the total exports remained the same.

(cc) *Austria and Roumania*

Austria's exports to Roumania developed very unfavourably. As in the case of Hungary, the drastic Roumanian tariff policy was the main cause of this decline up to 1929. By 1931 the high duties and the diminished purchasing power in Roumania had inflicted such injury upon Austrian exports that they lost 65% of their 1929 figure. Austrian semi-finished articles (chiefly textiles) had to overcome an actual Roumanian tariff level of 30–38% in 1927 and 20–59% in 1931, while duties on tissues and bar iron far exceeded these figures (70–150%). Already in 1929 the devastating effect of some of these high duties was shown by the sharp drop in the exports of cotton and iron goods compared with 1927. In 1931 the decline of exports was still much more severe. Since then the downward movement has been brought to a standstill, so that in 1933 Roumania bought as many Austrian exports as in 1931, while its relative share of the total Austrian exports increased from 3·4% to 5·8%.

(dd) *Austria and Poland*

Austria's exports to Poland were subjected to very high duties. Polish duties on semi-finished textile goods alone remained moderate (13–15%); the most important classes of Austrian exports of finished goods, such as textiles, paper goods, and machinery had to pay very high duties (22–56%). Consequently, exports in 1929 were only at the same figure as in 1927, but in 1931 they dropped almost by 50% compared with 1929. Between 1931 and 1933 the unfavourable tendency continued, so that Poland in 1933 imported no more than 30 Mill. Schillings' worth of Austrian goods, which was only 3·4% of Austria's total exports.

(d) *General Trend of Austrian Exports*, 1927–34
(See Table D, p. 285)

During the whole post-War period the development of Austrian exports has been decisively influenced by the tariff policy of Austria's customers in Border Europe.[1] The rising industrial tariff walls of these States (see Table D) drove Austrian exports more and more from their pre-War markets, and they had to seek compensation in Central Europe for the dwindling markets of South-Eastern and Eastern Europe. The changes in question were of a structural character, as this tendency was in operation long before the outbreak of the world economic crisis, which, however, accentuated it to a high extent. Textile exports to the south-east (Hungary, Yugoslavia, Roumania, Bulgaria) dropped from 132 to 95 Mill. Rm. between 1925 and 1929, and the relative share of the four States from 37·6% in 1924 to 26·7% in 1929.[2] From this position of increasing menace to Austria's economic structure, after the failure of the project of a Customs union with Germany in 1931, Austria, under the leadership of Dr. *R. Riedel*,

[1] Comp. *Ohlin*, op. cit., p. 110.
[2] *Enquête*, II, p. 106, and Report of Austrian Government in *Proceedings*, II, pp. 123–125.

has sought to develop new preferential plans for the South-Eastern States, only a modicum of which has so far been realized through the close economic union of Austria, Hungary, and Italy.

TABLE D: ACTUAL TARIFF LEVELS FOR AUSTRIA
(Only for Group C: Finished Goods)
(*In % of Prices*)

Country	1927	1931
Germany	[11] 18·8–22·0	24·5–35·0
Czechoslovakia	[9] 22·0–36·0	21·0–34·0
Hungary	[10] 26·0–37·0	33·0–47·0
Yugoslavia	[9] 19·0–28·0	23·0–30·0
Roumania	[7] 22·5–42·0	11·5–33·0
Poland	[9] 22·5–53·0	34·0–56·0

The trend of exports after 1931, therefore, has been very unsatisfactory, as in 1934 they amounted to no more than 860 Mill. Schillings, which was only 65% of 1931 and 41% of 1929, although the fall in the value of the Schilling seems to have caused an improvement in Austrian economic conditions recently (1935).

8. *Czechoslovakia and the Tariffs in Europe*

(a) *Composition of Czech Exports*

Czechoslovakia was one of those industrial States, like Italy, Germany, and Belgium, in which agrarian exports played an important part (see Table A, p. 286).

Semi-finished articles were more prominent among Czech industrial exports than among Austrian exports. Textile exports, which formed 33% of the total exports of finished goods in 1927, were the most important group in Czech industrial exports. The cotton and woollen trades were the great special branches of the textile industry. Textile exports showed a distinct tendency to favour yarns at the expense of tissues; this was undoubtedly due to the tariff policy of the most important customers of Czechoslovakia. Very remarkable was the rise of the shoe industry (Bata). In 1925 Czech exports amounted only to 10·8%, in 1929 to 32·6%, of

TABLE A: PRINCIPAL GROUPS OF CZECH
EXPORTS, 1927–31
(*In Mill. Crowns and % of Total Exports*)

Group	1927 Mill. Cr.	%	1931 Mill. Cr.	%
Total Exports	20135	100·0	13150	100·0
Of which:				
A. Agrarian exports . . .	2920	14·5	1136	8·7
B. Raw materials, semi-finished goods	3955	19·6	2040	15·5
C. Finished goods . . .	13250	65·8	9930	75·5
Including:				
Sugar, corn, malt . . .	2525	12·5	967	7·3
Cotton semi- and wholly-finished goods	3070	15·3	1580	12·0
Woollen semi- and wholly-finished goods	2020	10·4	1140	8·7
Glass, glass articles, ceramic .	1603	8·0	1294	9·8
Semi- and wholly-finished textiles *	3000	14·8	2668	20·2
Machinery, apparatus, metal goods †	2433	12·0	1974	15·1
Coal and timber	2036	10·0	951	7·2

* Textiles = silk, leather, flax goods, and clothing.
† Metal goods = semi- and wholly-finished articles.

world shoe exports. The glass trade likewise occupied a leading position. In 1913 it exported 27·6%, and in 1929 31·3%, of the world's export of this article. Czech industries depended in varying degree upon exports, but on the whole not so much as the Austrian industries. Thirty per cent. of the total output of finished goods was exported in 1929. Some industries, however, worked almost exclusively for the export trade. Thus over 66% of the production of the sugar industry was exported, over 75% of the output of the glass industry.

The proportion of exports to total output was still higher in the case of the shoe industry. The engineering trades also depended considerably upon export, although not to such an extent as the trades above mentioned, while about 33·3% of the output of the timber trades was exported.[1]

In order to calculate the important actual tariff levels for Czech exports, fifty-five articles have been selected, each of them having a minimum export value of 55 Mill. Crowns in 1927 or 1931, and the duties upon them have been calculated.

TABLE B: PROPORTIONS OF CZECH EXPORT
LIST TO CZECH TOTAL EXPORTS
(*In Mill. Cr. and %*)

Group	1927		1931	
	Mill. Cr.	%	Mill. Cr.	%
Total List . .	11755	58·5 of T.E.	6800	51·5 of T.E.
6 Agrarian articles .	2845	98·0 of A.E.	995	87·0 of A.E.
49 Industrial articles	8910	52·0 of I.E.	5805	48·5 of I.E.

T.E. = Total Exports.
A.E. = Agrarian Exports.
I.E. = Industrial Exports.

The considerable share of the products not included is again explained, as with Austria, first, by the omission of duty-free raw material exports, and secondly, by the very great differentiation of the Czech export statistics (2000 items), so that numerous export values remained below the export minimum of 55 Mill. Crowns.

(b) *Geographical Distribution of Czech Exports*

As Europe purchased over 82% of Czech exports in 1925–30, it can be said that Czechoslovakia had an overwhelming European orientation, although the development of a world-

[1] See *W.d.A.*, pp. 262–270, and *Enquête*, II, pp. 106, 236, 241.

wide trade for the products of some of her industries made the overseas proportion of Czech exports larger than in the case of Austria's exports: the U.S.A. was a particularly important market for Czech goods. By taking 64% of Czech exports in 1927 and 60% in 1931,[1] Central Europe kept the preponderance, but reduced its share in 1931 in contrast to the development of Austrian exports. As Table C shows, there were three States in industrial Europe (Germany, Austria, and England), and three countries in agrarian Europe (Hungary, Yugoslavia, and Roumania), which were of paramount importance for Czech exports.

TABLE C: PRINCIPAL MARKETS OF CZECHO-SLOVAKIA, 1927–31

In Mill. Cr. and % of Total Czech Export Goods were exported to:

Country	1927		1931	
	Mill. Cr.	%	Mill. Cr.	%
Total Exports . . .	20135	100·0	13100	100·0
Including:				
Germany	4850	24·1	2040	15·5
Austria	3070	15·2	1800	13·7
Great Britain . . .	1520	7·6	1360	10·3
Hungary	1620	8·1	289	2·2
Yugoslavia . . .	926	4·6	832	6·3
Roumania . . .	908	4·5	341	2·6
Hamburg . . .	866	4·3	452	3·5
U.S.A.	1012	5·0	805	6·1

The balance of the exports was distributed in smaller items among the remaining countries of industrial and agrarian Europe, as well as the overseas markets. Mention should be made of the exports consigned to the free ports of Hamburg, Triest, and Fiume, the destination of which is not indicated (mostly overseas exports).

[1] See *Gaedicke, Vol. of Text*, p. 153.

(c) *Actual Tariff Levels of the chief Markets of Czechoslovakia*

I. *Czechoslovakia and Industrial Europe*

(aa) *Czechoslovakia and Germany*

In 1927 Germany bought almost 25% of Czech exports. These exports consisted primarily of agrarian goods (sugar, barley, malt, hops), further, of timber and of cheap yarns and cotton and woollen tissues, leather shoes, glass and glassware. For agrarian exports the German actual tariff level in 1927 amounted to 26·5% and by 1931 it had risen to 136% (but sugar duties, 218%). These duties, some of which were very effective already in 1929, had brought about the practical collapse of the Czech agrarian exports by 1931. For semi-finished articles the actual German tariff level reached a height of 15–33% in 1929–31 (but duties on the cheap Czech cotton yarns and tissues up to 100%). For finished goods the German duties fluctuated between 31 and 36%. Here shoes were particularly hit by the increased German shoe duty in 1929, which was aimed at Bata's exports and amounted to 51%. And after 1925, glass products were affected by the very high duties (70–80%) which Germany had taken over from the inflation period.

Owing, therefore, to the composition of the Czech exports to Germany, not only agrarian exports had to pay very high duties since the beginning of the crisis, but long before, semi-manufactured articles and finished goods were heavily taxed by German duties. Exports therefore dropped between 1927 and 1929, while by 1931 they showed a decline of nearly 60% compared with 1927, a striking reduction in two industrial states at that time. By 1933 these exports had dropped to 1045 Mill. Cr., a further decline of almost 50% compared with 1931 (74% compared with 1929). Although Germany, by taking 17·7% of the total Czech exports, still held first place as a market for Czech goods, these exports were a shadow of what they were before the outbreak of the world economic crisis.

T

(bb) *Czechoslovakia and Austria*

Czech exports to Austria, the second-best market for Czech goods, showed a composition similar to those exported to Germany, except that coal played a greater part, while timber exports were absent. Favoured by moderate Austrian duties, agrarian exports to Austria developed far better. Only sugar exports, which were liable in 1931 to an Austrian duty of over 200%, dropped from 200 Mill. Cr. in 1927 to 28 Mill. in 1931. For Czech exports of semi-finished goods the Austrian actual tariff level amounted to 15–38% (but cotton tissues liable to 60–80%); for finished goods the Austrian actual tariff level reached 15–27% (but duties upon leather goods and shoes, 50–100%).

The export of a number of Czech goods thus encountered very high duties. But in spite of severe declines in such cases, total exports to Austria held their own up to 1931 much better than with Germany. (Decrease about 44% compared with 1927 and 1929.) On the other hand, by 1933 they had dropped to 722 Mill. Cr., which showed a 60% decline compared with 1931 (76% loss compared with 1929). This reduction was as severe as in the case of Germany.

(cc) *Czechoslovakia and Great Britain*

The growing pressure of the duties imposed by their best Continental customers had driven the export industries of Czechoslovakia to the great English market, to which they could send almost all their goods duty free up till November 1931. In fact, between 1927 and 1931 England became of increasing importance for Czechoslovakia's exports. For sugar it was the best European market, in spite of duties of 50–100% even in 1927, and it was only the rapid fall in price up to 1931 which raised the specific English duties to such a height (60–160%) that exports during this year only reached 25% of their 1927 figure. On the other hand, Czech exports of textile goods, as well as glass and leather articles, made such progress in the English market, remaining duty free, that in spite of the reduction of sugar exports, the total exports to England reached 90% of the figure of 1927 in 1931, which was a very satisfactory result compared with exports to Germany and to Austria.

The depreciation of the Pound and the English tariff of 1932 destroyed the favourable development of Czech post-War exports to England. In 1933 they were reduced to 360 Mill. Crs., which was only 25% of the exports in 1931.

II. *Czechoslovakia and Agrarian Europe*

(aa) *Czechoslovakia and Hungary*

In spite of the severe political tension which existed between Czechoslovakia and Hungary during the whole post-War period, Hungary was the best market for Czech goods in Border Europe up to 1930; this showed how the forces of economic integration of the mutilated pre-War Danubian area were striving to overcome the political obstacles. Hungary being poor in raw materials satisfied a great part of her fuel and industrial requirements by the purchase of Bohemian (or Austrian) products. These relationships showed signs of reviving during the first years after the War, so that a considerable portion of Czech exports of semi-finished textile goods found their way to Hungary. But here, Hungarian tendencies towards industrialization were manifest since 1919, and were responsible for the high duties which reduced Czech exports. (Average in 1927, 22–50%; duties on tissues up to 100%.) Exports of Czech industrial finished goods to Hungary were not substantial. Owing to the high Hungarian duties on semi-finished articles, Czech exports, especially of textiles, had sharply declined already in 1929 compared with 1927. When the commercial treaty between the two countries was denounced at the end of 1930 and a tariff war was started (mutual application of the autonomous duties), the Hungarian actual tariff level for industrial goods reached the prohibitive height of 35–68%, and even the Czech timber exports, hitherto on the free list, were now hampered by duties. The result was that by 1931 Czech exports to Hungary had been extensively destroyed, declining by no less than 78% of their figure in 1927. In 1933 Czech exports were reduced to 190 Mill. Cr., so that Hungary occupied only the tenth place as Czech customer instead of the fourth in 1929.

(bb) *Czechoslovakia and Yugoslavia*

Up to 1931 Czech exports to Yugoslavia remained much better than exports to Hungary (important export goods: yarns, tissues, shoes, and ironware). This was largely due to Yugoslavia's very stable tariff policy. (Actual tariff level for semi-finished Czech goods, 1927–31, between 18–47%.) But duties on tissues were higher (50–80%). In general these conditions were favourable to Czech exports. With the exception of the heavily taxed shoe exports (duties: 1927, 30–86%; 1931, 40–117%), exports of finished goods were insignificant, and distributed among numerous items. In contrast to the decline in the exports to Germany and Hungary, already in 1929 Czech exports to Yugoslavia increased considerably; in 1931 they declined to a very small extent compared with 1927, and with the large export losses of this year in nearly every other market, Yugoslavia's relative share of Czech exports in 1931 was considerably greater than in 1927. Between 1931 and 1933 this favourable tendency was not maintained, as in 1933 Yugoslavia bought only 3·3% of the total Czech exports, representing a value of 197 Mill. Crs.

(cc) *Czechoslovakia and Roumania*

In 1927 Roumania formed the third-best customer in Border Europe for Czech exports. Yarns, tissues, and semi-finished iron goods, in particular, were exported to Roumania, although with an actual tariff level of 31·5–40·4%, the Roumanian tariff walls were detrimental to the export of Czech semi-finished articles. Falling Czech export prices and heavier Roumanian duties combined to raise the Roumanian tariff level even in 1929, and still more in 1931, when it reached 37·5–71·5%. The duties on shoes amounted to 32–129% in 1927 and 45–180% in 1931, which had the effect of reducing such exports to a minimum.

It was mainly due to this industrial tariff policy of Roumania that Czech exports were already decreasing in 1929, while in 1931 they suffered a much greater reduction, which was only surpassed by that in Czech exports to Hungary. After 1931 this movement slackened; in 1933 Roumania bought goods to the value of 222 Mill. Crs., which represented 3·7% of the total Czech exports.

(d) General Trend of Czech Exports, 1927–34
(See Table D)

Both the composition and the geographical distribution of Czech exports had exposed them, even before the outbreak of the world economic crisis, to a heavy pressure from actual tariff levels on their most important markets, not only in Border but also in Central Europe.

TABLE D: ACTUAL TARIFF LEVELS FOR CZECHOSLOVAKIA
(Tariff levels of semi and wholly finished goods)
(In % of Prices)

Country	Semi-manufactured articles		Wholly manufactured articles	
	1927	1931	1927	1931
Germany .	[18] 15·0–27·6	17·6–33·0	[10] 34·0–41·0	35·0–46·0
Austria .	—	—	[14] 15·6–19·4	21·5–27·5
Hungary .	[10] 22·5–29·4	34·3–67·8	—	—
Roumania .	[12] 31·5–40·4	37·5–71·5	—	—
Yugoslavia .	[10] 18·3–44·0	26·0–47·0	—	—

Owing to the drastic policy of protection for the textile industry pursued by the States of South-Eastern Europe, Czech textile exports to these countries, like the similar exports from the other countries of industrial Europe, had fallen off between 1925 and 1929 from 296 Mill. Rm. to 196 Mill. Rm.[1] The decline had been so considerable, because the Czech exports chiefly consisted of cheap and heavy goods which were more affected by specific duties than articles of high prices. Czech exports therefore increased only very slightly between 1927 and 1929, while by 1931 they had dropped by 36% compared with 1929, although partial compensation for the losses in South-Eastern and Central Europe was found in larger sales to the U.S.A. and England. The American Tariff of 1930 and the English Tariff of 1932, combined with the depreciation of the Pound, in addition to the much more stringent import policy pursued by the States of Central and South-Eastern Europe after 1932, had very serious consequences for the total Czech exports. They suffered in 1933 a loss of no less than 71% compared with 1929 and 55% compared with 1931, and reached only 5·92 milliard Crs. Czechoslovakia sought to arrest this disastrous development by depreciating the Crown in 1934 to the extent of 16%, which had the effect of increasing exports to a value of 7·4 md. during this one year. The permanent high industrial unemployment of the country (1935), however, sufficiently indicates that, in spite of the remarkable initial success of devaluation, this Central European State, with its limited home market, will not be able to surmount the crisis by monetary measures alone.

[1] Comp. *Enquête*, II, p. 273.

V

ACTUAL TARIFF LEVELS FOR THE EXPORTS OF AGRARIAN EUROPE

PRELIMINARY REMARK: *Differences in composition and destination between exports from agrarian and industrial Europe*

THE exports of the ten pre-War and sixteen post-War states of agrarian Europe, during the years 1913, 1927, and 1931, were distinguished from the exports of the industrial states by the greater simplicity of their composition. They consisted, in general, of a few commodities of the agrarian or raw material category exported in large quantities. Consequently, often the classification of goods into agrarian products, semi and wholly finished industrial articles could be abandoned and the exports could be divided into raw materials and agrarian products. The geographical distribution was also less complicated. Whereas the exports of the industrial states went largely to Central Europe, the balance being distributed in varying degrees among Border Europe, both before and after the War more than 80% of the European exports of Border Europe went to Central Europe,[1] and here again mostly to Great Britain, Germany, Czechoslovakia, Austria, and Switzerland, much less to the remainder of Industrial Europe.[2] Consequently, as regards most Border States, we may restrict our analysis to their relations with a few countries. Moreover, the similar structure of the exports of single states (which was the reason for their very loose economic integration) enabled us to divide them in groups and to discuss the trend of their exports and the tariffs of their principal markets together. The following countries will be included in separate investigations in the order stated:

---

[1] See *Gaedicke, Vol. of Text*, pp. 166–167.
[2] See Summaries in *Gaedicke, Vol. of Text*, pp. 156–161.

1. Holland and Denmark.
2. Sweden, Finland, and Norway.
3. The Baltic States.
4. Poland.
5. The South-Eastern States.
6. The Mediterranean States (Greece, Spain, Portugal).

1. *Denmark and Holland and the Tariffs in Europe*

(a) *Composition of Danish and Dutch Exports*

Before and still more after the War Denmark's and Holland's European exports were determined to such an extent by the existence of a number of similar export products of dairy farming as to justify lumping these countries together, although, in spite of great agricultural similarities, their general economic structures revealed important differences. As Tables AI and II show, the most important goods of the largest export group of both countries (agrarian exports) were butter, eggs, live-stock, and meat, and, in the case of Holland, cheese.

In Denmark's case, not only the total agrarian, but also the total exports were wholly determined by the export of animal foodstuffs, especially butter, eggs, bacon, and meat, just as the general economic structure of the country, despite some post-War expansion in Copenhagen's industry (ship-building, engineering industry, cement, fats, and margarine industries) [1] was dominated by dairy farming. In the case of Holland, on the other hand, dairy produce only occupied the first place among other agrarian exports, and, as with Denmark, their export figures increased after the War, until 1929, to a great extent. Other products, however, such as sugar, margarine, cocoa, and vegetables, were important items in Dutch agrarian exports, and remained so until 1931, vegetable exports being especially prominent. At the same time, not only Dutch agriculture but the general economic system showed a much higher degree of differentiation than the Danish. In particular, the post-War period in Holland was marked

[1] See *W.d.A.*, pp. 407, et seq.

TABLE Aı: PRINCIPAL GROUPS OF DUTCH EXPORTS, 1927–31 *

(In Mill. Florins and % of Total Exports)

Group	1927 Mill. Fl.	%	1931 Mill. Fl.	%
Total Exports . . .	1900	100·0	1312	100·0
Viz.:				
A. Agrarian exports . .	940	49·3	532	40·6
B. Raw materials and semi-finished articles . .	348	18·3	260	19·8
C. Finished goods . .	575	30·2	415	31·6
Including:				
Milk products and meat .	383	20·2	260	19·8
Margarine, sugar, oils . .	226	11·8	88	6·7
Electro goods . . .	No information		48·6	3·7

* Figures for 1913 are omitted, because the Dutch statistics for this year contain a large proportion of transit trade. Even the improved post-War Dutch figures include a considerable percentage of transit trade, as the proportion of re-exports to total exports remained high because many imported articles were refined in Holland and then exported for overseas markets. Therefore detailed figures of Dutch industrial post-War exports have been omitted.

TABLE Aıı: PRINCIPAL GROUPS OF DANISH EXPORTS, 1913–31

(In Mill. Crowns and % of Total Exports)

Group	1913 Mill. Cr.	%	1929 Mill. Cr.	%	1931 Mill. Cr.	%
Total Exports . .	637	100·0	1616	100·0	1260	100·0
Viz.:						
Agrarian exports .	575	95·0	1340	82·0	1060	84·0
Including:						
Dairy produce . .	459	72·0	1173	72·5	945	75·0
Livestock . .	69	10·3	88	5·4	34	2·7

by a considerable industrialization, which resulted in the establishment of completely new industries (artificial silk industry, electro-industry, heavy iron industry, and chemical industry (fertilizer), and was responsible for great increases in the output of a number of pre-War industries (coal, engineering, margarine, and oils).[1]

In Holland's exports to Europe, however, only artificial silk, electro-wares, and fertilizers played a bigger part, and agrarian exports remained decisive compared with these. For the calculation of actual tariff levels seven agrarian products of Denmark and twenty-six of Holland were selected. Their export value represented about 90% in the case of Denmark and 80–90% in that of Holland of the agrarian exports. The highly specialized agriculture of the two countries, in which large amounts of capital were invested, depended very much on export. This may be inferred from the fact that during the period 1922–30 Denmark consumed on the average only 11–16% of the butter manufactured by her farmers, while in Holland the proportion was 50–60%. The new Dutch industries were likewise working largely for the export trade, the artificial silk trade exporting 80% of its output.[2]

(b) Geographical Distribution of Danish and Dutch Exports

By virtue of their great colonial empire and their economic history during recent centuries, the Netherlands belong to those European States which have important foreign trade connections outside Europe. (In the periods 1909–13 and 1925–30 on the average 25% of total exports went to overseas markets.) Denmark, on the other hand, selling 95% of her exports to Europe, was one of the Border States of Europe most closely integrated with Europe (see Table III of Appendix).

Both countries showed great similarities in the distribution of their European exports among Central and Border Europe,

---

[1] See *Schlier*, op. cit., pp. 26–27, 35; *Enquête*, I, p. 246, II, pp. 106–109, 188; *W.d.A.*, pp. 134 et seq.

[2] See *Enquête*, I, p. 105; *W.d.A.*, p. 140.

with an average of 85% destined for Central European markets, and the concentration of these 85% upon two countries of industrial Europe [1] (comp. Tables Bi and ii). Both countries were vitally dependent upon Germany and Great Britain; Denmark so exclusively that it was only necessary in analysing her export relationships to deal with these two countries; while for Holland, Belgium was such a substantial market before the War, and France became so important after it, that something had to be said about the relations between these three countries.

TABLE Bi: DENMARK'S PRINCIPAL MARKETS, 1913–31

In Mill. Cr. and % of Total Exports Denmark exported to:

Country	1913 Mill. Cr.	%	1929 Mill. Cr.	%	1931 Mill. Cr.	%
Total Exports . .	637	100·0	1616	100·0	1260	100·0
Viz. to:						
Great Britain . .	398	62·5	963	59·6	814	64·6
Germany . .	159	24·9	334	20·7	173	13·8

TABLE Bii: HOLLAND'S PRINCIPAL MARKETS, 1913–31

In Mill. Fl. and % of Total Exports Holland exported to:

Country	1913 Mill. Fl.	%	1929 Mill. Fl.	%	1931 Mill. Fl.	%
Total Exports . .	—	100·0	1990	100·0	1312	100·0
Viz. to:						
Germany	45·0		455	22·9	256	19·5
Great Britain	21·3		407	20·5	321	24·4
Belgium	10·0		204	10·3	169	12·9
France	1·0		117	5·9	177	8·9

(Absolute figures have no value — about)

[1] *Gaedicke, Vol. of Text,* pp. 152–153 and 166–167.

(c) Actual Tariff Levels of the chief Markets of Denmark and Holland

A. Actual Tariff Levels of Denmark's chief Markets

(aa) Denmark and Great Britain

Before and after the War Great Britain was by far Denmark's most important market. Between 1913 and 1931 the whole of her exports to England, consisting mainly of bacon, butter, and eggs, entered duty free, and increased materially, especially the bacon export which was exclusively destined for England, whereas Danish butter had been supplanted in the English market by New Zealand butter to an appreciable extent even before 1931, and was seeking a compensatory outlet in Germany.[1]   In view of this Danish dependence upon the English market, the abandonment of the Gold Standard and adhesion to the Sterling Block in September 1931 was perfectly justified, and this preserved Danish exports to Great Britain from excessive losses in 1931–33; for in 1933 they reached the sum of 783 Mill. Crowns, which represented 97% of the 1931 figures, a very satisfactory result compared with the decline of exports in other countries. In taking 64·5% of the total Danish exports, England's old position remained practically unchanged, so that the Anglo-Danish integration has so far remained undisturbed.

(bb) Denmark and Germany

The development of exports to Denmark's second-best market, Germany, was much more unfavourable, even before 1931.   Here, Danish exports, consisting chiefly of live-stock, butter, eggs, and meat, were largely reduced by the German agrarian tariff policy.   In 1913 the German actual tariff level for Danish agrarian products amounted to only 7·5–9·6%, but by 1927 it had risen to 13–20·6% (increased duties on

[1] Comp. Enquête, I, pp. 107–108.

live-stock and meat since 1925), and inflicted severe injury on Danish exports of live-stock and meat, which, however, was more than compensated by the enlarged exports of butter and eggs, still liable to moderate duties. Fresh duties on meat and live-stock, imposed after 1929 and raised up to 75%, brought Danish exports of these products to a standstill by 1931, while the very considerable decline in exports of butter and eggs must be attributed to the crisis, and not to the German duties, which remained still moderate (about 20%).

The decisive change took place 1932–33 when heavy German duties were imposed on dairy produce, and after March 1933 more comprehensive measures for reducing imports were adopted. In spite of the depreciation of the Crown, Danish exports to Germany fell to 158 Mill. Crowns in 1933, that is to say, to 91% of the already unsatisfactory result of 1931, and to only 47·5% of the export of 1929. Therefore the German market meant considerably less to Denmark in 1934 than it did before the world economic crisis, and this country was driven into the group of the Sterling Block.

B. *Actual Tariff Levels of the chief Markets of the Netherlands*

(aa) *The Netherlands and Germany*

Before and after the War (till 1931) Germany was the best market for the Netherlands. So far as exports of butter, eggs, live-stock, and meat were concerned, what has been said about the development in Denmark up to 1931 applied equally to Holland. Other products, however, played a great part in Dutch agrarian exports to Germany, especially cheese and vegetables, and to a lesser degree margarine, cocoa powder, and sugar. Sugar and cocoa powder were liable to duties of over 100%, but cheese and vegetables were moderately taxed up to 1931. The German actual tariff level for Dutch agrarian exports reached 25% in 1913 and 30% in 1927, but in 1931 it had risen to 50–54%, owing to the enormous duties on cocoa powder and sugar.

After the War artificial silk, radio apparatus, and fertilisers became increasingly important items of Dutch exports to Germany, where they were liable to moderate duties between 10 and 18%. The severe set-back to Dutch exports in 1931 was due mainly to the crisis, and not to high German duties. On the other hand, after 1931 Holland, like Denmark, was most severely hit by the new German duties on dairy produce and vegetables, by German quotas, and other measures. By 1933 Dutch exports had fallen to 157 Mill. Fl. which was only 61% of the 1931 result and 34·4% of the 1929 figures.

(bb) *The Netherlands and Great Britain*

Before the War England was an important market for Dutch butter, eggs and meat, sugar, margarine, and cocoa powder. After the War the Netherlands suffered considerable losses from the high English sugar duties (70–140%) and from competition of butter and cheese from New Zealand,[1] but exports of bacon and eggs and of artificial silk and electro-goods increased, so that in 1931 England was the best Dutch market.

The depreciation of the Pound, the new English duties since 1932 and the maintenance of the gold parity in Holland, brought about a great reduction in exports by 1933, when they reached a value of 126 Mill. Fl. which was only 39% of the export in 1931 or 31% of the export in 1929. As with Germany too, foreign trade relations were unduly disturbed, which had been flourishing till 1931.

(cc) *Holland and Belgium*

The close relationships between Holland and Belgium, which already existed in 1913, were consolidated during the post-War period, favoured by Belgium's very moderate tariff policy. Belgium bought Dutch agrarian and industrial products, imposing duties which amounted to about 10%

[1] See *Enquête*, I, pp. 107–108.

before and after the War. Between 1931 and 1933 Dutch exports developed much better than to Germany or England, and in the latter year reached a value of 100 Mill. Fl. which was 50% of the 1931 figures.

(dd) *Holland and France*

For a number of Dutch products, particularly butter, cheese, and meat, as well as coal, France proved to be an expanding market in the post-War period, particularly after the beginning of the world economic crisis. This tendency was favoured by low French duties on butter and cheese (about 7–16% up to 1931), while the duty on pork was as much as 75% even in 1931. Thus, during the whole post-War period France became increasingly important as a market for Dutch goods. In 1933 France was able to take as much as 73 Mill. Fl. worth of Dutch goods, which was 61·5% of the exports of 1931 and even of 1929. The reduction in Dutch exports to France was therefore smaller than that to England, Germany, and Belgium, so that in recent years (1933–34) the economic integration of the two most important countries of the European Gold Block has been obviously consolidated.

(d) *General Trend of Danish and Dutch Exports*, 1913–34

During the post-War period up to 1929, Denmark and Holland experienced a satisfactory development of their exports, which were based wholly or mainly upon intensive dairy farming. The assumption upon which this situation rested was the willingness of Great Britain and Germany to buy the exports of these two countries. When, therefore, Germany began (after 1929) to restrict imports, in order to protect German agriculture or for other reasons connected with the crisis, a set-back occurred in the exports of both countries in 1931. This set-back, however, was relatively mild in comparison with the development of agrarian exports from other countries of Border Europe, thanks to the free-trade policy and wealth of England and to the still moderate German duties on the chief export products.

Since 1932 new German defensive measures of a prohibitive nature came in force and almost annihilated the agrarian imports from both countries. So far (1934) Denmark has averted the loss of the English market. By 1934 Denmark's exports had fallen only to 1160 Mill. Crowns, i.e. by 7% compared with 1931, and her present position (1935) testifies that by the adhesion to the Sterling Block she has so far overcome the loss of the German market as to find a tolerable new economic equilibrium.

Dutch exports, on the other hand, had by 1934 dropped to 735 Mill. Fl., i.e. by 45% compared with 1931, or 63% compared with 1929. Holland lost not only the German but a large part of the English market. It is doubtful (1935) whether, in view of the depreciation of the Pound and the Dollar, the country can increase its volume of foreign trade, while remaining on the Gold Standard. Efforts to reach this aim are marked by closer union with its colonial empire, by reducing industrial imports in order to stimulate its own industrial production and by a thorough-going policy of deflation.

2. Sweden, Norway, Finland, and the Tariffs in Europe

(a) Composition of Swedish, Norwegian, and Finnish Exports

The general economic structure, as well as the nature of the exports, of the three Scandinavian States is determined by their vast forests, so that, in spite of other important differences, it seemed justified to group them together. As Tables AI–III show (pp. 305–306), wood in the form of timber, of semi-finished wooden and paper goods (cellulose), or in the form of paper, occupy first place among the exports of all three countries.

Finnish exports were most, Norwegian exports were least, determined by the export of timber and paper. Norway exported the products of her fisheries, and after the War large amounts of her new and prosperous aluminium and nitrogen industries. In post-War Sweden the engineering and electrical industries assumed increasing importance among exporting trades, while there were also substantial exports of iron ore. Swedish and Finnish agrarian exports consisted mainly of dairy produce (butter and cheese in Finland, butter and bacon in Sweden).

TABLE A1: PRINCIPAL GROUPS OF SWEDISH
EXPORTS, 1913–31
(*In Mill. Crowns and % of Total Exports*)

Groups	1913 Mill. Cr.	%	1929 Mill. Cr.	%	1931 Mill. Cr.	%
Total Exports	817	100·0	1816	100·0	1162	100·0
Viz.:						
A. Agrarian exports	104	12·8	174	9·5	99	8·5
B. Raw materials, semi-finished articles	516	63·0	902	49·7	500	43·0
C. Finished goods	197	24·1	737	40·6	525	45·1
Including:						
Timber and semi-finished wooden goods	165	20·3	312	17·2	164	14·0
Semi- and wholly-finished paper goods	142	17·3	460	25·4	354	30·4
Iron and steel *	127	15·5	300	16·5	262	22·6

* This group includes iron and steel semi- and wholly-finished articles, machinery, and apparatus.

Exports of timber from all three countries declined in the post-War period, but great exporting industries of semi-finished timber and paper goods developed instead, while the production and export of various kinds of finished paper goods attained great dimensions especially in Sweden, and also in Norway and Finland.[1]

The Scandinavian timber and paper trades depended very

[1] Comp. *Schlier*, op. cit., pp. 26, 35.

U

much on export. In Sweden 75–80% of the production was exported until the world economic crisis.[1]

TABLE AII: PRINCIPAL GROUPS OF FINNISH
EXPORTS, 1913–31
(*In Mill. Finnish Marks and % of Total Exports*)

Group	1913 Mill. Fmk.	%	1929 Mill. Fmk.	%	1931 Mill. Fmk.	%
Total Exports . .	410	100·0	6430	100·0	4456	100·0
Viz.:						
Timber, semi-finished wooden goods . .	176	43·0	3120	48·7	1520	34·6
Semi-finished and finished paper goods . .	53	12·9	1800	28·1	1720	39·1
Butter	36	8·7	540	8·4	392	8·9

TABLE AIII: PRINCIPAL GROUPS OF NORWEGIAN
EXPORTS, 1913–31
(*In Mill. Crowns and % of Total Exports*)

Group	1913 Mill. Cr.	%	1929 Mill. Cr.	%	1931 Mill. Cr.	%
Total Exports . .	393	100·0	744	100·0	487	100·0
Viz.:						
A. Agrarian exports .	144	36·6	211	28·5	124	25·4
B. Raw materials, semi-finished articles .	198	50·5	265	49·0	249	51·2
C. Finished goods . .	51	12·9	166	22·4	86	17·7
Including:						
Fish products * . .	93	23·6	165	22·2	100	20·6
Paper, timber † . .	125	31·9	229	30·8	123	23·3
Aluminium, nitrogen .	16	4·1	76	10·2	75	15·4

* Fresh and dried fish, fish conserves, and fish oil.
† Semi- and wholly-finished wooden and paper articles.

For calculating the important actual tariff levels for the three countries twenty-four export goods were selected for

[1] *W.d.A.*, p. 390.

Sweden, thirteen for Finland, and fifteen for Norway. The export value of each one of these articles was at least 10 Mill. Cr. in the case of Sweden and Norway in 1913, 1927, or 1931, and in the case of Finland, 6 Mill. Fmk. in 1913 and 100 Mill. Fmk. in 1927 or 1931. The export values of the selected goods represented in the case of Sweden about 38%, in the case of Finland about 70–80%, and in the case of Norway 50–60% of the total exports. In all three countries duty-free raw materials (rough timber, ore, and hides) formed a considerable part of the total exports not included in the export list. Moreover, the analysis of the geographical distribution of the exports of the three States will throw some light upon this phenomenon, especially with regard to Sweden's remarkably small percentage.

(b) *Geographical Distribution of Swedish, Norwegian,*
and Finnish Exports

In the post-War period all three States showed a striking reduction of their European exports at the expense of increasing sales in the U.S.A. (see Tables BI–III, pp. 307, 308). As regards their European exports, the markets in Central Europe were vital to all three countries. Sweden sold about 70%

TABLE BI: SWEDEN'S PRINCIPAL MARKETS, 1913–31
In Mill. Cr. and % of total Swedish exports, goods were exported to :

Country	1913 Mill. Cr.	%	1929 Mill. Cr.	%	1931 Mill. Cr.	%
Total Exports .	817	100·0	1812	100·0	1122	100·0
Viz.:						
England . .	238	29·1	457	25·2	305	27·1
Germany . .	179	21·9	275	15·2	114	10·2
France . . .	66	8·1	102	5·6	69	6·2
Denmark ⎫						
Norway ⎬ .	129	17·0	251	13·9	180	16·0
Finland ⎭						
U.S.A. . . .	34	4·2	198	10·9	133	11·8

of them to Central Europe, Finland 80–84% (after the War), and Norway 70–75%.[1] As Tables Bɪ–ɪɪɪ show, again, as with Denmark and Holland, England and Germany were the best customers of the three countries.

TABLE Bɪɪ: FINLAND'S PRINCIPAL MARKETS, 1913–31
In Mill. Fmk. and % of total Finnish exports, goods were exported to:

Country	1913 Mill. Fmk.	%	1929 Mill. Fmk.	%	1931 Mill. Fmk.	%
Total Exports .	405	100·0	6430	100·0	4460	100·0
Viz.:						
Russia . . .	113	28·0	Unimportant		—	—
Great Britain . .	108	26·8	2440	38·0	1990	44·7
Germany . .	52	12·9	925	14·4	375	8·4
France . . .	38	9·5	418	6·5	320	7·2
Denmark⎫ Sweden ⎬ . . Norway ⎭	30	7·4	300	4·7	290	6·6
U.S.A. . . .	No indication		453	7·0	413	9·3

TABLE Bɪɪɪ: NORWAY'S PRINCIPAL MARKETS, 1913–31
In Mill. Cr. and % of total Norwegian exports, goods were exported to:

Country	1913 Mill. Cr.	%	1929 Mill. Cr.	%	1931 Mill. Cr.	%
Total Exports .	381	100·0	744	100·0	460	100·0
Viz.:						
Great Britain . .	98	25·7	199	26·8	129	28·0
Germany . .	66	17·5	96	12·8	53	11·5
France . . .	14	3·8	38	5·1	27·2	5·9
Denmark⎫ Sweden ⎬ . . Finland ⎭	30	7·8	75	10·0	50	10·8
U.S.A. . . .	30	7·9	72	9·7	33	7·2

In Central Europe France was still of some importance. In Border Europe the inter-Scandinavian trade was not in-

[1] See *Gaedicke*, pp. 166–167.

significant as an outlet for exports, especially for Norway and Sweden, while Russia was of very little account, after the War, as a market for Finnish goods.

(c) *Actual Tariff Levels of the chief Markets of Sweden, Norway, and Finland*

PRELIMINARY REMARK: *As the exports of the three States showed great similarities not only as to their geographical distribution but also as to their composition, it was possible in the following section to group all three countries together as regards their exports*

(aa) *Great Britain as a Market for Sweden, Norway, and Finland*

With few exceptions, the exports of the three countries were not subjected to duties in England up to 1931, and, owing to a steadily growing demand for Scandinavian timber and paper goods increased rapidly until 1929. Even the set-back of 1931, due solely to the diminution in English purchasing power and the fall in prices, left the exports of all three countries on a much higher level than in 1913.

Despite the depreciation of the Pound and the existence of an English Tariff since 1932, the three Scandinavian countries, which immediately devalued their currencies to the same degree or more than England, on the whole maintained their exports to this country. In 1933 Finland's exports even exceeded the value of 1931 so much as to reach the record figures of 1929—certainly an exceptional case amid the general reduction of foreign trade during the years after 1931. The figures of Swedish and Norwegian exports to England in 1933 were only a little lower than those of 1931.

(bb) *Germany as a Market for Sweden, Norway, and Finland*

Germany was the second-best customer for those Scandinavian raw materials and industrial products which were exported to England, both before and after the War, while for Swedish and Finnish butter exports she was even the best market. Scandinavian exports to Germany had made astonishing progress between 1913 and 1929, but by 1931 such exports had decreased so much that neither of the three countries reached the level of its pre-War exports to Germany. For this decline German duties were not responsible, as they remained very moderate in respect of all important Scandinavian products until 1931. (Butter, 1913, 8·5%; post-War up to 22%; paper and wooden manufactures about 10–15%; semi-finished metal goods likewise 10–15%; printing paper and ball bearings, 1913, 6–11%; post-War about 22%.)

Between 1931 and 1933 the exports of the three States to Germany did not decline further in spite of the destruction of Finnish-Swedish butter exports by the new German duties and import policy in 1932–33, so that in 1933 Finland and Norway were even able to exceed their 1931 figures, while Sweden remained at the same level.

(cc) *Sweden, Norway, and Finland, and the rest of Europe*

Of European markets apart from Germany and England, only France, the Scandinavian countries themselves, and Spain deserve a passing reference with respect to their actual tariff levels. Even before, and still more after, the War, France was an important customer of all three States for semi-finished wooden and paper articles, as well as for printing paper. (French tariff level for semi-finished goods about 10–15% before and after the War; printing paper 30–40%, 1913; 40–50% in post-War times.) Between 1931 and 1933 the exports of the three countries to France did not change much, and 1933 yielded results similar to 1931.

The relatively brisk inter-Scandinavian trade (export of Swedish semi-finished wooden and paper goods to Denmark, of Finnish meat to Norway and Sweden, of Danish ships to Norway, etc.) usually encountered very low duties. (Danish actual tariff level for Swedish semi-finished articles 3–10%.)

Since the outbreak of the world economic crisis, however, protectionist tendencies have been growing even in these countries, provoking complaints from Finland about the high Norwegian meat duties.[1]

For semi-finished wooden and paper goods also Belgium, Holland, and Spain were good customers. In the former two countries these exports were mostly duty free, in Spain subjected to duties between 12% (1913) and 19% (1931).

(d) General Trend of Swedish, Norwegian, and Finnish Exports, 1913–34

In the post-War period the exports of Sweden, Finland, and, to a lesser degree, Norway showed a very satisfactory development, the cause of which was their composition and their geographical distribution. For in the first place these exports consisted primarily of raw materials, semi or finished goods required by the paper trades, and the immense growth in the demand for such goods compared with pre-War times was one of the characteristic features of the post-War boom which lasted until 1929. Consequently, these were goods which even in countries with a protectionist tariff policy were usually taxed moderately. Moreover, a large part of these exports was consigned to that greatest market of Europe which still pursued a far-reaching free trade policy. In addition the U.S.A. became a growing customer for these exports. These factors exerted a great influence upon Scandinavian exports (Denmark always excepted), also after the outbreak of the world economic crisis, and as the adhesion of these countries to the Sterling Block averted the greatest danger to their exports in 1931 from the geographical side, viz. the monetary seclusion of their vital customer, England, the Scandinavian countries to-day (1935) are among the most prosperous in Europe.

[1] See Report of Finnish Government to the League of Nations in *Proceedings*, II, pp. 153–154.

This was plainly shown by the figures of their exports during the year 1934. Whereas most of the industrial and agrarian States of Europe recorded severe shrinkages in their exports compared with 1931, let alone 1929, all three Scandinavian countries again exceeded the results of 1931, Sweden by 7%, Norway by 17%, and Finland by as much as 38% (see the absolute figures in Table I of Appendix). As the unemployment figures and the revenue returns in 1934 and 1935 were of a similar favourable character, it may be said that the world economic crisis has been most successfully overcome in North Scandinavian Europe, especially by Sweden and Finland.

3. The Baltic States and the Tariffs in Europe.

PRELIMINARY REMARK: *The three Baltic States, Lettland, Esthonia, and Lithuania were too insignificant, as exporting countries, to justify a detailed description of their exports and the duties imposed on them. Their export problems will therefore be discussed only shortly in the following sections*

(a) Composition of Baltic Exports

The exports of the Baltic countries included large quantities of raw materials and semi-finished articles as well as agrarian products. Agrarian exports were based almost wholly upon dairy farming, co-operatively organized.[1] Butter, bacon, and meat, in the case of Lithuania live-stock also, were the most important export products. Exports of raw materials and semi-finished goods are based on the great timber wealth of the three countries, and consist chiefly of logs or rough timber, and, in the case of Lithuania and Esthonia, also of cellulose, in addition to flax.

Upon the industrial foundations of their capitals, Tallin (Reval) and Riga, dating from the Russian domination of the Baltic, and under the protection of very high industrial duties,[2]

---

[1] See *Enquête*, I, pp. 120–121, 138–139.
[2] Ibid., II, pp. 218, 287; *W.d.A.*, pp. 457–459.

Esthonia as well as Lettland developed textile and rubber industries which exported high proportions of their output.

The importance of the exports of dairy produce increased between 1927 and 1931, while those of raw material and semi-finished exports declined.   In the case of Lithuania agrarian exports were 70% of the total exports, in the case of Esthonia and Lettland the proportion was between 30% and 50%.   The articles selected for calculating the actual tariff levels (15 for Lithuania, 10 for Lettland, 8 for Esthonia) formed about 60–75% of the total exports.   The exports omitted consisted of duty-free raw materials.

(b) Geographical Distribution of Baltic Exports

The exports of all three States went to Europe to the extent of almost 100%, and between 75% and 85% were bought by Central Europe.[1]   Great Britain and Germany formed the principal export markets.   Great Britain purchased 25% and 35% respectively of Esthonia's and Lettland's exports, Germany 25% and 30% respectively.   Germany received 40–50% of Lithuania's exports, and England 11–25%.   Belgium, Holland, and France were also important export markets for Lettish timber.

(c) Actual Tariff Levels of the chief Markets of the Baltic Countries

England, the best customer for Baltic raw material and semi-finished exports, as well as for the rapidly expanding bacon exports, remained open to Baltic produce, without imposing any duties, until 1931.   After 1931 the depreciation of the Pound and the English Tariff inflicted little injury upon the exports of the three States, chiefly owing to the large proportion of duty-free exports of timber, raw materials, and semi-finished articles for the production of paper.

[1] Comp. Gaedicke, Vol. of Text, p. 167.

In 1933 Great Britain was by far the most important customer for all three countries.

Although Germany was an important market for Baltic raw materials and semi-finished goods, she was a still larger customer for agrarian exports, of which she remained by far the largest consumer (except bacon) until 1931, especially as the shrinkage in German purchasing-power since the outbreak of the economic crisis led to her favouring Baltic butter in preference to the much more expensive Danish and Dutch product.[1] Between 1927 and 1929 German duties on the most important Baltic exports remained moderate (10–25%), but duties on Lithuania's exports of meat and live-stock were raised from about 25–30% in 1927, to 40–50% in 1931, and led to sharp declines.

Germany's drastic measures of agrarian protection in the sphere of live-stock breeding after 1932–33 disturbed severely Baltic exports to Germany. In 1933 Germany's share of the total exports of all three countries had dropped considerably in comparison with 1931, with the result that Germany was strongly supplanted by Great Britain as the best customer not only of Esthonia and Lettland, but also of Lithuania.

(d) General Trend of Baltic Exports, 1927–34

Thanks to the brisk German demand for the agrarian exports before and even during the first two years of the world economic crisis, as well as to the growing English demand up to 1929, the total exports of the three countries developed very favourably; the losses of 1931 were chiefly due to the effects of the crisis on their chief markets, and not to high tariff walls.

After 1932 the protectionist closing of the German market, which in the case of Lithuania was also influenced by political tension, was responsible for part of the very considerable reduction in Lithuanian and Lettish exports, in conjunction with the maintenance by all three States up to 1933, and by

[1] See *Enquête*, I, pp. 236–237.

Lettland and Lithuania afterwards, of the old gold parity, in spite of their intimate connections with the English market.

Thus by 1934 Lettland and Lithuania had seen their exports more than halved compared with the 1931 figures, while already in the first year of the devaluation Esthonia was able to increase her exports so much, compared with 1932–33, that in the year 1934 they reached 94·5% of the value of 1931.

4. *Poland and the Tariffs in Europe*

(a) *Composition of Polish Exports*

Poland was the most important representative of that type of Border European State with mixed exports, of which the Baltic States were small representatives. As will be seen from Table A, exports of raw materials and semi-finished goods played a dominant part, after which came agrarian products, and finally some exports of finished goods, which were not yet very important.

TABLE A: PRINCIPAL GROUPS OF POLISH EXPORTS, 1929–31
(In Mill. Zl. and % of Total Exports)

Group	1929 Mill. Zl.	%	1931 Mill. Zl.	%
Total Exports	2813	100·0	1880	100·0
Viz.:				
A. Agrarian exports . . .	940	33·4	612	32·6
B. Raw materials, semi-finished articles	1321	47·0	801	42·6
C. Finished goods . . .	551	19·5	447	23·8
Including:				
Sugar, etc.*	605	21·5	450	24·1
Coal, timber, semi-finished goods .	814	29·0	540	32·0
Textile and metal goods † . .	380	13·5	254	10·3

* Sugar, dairy produce, live-stock.
† Cotton goods, woollen yarns, semi-manufactured metal goods.

In view of the great fluctuations in the Polish corn harvests,[1] exports of corn were much less important than the steadily increasing exports of dairy produce (eggs, butter) and bacon. Sugar exports were very important, and between 1925 and 1931 reached about 40% of the total sugar production.[2]

Among raw materials and semi-finished articles, exports of timber and coal occupied an important place. Of industrial products the exports of semi-finished metal goods of the iron and zinc trades reached the highest figures; also exports of cotton and woollen goods were considerable. These trades were located in the Lodz district and, dating from the Russian era, were fostered by high tariffs.

For calculating the actual tariff levels for Poland's exports, those goods were selected the export of each of which reached at least 15 Mill. Zlotys in 1927 or 1931. These made up a list of 39 articles, whose export value represented 64–70% of the total and 85–90% of the agrarian exports. The excluded remainder consisted either of exports of duty-free raw materials or of goods which, in view of the great differentiation of the export statistics (4400 items), failed to reach the export minimum.

(b) Geographical Distribution of Polish Exports

Europe bought on the average about 96·4% of Polish exports in 1925–30, so that Poland was one of those Border States which were almost entirely dependent upon Europe. As Table B shows, these European exports went to a large extent to certain Central European countries. In 1927 Central Europe bought 78% and in 1930 72·3%[3] of Polish exports to Europe, which left, however, a considerable share for Border Europe.

England, Germany, Austria, and Czechoslovakia were so important for Polish exports that more than 50% of her total

[1] See Part II, p. 91 of this book.
[2] See *Enquête*, I, p. 126.
[3] See *Gaedicke*, p. 167.

exports were absorbed by these markets, while the remainder went chiefly to Holland, Belgium, Scandinavia, and South-Eastern Europe (in 1931 there were also considerable exports to Russia). The discussion of the important actual tariff levels for Polish exports can be confined to the States of industrial Europe and a few remarks about the position in agrarian Europe.

TABLE B: POLAND'S PRINCIPAL MARKETS, 1929–31
In Mill. Zl. and % of Total Exports, goods were sent to :

Country	1929		1931	
	Mill. Zl.	%	Mill. Zl.	%
Total Exports .	2813	100·0	1880	100·0
Including:				
Germany . .	877	31·2	315	16·8
Great Britain .	238	10·3	318	17·0
Austria . .	295	10·5	175	9·3
Czechoslovakia .	296	10·5	144	7·7
Sweden . .	107	3·8	91	4·9

(c) *Actual Tariff Levels of the chief Markets of Poland*

I. *Poland and Industrial Europe*

(aa) *Poland and Germany*

In the whole period between 1927 and 1931, Polish exports, alone among the exports of all the European States, to Germany were subjected to the autonomous German duties, which were applied in consequence of the Polish-German tariff war. If, nevertheless, Germany was Poland's most important market in 1927 as in 1929, this was due first to the predominance of logs and timber among Polish exports; even the autonomous German duties on these goods were not high (23–25%); further, to the fact that Polish zinc was on the German free list, and finally to the large volume of exports of eggs and butter, which were liable to very moderate autonomous duties (4–18%)

until 1929. Consequently, the actual German tariff level for Poland in 1927 reached not more than 14–19% in respect of agrarian, and 21–25% in respect of semi-finished, products.

But owing to the enormous increases in German agrarian duties of 1930–31, the actual agrarian tariff level for Poland rose to 135–137% by 1931, while the duties on semi-finished goods had increased to 27–31%. In consequence of these duties, but also owing to the crisis in Germany, Poland's exports in 1931 dropped by 64% compared with 1929. By 1933 they had again fallen by 47% compared with the already deplorable position of 1931, and in the year when the German-Polish Treaty of Friendship was concluded these exports were only 19% of the 1929 figures (167 Mill. Zl.). They had thus suffered extensive damage, as had likewise German exports to Poland.

(bb) *Poland and Great Britain*

Between 1927 and 1931 Great Britain developed into a very good market for Polish exports (chiefly bacon and eggs), whereas the market for Polish wood products had begun to contract even in 1929. In spite of heavy sugar export losses between 1929 and 1931 (50% decrease of exports compared with 1929, English duties between 60% and 100%), the increase in bacon exports was so great that in 1931 England bought more from Poland than in 1927 and 1929. The depreciation of the Pound and the English tariff of 1932, on the one hand, and Poland maintaining the old gold parity, on the other, inflicted severe injury to her exports to England, so that in 1933 they amounted to only 185 Mill. Zl., which was only 58% of the 1931 export. Yet this was a considerably better figure than that of the Polish export to Germany.

(cc) *Poland and the Tariffs of Austria and Czechoslovakia*

Between 1927 and 1929 Austria and Czechoslovakia were so important as Polish markets that they ranked next to Germany and Great Britain. They bought 97% of Poland's very considerable export of pigs (1929, 185 Mill. Zl.), Austria taking during this period 70% of the pork export,[1] and both countries imported from Poland large quantities of coal and other raw materials.   In both States the actual tariff levels for Polish exports were low up to 1929.   In 1927 they were between 13% and 16% for Polish agrarian products, and between 10% and 25% for Polish semi-finished goods, but by 1931 they had quickly risen to a great height.   In Austria the actual tariff level was now 23–27% for agrarian exports, but the duty on the most important product (pork) reached 120%.   The Czech actual tariff level for agrarian exports now amounted to 63–91%.   The great reduction in the Polish exports to both countries in 1931 was in the first place caused by heavy losses in agrarian exports due to these sharp duty increases, and in the second place by a decline in the exports of raw materials, caused by the crisis.[2]

Between 1931 and 1933 the still more drastic import policy of the two States effected a further reduction in Polish exports, so that in 1933 the exports to Austria and Czechoslovakia reached only 31·7% and 33·3% respectively of the exports in 1931 (18·8% and 16·2% respectively of 1929).   Here, too, we have to record, as in the case of Germany, an extensive reduction of an export trade which had been very brisk up to 1929.

II. *Poland and Border Europe*

Poland's exports to Border Europe went mainly to Scandinavia (coal), and to a much smaller extent to South-Eastern Europe, which bought chiefly Polish yarns, tissues, and semi-finished iron goods.   In 1927 the Roumanian duties on such goods were still moderate (13–25%).   Very quickly, however, the extreme tendencies of Roumanian tariff policy affected these exports; by 1931 Roumanian duties on Polish artificial

[1] See *Enquête*, I, pp. 123–128.
[2] Polish pig exports to Czechoslovakia declined from 116 Mill. to 6·8 Mill. Zl. between 1929 and 1931!

silk yarn had increased to 143%, and on iron sheets and pipes to 47–80%. The consequence was the almost complete prohibition of these exports, and a drop in Roumania's percentage of Polish exports by 50% between 1929 and 1931.

(d) General Trend of Polish Exports, 1927–34

Poland's exports, which developed favourably up to 1929 in spite of the tariff war with Germany, were increasingly injured after the outbreak of the world economic crisis by European tariff policy so far as agrarian products and finished goods were concerned. To this cause must be attributed the greater part of the 33·3% decrease in the total exports between 1929 and 1931, which, however, comprised declines of more than 50% in the exports of single and very important products (sugar, barley, pigs, eggs, etc.), although the favourable development of meat exports to England in 1931 compensated Poland to some extent for the loss of the Central European markets. Since this year the more drastic reduction of imports, especially of agrarian imports, by Germany, Austria, and Czechoslovakia, in conjunction with the depreciation of the Pound and the new English tariff policy of 1932, reduced still further the exports of the gold country Poland, so that in 1934 her total exports, valued at 980 Mill. Zlotys, were only 52% of the value of 1931, or no more than a good third of 1929. Deprived of the great Russian market of pre-War times,[1] surrounded by the insurmountable tariff walls of her neighbouring industrial countries and by depreciated currencies in Scandinavia and England, as well as by stringent immigration prohibitions in Germany and the U.S.A., Poland has remained up to this day in a state of severe economic depression, without showing any definite signs of recovery. (Beginning of 1936.)

[1] In 1913 Russia bought about 42% of what the present Polish territory then exported, but only 6·7% in 1931. Comp. Report of Polish Government to the League of Nations 1930, in *Proceedings*, II, p. 201.

5. The South-Eastern States and the Tariffs in Europe

(a) Composition of the Exports of the South-Eastern States

Among the four post-War States of South-Eastern Europe, Roumania, Hungary, Yugoslavia, and Bulgaria, the last named a representative of the pure agrarian States of Border Europe,[1] while Roumania and Yugoslavia are representatives of the States with mixed exports with important percentages of raw materials and goods only slightly manufactured. As regards Hungary, in spite of the decisive weight of agrarian exports, finished goods gained a steadily increasing percentage of her total exports.

Both the preponderance of agrarian exports over the other export groups, as Table A, p. 322, distinctly shows, and the recurrence of the same products justified the common treatment of the problems of these countries, although they show important differences, with regard to their general economic structures.

In the case of all four countries corn and flour were the most important items of agrarian exports up to 1929. (With exception of Bulgaria where after the War exports of eggs surpassed those of corn.) As regards Hungary and Yugoslavia exports of live-stock and animal foodstuffs (pigs, cattle, meat, and eggs) supplanted corn exports in the leading position of 1931, whereas these retained this position in Roumania during this year. Exports of cattle and pigs, however, were substantial for a time here, as in the case of Bulgaria. In the case of Yugoslavia hops and fruit, in the case of Hungary sugar, were important export goods. Hungary was the greatest exporter of flour.[2] The proportion of exports to total production was everywhere very great; in the case of Roumania's total agrarian production it amounted to 55% and was

---

[1] If tobacco is considered to be an agrarian product.

[2] Comp. *Enquête*, I, pp. 28, 74–75, 280, *W.d.A.*, pp. 283, 298, about changes in the agrarian exports of the European South-Eastern States in the post-War period.

estimated at much higher figures for certain branches. For the Hungarian sugar industry it was 50%.[1]

TABLE A: CLASSIFICATION OF SOUTH-EASTERN EXPORTS, 1913–31 *

In Mill. Leis, Pengös, Levas, or Dinars and % of Total Exports

Year	Country	T.E. Mill.	%	A.E. Mill.	% of T.E.	I.E.I Mill.	% of T.E.	I.E.II Mill.	% of T.E.
1913	Roumania	671	100·0	480	71·4	185	27·7	6	0·9
1929		29000	100·0	12700	44·0	14200	49·0	2100	7·0
1931		22200	100·0	11750	53·0	9100	41·0	1350	6·0
1913	Bulgaria	93	100·0	67	71·5	17	18·1	9·5	10·4
1929		6400	100·0	1860	29·1	4090	63·9	444	6·9
1931		5930	100·0	2600	43·7	3160	53·4	170	2·9
1929	Hungary	1040	100·0	691	66·7	136	13·1	212	20·4
1931		570	100·0	328	57·5	78	13·7	164	28·7
1929	Yugoslavia	7920	100·0	3730	47·2	3500	44·1	690	8·7
1931		4800	100·0	2440	50·7	2020	42·0	340	7·3

* Roumania has no classification into the four groups of the Brussels specification. The 1913 figures are from *Gaedicke, Vol. of Tables*, p. 19; the 1929 and 1931 figures are taken from the Roumanian Trade Statistics, and are only approximations. In the case of Yugoslavia the equivalent 1913 figures for Serbia have been omitted. Even for Roumania the 1913 figures are not strictly comparable to those of the post-War period.

    T.E. = Total Exports.
    A.E. = Agrarian Exports.
    I.E.I = Exports of industrial raw materials and semi-finished goods.
    I.E.II = Exports of finished industrial goods.

The substantial percentages of raw materials and semi-finished articles among the total exports of Roumania and Yugoslavia consisted in the first place of exports of large quantities of timber, logs, etc.; in the case of Roumania, of steadily increasing exports of mineral oils also. Further, Yugoslavia exported tobacco, ores, and copper, Bulgaria tobacco, which became by far her most important export article after the War.

[1] See Report of Roumanian Government to the League of Nations in *Proceedings*, II, p. 217.

Lastly, Hungary's exports of finished goods consisted chiefly of articles of the engineering and textile trades, which, protected by high tariff walls, not only supplied Hungarian requirements to an increasing extent, but also developed a considerable export.

For calculating the most important actual tariff levels, 16 leading export commodities were selected for Roumania, 18 for Hungary, 23 for Yugoslavia, and 8 for Bulgaria. In the case of Bulgaria and Roumania their export values reached 70–90%, in the case of Yugoslavia and Hungary about 60% of the total exports, and about 80–90% of the agrarian exports of these States.

(b) Geographical Distribution of the Exports of the South-Eastern States

About 90% of the exports of all four States were consigned to Europe in pre-War as in post-War times, which sufficiently indicated their overwhelming European orientation. (See Table III of Appendix.) Of these exports, Roumania and Bulgaria sold 88% and 78% respectively to Central Europe in 1913, after the War Hungary, Jugoslavia and Bulgaria sold on the average 75 to 85% to Central Europe, while Roumania's proportion was 70–76%.[1]

As may be seen from Tables BI–IV, pp. 324–325, Germany, Austria, and Czechoslovakia were the most important markets; Italy, too, was of considerable importance, while England was a valuable market for Hungary and Roumania, especially in the post-War period. Finally, France was an important market for Roumania.[2] In Border Europe Hungary was of some importance for Roumania and Yugoslavia, and Greece for Bulgaria and Yugoslavia. The following sections are confined

[1] For exact figures see *Gaedicke, Vol. of Text*, pp. 166–167.

[2] Belgium and Holland too were important markets for the South-Eastern States, especially before the War, but most of the imports of the two countries from the Balkan States were *transit*-imports.

to the above-mentioned countries in Central and Border Europe.

TABLE BI: ROUMANIA'S PRINCIPAL MARKETS, 1913-31

In Mill. Lei and % of Roumanian Total Exports, goods were sent to:

Country	1913 Mill. L.	%	1929 Mill. L.	%	1931 Mill. L.	%
Total Exports .	671	100·0	29000	100·0	22200	100·0
Including:						
Belgium . .	182	27·1	450	1·6	1700	7·6
Austria-Hungary *	96	14·3	8200	28·3	6500	29·0
Austria . .	—	—	2700	9·4	2400	10·7
Czechoslovakia .	—	—	1800	6·2	1560	7·0
Hungary . .	—	—	3200	11·0	2300	10·2
France . .	63	9·5	1300	4·5	2410	10·9
Germany . .	52	7·8	8000	27·6	2540	11·5
Great Britain .	45	6·7	1900	6·4	2250	10·0

TABLE BII: BULGARIA'S PRINCIPAL MARKETS, 1913-31

In Mill. Leva and % of Bulgarian Total Exports, goods were sent to:

Country	1913 Mill. L.	%	1929 Mill. L.	%	1931 Mill. L.	%
Total Exports .	93	100·0	6400	100·0	5930	100·0
Including:						
Germany . .	17	18·4	1910	29·9	1750	29·5
Austria-Hungary *	14	15·4	1300	20·3	1450	24·4
Austria . .	—	—	800	12·5	993	16·7
Italy . . .	4	4·5	670	10·5	344	5·8

* In the case of Bulgaria and Roumania, for the years 1929 and 1931 the totals of exports to Austria, Hungary, Yugoslavia, and Czecho-slovakia were added for comparison with 1913.

TABLE Bɪɪɪ: HUNGARY'S PRINCIPAL MARKETS, 1929–31

In Mill. Pengö and % of Hungarian Total Exports, goods were sent to:

Country		1929 Mill. P.	%	1931 Mill. P.	%
Total Exports	.	1040	100·0	570	100·0
Including:					
Austria	.	316	30·4	170	29·8
Czechoslovakia	.	170	16·4	23·8	4·2
Germany	.	121	11·7	72·6	12·7
Italy .	.	71·5	6·9	55·6	9·8
Great Britain	.	19	2·4	56	9·8

TABLE Bɪᴠ: YUGOSLAVIA'S PRINCIPAL MARKETS, 1929–31

In Mill. Dinars and % of Yugoslav Total Exports, goods were sent to:

Country		1929 Mill. D.	%	1931 Mill. D.	%
Total Exports	.	7920	100·0	4800	100·0
Including:					
Italy .	.	1970	24·9	1200	25·0
Austria	.	1240	15·6	727	15·1
Czechoslovakia	.	426	5·4	744	15·5
Germany	.	675	8·5	543	11·3
Hungary	.	538	6·8	318	6·6

(c) *Actual Tariff Levels of the chief Markets of the South-Eastern States* [1]

I. *The South-Eastern States and Industrial Europe*

(aa) *The South-Eastern States and Germany*

Before and after the War until 1929 Germany was an important market for South-East European agrarian products; she was Bulgaria's best customer in 1931. Before the War

[1] As the Bulgarian export statistics for 1931 had not been published at the time of writing, the actual tariff levels for this country could be calculated only for 1913 and 1927.

both Roumania and Bulgaria exported substantial quantities of wheat, barley, and maize, as well as eggs, and, in the case of Bulgaria, tobacco to Germany. After the War wheat exports lagged considerably behind the expanding exports of barley and maize, except in the case of Hungary, while Bulgaria's exports of eggs and tobacco increased. As regards raw materials and semi-finished articles Germany was a great market even before the War for Roumanian mineral oil and timber, while after the War she became a large buyer of Yugoslavia's timber and copper. Up to 1929 the German duties on these products were generally moderate. (Corn duties, 1913 and 1927, between 25% and 37%; timber products, 1913 about 7·5%, 1927 about 15–20%; oil products, 1913: 19–28%, 1927: 54%; tobacco, 1913: 73%, 1927: 36%.)

The year 1929 witnessed a fundamental change in connection with the most important group of South-Eastern European exports to Germany (corn). By 1931, in fact, the German corn duties had risen to about 120–190%. On the other hand, the duties on eggs, fruit, and wood products had altered very little, but the huge increases in the oil duties of 1930 had raised them up to over 250–450%.

Owing to these duties, the exports of Roumania and Hungary suffered severe reductions in 1931. Yugoslavia's exports were less affected, and Bulgaria's exports least of all. Between 1931 and 1933 the exports of all countries dropped, in consequence of more restrictive measures of German agrarian protection, which now included animal foodstuffs. By reason of Germany's far-reaching self-sufficiency in corn, the South-Eastern States lost one of their most important markets for their grain exports. Consequently, they bought fewer industrial products from Germany (1934–35).

(bb) *The South-Eastern States and Austria*

The large imports of the small post-War Austria from the South-Eastern States were the expression of the natural cohesion of the old Danubian area. With a low actual tariff level (1927, 7–19%), Austria was an important customer for corn and flour, above all for live-stock and dairy produce of Hungary, Yugoslavia, and Roumania and for the sugar of Hungary. Even in 1931 live-stock and dairy produce were not excessively taxed (up to 20%). On the other hand, the duties on corn and flour had risen by then to 80–120%, while sugar was taxed 200% and mineral oil as much as 175%.

Thanks to the large proportion of exports consisting of live-stock and dairy produce in the South-Eastern total exports to Austria, these developed fairly well until 1931. The heaviest losses were suffered by Hungary in view of her large flour and corn exports (Austrian flour duty, 1931, 120%). Already before the crisis Austria had imposed heavy duties on flour to protect Austrian milling; this had severely injured the Hungarian flour industry, which had been organized from pre-War times for supplying the requirements of Austrian and Yugoslavian territory, and consequently this industry was working at no more than 25–33% of its capacity in 1927, while by 1931 Yugoslavian flour exports to Austria had been almost completely destroyed.[1] By 1933 Bulgarian exports had fallen considerably compared with 1931, while the shrinkage was less severe in the case of Hungary and Roumania, and Yugoslavia even managed to exceed the figures of 1931. Austria's dependence on imports from Hungary and Yugoslavia, which no political frontiers could destroy, prevented such great displacements of exports to Austria as have been recorded in the case of Germany.

(cc) *The South-Eastern States and Czechoslovakia*

Up to 1931 Czechoslovakia was Hungary's second-best customer, as well as an excellent market for the corn and flour surplus, the live-stock and dairy produce of Roumania and Yugoslavia (duties on corn and flour between 17% and 25%). The outbreak of the world economic crisis and the Czecho-

[1] See *Enquête*, I, p. 28; *W.d.A.*, pp. 283, 287, 300.

Hungarian tariff war of 1930 put an end to this state of affairs. Apart from the rapid rises in the corn duties of Czechoslovakia after 1929, this country also enforced its autonomous duties against Hungary, with the result that the Czech duties on Hungarian corn were raised to more than 90% in 1931, while the duties on live-stock and dairy produce were considerably higher. By 1931 this tariff war had nearly destroyed Hungarian exports, while Yugoslavia, in spite of the much higher Czech actual tariff level for her agrarian exports (60–65%), profited from this struggle so greatly as to be able to export far more goods to Czechoslovakia in 1931 than in 1929. In spite of similar heavy corn duties, Roumania was able to increase her corn exports to Czechoslovakia so extensively as nearly to reach the level of total exports of 1929, so that Czechoslovakia took a larger percentage of the Roumanian total exports in 1931 than in 1929. Between 1931 and 1933 this situation underwent little change; the once brisk exchange of goods between Czechoslovakia and Hungary has not yet been resumed (1934).

(dd) *The South-Eastern States and Italy*

After the War Italy became an important customer for all the South-Eastern States. She was by far Yugoslavia's best customer, and in the case of Hungary she more than doubled her share of that country's total exports between 1927 and 1931. The Italian share in Bulgarian exports was higher in 1931 than in 1913, and only in the case of Roumania it was a little lower than in 1913. This favourable position was stimulated by the composition of South-Eastern exports to Italy. The principal goods exported were maize, barley, live-stock, and meat, as well as timber and mineral oil. For all these commodities, which could not be produced in sufficient quantities in Italy, the Italian duties both before and after the War remained very moderate (for live-stock and dairy produce about 8–25% before and after the War; for Yugoslavia's total agrarian exports, 1927, 11–29·5%; 1931, 13–20·5%).

The sole exceptions were the Italian wheat duties, which already in 1929 reached 60–65%, but were raised to 180–260% by 1931; this led to the complete destruction of these exports; further, the Italian duties on mineral oils which were over 100% in 1927 and more than 300% in 1931, but did not lead to any appreciable decline in exports. For Roumanian and Yugoslav timber the Italian duties were very low (about 5%). Between 1931 and 1933 Italy's importance somewhat diminished in the case of Yugoslavia, but it remained what it was for the other South-Eastern States.

(ee) *The South-Eastern States and France*

Before and after the War France was an important customer for Roumanian wheat, and in 1931 for barley and mineral oil as well. For corn the French actual tariff level in 1913 was about 31%, in 1927 about 20%, but in 1931 about 75%. Compared with other States, the duties on mineral oil were very moderate (in 1913 between 35% and 65%, in 1931 between 90% and 120%). Even after 1931 France remained an important market for Roumanian products, so that in the year 1933 she bought 12·5% of Roumania's total exports, the highest percentage since 1927. For the other States France was an unimportant customer.

(ff) *The South-Eastern States and Great Britain*

Before the War Great Britain was a good customer for Roumanian corn and mineral oil, and after the War for Roumanian and Hungarian corn and Roumanian mineral oil, as these commodities were exported to England duty free.[1] Since 1931 trade relations between Roumania and England have been considerably improved, with the result that in 1933 England was Roumania's best customer. On the other

[1] Apart from the mineral oil, for which the high English post-War fiscal duties represented a tax of 70% in 1927, and of more than 200% in 1931.

hand, Hungary has lost much ground in England since the depreciation of the Pound and the English Tariff of 1932.

II. *The South-Eastern States and Agrarian Europe*

There were two noteworthy features of the exports of the South-Eastern countries to Border Europe. In the first place, Greece, largely deficient in corn, dairy produce, and timber, imported her requirements from Bulgaria, Roumania, and Yugoslavia, so that for the time being she took a considerable share of the total exports of these States (9·7% of Yugoslav exports in 1927, 14·8% of Bulgarian). Further, Hungary was obliged to import her timber requirements mainly from Roumania and Yugoslavia, and this was done without imposing duties. Roumanian and Bulgarian exports to Greece consisted chiefly of flour exports, which in 1913 were liable to duties of about 30–35%, falling to 21% in 1927, but rising to 80% in 1931, owing to heavy increases in the Greek flour duties, the effect of which was to paralyse the exports to Greece. For Yugoslavian corn exports the Greek actual tariff level in 1927 was 21%, but by 1931 it had risen to 50%.

The second noteworthy feature of the export trade of South-Eastern Europe with Border Europe was Hungary's industrial exports to the neighbouring countries, for which she became increasingly important as a supplier of semi and wholly finished goods, machinery, apparatus, and even textiles. Except for agricultural machinery and electrical goods Hungary had here to contend with a growing industrial protectionism which she herself practised extensively. (Example: duties on Hungarian steel in Yugoslavia, 1927, 41%; 1931, 48%.) In view of increasing general economic difficulties, the mutual relationships of the South-Eastern countries were scarcely intensified between 1931 and 1933, in spite of all the efforts in the direction of a closer political and economic unity.

(d) *General Trend of South-Eastern Exports*, 1913–34
(See Tables DI and DII, p. 332)

In surveying the post-War movements of the exports of the four South-Eastern countries with respect to the tariff policies of their customers, it must be acknowledged that since 1929 high duties have exerted a very unfavourable effect upon them. The export position of all these States (except Bulgaria) became very serious after 1929, when their most important exports were increasingly excluded from the markets of industrial countries by unprecedented duties on corn; a tariff war between Hungary and Czechoslovakia worsened the situation for Hungary after 1930. Consequently, the latter's export losses in 1931 were the greatest, although both Roumania's and Yugoslavia's export losses were likewise very considerable, while Bulgaria's tendency to concentrate upon exports of tobacco and eggs—two products not so heavily hit by duties till 1931—averted a severe set-back. As agrarian protection was still further reinforced in all industrial countries between 1931 and 1933, the recent trend of South-Eastern exports (1935) has been anything but satisfactory, especially as regards Hungary and Bulgaria, which have no exports of industrial raw materials to compensate them for their shrinking agrarian exports.

Assuming 1931 to be 100, 1934 Hungary and Bulgaria only reached 48·6% and 43·2%, Yugoslavia and Roumania only 80% and 61% respectively of the exports of this year. The full extent of the shrinkage can only be perceived if 1929 be selected as the basis of comparison, in which case Hungary and Bulgaria reached only 26·6% and 40%, Roumania and Yugoslavia only about 48% respectively of the last normal European post-War year. It was remarkable that this South-Eastern State, whose exports recently developed most favourably (1935) was the only one of the four which devalued its currency after 1931 (Yugoslavia, 1934, about 23% depreciation). On the whole, the situation of these four States which are dependent upon agrarian exports, has remained unsatisfactory up to the present day (beginning of 1936).

TABLE D1: ACTUAL TARIFF LEVELS FOR HUNGARY
(Only for Group A, foodstuffs)
(*In % of Prices*)

Country	1927	1931
Austria . .	[9] 16·8–19·2	[11] 79·0
Czechoslovakia .	[9] 10·0–13·0	47·0–53·0

TABLE D11: ACTUAL TARIFF LEVELS FOR YUGOSLAVIA
(Only for Group A, foodstuffs)
(*In % of Prices*)

Country	1927	1931
Italy . . .	[10] 10·8–29·5	13·1–20·5
Austria . .	[9] 7·2–10·3	34·8–38·0
Czechoslovakia .	[9] 33·0–35·0	60·0–65·0

6. *The Mediterranean Border States (Greece, Spain, Portugal) and the Tariffs in Europe*

(a) *Composition of Exports of the Mediterranean Border States*

Foodstuffs (Southern fruits) play the chief part in the exports of the three Mediterranean Border States, Greece, Spain, and Portugal, as Table A, p. 333 shows. Spain only exported considerable quantities of raw materials and semi-finished goods (ore and metals). The preponderance of the same or similar products among their agrarian exports justified a common discussion of the export problems of the three countries. All three exported large quantities of wine. Between 1913 and 1931 wine exports varied between 35% and 27% of Portugal's total exports, 17% and 11% of Spain's total exports, and 14·5% and 4% of Greece's total exports.

Fruits and olive oil were the most important part of the agrarian exports of Greece and Spain. Portugal and, to a lesser extent, Spain exported considerable quantities of tinned fish (sardines). After the War tobacco became the chief item in Greece's exports, being 53–56% of the whole, compared with 15% in 1913. Among the (less important) exports of finished goods from Spain and Portugal, cork articles played the chief part. Before and after the War the export values of the goods selected for calculating the most important actual tariff levels (7 goods for Greece, 19 for Spain, and 10 for Portugal) reached about 45–60% of the total exports in the case of Portugal and Spain, and 70–85% in the case of Greece. So far as the goods omitted were not raw materials on the free list, an analysis of the geographical distribution of exports will afford some explanation of the very low percentage of the selected goods in the case of Spain and Portugal.

TABLE A: CLASSIFICATION OF EXPORTS OF THE MEDITERRANEAN BORDER STATES, 1913–31

(In Mill. Drachmas, Pesetas and Escudos and % of Total Exports)

		T.E.		A.E.		I.E.I		I.E.II	
Year	Country	Mill.	%	Mill.	% of T.E.	Mill.	% of T.E.	Mill.	% of T.E.
1913	Greece	119	100·0	94	79·0	23	19·0	unimportant	
1929		7000	100·0	2370	34·0	4470	64·0		
1931		4200	100·0	1485	35·3	2580	61·4		
1913	Spain	1058	100·0	473	44·5	333	31·4	215	23·3
1929		2108	100·0	1200	57·0	436	20·8	472	22·2
1931		961	100·0	673	69·0	162	16·5	137	14·5
1913	Portugal	35	100·0	23	64·5	9	25·0	4	10·5
1929		1073	100·0	620	57·8	325	30·3	128	11·9
1931		812	100·0	557	68·6	184	22·7	71	8·7

T.E. = Total Exports.
A.E. = Agrarian Exports.
I.E.I = Exports of raw materials and semi-finished goods.
I.E.II = Exports of finished goods.

(b) Geographical Distribution of the Exports of the Mediterranean Border States

In the main features of the geographical distribution of their exports, all three countries showed great similarity, as they were more loosely integrated with Europe than the other states of Border Europe, as regards both imports and exports.

Europe's share of the total exports of Spain and Portugal, before and after the War, fluctuated between 62% and 71%. In the case of Greece the proportion was 83% before the War, but only about 74% after the War.[1] Colonies and old relations to South America in the case of Spain and Portugal, and the long distances by land from the European trading centres in the case of all three countries exerted a disintegrating effect on their European commerce. Central Europe's share among the European exports of all three countries was preponderant, being 85–93% in 1913 as well as after the War. This share was less only in the case of pre-War Portugal (66·5%) owing to that country's closer integration with Spain.[2] As Tables BI–BIII show, these exports went largely to England, France, and Germany, although Italy was of great importance to Greece after the War.

TABLE BI: GREECE'S PRINCIPAL MARKETS, 1913–31

In Mill. Drachmas and % of Total Greek Exports, goods were sent to:

Country	1913		1929		1931	
	Mill. Dr.	%	Mill. Dr.	%	Mill. Dr.	%
Total Exports Viz. to:	119	100·0	7000	100·0	4200	100·0
Great Britain .	28	24·0	826	11·8	628	15·0
Germany .	12	10·2	1614	23·1	587	14·0
Italy . .	4	3·2	1280	18·3	696	16·5
U.S.A. . .	10	8·2	1114	15·9	724	17·2

[1] For exact figures see *Gaedicke*, p. 20.
[2] For exact figures see *Gaedicke*, pp. 166–167.

TABLE Bɪɪ: SPAIN'S PRINCIPAL MARKETS, 1913–31
In Mill. Pes. and % of Total Spanish Exports, goods were sent to :

Country	1913		1929		1931	
	Mill. P.	%	Mill. P.	%	Mill. P.	%
Total Exports Viz. to:	1058	100·0	2108	100·0	961	100·0
France . .	244	23·0	462	21·9	196	20·4
Great Britain .	229	21·6	399	18·9	237	23·6
Germany .	73	7·0	157	7·4	87	9·0
U.S.A. . .	72	6·8	258	12·2	74	7·7

TABLE Bɪɪɪ: PORTUGAL'S PRINCIPAL MARKETS, 1913–31
In Mill Esc. and % of Total Portuguese Exports, goods were sent to :

Country	1913		1929		1931	
	Mill. E.	%	Mill. E.	%	Mill. E.	%
Total Exports Viz. to:	35·3	100·0	1073	100·0	812	100·0
Great Britain .	7·6	21·5	251	23·4	189	23·3
France . .	1·3	3·8	119	11·1	150	18·4
Germany .	3·4	9·7	118	11·0	82	10·1
U.S.A. . .	1·1	3·1	60	5·6	37	4·6

Among overseas exports of all three countries the share of the U.S.A. increased to a striking extent.   The analysis of export trends and actual tariff levels could be confined to the markets of Central Europe, and once again the method of simultaneous comparisons of the relations of all three countries to a single important market was employed.

(c) *Actual Tariff Levels of the chief Markets of the*
Mediterranean Border States

(aa) *Great Britain as a Market for the Three Countries*

Before and after the War Great Britain was a very important market, in fact, the most important market for Greece and Portugal's foodstuffs and wines.   Apart from light fiscal duties on dried currants and raisins (29% before, 13–17% after, the War), these exports (with exception of wines) entered duty free, and after the War considerably increased in value and quantity until 1929, while they maintained their position up to 1931. Wine exports, however, developed unfavourably. Here, the English wine duties were very high even in 1913, being about 40–55% for the more expensive Spanish and Portuguese wines (according to alcoholic content), and between 150% and 350% for the cheaper Greek wines.[1]

After the War England raised her wine duties considerably, so that for Greek exports between 1927 and 1931 they reached a height between 300% and 900%, for Spanish and Portuguese exports between 75% and 200%, and as much as 1000% in the year 1931.[2] Those enormous duties had the effect, in conjunction with the economic crisis, of practically preventing Greek and Spanish wine exports to England in 1931, and inflicting heavy losses on the Portuguese exports.

Between 1931 and 1933 England's importance as a market for Spanish and Portuguese exports remained unchanged. In the case of Portuguese exports to England the absolute figure of exports was almost the same as in 1931, but Spain recorded a sharp absolute decline in 1933, which, however, did not exceed the general reduction in her total exports.[3]

(bb) *France as a Market for the Three Countries*

In spite of her own wine surplus, France was an important customer of all three States, before and after the War—in the case of Spain, even the largest customer for wines and other

---

[1] This did not check exports to England, in view of the high English purchasing power.

[2] The falling gold price of Spanish and Portuguese wines in pesetas and escudos which were considerably below the gold parity helped to bring about this rise, English duties on wine being specific ones.

[3] Data of the geographical distribution of Greece's exports of 1933 were not available.

exports [1] until 1931, when she was supplanted in this position by England, largely owing to the French wine tariff policy. Although the French wine duties were considerably high in 1913 and 1927 (on Greek wines about 50% and 44–88%, on Spanish 37% and 19–33%), heavy increases between 1929 and 1931 raised them to 60–120% for Greek and 100–200% for Spanish wines. In addition to which there was the French prohibition of wine mixing of December 1929, before referred to.[2] This policy had almost paralysed Greece's as well as Spain's wine exports to France by 1931.[3]

It was also largely responsible for the severe set-back in Spain's total exports to France and aroused great resentment in Spain.[4] This unfavourable trend in Spanish exports was also influenced by the rise of the French duties on the other Spanish agrarian exports in 1931, due, except in the case of wine, more to the fall in prices than to an increase in rates. In 1913 and 1927 the French actual tariff level for all Spanish agrarian exports was about 17–20%, in 1931, 35–61%. In contrast to Spain, Portugal was able to develop her export trade with France in the post-War period to a remarkable extent, as the chief item in this trade—tinned fish—was subject to much lower duties between 1927 and 1931 than in 1913, and even the Portuguese exports of more expensive wines were less hit by the French duties and the wine mixing prohibition, and steadily expanded. Up to recent times (1934) France has not recovered her place as the largest market for Spanish goods. In 1933 the French relative share was the same as in 1931. On the other hand, Portugal's exports to France have suffered severely since 1931, owing to French quota restrictions, etc., so that in 1933 they were only half the figures of 1931.

---

[1] This is explained by the general custom of mixing French with foreign wines.

[2] See p. 68 of this study.

[3] Spanish wine exports to France declined from 152 Mill. pesetas in 1929 to 45 Mill. pesetas in 1931.

[4] See *Jones*, op. cit., pp. 47 et seq.

(cc) *Germany as a Market for the Three Countries*

Germany was Greece's second best, and Spain's and Portugal's third-best, customer in the post-War period, an important market especially for the wines of all three countries. Before the War, the German duties on the agrarian products of these countries were fixed rather high [1] (for wine 30–85%; for Greek fruit and tobacco 40–50%), but fell considerably in 1927 (to about 20–30% for all goods, owing to a sharp upward trend in prices; the height of the wine duties remaining unchanged). After the beginning of the world economic crisis, this position changed for the worse as regards the exports of wine and tobacco, owing to heavy increases in the German duties during 1930 and 1931. By the latter year the tobacco duty for Greece had risen to about 63%, and wine duties for Greece and Spain to about 200–300%, whereas the duties on fruit continued to be low (9–23%). The result was a severe shrinkage in the exports of tobacco and wine in 1931, while the Spanish exports of fruit held their own. Between 1931 and 1933 Portuguese exports to Germany remained very stable, but Spanish exports to Germany declined somewhat more than Spanish total exports.

(dd) *Italy as a Market for Greece*

In the post-War period Italy developed from the small customer that she was in 1913 into an important buyer of Greek fruit, wines, and tobacco, Italian post-War duties on Greek exports with exception of the wine duties being much lower than those of 1913.[2]

Greek exports to Italy sustained considerable losses after the outbreak of the world economic crisis until 1931, but Italy's very important position as a market for Greek goods remained unimpaired.

[1] With exception of the low duties on Spanish fruit.
[2] On fruits, 1913, 60%; on wines, 50%; 1927–31, on fruit, 20–25%; on wines 100–120%.

(d) *General Trend of the Exports of the Three Countries,* 1913–34

By their composition and geographical distribution the exports of the three States were preserved until 1929 from severe injury by any protectionist tariff policy in their main European markets. Moreover, the tendency observable throughout Europe to eat more fruit and the currency devaluations which had taken place in Spain and Portugal, even before 1927, gave a special impetus to their export trade. After 1929 great increases in the wine and tobacco duties, combined with the fact that the consumption of such goods was peculiarly susceptible to any crisis, inflicted heavy losses on the exports of the three States. In the case of Spain in spite of a marked depreciation of her currency the development of exports was very unfavourable; her great export to the U.S.A. suffered heavy losses after the introduction of the American tariff of 1930, and the Spanish revolution of 1931 hampered foreign trade. Thanks to a progressive depreciation of the currency, Portugal's exports developed better, while Greece, with a stable currency, suffered substantial losses. The depreciation of the currency, which continued in Spain and Portugal even after 1931, and began in Greece in 1932, preserved the exports of the three countries from excessive declines in the following years (1933–34). The figures of 1934 showed that their exports exceeded the results of 1931 (Greece by 30%, Spain by 50%, and Portugal by 12%) and had reached about 70–85% of the figures of 1929 (see Table I of Appendix). These results were favourable, compared with the export position of the gold countries of industrial Europe or the Eastern and South-Eastern Border States of agrarian Europe.

SUMMARY: THE ECONOMIC INTEGRATION OF EUROPE UP TO 1931 AS AFFECTED BY EUROPEAN TARIFFS

(*See Tables B1–IV, IVA, B of Appendix*)

WITH the discussion of the export problems of the three Mediterranean countries we have concluded the series of detailed inquiries into the export structures and actual tariff levels of post-War Europe between 1927 and 1931.[1]

It is now possible to summarize the results of the third part of our inquiry, i.e. to give a more general answer to the question how European tariff policy affected the economic integration of Europe between 1927 and 1931.

A glance, however, at the very incomplete number of countries, groups, and classes of goods in Table B or D of actual tariff levels is sufficient to show that this cannot be adequately done with the aid of statistical inquiries into actual tariff levels alone.

At this stage of the inquiry, therefore, we must revert to what was elucidated in the analysis of the potential tariff levels in the second part.

Since the tariff policy of the single countries has been discussed in detail in the separate sections, we can now base our results on the figures of the *general* tariff levels.[2]

The years before the beginning of the world economic crisis in the autumn of 1929 and the period afterwards up to the

[1] No analysis has been made of Ireland's exports, as up to 1931 that country was mainly dependent on the English market which admitted Irish (agrarian) produce duty free. A discussion of the export position of Iceland, Albania, and European Turkey is also omitted, owing to the small importance of the export trade of these three countries.

[2] Statistically set forth in Table IVB of the Appendix.

end of the year 1931 must be sharply separated. The first period, in which, between 1925 and 1929, an extensive reconstruction of world and European economy took place, has been aptly called the "*Period of Reconstruction.*" [1] For this the figures of the tariff levels of 1927 were taken as representative figures. The second period (autumn of 1929 to end of 1931) in which the world economic crisis began in ever-increasing degree to shake the economic foundations of first a few and then almost all European States, could only be called the "*Period of Destruction.*"

1. *The Period of Reconstruction, 1925–29*

Among the most important results of the investigations of *Gaedicke* and *von Eynern* was the conclusion that "in the rebuilding of European Integration after the War only gradual dislocations occurred, which could alter in no wise the fundamental equilibrium within European trade relationships," and that the political disintegration by the peace treaties of economic areas which were compact in 1913 "did not go nearly as far as might have been expected from the disruption of great European markets, and the consequent mutual exclusion, prompted by attempts at self-sufficiency." "During the years which immediately preceded the outbreak of the world economic crisis, there was obviously a tendency to restore the conditions existing before the War." [2] These conclusions applied to the trend of trade between 1925 and 1929.

If we compare the figures of the general tariff levels in 1927 with those of 1913, these conclusions of Gaedicke and von Eynern can only be confirmed by the reservation of important changes (plainly perceptible even in 1927 or 1929) in the tariff situation of Europe compared with 1913 so far as the European tariffs of the period of reconstruction were concerned.

[1] *Alfred Weber*, in Preface to *Gaedicke, Vol. of Text*, p. v.
[2] *Gaedicke, Vol. of Text*, p. 125.

In industrial Europe the most important changes consisted of the appearance of very appreciable English industrial duties on goods which entered duty free in 1913 and of the almost general rise of the duties on industrial finished goods causing a rise of the general tariff levels of Germany, Italy, Czechoslovakia, and Switzerland. In agrarian Europe they consisted of a heavy rise of general tariff levels throughout the European East, South-East, and in Spain, effected mainly by the sharp increases in industrial duties.

Thus, in spite of the rebuilding of the economic pre-War integration of Europe, the close observer became aware of dangerous tendencies in the growing protectionism of many European countries, even in the period of reconstruction, especially in connection with certain groups of goods. The level of world prices, however, of this period, which in 1927 and 1929 was respectively 39·2% and 36·5% higher than that of 1913 according to calculations of the "Deutsche Reichsstatistische Amt," [1] and the favourable export positions of all those branches of agriculture and industry which catered for specific post-War needs, spread a kind of veil over these dangerous fractures in the edifice of European integration now in course of rebuilding.

2. The Period of Destruction, 1929–31

Since the memorable collapse of the New York exchange in the autumn of 1929 a heavy fall in prices, first of world agrarian commodities then of the industrial ones also, set in which by 1931 had deflated the world agrarian price level, and by 1932–33 the whole price level of world trade commodities to such an extent as to exclude all comparisons drawn from modern economic history. Assuming the period 1925–29 to be 100, world agrarian prices fell from 98·4% in the year 1927 to 48·2% in 1931, that is by more than 50%, the index of world industrial prices during the same period from 92·9% to 60·8%, that is by 34·5%. [2]

[1] Comp. *Stat. Jahrbuch*, 1934, p. 121.   [2] *Ibid.*, p. 144.

This development with ever-increasing severity destroyed that veil which had concealed the rise in European tariffs during the period of reconstruction. The example of some Swedish tariff levels shows the rises in tariffs that this fall in prices would occasion in 1931, with specific duties remaining unaltered. This is also shown by the rapid automatic growth of all those tariff levels in Border Europe where duty rates were changed very little after 1929.[1]

But the unusually violent and swiftly growing agrarian protectionism of the industrial states of Central Europe [2] was still more disastrous to the economic integration of Europe between 1929 and 1931 than the above-mentioned development.

It was mainly the increases in the agrarian duties which were responsible for the enormous rise in the general tariff levels recorded in 1931 in industrial Europe.[3]

Until the autumn of 1931 the existence of a large English market still almost duty free formed a corrective of great importance to the industrial as well as the agrarian countries of Europe, which was plainly expressed in the growth of England's importance as a market for nearly all European States.[4]

With England's departure from the Gold Standard in September 1931, far-reaching changes in the economic integration of Europe began to be discernible, compared with the picture presented by Gaedicke and von Eynern for the period till 1929. These were due to a large extent to the European tariff policy between 1929 and 1931. Recalling the division of Europe into the two great spheres of integration—that of the industrial countries of Central Europe among each other and that of industrial Europe with the agrarian Border Europe

[1] See the figures for Hungary, Yugoslavia, Spain, etc., in Tables IVA–B of the Appendix.

[2] Great Britain and Belgium excluded.

[3] Extreme industrial protection played a large part only in the case of Italy and Czechoslovakia.

[4] This also applied to a lesser degree to the free-trade markets of Scandinavia, Belgium, and Holland.

as well as the subdivisions of the latter into several spheres—
these changes may be summarized as follows:—

1. The sphere of economic integration of the industrial
countries was menaced by the new English tariff of 1931–32,
by drastic Italian and Czech industrial protection with a far-
reaching loss of these three countries as markets, concealed in
1931 in the case of England by large coverings in anticipation
of the coming duties. Among the remaining states, industrial
exports which were still liable on the whole to moderate duties
kept up fairly well. So far as these countries had any substantial agrarian exports (corn, sugar, or wines) they had been
extensively destroyed by 1931.

2. The connections between Central and Border Europe
were to a large extent threatened, on the one hand, by the new
agrarian protectionism of Central Europe; this was a serious
menace to the exports of the Eastern and South-Eastern
countries to Germany, Austria, Czechoslovakia. On the
other hand, the industrial protectionism of the Eastern and
South-Eastern countries as well as of Spain inflicted extensive
damage to the industrial exports of industrial Central Europe.

3. The integration of the northern and north-eastern
countries and of Holland with Germany and England, based
chiefly upon the exchange of timber and timber products,
dairy produce, and meat for industrial products was well
maintained up to 1931, duties on these articles still remaining
moderate.

4. Lastly, the trend of trade between the three Mediterranean
Border States and industrial Europe (England, Germany, and
France) remained relatively favourable, as one of the most
important export groups of these countries, Southern fruit,
was less hit by duties.

These conclusions regarding the economic integration of
Europe at the end of 1931 show how within a period of only
two and a half years (1929–31) its painfully gained restoration
to the pre-War level could be shaken to its foundations and
threatened with far-reaching disaster, so that at the end

of 1931 the complete destruction of the economic unity of Europe seemed no longer impossible.

Large parts, however, of the inter-European trade relations were still intact in this year in spite of an extreme tariff policy. The worst happened during the next years (1932–35). Then the fruits of the protectionist policy of 1929–31 ripened. From the following description of the main tendencies of European commercial policy up to 1931, and from the sketch of the evolution of trade policy between 1932 and 1935, it will be realized to what extent much that has happened in Europe and overseas up to the present time was implicit in the events of the years 1929–31 and prepared by the commercial policy of this period.

VII

CONCLUDING CHAPTER: TENDENCIES AND DANGERS OF EUROPEAN POST-WAR TARIFF POLICY

THE strength of the protectionist forces of post-War Europe and their influence upon European commercial policy has been revealed by the detailed inquiries of the second and third part of this study. If, however, we want to understand the underlying motives of this policy and the dangers connected with it, it will be useful to mention the anti-protectionist forces which sought to impede the actual course of events. This could best be done by giving a general description of the most important collective actions in the field of commercial policy which were taken in Geneva between 1927 and 1931 under the auspices of the League of Nations. Up to 1931 tariffs were the most important instrument of the international commercial policy of nearly all European countries ; tariff policy was of such importance for all states that its analysis could not fail to cast light upon essential problems of their *general* economic policy. This can be shown by numbers and weight, of those factors which must be enumerated in order to understand the nature of European commercial policy.

In support of the contention that many elements of the present (beginning of 1936) European and world situation were already implicit in the state of affairs in 1931, a general sketch of European commercial policy and its effects upon the European situation between 1932 and 1935 must be added to the description of the course of events up to 1931. This summary will be followed by a survey of the most important factors of European tariff policy.

Our inquiry will end with an outline of the great dangers of such a policy for Europe and the world.

1. *Outlines of European post-War Tariff Policy*

(a) *Course of Development up to the Outbreak of the World Economic Crisis* (1929)

The outcome of the World War in the year 1919 left European economy in a state of complete anarchy. This lasted about six years until, after numerous difficulties, in the year 1925 Europe entered upon a period of tolerably stable economic conditions, during which the restoration to which we have already referred was carried out, although under political and economic conditions which were fundamentally different.

This fact, however, as well as the extremely slow removal of obstacles to trade, such as import prohibitions, quotas, etc. (then regarded as abnormal post-War emergency measures), alarmed free-trade circles of all countries in Europe concerned for the development of international trade. Their decisive counter-attack was the *World Economic Conference* of 1927, carefully prepared by the best economic experts of the world, who, however, were not armed with plenipotentiary powers. The reports prepared for this Conference, the debates both in full session and committees, and lastly the report of the Conference itself, to which fifty nations sent delegates, constitute a broad survey of the economic situation in post-War Europe.[1] The Conference was unanimous in condemning all obstacles which impeded the development of international trade, and regarded the European industrial tariffs which were much higher than the pre-War tariffs as the most dangerous of such obstacles. A recovery of world economy and a lessening of the dangerous political tension in Europe could only be hoped from an increasing turnover in foreign trade. The sum and substance of the Conference discussions may perhaps be best summarized in the famous sentence of the final report, which was adopted unanimously:

---

[1] See *Report and Proceedings of the World Economic Conference,* hereafter cited as *W.E.C.* 27, I, II.

"The main conclusion to be drawn from this work of the Conference in the field of commercial policy is that the time has come to put a stop to the growth of customs tariffs and to reverse the direction of the movement." [1]

The Conference recommended the reduction of autonomous tariff rates, the lowering of tariff levels by commercial treaties and collective agreements. . . . In the years 1927–28 these recommendations influenced the character of numerous European commercial treaties, by which the duties on semi- and wholly-finished goods, but not so much the agrarian duties, were consolidated. A lowering of the autonomous tariffs or a really drastic reduction in conventional rates, on the other hand, was not brought about, and tariff levels remained, as the foregoing inquiry has shown, mostly above pre-War levels.

This half-hearted attempt to carry out the recommendations so enthusiastically adopted by the Conference in 1927 soon aroused alarm among the most experienced economists in Europe, especially as the signs of a turn in the trade cycle were visible in 1929. The Economic Committee of the League of Nations pressed for more collective action for the lowering of tariff walls. It was characteristic of the situation that the committee appointed by the Council of the League to make preparations for fresh economic action was obliged to confess in its report to the latter (September 1929):

"We are now nearing the end of 1929 and are obliged to admit that in spite of a few sporadic efforts no decisive movement has occurred in this direction." [2]

In the assembly of the League of Nations in 1929 such statesmen as *Stresemann, Briand,* and others were visibly alarmed at the situation, especially in view of the growing American industrial competition in Europe; *Stresemann* advocated "a new European economy as the basis of a new

---

[1] See *W.E.C.* 27, I, p. 39.
[2] See *Proceedings of the Preliminary Conference*, pp. 78, 367, hereafter cited as *Proc.* I.

European peace policy " ;[1] *Briand* produced his plan for the economic unification of Europe, which became the subject of futile negotiations in Geneva in 1930–31. The Assembly adopted a resolution, which instructed the Economic Committee to summon a conference in the beginning of 1930, at which a tariff truce of two to three years should be concluded. The commercial convention to be entered into was "to inaugurate an era of peace and stability."[2]   Meanwhile the collapse of the New York Stock Exchange in September 1929 announced the beginning of the general economic crisis.

(b) *The Course of Events in* 1930 *and* 1931

From the 17th February to the 24th March 1930 the Economic Conference, summoned to give effect to the tariff truce idea of 1929, met in Geneva. Thirty states sent delegates with full powers, seven (including the U.S.A.) only observers. The result of the Conference was a draft of a trade convention, the chief clause of which consisted in the obligation imposed on all parties not to denounce any of their commercial treaties at present in force before the 1st April 1931, thereby protecting the consolidated part[3] of their tariff rates from increases, and only to increase duties "in cases of emergency" and after previous notice. In November 1930 a later conference was to meet, which was to give practical effect to this convention.   The Convention of March 1930 was signed by all the important states of Europe.[4]

This Conference of the Spring of 1930 signified a complete abandonment of the tariff truce idea of 1929, which had aimed at the stabilization of tariff rates for two to three years. Nine months of world economic crisis, which meant in the first

---

[1] See *Proc.* I., p. 78, and *Hauser*, op. cit., pp. 240 et seq.

[2] See *Proc.* I., p. 377.

[3] The free-trade states of Europe, which had entered into no tariff conventions, were to undertake not to raise their autonomous tariffs.

[4] See text of Trade Convention in *Proc.* I, pp. 19–24.

place a world agrarian crisis, had sufficed to show that many of the States of Europe were by no means prepared to fix their autonomous rates, especially not the agrarian rates.

How deeply the free-trade States of Europe were disappointed by this dilution of the 1929 idea was shown by the warning of the English Minister, Mr. *Graham*, against an "ample" interpretation of the emergency tariff clause, which would frustrate the collective action.[1] If England, nevertheless, signed, it was only to keep alive tendencies which aimed at lowering tariffs. For the serious fall in prices had strengthened the desire for tariffs or protectionism even in countries which were largely on a free-trade basis.[2] Before the summoning of the second Conference of 1930, questionnaires concerning the main problems of their foreign trade position were sent to all countries. The answers to these questions in the form of reports to the League of Nations contained valuable informations about difficulties of the commercial policy of the single States.

Before this second Conference of 1930 met, the ever deepening economic crisis prompted the Assembly of the League of Nations of September 1930 to empower the Conference not only to set in force the Convention, but to take "concerted economic action."[3] Meanwhile, the menacing economic situation in the Eastern and South-Eastern agrarian States of Europe had driven the latter to hold an *agrarian conference* in Warsaw (August 1930), at which the eight states represented (Baltic States, South-Eastern States, Poland and Czechoslovakia), by a resolution of the 30th August 1930, announced the common organization of their agrarian foreign trade policy and requested the grant of agrarian preferential duties by their chief European markets.[4]

On the 17th November 1930 the second International

[1] See *Proc.* I, pp. 87, 99, and 126.

[2] See Graham's speech on the 14th March 1930, *Proc.* I, p. 127.

[3] See *Proc.* of the second conference with a view . . ., p. 9, cited as *Proc.* II.

[4] Text of resolution, *Proc.* II, pp. 211–213.

Economic Conference of that year met presided over by the Dutch delegate, Dr. *Colijn*. Only twenty-six European States had sent delegates with full powers. The subjects of the Conference were:

1. To set in force the Convention of the Spring of 1930.
2. The problem of agrarian preferences.
3. The decision upon two proposals for lowering tariffs, one of which was contained in the Memorandum of the English Government, and the other in that of the Dutch Government to the League of Nations.

England, who together with all free-trade states, with Germany and Switzerland, regarded high tariffs as the decisive obstacle to foreign trade, while France and Italy laid great stress on indirect protectionism, proposed a general reduction of the duties of all countries on certain groups of commodities, at first on textiles and machinery. Holland recommended the granting of tariff concessions by the protectionist states, in return for assurances by the free-trade countries to maintain their free-trade policies.[1]

The result of the Conference again was completely abortive. A fresh arrangement was made, by virtue of which a second session of the Conference was to determine the date when the convention would come into force. For in view of the small number of states which were prepared to ratify, no date could then be fixed. Neither the English nor the Dutch proposal was accepted, as important countries, like France, Poland, and the South-Eastern States, were not prepared to fix their industrial tariffs, while no great industrial country was willing to stabilize, let alone reduce, its agrarian duties. The problem of agrarian preferences was to be re-examined without delay, and without provoking conflicts with the most favoured overseas states. It appeared that none of the European States with important overseas exports (e.g. England, Italy, Holland, Sweden, and Switzerland) was prepared to offend its customers

---

[1] See in *Proc.* II, the proposals of England, pp. 132–133, and of Holland, p. 190.

outside Europe and provoke them into retaliatory measures by granting preferences to European agrarian countries.[1]

The Dutch delegate, Mr. *Nederbragt*, uttered the warning that "Holland, the last fortress of the liberal régime, would be destroyed and forced to abandon her policy"; the Danish delegate prophesied similar things for the policy of all free-trade countries, in addition to strengthened industrial protection in the agrarian countries in answer to the agrarian protection of the industrial countries.[2] Dr. *Colijn* feared a "general tariff war." [3]

From the 16th to the 18th March 1931, at the second session of this Conference, the attempt was again made at least to put the Convention of the Spring of 1930 into force.[4] As only twelve countries had ratified, and these were not prepared to put the Convention into force even among themselves, the whole attempt failed.[5] Thus in the Spring of 1931 all the attempts made on the initiative of the League of Nations Assembly of the Autumn of 1929, to give effect to the urgent exhortations of the World Economic Conference of 1927 to effect a reversal in tariff policy ended in a complete fiasco. At the concluding session Dr. *Colijn* drew up the balance of the European commercial policy between 1927 and 1931 in the following memorable words: "All would agree that on looking back over the four years since 1927 the efforts to carry out the recommendations of the World Economic Conference of 1927 had entirely failed." [6] In the final protocol of the Conference thirteen European States acknowledged "that they were unable to agree upon a date for putting the commercial convention into force." [7]

[1] See Memoranda of the states concerned, pp. 178, 191, 225, 227.
[2] See *Proc.* II, pp. 48–49, 141.
[3] *Proc.* II, pp. 48–49, 90.
[4] See *Proc.* of the second conference with a view to concerted economic action. Geneva (*Proc.* III).
[5] Ibid., pp. 8, 18.
[6] Comp. *Proc.* III, p. 36.
[7] Ibid., p. 8.

Meanwhile, the bilateral negotiations for lowering tariffs, recommended by the Economic Conference in November 1930, had been begun. Two attempts of the year 1931 deserve mention. First the conclusion of the preferential treaties between Germany, Austria, and France, on the one hand, and a number of South-Eastern States, on the other. The industrial states expressed their readiness to import certain quantities of South-Eastern corn at preferential duties, provided no objection was raised from overseas. The most hopeful of these attempts, the treaties with Germany, failed, as the acquiescence of the overseas most favoured agrarian countries could not be obtained.[1] More radical was the project of the Austro-German Customs Union which surprised Europe in March 1931, and which had to be abandoned in September 1931, owing to political opposition, chiefly from France and Italy. The considerable worsening of the economic situation in 1931 led very quickly to that general European tariff war predicted by Dr. *Colijn* in 1930, which after the abandonment of the Gold Standard in England and Scandinavia culminated in a general competition for the most successful import-hampering measures *besides* tariffs. The last months of the year 1931 found Europe in a state of extensive commercial isolation, either already accomplished or in course of preparation.

(c) *The Course of Events in the Recent Past* (1932–35)

The year 1932 and the first half of 1933 brought a further intensification of the commercial struggle. There were not only fresh increases in the duties on agricultural and industrial products, some of them of unprecedented dimensions,[2] throughout Europe (and in numerous overseas states), but practically all European States proceeded to employ the oft-mentioned much more drastic new weapons of commercial

[1] See *Greiff*, op. cit., pp. 20–23.
[2] *World Economic Survey*, 1933–34, p. 203, quoted as *Survey* II.

war, in such a degree as to surpass all that happened in European post-War commercial policy, even in the first post-War years.[1]

The denunciation of numerous commercial treaties, based upon the most-favoured nation principle, or their supersession by the discriminatory application of new methods of commercial warfare, signified a general departure from the previous collective and international attitude towards foreign trade and an approach to the regional or bilateral principle; this was the logical consequence of the tendency towards self-sufficiency, which was welcomed in strongly nationalist states, and in other countries regarded as inevitable and enforced.

In vain the still relatively liberal countries of Holland and Belgium attempted to stem the protectionist flood in Europe by concluding the Convention of *Ouchy* in February 1933 by which they undertook to lower their tariffs gradually, inviting other States to join them. As no other European State signed the Convention, the attempt completely failed.[2]

The rapid progress of the world crisis, in particular the alarmingly swift fall in the volume and values of world trade in 1932–33, led in 1933 to a new attempt by all the forces in the world which were convinced of the vital importance of a revival of foreign trade. Strongly supported by President *Roosevelt*, the English Government invited all the states in the world to send delegates to a World Economic Conference in London.[3] From the 12th June 1933 to the 27th July 1933 the ministers and delegates of sixty-six states sought ways and means of ending the appalling crisis. On Mr. *Roosevelt's* initiative, a tariff truce was concluded for the duration of the Conference, the states undertaking not to increase duties nor to impose fresh restrictions on trade.[4] The aim of the Conference was described by the King of England on the occasion of its

[1] See *Survey* I, p. 197.
[2] Ibid., p. 195.
[3] See proceedings of the Monetary Conference, 33, in *League of Nations Journal*, Nos. 1–39, cited as *W.E.C.* 33.
[4] *Survey* I, p. 196; *W.E.C.* 33, p. 22.

ceremonial opening in the following terms: "It cannot be beyond the power of man so to use the vast resources of the world as to ensure the material progress of civilization."[1]

The existing economic situation could not be improved until two great problems were solved, and these problems were described by Mr. *Colijn*, the Dutch Prime Minister, as being so closely interconnected "that they formed a single complex of questions": the stabilization of currencies and the removal of intolerable hindrances to trade.[2] All the discussions then in reality turned upon these problems.[3]

Exactly as in 1927 all the delegates declared in favour of international trade and against economic nationalism and protection. Despite this universal condemnation of protectionist economic policy, the Conference failed completely, because the stabilization of currencies, which was a *conditio sine qua non* for the gold countries, was defeated by the opposition of America and England, which held that the time was not yet ripe for such a step.[4] Again it was Dr. *Colijn* who frankly admitted the negative result of the Conference and justifiably recalled his previous warnings.[5]

The failure of the Conference was swiftly followed by the denunciation of the tariff truce by all states, and fresh increases of duties in Europe, even in the free-trade countries of Belgium and Holland; but such increases were no longer so great as during the preceding years. The new outbreak of economic nationalism, so lately the subject of general condemnation, found expression rather in the ever-growing tendency to conclude bilateral trade agreements by way of exchange clearings and quotas, which has so much determined the

[1] *W.E.C.* 33, p. 8.
[2] Ibid., p. 30.
[3] The collateral discussions regarding restrictive plans for wheat, wine, etc., were of secondary importance.
[4] See the remarks of the French Minister, Bonnet, of the German Delegate, Posse, and of the Italian Minister, Jung, in *W.E.C.* 33, pp. 133, 160, 230.
[5] Comp. *W.E.C.* 33, p. 229.

aspect of European commercial policy in the recent past (1934–36), and which, by the deliberate destruction of the most-favoured nation principle and the triangular trade, has caused further severe reductions in the foreign trade of many European States and in world trade.[1]

In this state of general trade paralysis, the greater part of Europe has persisted to the present day (beginning of 1936), and this gloomy situation is only relieved by the much freer commercial intercourse between the Scandinavian countries, adhering to the Sterling Block, and England.

(d) The Result of the European Trade Policy of 1932–35

A glance at the development of the economic situation in Europe in the four years between 1932 and 1936 seems to show that in many of the countries of Europe there has been a decided upward movement from the depths of the depression reached in 1932–33. A somewhat closer analysis, however, and reflection upon the most important foundations of this recovery must arouse serious apprehensions regarding this interpretation of the present state of Europe and the world (beginning of 1936).

The first symptom, which raises grave doubts as to how far the crisis has been really overcome, is the visible discrepancy between the higher figures of home trade revival and the considerably less favourable growth of exports.

This discrepancy, supplemented by corresponding reduced import figures, is reflected in the picture of the further decay of European foreign trade between 1932 and 1935, and is a process which was repeated in the trend of world trade. From 68·6 Milld. gold dollars in 1929 the latter fell to 26·9 Milld. in 1932 and 23·4 Milld. in 1934, i.e. by 61% and 66% respectively, to no more than 34% of the value of 1929. In the first quarter of 1935 it reached only 33%.[2]

[1] *World Economic Survey*, 1934–35, pp. 179–181, hereinafter cited as *Survey* III.

[2] See *Survey* III, pp. 157–158.

This enormous reduction of world trade between 1929 and 1935 [1] could not be surprising, in view of the trade policy above described.

Assuming that the duties in force in 1931 had not been raised in Europe between 1932 and 1933, then, by a very rough calculation, *European specific duties would have been 25% higher at the commencement of 1934 than the figures of tariff levels here submitted for* 1931, owing only to the fall in the world price level from 100·8 in 1931 (1913 = 100) to 75 in 1933.[2]

However, not only were duties further increased between 1932 and 1935, but numerous additional restrictions were imposed upon imports, and the result of this destructive policy was that the foreign trade of many European States became a mere exchange of absolutely indispensable commodities, and dropped to a minimum never before known. Consequently, the crisis was "overcome" only to the extent of the home trade revival, except in the Sterling countries.[3] This was also reflected in the considerable discrepancy shown by the index figures for the quantitative trends of world trade and world production in the agrarian and industrial spheres, as Table B, p. 358, shows.

In view of the vital importance of exports to many branches of agrarian and industrial production, it is permissible to entertain serious doubts as to the solidity of these national economic recoveries in Europe, and to endorse the warning words of Professor *Robbins* that "it is impossible to feel any confidence in a continuance of stability" (1934)[4] or of the 1935 Report of the League of Nations on world economic conditions "that the recovery thus registered has been superficial rather than fundamental" and "without a truce to currency and trade manœuvring the limits of recovery may

[1] Even reckoned in paper pounds world trade in 1934 had lost 45% of its 1929 value.
[2] See *Stat. Jb. f. d. dt. Reich*, 1934, p. 121.
[3] See *Survey* III, p. 10.
[4] Comp. *Robbins, The Great Depression*, 1934, pp. 195–196.

prove narrow," "until some significant expansion of international trade is achieved, there will remain a hard core of unemployment in practically every industrial country." [1]

TABLE B: QUANTITATIVE DEVELOPMENT OF WORLD TRADE AND WORLD PRODUCTION, 1929–34

If 1929 = 100, world trade and world production amounted to:

Year	Agrarian products		Raw materials, semi-finished goods		Finished goods	
	W.T.	W.P.	W.T.	W.P.	W.T.	W.P.
1932	89·5	102·0	81·0	80·5	58·0	62·0
1934	84·5	98·5	88·0	89·5	64·0	75·5

W.T. = World Trade.
W.P. = World Production.
See *World Production and Prices*, p. 94.

This serious view of the European situation at the beginning of 1936 is reinforced by a consideration of the main factors which have caused the strong revival of the home trade since 1933. Two chief factors may be mentioned: First, the incurring of enormous *public debts* in order to lower unemployment, a policy which has been pursued, e.g. by Germany, Italy, and Belgium.[2] Much could be said for this policy in the countries concerned, in view of the widespread unemployment, but the necessary supplement was a corresponding revival of private enterprise, which again increased foreign trade especially in those densely populated European States where adequate supplies of raw materials are lacking.

The second source of the national recoveries of many countries is the *large armaments* expanding month by month since 1933.[3] In view of such conditions many doubts must be expressed about the economic situation of all those countries

[1] Comp. *Survey* III, pp. 7, 10, 11.
[2] Comp. *Survey* II, pp. 25–29, 31; III, pp. 35–37.
[3] Comp. *Survey* III, pp. 201, 272–273; Further: *Remarks on the Present Phase of International Economic Relations*, p. 20, cited as *Remarks*.

which are believed to have overcome the crisis merely by the revival of the home markets without any signs of a strong recovery in their imports and exports.

2. Decisive Factors of European Post-War Tariff Policy

PRELIMINARY REMARK : *The Gulf between Theory and Practice*

In the year 1927 the leading economists and statesmen of the whole world, at the World Economic Conference, condemned protectionist tariff policy and warned the peoples of the earth of its dangerous consequences. Nearly all the governments which applauded the exhortations of the Conference to lower tariffs did next to nothing during the following $2\frac{1}{2}$ years to carry out these recommendations, and during the subsequent period of $3\frac{1}{2}$ years up to the middle of 1933 waged a trade war which assumed increasingly sharper forms year by year.

In the summer of 1933 the plenipotentiaries of sixty-six states of the earth again uttered a unanimous warning against the disastrous consequences of protectionism and economic nationalism, only, immediately after the failure of the World Economic Conference, to adopt a much more drastic trade policy lasting until most recent times (1936), the fearful results of which may be observed in the figures of the fettered world trade of 1935.

How is such a gulf between theory and practice possible? In order to understand this contradiction it may be useful to specify the most powerful motives which lay behind this policy and frustrated all anti-protectionist efforts.

The great intricacy of the capitalist national economies, expressed not only in an increasing interdependence of all their parts, but also in the ever-tightening bonds of the common economic fate of all the peoples of the earth, made it impossible to achieve any more than a brief survey of the driving forces of European tariff policy, so that only the most important features could be mentioned.

(a) *Differences in Costs of Production as Causes of Tariff Policy*

If "foreign trade is determined by the different structures and conditions of production and consumption in various countries,"[1] we must seek the foundations of protective tariffs in Europe in the purpose to equalize partially or, in the case of prohibitive duties, entirely these differences of production. In other words, these duties are intended to equalize productivity of labour, land, and capital of a national economy with the superior productivity of other countries, with which the former may enter into commercial relations.

The partial adjustment of higher costs of production was the main purpose of all European pre-War tariffs, and has also remained so in the post-War period, although after 1919, especially after the outbreak of the world economic crisis, other reasons for the tariff policy of many states emerged. Into this category of partial or entire adjustment of differences in costs of production fell, for example, most of the industrial post-War duties imposed by many of the agrarian and industrial countries of Europe in order to develop new industries and to protect these from the competition of old industries. This category also includes the high agrarian duties imposed by the industrial countries after the onset of the world economic crisis, to save their agriculture from the dangerous competition of the best European and overseas agrarian producers, as well as many important industrial duties, either newly imposed or increased, before and after 1929, by the European industrial states to combat superior American mass production (e.g. duties on motor-cars).

What was involved in these proceedings, both in the agrarian and in the industrial sphere, is the use of tariffs as a weapon against *technical progress*, of which it has been justly said that it has brought about a second "industrial revolution" in the post-War period.

---

[1] Comp. *Enquête*, II, p. 16.

The great and swiftly progressing fall in prices of many important commodities during only one post-War decade which it made possible was more startling in the agrarian than in the industrial sphere. Its result in the tariff field was, on the one hand, numerous duty increases by countries which, for various reasons, were backward in technical progress; on the other hand, this phenomenon produced one of the most disturbing features of post-War tariff policy, viz. the much shorter duration of commercial treaties. Even in 1927 both Dr. *Colijn* and Mr. *Runciman*, who was to become President of the Board of Trade, called attention to the instability of commercial treaties, as contrasted with the pre-War treaties which were mostly valid for twelve years.[1]   If numerous trade agreements lasted for a period between three and five years up to the outbreak of the world economic crisis, since 1932 the period has mostly been no more than one to two years, and although political considerations connected with exchange control may have played a big part in this drastic curtailment of the terms, con&iderable importance must be ascribed to the fear to consolidate rates of duty for a longer time because they might quickly become inadequate in a world of rapid technical progress.[2]

(b) *Monetary Factors as Causes of Tariff Policy*

The great changes which have developed in the sphere of currencies and international indebtedness during the post-War period have exerted a deep influence upon the shaping of European tariff policy.[3]   The collapse of most of the currencies of Europe immediately after the War, the subsequent inflations followed by the stabilization of most of them upon an old or

[1] See speeches of Colijn and Runciman at World Economic Conference, 1927, in *W.E.C.*, 1927, I, pp. 70, 88.

[2] See Sir *Arthur Salter's* article, "Stabilization and Recovery," pp. 18–19 in *Foreign Affairs*, vol. xiv, 1, October 1935.

[3] Logically the duties discussed here belong to those mentioned in the preceding section to adjust differences in costs of production. The close connection of these duties, however, with mainly monetary ends, justifies their inclusion in a special section.

new gold parity between 1924 and 1927, led in numerous states to rapid duty increases, designed to maintain the gold value of the duties,[1] or to protect countries remaining on pre-War parity against the *valuta* dumping of the countries with devaluated currencies.

After the fresh outbreak of currency warfare in Europe (since September 1931), tariffs became a very important weapon, next to the new trade expedients, of the gold countries in meeting the competition of the European and overseas devaluation countries and protecting their currencies.[2]

The second factor of a mainly monetary kind which exerted a great influence upon the tariff policy was international (public and private) indebtedness. First the pressure of reparations, which since the Dawes Plan had actually represented for the greater part the payment of interallied War debts to the U.S.A. by Germany, considerably accentuated the pace of German agrarian tariff policy when the flow of international credits into Germany was stopped in the autumn of 1929. It was essential to cut Germany's agrarian import deficit, which then ran into milliards, in order to rectify the German balance of trade and provide the necessary foreign currency for reparations.

Further, a number of European agrarian states (e.g. Poland and Bulgaria), which were heavily indebted to foreign countries, based their policy of extreme tariff protection upon their obligation to cut all superfluous imports in order to maintain their balance of trade and consequently their currency, as, in the absence of "invisible exports," a deficit in their balance of trade was equivalent to a deficiency in their balance of payments.[3]

---

[1] A typical example of such duties and their being taken over as extremely high gold duties is provided by Germany after 1924–25. See pp. 115, 116 of this study.

[2] Comp. declaration of the German Delegate, Posse, on the World Economic Conference, 1933. *W.E.C.*, p. 133.

[3] See Memorandum of Bulgarian and Polish Governments to the League of Nations in *Proc.* II, pp. 134, 199. Recently *Viner*, loc.

In this connection, nothing has contributed more to the impeding of international trade relations and the reinforcement of European tariffs imposed for monetary reasons than the *American Tariff* of 1930, by which the greatest creditor nation in the world surrounded itself at the moment of severe crisis with the highest tariff walls in its history, intending to exclude entirely all imports.[1]

The recently published inquiry of the American, Mr. *Jones*, into the world-wide repercussions of this tariff, against which thirty-three states protested in Washington when it was being drafted,[2] shows that numerous industrial duty increases in Europe (Italy, Switzerland, and Spain) in 1931 were retaliatory measures against it. For Germany, obliged to achieve a large export surplus and already severely injured by European industrial protection, even when not directly aimed at her, this American Tariff signified a fresh and unprecedented accentuation of the trade depression.[3]

(c) *Population Problems as Causes of Tariff Policy*

The increasing restrictions which since the War have been imposed upon immigration into the sparsely peopled areas of the earth must be reckoned among the most important events of the post-War period.[4] The earliest step taken in this direction, bearing great political and economic consequences, the extensive stoppage of immigration chiefly from the Eastern and South-Eastern States of Europe to the

cit., pp. 73–77; *Pasvolsky*, Memoranda: *Comments on the Improvement of the Commercial Relations between Nations*, pp. 86–87; Prof. *Gregory's* survey, pp. 189, 194, 204, in *Carnegie Report*.

[1] See *Roosevelt: Looking Forward*, p. 186, and speech of State Secretary *Sayre* of 2nd July 1935 on tariff policy, quoted in *Remarks*, p. 28.

[2] *Roosevelt*, op. cit., p. 183.

[3] See *Haberler*, op. cit., p. 70.

[4] See an article by Professor *Robbins*: "The Nature of National Planning in the Sphere of International Business," pp. 8–9, and an article by L. *Hennebicq*: "La Crise et les Banquiers Anglais," in *Rev. Economic Inter.*, March 1936, pp. 536–537.

U.S.A. by the American law of 1924, was followed by similar impediments on immigration in Europe. These obstacles became quite general after the outbreak of the crisis, also spreading over countries hitherto regarded as most liberal States (France, Belgium, Holland).[1]

At the World Economic Conference of 1927 Sir Walter *Layton*, in his analysis of the European post-War situation, had impressively indicated the dangers for Europe which lurked in the decline of European annual overseas emigration from an average of $1-1\frac{1}{4}$ Mill. between 1911 and 1914 to 0·6 Mill. in 1924.[2] These immigration restrictions, applied by the most important settlement areas of the world, could not fail to have profound repercussions on the tariff policy of the traditional emigration countries of Europe—Italy, Poland, and the Balkan countries. Already in 1927 the Greek delegate, Mr. *Tournakis*, stated that the Balkan States were obliged to introduce industrial tariffs, in order to build up industries under their shelter, to give employment to the surplus population which before the War had an opportunity to emigrate, and the Italian delegate, Mr. *Nola*, justified Italian industrial tariffs on similar lines.[3] In 1930 the Polish Government again justified their industrial tariffs by pointing to the immigration barriers in Europe and overseas.[4]

It may be said that since the extensive embargo on agrarian imports by the great European industrial countries a considerable part of the retaliatory increases in industrial duties by agrarian Europe was likewise designed to build up home industries to absorb the unemployed agrarian population. In excluding the goods of these agrarian states the old European industrial countries were behaving towards them like the overseas settlement areas in excluding their people.

[1] Restrictions on foreign labour were imposed in Belgium in 1935 ; a new law to regulate foreign labour was introduced in Holland in 1936.

[2] See *W.E.C.*, 27, I, p. 107.

[3] See ibid., p. 163, and II, p. 69.

[4] See *Proc.* II, p. 197.

Another population motive behind the extreme agrarian tariff policy of certain industrial states since 1929 has been the desire to preserve the composition of the population by preventing the decay of the peasantry, or even strengthening that part of the population. This motive was inspired by national rather than economic considerations, in view of the great productive superiority of other countries. There are distinct indications of agrarian tariff policy being influenced by a social regard for the peasantry in several industrial states of Europe, e.g. Germany, France, Switzerland, etc.[1]

(d) *Military Factors as Causes of Tariff Policy*

In dealing with tariff policy inspired by a desire to maintain a peasantry our analysis has already touched upon non-economic motives behind European post-War tariff policy. A second group of such duties must be mentioned when enumerating the important causes of European tariff policy, because this has played and still plays a great part. These duties, which in detail can only be ascertained by having an exact knowledge of individual economic conditions, have been introduced by many States, in the interest of their military independence, and are proportional, so to speak, to their (real or supposed) political insecurity against the hazard of war. Their object is to develop in peace time those branches of production which are considered to be important for war. A classic example of such duties are the duties of the key industries imposed by England in 1921.[2] A considerable part of the almost generally high chemical duties must also be reckoned in this category, as well as the usually high duties on motor-cars, motors, electrical appliances, etc. It must be admitted that, in view of the increasingly totalitarian form of the modern war, the number of branches of a national economy to be considered as "vital" in a military sense might

[1] See Memorandum of the Swiss Government to the League, 1930, in *Proc.* II, p. 227.
[2] See p. 132 of this study.

be very large, according to its lack of self-sufficiency and the degree of political tension.[1] A great part of the protectionist agrarian tariff policy of a number of European agrarian deficit countries must be ascribed to the desire to be able to feed themselves in times of military danger.[2] These military reasons of tariffs were already recognized by the World Economic Conference of 1927,[3] but as the political tension has become much more acute in recent years, an increasing importance must be attributed to these factors in modern European tariff policy.

(e) *Fiscal Needs as Causes of Tariff Policy*

Lastly, because least important, we must revert to a purely economic motive behind European tariff policy, viz. to the financial needs of States which have steadily increased, especially since the War. Yet the raising of revenue by means of tariffs is the weakest motive for imposing or raising any of all those duties (constituting by far the majority of European duties) which were designed to cut imports as much as possible, and were therefore obviously opposed to revenue purposes. Revenue requirements were the most important motive only in the case of the steady increase in the duties on colonial produce, mineral oils, alcohol, etc., as well as the greatest obstacle to their reduction. In this connection, we must mention a number of small agrarian countries in Europe, whose finances were based so much on revenue from duties that they opposed, on financial grounds, every request to lower their tariffs, even proposals to abate their protectionist duties only (e.g. Bulgaria and Portugal).[4]

---

[1] See E. *Lederer's* article, "European Intern. Trade," in *The Annals*, July 1934, p. 110.

[2] See *Survey* III, p. 78; *Considerations*, p. 10; *Röpke*, loc. cit., pp. 46–47.

[3] See final report, *W.E.C.*, 27, I, p. 40.

[4] See Memorandum of Bulgarian Government to the League 1930, and speech of Portuguese Delegate in Second Econ. Conference, 1930, in *Proc.* II, pp. 134, 171.

Concluding Remark

With the mention of financial requirements as a cause of European post-War tariff policy our survey of some of its most important factors should conclude. To avoid misunderstanding, however, it should be emphasized that all or several of the tendencies enumerated might be simultaneously operative whenever one of the many thousand single duties was imposed or increased, so that it implies no contradiction if the same duties appear in several or all of the defined categories.

3. The Dangers of European Protectionism

PRELIMINARY REMARK : *Protectionism from the standpoint of free trade and the theory of location of industries*

European (and North American) protectionism in the post-War period is largely responsible [1] for the very serious economic position of Europe (beginning of 1936) which cannot be concealed by the substantial revival of trade in the Sterling countries as well as national recoveries in a number of gold countries.   In creating this serious situation tariffs have been assisted by other important causes, chiefly by the policy of agrarian and raw material restrictions, valorisations, and price agreements on the part of all the great economic Powers before and after 1929, all being measures designed to maintain a price level before and during the economic crisis, which, in view of technical progress in agriculture as well as in industry, was far too high up to 1931.[2]

In order to show some of the chief dangers of the position of present Europe (1936), it is desirable to recall the most important objections of the free-trade theory, as well as of the modern theory of the location of industry to protectionism.

[1] It goes without saying that other causes before the outbreak of the crisis, such as War debts and reparations, credit policy, political tension, etc., should not be overlooked.

[2] See the remarks in the *Macmillan Report*, p. 136, and *Robbins, The Great Depression*, pp. 48–49.

The substance of the free-trade theory is even to-day acknowledged to be indisputable by the overwhelming majority of all the scientific economists in the world.

As Sir *William Beveridge* defined it, the fundamental principle of free trade is as follows: The average productivity of all the labour of a country will be higher, that is to say, its standard of life will be higher, the more its efforts can be concentrated on those things it can do best. This is the purpose and justification of international trade and the fundamental reason for leaving trade as free as possible.[1]

According to the free-trade theory, the opposite policy of protection leads to a lowering of the standard of life of the nations who adopt it, and the various stages towards such impoverishment may be summarized as follows: Concentration of labour and capital in branches of industry which sell their products above world market prices, with consequent rise in the cost of living, especially in view of the interdependence of modern economic systems, pressure to protect more and more industries, shrinkage of imports of taxed goods, shrinkage of exports owing to lessened imports, unemployment in the export industries, gradual over-production in the protected trades, with consequent unemployment, and a pressure to grant subsidies or adopt fresh protective measures in their favour in a vicious circle.[2]

The contention of protectionist advocates that tariffs relieve the home labour market, either by fostering new industries until they no longer need protection or by protecting existing industries from undercutting, is rejected by free-trade theory for this reason: Even if this method of creating employment should afford such relief, and, in the case of a less elastic home demand, even lead to isolated booms and monopolistic gains, it still signifies no relief for the economic system and the labour market as a whole owing to the rise in the cost of

[1] Comp. Sir William Beveridge, *Tariffs*, pp. 41–42.
[2] See the analysis of protectionist policy in the first ten chapters contributed by Sir William Beveridge in the book just quoted, *Tariffs*.

living and the depression in other (export) trades. When employment can be created only by protection of this kind it is a sure symptom that the productivity of labour is a long way from its optimum. A steady decrease in the standard of living is the only condition under which in the long run this form of creation of employment is possible. If it be desired to protect infant industries, duties should be rejected because, *once introduced, they are never voluntarily relinquished by the interested parties*, and the struggle that rages around them is productive of corruption in political and economic life. The method of direct and strictly limited subsidies for such industries is decidedly to be preferred to them.[1]

The doctrines of free trade found extensive practical application only in the period between 1860 and 1880 when, after the pattern of the Franco-British Treaty negotiated by Cobden in 1860, Europe was covered with a network of free-trade agreements, and European foreign trade flourished accordingly. In view of the quoted figures of European tariff levels in the post-War period, particularly the high figures of 1931 and the much higher tariff walls of to-day, it is surprising to learn that after 1860 the European tariff levels could be reduced by these treaties to about 8–15% with a maximum of 25%.[2]

The theory of location of industry is likewise hostile to the claims of tariff protection, as is shown by its founder's— Prof. *Weber's*—article on "Theory of Location of Industries and Commercial Policy,"[3] which was published in 1911.

According to this theory industrial tariffs may be introduced, with a prospect of fostering new industries, where undeveloped

---

[1] See *Beveridge*, loc. cit., pp. 51, 61, 101, 103, and 121, on the question of a lowered standard of living under protection; also A. *Marshall's* Memorandum, *Zur Zollpolitischen Regelung des Aussenhandels*, p. 25.

[2] See *Nogaro*, op. cit., pp. 52 et seq.

[3] Comp. essay of Alfred Weber: "Die Standortslehre und die Handelspolitik," in *Archiv fuer Sozialwissenschaft u. Soz. Politik*, Bd. 32, pp. 667–688.

countries possess raw materials and all the natural and economic resources required for industrialization. The theory of location was able to designate certain industries in the old industrial countries of Europe to which dangerous competitors might arise from the application of tariffs by still little-developed industrial countries. In view of the notorious distribution of raw materials and coal deposits throughout the world, this could apply only to part of the old European industries of labour and consumption orientation. The bulk of the old European industries, the heavy industries of the transport orientation and the great mechanised industries with labour orientation (closely dependent on coal consumption) were hardly vulnerable, and consequently the advantages of their location were not threatened by tariff policy. No tariff could alter the distribution of coal deposits favourable for the development of new industries save in U.S.A. and China, and none but the highest tariffs could destroy the natural advantages of location of the old European industries.

Consequently, protective duties upon the products of these most important industries would lead to nothing but decreases in purchasing power, both in the exporting countries and in the protectionist states, without facilitating the organization of new industries.[1]

We shall try to give some illustrations taken from the economic development of Europe and the world since 1929 up to recent years (1934–35) which are alarming confirmations of these warnings.

(a) *Lowering of the Standard of Life*

Drastic agrarian protection has led to very high prices of important foodstuffs, and thus to a considerable increase in the cost of living in protectionist countries. Tables AI and AII, p. 371, give a few characteristic examples. Owing to the great differentiation of the industrial production, it was

[1] See *A. Weber*, op. cit., pp. 668, 681, 684, 686–688.

difficult to obtain information about the corresponding raising of prices of industrial goods by protectionist tariffs of the agrarian countries.

TABLE AI: PRICES OF IMPORTANT FOODSTUFFS, 1931–34, IN WORLD MARKET AND IN PROTECTED COUNTRIES

World market prices (London) = 100; prices in Berlin, Paris, Milan amounted to:

Commodities		Berlin	Paris	Milan
Wheat	1929	106	116	135
	1934	276	300	268
Butter	1931	117	143	—
	1934	271	283	—
Beef	1929	123	93	—
	1934	144	111	—

TABLE AII: PRICES OF IMPORTANT AGRARIAN PRODUCTS, DECEMBER 1934, IN BERLIN AND IN WORLD MARKET

(*In Rm. per* 100 *kilos*)

Commodities	Berlin	World market	Berlin in % of world markets
Lard . .	181·00	66·86	270
Barley .	15·45	8·17	188
Maize .	15·50	5·84	265
Pork . .	96·00	28·37	338
Butter .	260·00	121·77	212
Sugar . .	44·00	9·17	480

See *Considerations*, pp. 21–22.

An example taken from the Roumanian tariff, however, gives some idea of the way in which protection raised industrial prices. In the year 1929 the Roumanian duty on iron pipes (item 1080 of Roumanian tariff) amounted to 540–700 Lei per 100 kilogrammes. So long, however, as Roumanian iron works were unable to supply the home market, a preference duty of 120 Lei was in force. In 1931 this was abolished, for it was established that "Roumanian works manufactured pipes in sufficient quantities from cast iron."[1]

Roumanian industry was henceforth compelled to use pipes which were at least 420 Lei per 100 kilos more expensive (540–120) than those imported prior to 1931, the sole consolation being that they were Roumanian pipes. These high prices of agrarian as well as industrial products brought about by protection lead to sharp declines in consumption of the protected commodities in the protectionist countries. Thus the *per capita* fat consumption in Germany fell from 41·3 lbs. in 1929 to 34·3 lbs. in 1933, and the dearness of food has generally driven demand from the foodstuffs of the higher to that of the lower nutrition value (corn, potatoes).[2]

Another form of lowering the standard of life by protection was the heavy dislocation of capital into the protected trades, which raised production far above the declining home consumption, and were therefore compelled to export their products at world market prices, where these prices, thanks to the protection of the great import countries, were depressed to a very low level. Thus France's loss from wheat exports of this kind in 1934 was at least 1·5 Md. Frs. Further, large sums, which are very difficult to ascertain, were diverted as direct subsidies to the development of production in the protected trades. England, for example, spent 39·5 Million Pounds between 1925 and 1935 upon the development of the sugar industry, employing 32,000 workers. Even in the exporting states the protectionist policy of the importing countries leads to direct subsidies, if exports of vital importance are involved.[3]

[1] See Decree of Roumanian Government in *H.-A.*, 1931, p. 1475.
[2] Comp. *Considerations*, p. 23; *Survey* III, pp. 87–89.
[3] Lettland, e.g., paid in 1934 subsidies to maintain her butter exports which were larger than the value of this export (comp. *Survey* III, pp. 85–87, 95). In a similar way Holland could only maintain her butter exports to England by paying large subventions.

(b) *Destruction of the Economic Location of Production*

Between 1929 and 1931 the exports and imports of most European countries decreased to an alarming extent. Between 1932 and 1935, again, the foreign trade of many European states has taken a turn which can only be described as a collapse. If it could be said in 1911, from the standpoint of the theory of location, that "unusually high tariffs and consequently unusual restriction of home consumption" were necessary to divert European industry, in view of its great advantages of location both as regards transportation as well as labour factors, and only "very high duties could threaten its position."[1] This situation then deemed highly improbable has in fact been brought about by European protection between 1929 and 1931, and even more so between 1932 and 1935, and, what is very important, in the industrial as well as in the agrarian sphere. The consequence is a threat to the foundations of the economic location of European production, which was slowly built up in pre-War years and painfully reconstructed after the World War up to 1929. In other words, what was proceeding rapidly was the destruction of Europe's division into a (predominantly) industrial Central and a (predominantly) agrarian Border Europe, accompanied by an extensive conflict of the industrial countries with each other.

Sheltered by these tariff walls of unprecedented height industries are being fostered in numerous European countries for which the natural and economic conditions of location are entirely unsuitable. In view of the post-War transformation of the technique of the heavy industries, which has rendered them more dependent on electricity and oil than on coal, a number of states which are poor in coal and raw materials have found it possible, by means of high tariffs and high costs, to develop such industries. (Examples are the Italian iron and steel duties, and the duties on semi-finished metal goods in South-Eastern Europe.)

[1] *Alfred Weber*, loc. cit., p. 686.

In the agrarian sphere the protectionist policy of the importing countries caused a diminution in the production of the most fertile exporting countries. Between 1928 and 1934 wheat product in the Danubian states declined by 33·3% (in the U.S.A., Canada, Argentine, and Australia by 18%), but in the importing countries of industrial Europe it increased by more than 20%, at prices between 200% and 300% above world market level. Barley, oats, beef, and sugar all present the same picture. The most favourable areas of production are restricting output, which rises in the less fertile districts, at prices which gradually lower home consumption.[1] To the destruction of their agrarian exports the agrarian states of Europe and the world have replied by reducing their industrial imports to a large extent. Warnings against this tendency were uttered at the Conferences at Warsaw and Geneva in 1930 by the representatives of all South-Eastern countries as well as Denmark.

TABLE A: DEVELOPMENT OF INDUSTRIAL PRODUCTION IN INDUSTRIAL AND AGRARIAN EUROPE, 1929–34

1925–29 = 100

Country		Total Industrial Production			Textile Industrial Production		
		1929	1932	1934	1929	1932	1934
I Industrial Europe	Germany	110	66	93	98	84	104
	Italy	109	73	88	102	67	74
	France	104	79	81	98	64	67
	England	105	88	104	99	85	92
II Agrarian Europe	Denmark	117	106	131	112	126	168
	Roumania	120	106	149	108	139	182
	Hungary	103	179	101	108	95	136
	Greece	108	109	136	117	140	178

See *World Production and Prices*, pp. 133–134.

Table A shows to what an extent the relative growth in the industrial production of agrarian Europe between 1929

[1] See *Survey* III, pp. 81, 96–97, 162–163.

and 1934 surpassed the development of the industrial states, especially in connection with the textile trades which are easily fostered by duties. And as the same process was going on in overseas agrarian states, and particularly in Japan, the result was a continuous depression in the old European export textile trades, as well as in other industries. Here too output rose only in the shelter of high tariff walls in those parts of Europe which are the least favourable to the development of industry.

The discrepancies between industrial production and industrial exports shown in Table B provide an analogy to the shrinking corn areas in South-Eastern Europe and the extensive pastures in Holland and Denmark which were not fully utilized.

TABLE B: INDUSTRIAL PRODUCTION AND INDUS-
TRIAL EXPORTS IN INDUSTRIAL EUROPE

1929 = 100

Group	England 1932	1934	Germany 1932	1934	France 1932	1934	Italy 1932	1934
Total Industrial Production .	82·5	100	64·5	88·0	65·5	70·5	68·0	75·0
Industrial Exports (volume) . .	61·5	68·5	59·0	49·5	56·0	57·5	76·0	69·0

See *World Production and Prices*, p. 96; Survey III, p. 123.

Thus the new progress of agriculture of industrial Europe was matched by the industrialization of agrarian Europe,[1] both processes which were being carried out under the pressure of excessive protectionism in contradiction to economic laws governing the location of production, accompanied by a growing impoverishment of Europe, especially of its densely peopled countries which are poor in raw materials and land. This aspect becomes yet more serious when it is borne in mind that

[1] Comp. *Survey* III, pp. 160, 163; *Considerations*, pp. 34–35; *World Production and Prices*, pp. 92–96. Recently Prof. *Ohlin* has stressed this point in his report, *International Economic Reconstruction*, pp. 93, 119. Paris, 1936.

the same process on a larger scale is being repeated outside
Europe, as may be gathered from the fall from 35% to 32%
in the share of industrial Europe in world industrial production
between 1928 and 1934 and the fall from 47% to 37% of the
non-European industrial states, accompanied by a rise in the
share of *agrarian* countries outside Europe from 11% to 24%.[1]

Moreover this protectionist trade policy by fostering bilateral
trade inflicted great damage on such countries as Belgium and
Holland, where a considerable section of the population lived
upon the proceeds of a transit trade established long since.[2]

This extensive destruction of European exchange relationships is expressed in the unprecedentedly low figures of the
European exports and imports of nearly all European states
during 1933 and 1934. Although a great part of the Central
European and the Dutch-Scandinavian-Baltic-German integration, of the Scandinavian-English integration and, to a
lesser extent, also that between the Mediterranean states and
England, was fairly well maintained up to 1931, still at the end of
this year there were indications of a general collapse from which
only the Sterling countries were exempt. At the beginning
of 1936 only the integration between England, Scandinavia,
and the Mediterranean countries remained intact although
Denmark, at least, had considerably suffered from the English
preferences in favour of New Zealand dairy produce. All the
other areas of the economic integration of Europe had largely
succumbed by 1933–34 to the trade war of all against all.
Europe as a closely integrated economic body was battered
to pieces by a drastic protectionist policy. Such was the
state of affairs at the commencement of 1936.

(c) *Empire and Regional Tendencies in Europe*

With the injuries which European protection has inflicted
upon the inner economic structures of almost all European
states summarized in the terms "lowering the standard of

---

[1] Comp. *Survey* III, p. 162.   [2] Ibid., p. 182.

life" and "destruction of the natural foundations of the location of production," our analysis of the dangerous accentuation of present-day economic problems in Europe (spring 1936) is not yet concluded. Protectionism is also largely responsible for the growth of an antagonism between two groups of states which displayed itself in the response of commercial policies to the destruction of the economic integration of Europe. Those nations which, like England, France, and Holland, possessed colonies and dominions and which may be called "Empire states," replied, with more or less emphasis to the European protectionism of recent years by tightening commercial bonds with their colonial areas and loosening their trade connections with Europe. Whereas France and Holland were in 1935–36 still more closely knit with Europe in respect to foreign trade than with overseas countries, in spite of the increasing economic penetration of their colonies systematically and successfully pursued by means of preferences, England, by means of the Ottawa Preferences of 1932, broke away, together with her Empire, from Europe and the rest of the world, to such an extent that in 1932–33 Europe wondered whether she intended to create a great economically self-sufficient area (without Europe and the rest of the world but including the Scandinavian countries) thus admitting the futility of her many attempts between 1929 and 1931 to break down European protection.

To the remaining states of Central, East, South, and South-Eastern Europe the path of empire policy remained closed as they either lacked colonies completely or possessed colonies which are capable of only slight development (Italy). After the failure of the preferential plans of 1930–31 these European countries have reacted in a twofold way to the ever-increasing disintegration of Europe. The countries of the South-East have been seeking without pause, and so far without success, for new regional pacts. Germany, Italy, and Poland pursued a policy of far-reaching economic self-sufficiency, but showed great interest in all attempts to draw closer to South-Eastern

Europe, by means of regional or bilateral trade pacts, or to draw closer to each other (Italian tripartite treaties, Germano-Polish economic agreement of 1934, etc.). These states may be called "Regional States" as opposed to the "Empire States." If during the same period (1932–35) when nearly all European countries have pursued a policy of commercial exclusion, those same countries have deliberately striven to realize an Empire or a regional trade policy, this state of affairs indicated that no European state could actually pursue a policy of complete self-sufficiency ; all attempts of this kind were a "flight from reality." [1] Both the empire and regional states of Europe had this in common.

If, however, we inquire into the economic conditions of the two groups, and proceed to investigate the questions of population, area, raw materials, etc., we find a fundamental distinction of great importance. If European protection persists in its present proportions, i.e. if the almost complete disintegration of Europe is perpetuated, the empire states, by making heavy sacrifices, could perhaps survive economically. *The regional states of the rest of Europe, however, could not survive economically.* From this point of view Sir *Arthur Salter* uttered an urgent warning in the spring of 1932 against the dangers of a policy which threatened to lead to the autarctic separation of the U.S.A. and of the British Empire, and thus to a dissolution of the whole world economy, into larger or smaller national economic units, as such a shattering of world economy, in view of the inevitable impoverishment of all small countries or states without raw materials, "would soon be dangerous and ultimately fatal to world peace." [2] This is the most dangerous side of European and world protection. The great differences in the economic structures and colonial possessions of the European states may lead to a political catastrophe if the existing system of protection is maintained, i.e. to a new *world war.*

[1] Comp. *Survey* III, p. 192.
[2] See Sir *Arthur Salter: Recovery*, p. 193.

(d) *Protectionism and War*

Mutual relationships between the economic and political spheres have existed at all times; in no epoch of human history have they become so inseparable as in the age of the modern capitalistic state.[1]

This interdependence was plainly revealed at the World Economic Conferences of 1927 and 1933. In his opening speech President *Theunis* said that it could not be too often repeated that political action and economic action were interdependent, and that the inquiry of the Conference would probably bring out more clearly the close relationship that existed between the economic policies of nations and international peace.[2]

Six years later General *Smuts*, at the 1933 Conference, warned the world against its failure to perform the chief tasks imposed upon the Conference:

"Things would become worse not merely financially, but also in the political sphere." [3]

The scientific economist who is confined within the limits of pure economic analysis cannot discern when severe economic depression and crisis in a social system may precipitate the nations into warlike complications. He can only indicate the consequences, either positive or negative (i.e. raising or depressing the material standard of life) of a given economic policy.

But all economic and sociological inquiries into the European situation during recent years (1929–36) must lead to the conclusion that protection is largely responsible for the growing political tension in Europe and the world,[4] as it can have no other effect than to depress the standard of living and damage the economic texture in all the regional states of

---

[1] See the paper of Sir *Alfred Zimmern*, read in Chatam House, 1924, on "Fiscal Policy and International Relations," in A. Zimmern's *The Prospects of Democracy*, pp. 233–256, especially pp. 234, 238–240.

[2] *W.E.C.*, 27, I, pp. 62–63.   [3] *W.E.C.*, 33, pp. 13–14.

[4] See *Robbins, The Great Depression*, pp. 196–198.

Europe to such an extent as to make a warlike explosion a probable outcome of the relations between economics and politics.

The political and economic problems of these states, i.e. Central, East, South, and South-Eastern Europe, have been clearly outlined in a recently published sociological work by *Alfred Weber*, in which he stated that the temporary end of capitalist world economy (not of capitalism) presented the most serious difficulties, first for all countries specializing in the production of raw materials and foodstuffs, secondly for the densely populated states of Central Europe.[1]

Political developments during 1935 completely justified the apprehensions of all those who, like Sir *Arthur Salter* or General *Smuts*, saw a grave menace to world peace in the increasing destruction of world trade by a more ruthless protectionist policy.[2] The fact that Europe's most important regional state next to Germany, viz. Italy, was starting a colonial war in October 1935, which was openly justified on the grounds of the necessity for economic expansion, showed more vividly than everything else how acute the economic situation had become in that country (and also in the rest of Central, Eastern and South-Eastern Europe, where serious political tension of a non-economic nature was already abundant!). This appearance of a political danger zone in that part of Europe suffering most severely in an economic sense, taken in conjunction with the question of protectionism, means that, with the possible exception of the Empire States, the rest of Europe cannot in the long run exist without restoring the economic integration of production in Europe. In other words, the most serious political consequences must be envisaged if radical European protectionism remains unchanged.

In concluding this study it must therefore once more be

[1] See *Alfred Weber*: *Kulturgeschichte als Kultursoziologie*, Leiden, 1935, p. 387.

[2] Loucheur's phrase at the W.E.C., 1927, "Competition in tariff increases bears the greatest resemblance to competition in armaments," should never be lost sight of. *W.E.C.*, 27, 1, p. 130.

clearly emphasized that European protectionism of the years 1929–35 implies the end of the economic integration of Europe, unless the prohibitive tariff walls and other protective barriers can be broken down in the near future.

If it should prove possible to break them, the economic integration of Europe in the framework of a world economy which is again functioning may be restored.

For practically all the states of Europe are unable to live without each other, or without the world, or the world without Europe, in economic and political peace.

APPENDIX

EXPLANATION OF TABLES AND GRAPHS

1. In the Tables AI, AII, BI–IV, each year is shown with two rows of figures, which indicate the lowest and highest limits of the tariff levels of the classes or groups of goods in question. (Comp. p. 33 of text.)

2. An "fr" in Tables AI and AII signifies that the goods in question were on the free list.

3. An "I" in Tables AII and BI–IV signifies that for various reasons comparative figures could not be calculated in respect of the goods in question.

4. When a class of goods or a whole group (A, B, C) in Tables BI–IV is shown without figures, it means that the actual imports in the cases concerned have been insignificant. (Comp. pp. 89–90 of text.)

5. The index figures in Tables BI–IV in front of the tariff level figures indicate the number of goods the duties on which could be included for computing the tariff levels in question. (Comp. p. 226, Table D, of text.)

6. Three graphs have been made to show the potential tariff levels of 15 countries in 1913, 1927, and 1931 respectively. They are indicated by the three columns for each country. (Graph A, tariff levels for foodstuffs; graph B, tariff levels for semi-manufactured goods; graph C, tariff levels for manufactured goods.) (Comp. p. 102 of text.)

TABLE A1: POTENTIAL TARIFF LEVELS OF GERMANY

(*In % of Prices*)

Group of Goods	1913		1927		1931	
A. Foodstuffs:						
I. Cereals and flour	27·0	28·0	28·4	28·4	186·0	186·0
II. Live-stock	11·5	14·6	19·3	35·2	41·0	63·0
III. Animal foodstuffs	*19·0	19·0	20·0	21·0	28·0	29·0
IV. Fruit and vegetables	19·0	20·0	11·0	20·0	12·0	24·0
V. Other foodstuffs	30·0	30·0	45·0	46·0	128·0	129·0
Average of I–V = average of A¹	21·3	22·3	24·7	30·0	79·0	86·0
VI. Alcoholic drinks and tobacco	58·0	64·0	54·0	63·0	76·0	103·0
Average of I–VI = average of A²	27·4	29·3	29·6	35·6	78·5	89·0
B. Semi-manufactured goods:						
I. Textiles	7·6	14·4	6·1	15·0	9·2	19·6
II. Timber, paper, cork	21·0	21·0	15·0	24·5	13·0	21·0
III. Metals	14·0	17·5	13·0	22·0	15·0	27·0
IV. Chemicals	10·4	17·0	7·6	12·8	39·0	43·5
V. Mineral oils	19·1	28·5	54·0	54·0	265·0	450·0
Average of I–IV = average of B¹	13·2	17·5	10·4	18·6	19·0	27·8
Average of I–V = average of B²	14·4	19·7	19·1	25·7	66·0	120·0
C. Manufactured industrial goods:						
I. Textiles	10·0	14·5	21·0	43·0	26·0	45·0
II. Paper	17·5	17·5	12·1	12·1	15·8	15·8
III. Glass, china, cement	14·0	14·0	20·0	20·0	16·5	16·5
IV. Metal goods	6·7	13·0	9·5	15·0	12·5	18·5
V. Machines	4·3	14·2	3·7	15·0	3·7	15·0
VI. Vehicles	3·3	8·2	24·0	40·0	8·8	22·0
VII. Apparatuses, instruments	6·0	6·0	19·0	19·5	20·0	20·0
VIII. Toys and tires	6·1	6·1	14·5	17·0	17·0	20·0
Average of I–VIII = average of C	8·5	11·7	15·5	22·7	15·0	21·6
General tariff level (average of A¹, B¹, C)	14·3	17·2	17·0	23·8	37·5	44·0

* Sardines in oil excluded as dishomogeneous price element.

TABLE AII: RELATIVE CHANGES IN PRE-WAR AND POST-WAR DUTY RATES AND TARIFF LEVELS OF GERMANY

1913 = 100, *duty rates and tariff levels amounted to :*

Group of Goods	1927				1931			
	Duty Rates		Tariff Levels		Duty Rates		Tariff Levels	
A. Foodstuffs:								
I. Cereals, flour	115	120	100	105	390	480	665	690
II. Live-stock	255	285	170	240	300	310	355	430
III. Animal foodstuffs	135	135	105	110	175	180	145	155
IV. Fruit, vegetables	140	155	58	100	130	155	63	120
V. Other foodstuffs	180	180	150	150	200	200	430	430
Average of I–V = average of A[1]	165	175	115	135	240	265	370	385
VI. Alcoholic drinks, tobacco	110	110	93	98	125	160	130	160
Average of I–VI = average of A[2]	155	165	110	120	230	250	285	300
B. Semi-manufactured goods:								
I. Textiles	105	160	80	105	110	160	120	135
II. Timber, paper, cork	64	98	71·5	117	64	98	62	100
III. Metals	98	110	93	125	175	180	107	155
IV. Chemicals	215	305	73	75	235	340	255	375
V. Mineral oils	200	300	190	280	500	565	1400	1600
Average of I–IV = average of B[1]	120	170	80	105	150	200	145	160
Average of I–V = average of B[2]	140	195	130	135	220	270	460	610
C. Manufactured goods:								
I. Textiles	350	395	210	300	335	400	260	310
II. Paper	97	97	69	69	97	97	90	90
III. Glass, cement, china	255	275	145	145	255	275	120	120
IV. Metal goods	160	180	115	140	160	180	145	190
V. Machines	125	140	86	105	125	140	86	105
VI. Vehicles	340	530	490	725	180	190	270	270
VII. Apparatuses, instruments	150	150	320	320	150	150	330	330
VIII. Toys and tires	170	210	240	280	170	210	280	330
Average of I–VIII = average of C	205	245	180	195	185	205	175	185
General tariff level (average of A[1], B[1], C)	165	195	120	140	190	225	255	260

TABLE AI: POTENTIAL TARIFF LEVELS OF FRANCE
(In % of Prices)

Group of Goods	1913		1927		1931	
A. Foodstuffs:						
I. Cereals and flour . .	27·2	30·0	19·8	21·6	98·0	102·0
II. Livestock . . .	13·1	15·0	8·0	10·1	18·7	21·6
III. Animal foodstuffs .	24·2	25·7	13·4	16·0	29·7	32·8
IV. Fruit and vegetables .	19·5	33·4	9·7	15·8	22·5	31·6
V. Other foodstuffs . .	54·5	60·0	28·8	30·3	90·0	99·0
VI. Alcoholic drinks * .	25·0	25·0	26·4	30·0	35·0	55·0
Average of I–VI = average of A .	27·2	31·3	17·7	20·6	49·0	57·0
B. Semi-manufactured goods:						
I. Textiles	13·0	62·2	10·7	59·0	14·5	76·5
II. Timber, paper, cork .	12·3	18·0	9·7	18·6	19·3	38·0
III. Metals . . .	27·6	41·2	18·3	58·0	21·3	64·0
IV. Chemicals . .	12·8	16·0	9·5	10·8	9·8	11·2
V. Mineral oils . .	138·0	194·0	37·7	62·7	130·0	182·0
Average of I–IV = average of B¹	16·4	34·3	12·0	36·6	16·2	47·4
Average of I–V = average of B² .	40·7	66·0	17·2	41·8	39·0	74·3
C. Manufactured goods:						
I. Textiles . . .	21·0	34·3	19·8	29·0	21·3	32·0
II. Paper	19·4	23·8	33·0	33·0	42·6	42·6
III. Glass, china, cement .	10·0	11·3	18·2	21·0	17·4	20·0
IV. Metal goods . .	7·0	23·0	17·4	22·7	18·6	24·0
V. Machines . . .	9·0	18·5	12·3	37·0	11·8	36·0
VI. Vehicles . .	9·6	15·4	34·0	35·8	35·0	52·0
VII. Apparatuses, instruments	10·1	14·0	15·1	18·3	15·5	19·0
VIII. Toys and tires . .	17·0	17·7	23·0	43·3	26·6	50·0
Average of I–VIII = average of C	12·9	19·7	21·6	30·0	23·6	34·4
General tariff level (average of A, B¹, C)	18·8	28·4	17·1	29·1	29·6	46·3

* Tobacco excluded, because of tobacco monopoly, 1913–31.

TABLE A1: POTENTIAL TARIFF LEVELS OF ITALY
(*In % of Prices*)

(Compare p. 70, note 1, and p. 71, note 1, of text.)

Group of Goods	1913		1927		1931	
A. Foodstuffs:						
I. Cereals and flour	30·0	37·6	21·0	26·3	89·0	131·0
II. Livestock	9·4	13·1	6·1	19·6	8·3	26·1
III. Animal foodstuffs	14·0	15·0	21·8	23·5	21·7	24·0
IV. Fruit and vegetables	15·2	15·2	14·5	18·6	11·7	16·0
V. Other foodstuffs	114·0	127·0	35·3	38·5	107·0	141·0
VI. Alcoholic drinks and tobacco	30·0	32·0	29·0	41·0	33·5	46·0
Average of I–VI = average of A	30·0	40·0	21·3	28·0	57·6	74·3
(Without Av)	19·7	24·0	—	—	45·2	64·0
B. Semi-manufactured goods:						
I. Textiles	9·2	15·5	6·6	18·7	9·9	29·0
II. Timber, paper, cork	*(39·0	44·5)	†26·3	29·0	†60·0	62·3
III. Metals	28·2	34·0	38·3	63·0	45·0	85·0
IV. Chemicals	9·2	10·2	17·7	29·5	44·6	59·6
V. Mineral oils	103·0	103·0	119·0	125·0	395·0	400·0
Average of I–IV = average of B¹	21·4	28·5	22·2	35·0	40·0	59·0
Average of I–V = average of B²	37·7	43·4	41·6	53·0	111·0	127·0
C. Manufactured goods:						
I. Textiles	15·6	19·4	19·4	29·6	19·6	31·6
II. Paper	17·1	27·1	18·7	29·1	23·1	36·9
III. Glass, china, cement	23·7	32·4	39·6	58·4	42·6	61·0
IV. Metal goods	11·6	15·5	16·7	31·4	21·8	49·4
V. Machines	6·4	7·5	11·5	21·3	15·3	25·4
VI. Vehicles	5·1	6·6	43·0	53·0	93·0	111·0
VII. Apparatuses, instruments	6·8	6·8	9·4	10·3	21·4	25·0
VIII. Toys and tires	16·2	18·5	21·7	43·0	33·4	58·0
Average of I–VIII = average of C	12·6	16·7	22·2	34·5	33·8	49·8
General tariff level (average of A, B¹, C)	21·3	28·4	22·6	33·7	39·3	57·3

* Only wood pulp; cellulose, timber, cork duty free.
† Planks soft, not planed, and cork; other goods duty free.

TABLE AII: RELATIVE CHANGES IN PRE-WAR AND POST-WAR DUTY RATES AND TARIFF LEVELS OF ITALY

1913 = 100, *duty rates and tariff levels amounted to:*

Group of Goods	1927 Duty Rates	1927 Tariff Levels	1931 Duty Rates	1931 Tariff Levels
A. Foodstuffs:				
I. Cereals, flour	100 115	70 70	210 225	300 350
II. Livestock	145 250	65 150	145 250	88 200
III. Animal foodstuffs	160 170	155 160	165 180	155 160
IV. Fruit, vegetables	105 145	95 120	105 150	77 105
V. Other foodstuffs	82 92	30·2 31	120 125	94 110
VI. Alcoholic drinks and tobacco	150 190	130 140	170 215	340 360
Average of I–VI = average of A	120 160	70 71	150 190	150 160
(Without Av)	— —	(110 115)	— —	(200 265)
B. Semi-manufactured goods:				
I. Textiles	I	72 120	I	108 186
II. Timber, paper, cork	120 120	65 65	120 120	140 155
III. Metals	140 210	135 185	170 265	160 250
IV. Chemicals	I	190 290	I	485 585
V. Mineral oils	105 115	115 120	120 135	385 390
Average of I–IV = average of B¹	150 210	105 125	175 250	190 205
Average of I–V = average of B²	140 185	110 120	160 220	290 295
C. Manufactured goods:				
I. Textiles	180 200	125 155	190 190	100 165
II. Paper	115 135	110 110	115 135	135 135
III. Glass, cement, china	390 395	165 180	420 430	180 190
IV. Metal goods	175 240	145 200	185 260	190 320
V. Machines	250 440	180 285	380 540	240 340
VI. Vehicles	I	800 840	I	1680 1820
VII. Apparatuses, instruments	I	140 150	I	315 370
VIII. Toys and tires	185 270	135 230	200 290	205 310
Average of I–VIII = average of C	215 285	175 205	245 310	270 300
General tariff level (average of A, B¹, C)	160 215	105 120	180 250	205 215

TABLE A1: POTENTIAL TARIFF LEVELS OF BELGIUM
(In % of prices)

Group of Goods	1913		1927		1931	
A. Foodstuffs:						
I. Cereals and flour	8·1	8·1	2·4	2·4	15·7	15·7
II. Livestock	fr.		fr.		fr.	
III. Animal foodstuffs	20·0	20·0	7·3	7·3	12·1	12·1
IV. Fruit and vegetables	39·0	39·0	13·6	27·5	13·6	32·6
V. Other foodstuffs	35·0	35·0	16·2	17·7	43·0	45·0
Average of I–V = average of A¹	25·5	25·5	9·9	13·7	21·0	26·4
VI. Alcoholic drinks and tobacco	95·0	95·0	28·5	38·6	44·0	60·0
Average of I–VI = average of A²	39·0	39·5	13·6	18·7	25·7	33·0
B. Semi-manufactured goods:						
I. Textiles	4·8	11·4	3·7	6·6	4·8	8·1
II. Timber, paper, cork	7·6	7·6	9·7	9·7	17·2	17·2
III. Metals	4·7	6·7	4·6	6·0	5·5	6·7
IV. Chemicals	*(9·1	9·1)	21·7	21·7	32·6	32·6
V. Mineral oils	fr.		60·5	75·0	232·0	232·0
Average of I–IV = average of B¹	6·5	8·7	9·9	11·0	15·0	16·1
Average of I–V = average of B²	6·5	8·7	20·0	23·8	58·5	59·0
C. Manufactured goods:						
I. Textiles	12·3	13·3	14·5	17·4	14·4	18·7
II. Paper	12·6	12·6	3·8	5·3	5·1	6·8
III. Glass, china, cement	10·6	10·6	5·6	8·3	6·1	9·1
IV. Metal goods	11·0	11·0	9·6	17·7	11·0	23·4
V. Machines	1·4	8·6	7·4	15·3	7·7	15·3
VI. Vehicles	3·3	7·3	10·3	20·3	12·5	24·8
VII. Apparatuses, instruments	6·9	6·9	7·2	9·5	7·8	9·9
VIII. Toys and tires	11·5	11·5	7·8	18·4	9·4	23·3
Average of I–VIII = average of C	8·7	10·2	8·3	14·0	9·2	16·5
General tariff level (average of A¹, B¹, C)	13·6	14·8	9·4	12·9	15·1	19·7

* Duty of only one commodity: soap.

TABLE A1: POTENTIAL TARIFF LEVELS OF SWITZERLAND

(In % of prices)

Group of Goods	1913		1927		1931	
A. Foodstuffs:						
I. Cereals and flour	4·3	24·7	5·8	45·6	13·0	101·0
II. Livestock	8·4	8·4	21·4	23·6	28·7	32·7
III. Animal foodstuffs	6·6	6·6	22·6	24·3	38·4	40·0
IV. Fruit and vegetables	28·0	28·0	15·7	18·4	30·3	32·3
V. Other foodstuffs	15·5	16·5	18·1	20·1	52·0	54·4
Average of I–V = average of A¹	12·6	16·8	16·7	26·4	32·5	52·0
VI. Alcoholic drinks and tobacco	11·2	12·7	26·2	94·0	29·1	112·0
Average of I–VI = average of A²	12·3	16·1	18·3	39·3	32·0	62·0
B. Semi-manufactured goods:						
I. Textiles	4·4	4·5	5·7	7·0	8·9	10·8
II. Timber, paper, cork	14·1	14·8	21·4	22·1	23·0	25·8
III. Metals	2·7	9·5	4·4	15·5	9·4	21·8
IV. Chemicals	4·6	4·6	7·8	7·8	9·3	9·3
V. Mineral oils	7·0	7·0	56·0	56·0	133·0	133·0
Average of I–IV = average of B¹	6·4	8·3	9·8	13·1	12·6	17·0
Average of I–V = average of B²	6·6	8·1	19·1	21·6	36·7	40·0
C. Manufactured goods:						
I. Textiles	4·7	5·1	7·7	8·9	10·4	12·7
II. Paper	17·2	18·9	33·2	33·2	56·0	56·0
III. Glass, china, cement	12·4	23·0	23·0	33·3	20·5	21·2
IV. Metal goods	8·2	12·2	16·7	22·5	24·5	31·4
V. Machines	3·9	8·4	7·5	13·0	7·4	12·0
VI. Vehicles	6·3	6·3	22·7	32·7	27·1	40·2
VII. Apparatuses, instruments	4·5	8·0	4·0	6·4	6·5	6·5
VIII. Toys and tires	3·5	6·6	7·8	9·4	9·5	11·5
Average of I–VIII = average of C	7·6	11·1	15·3	20·0	20·3	24·0
General tariff level (average of A¹, B¹, C)	8·9	12·1	13·9	19·7	21·8	31·0

TABLE Aɪɪ: RELATIVE CHANGES IN PRE-WAR AND POST-WAR DUTY RATES AND TARIFF LEVELS OF SWITZERLAND

1913 = 100, *duty rates and tariff levels amounted to:*

Group of Goods	1927 Duty Rates		1927 Tariff Levels		1931 Duty Rates		1931 Tariff Levels	
A. Foodstuffs:								
ɪ. Cereals, flour	185	220	135	185	185	220	300	410
ɪɪ. Livestock	530	555	255	280	510	530	340	390
ɪɪɪ. Animal foodstuffs	350	425	340	370	435	530	580	610
ɪv. Fruit, vegetables	130	140	55	65	140	145	110	115
v. Other foodstuffs	170	185	120	125	190	205	330	335
Average of ɪ–v = average of A[1]	275	305	135	160	290	320	260	310
vɪ. Alcoholic drinks and tobacco	385	1470	235	740	370	1440	260	880
Average of ɪ–vɪ = average of A[2]	290	500	140	245	305	510	260	385
B. Semi-manufactured goods:								
ɪ. Textiles	240	240	130	155	260	270	200	240
ɪɪ. Timber, paper, cork	230	260	150	155	230	260	165	175
ɪɪɪ. Metals	220	260	160	165	525	760	230	350
ɪv. Chemicals	160	200	170	170	160	200	200	200
v. Mineral oils	1530	1530	800	800	1530	1530	1900	1900
Average of ɪ–ɪv = average of B[1]	210	240	155	160	295	370	195	215
Average of ɪ–v = average of B[2]	470	500	265	290	540	605	495	550
C. Manufactured goods:								
ɪ. Textiles	290	290	165	175	300	305	220	250
ɪɪ. Paper	230	260	175	195	230	260	295	325
ɪɪɪ. Glass, cement, china	250	385	145	185	180	345	92	165
ɪv. Metal goods	230	250	185	205	230	250	300	355
v. Machines	240	300	155	190	240	300	140	190
vɪ. Vehicles	270	405	360	520	270	405	430	640
vɪɪ. Apparatuses, instruments	170	210	80	90	180	240	80	145
vɪɪɪ. Toys and tires	300	300	140	220	300	300	175	270
Average of ɪ–vɪɪɪ = average of C	250	305	180	200	245	305	215	270
General tariff level (average of A[1], B[1], C)	245	285	155	165	275	335	245	255

TABLE A1: POTENTIAL TARIFF LEVELS OF AUSTRIA
(1913: AUSTRIA-HUNGARY)
(*In % of Prices*)

Group of Goods	1913		1927		1931	
A. Foodstuffs:						
I. Cereals and flour	43·0	43·0	3·7	3·7	96·0	96·0
II. Livestock	6·8	22·5	5·4	5·4	16·4	22·0
III. Animal foodstuffs	30·0	30·4	15·2	15·8	35·0	38·5
IV. Fruit and vegetables	23·3	26·1	13·4	21·1	17·5	17·5
V. Other foodstuffs	32·5	32·5	41·5	42·0	118·0	144·0
Average of I–V = average of A¹	27·0	31·2	15·8	17·2	57·0	62·0
VI. Alcoholic drinks and tobacco	64·0	64·0	42·0	52·0	64·0	82·0
Average of I–VI = average of A²	33·2	36·7	20·2	23·3	58·0	66·0
B. Semi-manufactured goods:						
I. Textiles	8·5	17·7	5·1	11·5	7·8	20·0
II. Timber, paper, cork	20·7	20·7	10·1	10·1	14·3	14·3
III. Metals	29·3	33·0	21·2	29·5	30·5	37·0
IV. Chemicals	15·7	15·7	17·4	17·4	20·3	21·7
V. Mineral oils	65·8	65·8	24·3	29·0	61·0	78·0
Average of I–IV = average of B¹	18·5	21·8	13·4	17·1	18·2	23·2
Average of I–V = average of B²	28·0	30·6	15·6	19·5	26·2	34·2
C. Manufactured goods:						
I. Textiles	16·0	21·0	19·5	28·3	22·6	36·6
II. Paper	14·8	19·8	11·7	14·4	18·1	25·3
III. Glass, china, cement	23·5	40·3	15·1	15·7	25·7	25·7
IV. Metal goods	17·0	27·8	25·6	43·0	28·4	45·4
V. Machines	14·1	24·0	9·6	13·0	12·3	21·0
VI. Vehicles	14·0	19·0	32·0	32·0	31·6	58·7
VII. Apparatuses, instruments	9·6	11·5	17·0	17·0	19·5	19·5
VIII. Toys and tires	7·8	28·2	12·3	30·5	12·3	41·6
Average of I–VIII = average of C	14·6	24·0	17·8	24·2	21·5	34·2
General tariff level (average of A¹, B¹, C)	20·0	25·7	15·6	19·4	32·1	39·7

TABLE A1: POTENTIAL TARIFF LEVELS OF CZECHOSLOVAKIA
(1913: AUSTRIA-HUNGARY)
(In % of Prices)

Group of Goods	1913		1927		1931	
A. Foodstuffs:						
I. Cereals and flour . .	43·0	43·0	22·0	22·0	111·0	111·0
II. Livestock . . .	6·8	22·5	13·2	18·1	23·6	63·0
III. Animal foodstuffs .	30·0	30·4	19·0	19·6	56·0	57·0
IV. Fruit and vegetables	23·3	26·1	43·2	49·7	39·8	50·0
V. Other foodstuffs . .	32·5	32·5	78·0	79·0	161·0	164·0
Average of I–V = average of A^1 .	27·0	31·2	35·0	37·7	78·5	89·0
VI. Alcoholic drinks and tobacco	64·0	64·0	96·0	96·0	150·0	150·0
Average of I–VI = average of A^2	32·2	36·7	45·0	47·4	90·0	99·0
B. Semi-manufactured goods:						
I. Textiles	8·5	17·7	9·4	18·5	12·6	24·6
II. Timber, paper, cork . .	20·7	20·7	19·2	19·2	22·5	22·5
III. Metals	29·3	33·0	34·0	39·6	39·0	48·0
IV. Chemicals . . .	15·7	15·7	17·0	17·0	33·0	33·0
V. Mineral oils . .	65·8	65·8	31·5	31·5	71·0	71·0
Average of I–IV = average of B^1	18·5	21·8	19·9	23·5	26·8	32·2
Average of I–V = average of B^2 .	28·0	30·6	22·0	25·1	35·6	40·0
C. Manufactured goods:						
I. Textiles . . .	16·0	21·0	28·2	37·4	32·4	40·5
II. Paper	14·8	19·8	25·6	28·1	32·4	33·5
III. Glass, china, cement .	23·5	40·3	35·3	44·0	33·0	41·0
IV. Metal goods . . .	17·0	27·8	31·6	59·4	38·0	55·7
V. Machines . . .	14·1	24·0	19·4	29·7	19·4	30·0
VI. Vehicles . . .	14·0	19·0	55·0	70·0	47·7	47·7
VII. Apparatuses, instruments	9·6	11·5	16·2	21·2	18·0	21·3
VIII. Toys and tires . .	7·8	28·2	9·0	79·5	12·9	83·0
Average of I–VIII = average of C	14·6	24·0	25·5	46·0	29·2	44·0
General tariff level (average of A^1, B^1, C)	20·0	25·7	26·8	35·8	44·8	55·0

TABLE A1: POTENTIAL TARIFF LEVELS OF SWEDEN
(*In % of Prices*)

Group of Goods	1913		1927		1931	
A. Foodstuffs:						
I. Cereals and flour .	30·3	30·3	17·8	17·8	54·0	54·0
II. Livestock .	10·8	10·8	7·6	7·6	12·3	12·3
III. Animal foodstuffs	25·6	25·6	15·6	15·6	23·5	23·5
IV. Fruit and vegetables	67·0	72·0	39·0	41·5	52·0	56·0
V. Other foodstuffs .	28·4	32·0	24·7	27·0	47·4	53·0
Average of I–V = average of A¹ .	32·4	34·0	21·0	22·0	38·0	40·0
(Without AIV)	*(23·8	24·7)				
VI. Alcoholic drinks and tobacco	80·0	101·0	68·0	83·0	88·0	88·0
Average of I–VI = average of A² .	40·3	45·3	28·8	32·0	46·2	48·0
B. Semi-manufactured goods:						
I. Textiles .	12·4	17·3	7·1	10·3	11·5	17·0
II. Timber, paper, cork .	fr.		fr.		fr.	
III. Metals .	16·8	31·7	16·6	33·2	17·8	29·2
IV. Chemicals .	36·7	36·7	20·7	20·7	22·2	29·8
V. Mineral oils	fr.		fr.		4·2	4·2
Average of I–IV = average of B¹ .	22·0	28·6	14·8	21·4	17·2	18·7
Average of I–V = average of B² .	—	—	—	—	14·2	15·2
C. Manufactured goods:						
I. Textiles .	16·6	21·0	24·4	35·2	28·8	39·0
II. Paper .	24·5	24·5	19·4	19·4	27·4	27·4
III. Glass, china, cement .	38·5	45·5	24·0	29·2	24·4	30·4
IV. Metal goods .	16·6	31·6	11·0	23·0	13·5	33·7
V. Machines .	9·5	15·0	8·2	12·0	8·1	11·3
VI. Vehicles .	13·3	13·3	13·3	13·3	13·3	13·3
VII. Apparatuses, instruments .	14·0	16·5	11·3	12·6	13·4	14·3
VIII. Toys and tires .	45·0	45·0	38·0	38·0	37·8	37·8
Average of I–VIII = Average of C .	22·5	26·5	18·7	23·0	21·0	26·0
General tariff level (average of A¹, B¹, C) .	25·6	29·7	18·2	22·0	25·4	28·3

* Compare p. 86, note 1, of text.

TABLE A1: POTENTIAL TARIFF LEVELS OF FINLAND
(In % of Prices)

Group of Goods	1913		1927		1931	
A. Foodstuffs:						
I. Cereals and flour . .	*(21·0	21·0)	22·0	29·0	124·0	156·0
II. Livestock . . .	fr.		8·8	8·8	20·6	20·6
III. Animal foodstuffs . .	†52·3	52·3	43·4	43·4	84·0	84·0
IV. Fruit and vegetables .	‡40·0	40·0	124·0	124·0	79·0	93·0
V. Other foodstuffs . .	82·0	82·0	86·0	87·0	188·0	191·0
Average of I–V = average of A¹	49·0	49·0	57·0	58·0	95·0	109·0
VI. Alcoholic drinks, tobacco .	73·0	73·0	121·0	121·0	145·0	145·0
Average of I–VI = average of A²	45·0	45·0	67·5	69·0	107·0	115·0
B. Semi-manufactured goods:						
I. Textiles . . .	19·0	23·2	13·6	19·7	21·8	29·4
II. Timber, paper, cork .	fr.		fr.		fr.	
III. Metals . . .	19·0	22·0	10·6	17·5	15·2	24·2
IV. Chemicals . . .	33·5	33·5	33·6	46·6	30·0	40·6
V. Mineral oils . . .	53·0	53·0	20·4	20·4	308·0	308·0
Average of I–IV = average of B¹	17·9	19·7	19·4	21·0	16·7	23·5
Average of I–V = average of B²	31·1	33·0	19·5	26·0	94·0	100·0
C. Manufactured goods:						
I. Textiles . . .	26·4	34·0	26·4	38·0	39·0	58·0
II. Paper . . .	74·0	74·0	9·6	13·5	9·7	14·6
III. Glass, china, cement .	106·0	106·0	31·0	34·3	34·5	37·3
IV. Metal goods . .	16·0	35·3	14·7	23·2	17·2	26·5
V. Machines . . .	19·8	21·0	6·5	9·5	5·9	9·5
VI. Vehicles . . .	6·1	6·1	9·0	9·0	13·2	22·5
VII. Apparatuses, instruments	10·4	10·4	11·5	13·0	13·9	15·6
VIII. Toys and tires . .	32·6	32·6	202·0	202·0	240·0	240·0
Average of I–VIII = average of C	36·4	38·8	§15·5	20·1	§19·1	26·3
General tariff level (average of A¹, B¹, C) . . .	34·4	35·8	30·7	33·0	43·7	52·8

* Only duty on maize, other goods duty free in 1913.
† Butter, eggs, beef, pork, duty free in 1913.
‡ Potatoes, cauliflower, tomatoes, beans, duty free in 1913.
§ Tariff level of CVIII excluded as dishomogeneous element.

TABLE AI: POTENTIAL TARIFF LEVELS OF POLAND (1913: RUSSIA)

(*In % of Prices*)

Group of Goods	1913		1927		1931	
A. Foodstuffs:						
I. Cereals and flour	*30·5	30·5	*24·0	24·0	97·0	97·0
II. Livestock	fr.		12·5	15·0	20·0	23·5
III. Animal foodstuffs	34·6	34·6	31·6	36·2	77·0	85·0
IV. Fruit and vegetables	80·4	80·4	213·0	242·0	155·0	226·0
V. Other foodstuffs	132·0	132·0	61·0	61·0	160·0	160·0
Average of I–V = average of A¹	69·5	69·5	68·5	75·5	102·0	118·0
VI. Alcoholic drinks, tobacco	110·0	131·0	146·0	146·0	118·0	128·0
Average of I–VI = average of A²	77·5	82·0	81·0	87·0	105·0	120·0
B. Semi-manufactured goods:						
I. Textiles	42·0	71·5	26·6	49·5	34·0	63·0
II. Timber, paper, cork	36·6	55·5	10·2	13·4	19·0	22·5
III. Metals	84·0	95·5	40·6	54·5	51·5	67·0
IV. Chemicals	62·0	62·0	35·5	36·0	32·0	32·5
V. Mineral oils	166·0	166·0	64·0	64·0	420·0	420·0
Average of I–IV = average of B¹	56·0	71·0	28·2	38·3	34·0	46·2
Average of I–V = average of B²	78·0	90·0	35·4	43·5	111·0	121·0
C. Manufactured goods:						
I. Textiles	43·0	46·4	78·0	96·0	83·0	106·0
II. Paper	247·0	247·0	21·7	25·3	24·4	29·5
III. Glass, china, cement	140·0	186·0	37·5	74·5	29·0	47·0
IV. Metal goods	59·0	66·5	52·0	75·0	48·4	83·0
V. Machines	34·6	59·0	20·4	46·6	18·5	42·0
VI. Vehicles	22·2	23·6	21·6	32·7	27·5	45·0
VII. Apparatuses, instruments	31·5	33·3	61·0	67·0	70·0	77·4
VIII. Toys and tires	56·5	56·5	490·0	650·0	557·0	746·0
Average of I-VIII = average of C	79·0	90·0	†41·7	69·5	†43·0	61·4
General tariff level (average of A¹, B¹, C)	68·0	77·0	46·0	61·0	60·0	75·0

* Only duties on flour; cereals duty free in 1913 and 1927.
† Tariff level of CVIII excluded as dishomogeneous element.

TABLE A1: POTENTIAL TARIFF LEVELS OF ROUMANIA
(In % of Prices)

Group of Goods	1913		1927		1931	
A. Foodstuffs:						
I. Cereals and flour	*(39·0	39·0)	13·8	13·8	36·4	36·4
II. Livestock	6·6	11·1	3·8	8·8	3·7	11·1
III. Animal foodstuffs	47·3	47·3	48·0	48·0	85·5	88·5
IV. Fruit and vegetables	19·0	19·0	81·0	85·0	152·0	161·0
V. Other foodstuffs	59·0	60·0	72·0	83·0	148·0	155·0
Average of I–V = average of A¹	34·2	35·3	43·6	47·6	85·0	90·0
VI. Alcoholic drinks and tobacco	72·0	72·0	118·0	118·0	136·0	136·0
Average of I–VI = average of A²	40·5	41·4	56·0	59·4	93·5	98·0
B. Semi-manufactured goods:						
I. Textiles	10·0	22·8	15·3	32·6	25·3	54·0
II. Timber, paper, cork	61·0	61·0	25·0	80·0	36·4	42·2
III. Metals	12·1	15·4	26·2	30·2	32·0	47·5
IV. Chemicals	22·0	35·2	16·6	35·4	51·0	82·0
V. Mineral oils	27·3	27·3	17·1	19·5	41·0	42·0
Average of I–IV = average of B¹	26·3	33·6	20·8	44·5	36·2	56·4
Average of I–V = average of B²	26·5	32·3	20·0	39·9	37·1	53·5
C. Manufactured goods:						
I. Textiles	18·3	27·0	87·0	163·0	110·0	232·0
II. Paper	61·3	61·3	46·2	53·2	73·7	88·0
III. Glass, china, cement	25·0	31·0	63·5	66·6	43·4	48·0
IV. Metal goods	22·7	45·2	21·3	58·5	24·3	65·0
V. Machines	5·7	8·0	6·5	14·4	6·6	13·2
VI. Vehicles	18·8	27·0	13·0	27·4	19·7	29·3
VII. Apparatuses, instruments	8·3	8·3	35·7	39·0	20·7	28·7
VIII. Toys and tires	20·6	20·6	19·5	60·5	25·0	52·0
Average of I–VIII = average of C	22·5	28·5	36·8	60·3	40·4	69·5
General tariff level (average of A¹, B¹, C)	27·7	33·0	33·7	51·0	54·0	72·0

* Cereals duty free; only duties on flour.

TABLE AI: POTENTIAL TARIFF LEVELS OF HUNGARY
(1913: AUSTRIA-HUNGARY)
(In % of Prices)

Group of Goods	1913		1927		1931	
A. Foodstuffs:						
I. Cereals and flour	43·0	43·0	26·7	26·7	59·0	59·0
II. Livestock	6·8	22·5	13·3	22·7	23·1	40·0
III. Animal foodstuffs	30·0	30·4	30·0	31·6	45·4	50·0
IV. Fruit and vegetables	23·3	26·1	20·4	35·2	30·0	44·5
V. Other foodstuffs	32·5	32·5	52·0	56·5	122·0	129·0
Average of I–V = average of A¹	27·0	31·2	28·4	34·5	56·0	64·4
VI. Alcoholic drinks and tobacco	64·0	64·0	64·0	77·0	116·0	133·0
Average of I–VI = average of A²	33·2	36·7	34·3	41·6	66·0	76·0
B. Semi-manufactured goods:						
I. Textiles	8·5	17·7	9·5	26·0	16·0	33·6
II. Timber, paper, cork	20·7	20·7	fr.		fr.	
III. Metals	29·3	33·0	35·0	38·6	42·6	55·5
IV. Chemicals	15·7	15·7	33·0	56·3	34·3	54·0
V. Mineral oils	65·8	65·8	45·0	51·3	123·0	141·0
Average of I–IV = average of B¹	18·5	21·8	21·1	32·0	24·4	40·6
Average of I–V = average of B²	28·0	30·6	26·0	36·0	44·0	60·7
C. Manufactured goods:						
I. Textiles	16·0	21·0	25·0	44·0	30·4	49·0
II. Paper	14·8	19·8	16·8	43·0	24·0	55·0
III. Glass, china, cement	23·5	40·3	24·2	25·8	28·0	31·0
IV. Metal goods	17·0	27·8	55·0	61·0	67·5	95·0
V. Machines	14·1	24·0	14·5	30·7	24·0	50·5
VI. Vehicles	14·0	19·0	21·7	27·7	31·0	43·0
VII. Apparatuses, instruments	9·6	11·5	13·0	19·0	18·0	24·7
VIII. Toys and tires	7·8	28·2	11·0	77·0	14·6	97·0
Average of I–VIII = average of C	14·6	24·0	22·7	41·0	29·7	55·5
General tariff level (average of A¹, B¹ C)	20·0	25·7	24·0	35·8	36·7	53·5

TABLE A1: POTENTIAL TARIFF LEVELS OF YUGOSLAVIA
(1913: SERBIA)
(In % of Prices)

Group of Goods	1913		1927		1931	
A. Foodstuffs:						
I. Cereals and flour . . .	25·7	25·7	9·2	9·2	80·0	80·0
II. Livestock	4·0	20·0	18·4	24·0	26·6	34·0
III. Animal foodstuffs . .	23·6	24·7	60·0	60·0	100·0	103·0
IV. Fruit and vegetables . .	20·8	35·0	20·4	25·4	32·7	38·2
V. Other foodstuffs . . .	71·0	71·0	66·3	66·3	116·0	125·0
VI. Alcoholic drinks and tobacco .	25·8	31·0	74·0	91·0	63·0	98·0
Average of I–VI = average of A .	28·5	34·6	41·4	46·0	70·0	80·0
B. Semi-manufactured goods:						
I. Textiles	9·4	20·0	8·1	16·3	13·3	22·6
II. Timber, paper, cork . .	16·5	20·7	24·3	24·3	25·3	25·3
III. Metals	17·0	17·8	32·0	36·2	36·8	42·0
IV. Chemicals	17·8	18·3	28·5	28·5	40·0	40·0
V. Mineral oils . . .	9·5	76·0	40·3	93·0	142·0	238·0
Average of I–IV = average of B¹ .	15·2	19·2	23·2	26·3	29·0	32·5
Average of I–V = average of B² .	14·0	30·6	26·6	39·6	51·5	73·6
C. Manufactured goods:						
I. Textiles	16·8	21·8	27·7	38·5	27·7	40·0
II. Paper	20·3	32·3	20·4	29·2	37·0	37·0
III. Glass, china, cement . .	30·0	37·0	32·8	40·7	31·0	38·0
IV. Metal goods . . .	14·0	26·8	25·4	43·0	31·2	63·0
V. Machines	3·9	6·0	10·6	12·0	11·3	12·7
VI. Vehicles	7·3	7·3	16·8	16·8	16·3	16·3
VII. Apparatuses, instruments .	6·8	6·8	18·5	23·5	21·0	26·4
VIII. Toys and tires . . .	21·0	34·5	32·0	61·0	42·0	75·0
Average of I–VIII = average of C .	15·0	21·5	23·0	33·0	27·2	38·5
General tariff level (average of A, B¹, C)	19·4	25·0	29·2	35·0	42·0	50·0

TABLE AI: POTENTIAL TARIFF LEVELS OF BULGARIA
(*In % of Prices*)

Group of Goods	1913		1927		1931	
A. Foodstuffs:						
I. Cereals and flour	9·7	9·7	18·0	18·0	66·0	66·0
II. Livestock	2·5	9·7	10·0	21·4	16·0	37·6
III. Animal foodstuffs	24·0	30·5	82·5	123·0	142·0	196·0
IV. Fruit and vegetables	25·0	25·0	94·5	110·0	129·0	148·0
V. Other foodstuffs	55·0	56·0	152·0	157·0	264·0	270·0
Average of I–V = average of A¹	23·2	26·2	71·5	86·0	123·0	144·0
VI. Alcoholic drinks and tobacco	94·5	117·0	278·0	380·0	325·0	421·0
Average of I–VI = average of A²	36·4	41·3	106·0	135·0	157·0	190·0
B. Semi-manufactured goods:						
I. Textiles	18·2	23·0	76·0	99·0	106·0	141·0
II. Timber, paper, cork	16·4	16·4	26·2	26·2	44·0	44·0
III. Metals	19·7	20·4	28·5	39·0	31·2	42·0
IV. Chemicals	30·0	49·0	44·0	55·4	48·5	63·0
V. Mineral oils	28·5	32·5	17·3	187·0	40·7	450·0
Average of I–IV = average of B¹	21·2	27·2	44·0	55·0	57·4	72·5
Average of I–V = average of B²	22·6	28·3	38·4	81·0	54·0	148·0
C. Manufactured goods:						
I. Textiles	19·2	22·2	121·0	166·0	149·0	200·0
II. Paper	31·3	31·3	29·7	62·0	37·7	78·0
III. Glass, china, cement	21·0	22·4	77·0	77·0	66·6	66·6
IV. Metal goods	10·7	19·5	28·5	63·5	36·0	73·0
V. Machines	3·8	3·8	7·8	7·8	6·6	6·6
VI. Vehicles	8·6	8·6	13·3	13·3	13·3	13·3
VII. Apparatuses, instruments	12·4	12·4	47·0	47·0	51·5	51·5
VIII. Toys and tires	42·5	42·5	162·0	314·0	203·0	396·0
Average of I–VIII = average of C	18·7	20·3	55·8	94·0	70·4	110·0
General tariff level (average of A¹, B¹, C)	21·0	24·6	57·0	78·0	83·0	109·0

TABLE AI: POTENTIAL TARIFF LEVELS OF SPAIN
(In % of Prices)

Group of Goods	1913		1927		1931	
A. Foodstuffs:						
I. Cereals and flour	32·0	32·0	41·0	41·0	99·0	99·0
II. Livestock	11·4	13·4	19·3	28·0	35·0	46·0
III. Animal foodstuffs	23·0	35·0	28·7	37·3	45·4	56·0
IV. Fruit and vegetables	9·4	9·4	9·8	9·8	14·2	14·2
V. Other foodstuffs	125·0	125·0	114·0	125·0	199·0	199·0
Average of I–V = average of A¹	40·0	43·0	42·5	48·0	78·0	83·0
VI. Alcoholic drinks and tobacco	63·0	63·0	76·0	76·0	85·0	85·0
Average of I–VI = average of A²	44·0	46·0	48·0	52·5	79·5	83·0
B. Semi-manufactured goods:						
I. Textiles	25·0	64·0	33·3	62·4	40·0	88·0
II. Timber, paper, cork	7·9	8·3	8·1	6·0	14·4	14·4
III. Metals	32·0	36·6	70·0	86·0	87·5	98·0
IV. Chemicals	16·3	19·2	21·4	24·0	25·3	27·5
V. Mineral oils	137·0	137·0	133·0	133·0	253·0	253·0
Average of I–IV = average of B¹	20·3	32·0	32·2	45·2	41·8	57·0
Average of I–V = average of B²	43·4	53·0	53·3	63·0	84·0	96·0
C. Manufactured goods:						
I. Textiles	45·0	57·3	63·5	118·0	81·5	131·0
II. Paper	34·0	86·0	57·0	120·0	72·0	152·0
III. Glass, china, cement	41·5	68·0	59·5	73·0	57·0	72·0
IV. Metal goods	36·4	48·5	42·0	60·0	56·5	77·0
V. Machines	16·2	20·0	21·0	36·0	33·0	46·0
VI. Vehicles	7·5	11·5	29·0	43·5	37·0	55·0
VII. Apparatuses, instruments	19·5	19·6	20·5	22·0	25·0	27·0
VIII. Toys and tires	85·0	85·0	65·0	174·0	77·0	208·0
Average of I–VIII = average of C	35·7	49·5	44·4	81·0	55·0	96·0
General tariff level (average of A¹, B¹, C)	32·0	42·0	40·0	58·0	58·0	79·0

TABLE B1: ACTUAL TARIFF LEVELS OF GERMANY

Group of Goods	1913		1927		1927 as % of 1913		1931		1931 as % of 1913	
A. *Foodstuffs*										
I. Cereals, flour	[9] 21·0	25·5	[14] 25·5	26·3	103	121	[12] 142·0	149·0	535	670
II. Livestock	[3] 7·8	29·6	[4] 38·3	97·0	337	490	38·2	96·0	324	490
III. Animal foodstuffs	[24] 20·0	20·4	[39] 13·8	16·0	69	78	19·4	19·7	96	97
IV. Fruit, vegetables	[19] 13·4	15·0	[32] 14·7	21·0	110	140	24·8	44·0	185	290
V. Other foodstuffs	[7] 30·8	30·8	[9] 27·0	28·7	88	93	103·0	105·0	334	340
Average of I–V =average of A[1]	18·6	24·3	24·0	38·0	130	156	65·5	82·5	340	350
VI. Alcoholic drinks and tobacco	[9] 42·7	57·0	[10] 37·5	63·0	88	110	104·0	111·0	193	242
Average of I–VI =average of A[2]	22·6	29·7	26·1	42·0	115	140	72·0	87·0	292	320
B. *Semi-manufactured goods.*										
I. Textiles	[46] 6·7	12·7	[68] 7·3	16·8	109	132	12·0	26·2	180	206
II. Timber, paper, cork	[18] 18·7	18·7	[34] 18·0	22·8	96	122	18·6	25·7	100	138
III. Metals	[18] 14·2	20·3	[17] 14·5	22·6	102	111	18·5	29·4	130	145
IV. Chemicals	[4] 39·6	47·7	[5] 19·9	25·5	50	53·5	[6] 43·0	47·5	100	109
V. Mineral oils	—		—		—		—		—	
Average of I–IV =average of B	19·8	24·8	15·0	22·0	76	89	23·0	32·0	116	124
C. *Manufactured Goods*										
I. Textiles	[9] 6·3	6·5	[22] 18·6	25·5	295	390	24·1	35·4	380	545
II. Paper	[8] 15·0	16·7	[9] 12·6	12·7	76	84	13·4	14·0	84	89
III. Glass, china, cement	—		[8] 56·0	62·0	I		61·0	67·0	I	
IV. Metal goods	—		—		—		—		—	
V. Machines	[7] 3·5	10·4	3·8	11·2	108	108	4·1	10·8	104	117
VI. Vehicles	[3] 2·6	6·8	[4] 24·3	40·6	595	935	9·3	23·7	350	360
VII. Apparatuses, instruments	[10] 13·0	13·0	[14] 18·8	19·6	145	150	24·5	26·0	188	200
VIII. Toys and tires	[3] 7·9	7·9	15·8	21·3	200	270	18·6	28·2	235	386
Average of C	8·0	10·2	21·4	27·6	270	275	22·1	29·5	275	290
General tariff level (average of A,[1] B, C)	15·5	19·8	20·1	29·2	130	148	36·9	48·0	238	242

TABLE Bɪɪ: ACTUAL TARIFF LEVELS OF ITALY

Group of Goods	1913		1927		1927 as % of 1913		1931		1931 as % of 1913	
A. Foodstuffs										
I. Cereals, flour	[6] 25·0	35·0	[9] 19·0	27·0	76	77	[8] 122·0	123·0	350	490
II. Livestock	—		[5] 3·7	10·0	I		·5·3	14·2	I	
III. Animal foodstuffs	[6] 14·6	15·3	[9] 33·6	54·6	230	360	54·0	72·0	370	470
IV. Fruit, vegetables	[4] 33·3	33·3	13·2	15·8	40	47	17·6	18·0	53	54
V. Other foodstuffs	[3] 19·0	19·0	18·0	18·0	95	95	53·0	53·0	280	280
Average of A	23·0	26·0	17·5	25·0	76	96	50·4	54·0	210	220
B. Semi-manufactured Goods										
I. Textiles	[9] 6·3	9·5	[14] 10·2	16·4	161	172	16·4	27·5	260	290
II. Timber,paper,cork	—		[5] 3·2	3·3	I		3·8	3·8	I	
III. Metals	[16] 18·8	25	[21] 32·0	54·0	170	215	43·4	69·5	230	280
IV. Chemicals	[5] 7·3	9·9	[10] 16·3	36·4	210	370	22·0	44·6	300	450
V. Mineral oils	—		[3] 109·0	165·0	I		318·0	400·0	I	
Average of B	10·8	14·8	15·4	27·7	142	187	21·4	36·3	200	245
C. Manufactured Goods										
I. Textiles	[6] 11·5	16·3	[7] 11·7	25·3	102	155	9·7	19·0	84·5	116
II. Paper	—		[3] 22·5	29·0	I		31·6	39·1	I	
III. Glass, china, cement	—		[5] 27·2	33·0	I		29·0	36·0	I	
IV. Metal goods	[9] 11·7	16·4	[11] 17·4	38·4	147	234	21·0	48·0	180	290
V. Machines	[22] 6·5	7·1	8·8	19·0	135	270	12·7	23·6	195	330
VI. Vehicles	—		—		—		—		—	
VII. Apparatuses, instruments	[7] 3·6	3·7	[9] 9·0	12·7	250	342	26·0	41·0	720	1100
VIII. Toys and tires	[5] 8·1	8·1	[7] 17·2	24·4	212	300	28·3	37·7	350	465
Average of C	8·3	10·3	16·4	26·0	198	250	22·6	35·0	270	350
General tariff level (average of A, B, C)	12·7	15·9	16·4	26·3	130	165	43·3	52·8	330	340

TABLE BIII: ACTUAL TARIFF LEVELS OF SWITZERLAND

Group of Goods	1913		1927		1927 as % of 1913		1931		1931 as % of 1913	
A. Foodstuffs										
I. Cereals, flour	[3] 3·7	23·5	[7] 9·1	42·2	180	246	43·0	88·0	375	1160
II. Livestock	—		—		—		—		—	
III. Animal foodstuffs	[8] 1·6	3·6	[11] 6·9	8·3	230	430	[10] 18·1	26·4	730	1130
IV. Fruit, vegetables	[4] 40·0	40·0	[6] 23·6	25·4	59	64	35·7	35·7	89	89
V. Other foodstuffs	[4] 19·7	22·3	[5] 13·2	19·0	67	85	28·0	34·0	142	152
Average of A¹	16·0	22·3	13·2	23·7	83	106	31·2	46·0	195	205
VI. Alcoholic drinks and tobacco	[5] 23·7	29·7	[6] 47·0	83·0	198	280	73·5	98·0	310	330
Average of A²	17·7	24·0	20·0	35·6	113	148	40·0	56·0	225	235
B. Semi-manufactured Goods										
I. Textiles	[22] 3·6	6·5	[24] 5·5	6·7	103	155	7·9	9·6	147	220
II. Timber,paper,cork	—		—		—		—		—	
III. Metals	[19] 1·4	5·9	[20] 2·8	10·3	175	200	12·3	23·0	390	880
IV. Chemicals	[9] 4·7	7·4	4·6	9·6	100	130	5·9	12·3	125	166
Average of B	3·9	6·6	4·3	8·9	135	135	9·4	15·0	230	290
C. Manufactured Goods										
I. Textiles	[17] 3·5	4·3	[24] 6·8	8·6	195	200	8·4	12·1	240	280
II. Paper	—		—		—		—		—	
III. Glass, china, cement	—		—		—		—		—	
IV. Metal goods	[12] 6·3	16·4	13·0	29·8	180	206	13·4	31·0	188	210
V. Machines	[6] 2·3	6·5	4·9	10·8	166	212	4·9	9·3	143	212
VI. Vehicles	[4] 10·3	10·3	3·0	43·0	290	415	35·4	50·0	345	485
VII. Apparatuses, instruments	[10] 5·1	6·7	7·5	8·0	120	147	5·6	5·8	86·5	109
VIII. Toys and tires	[9] 1·4	2·0	5·9	6·0	300	420	7·2	7·4	360	515
Average of C	4·8	7·7	11·3	17·7	230	235	12·3	17·5	230	255
General tariff level (average of A¹, B, C)	8·0	12·3	9·6	16·8	120	136	17·6	26·2	212	220

TABLE BIV: ACTUAL TARIFF LEVELS OF SPAIN

Group of Goods	1913		1927		1927 as % of 1913		1931		1931 as % of 1913	
A. *Foodstuffs*	No figures available									
B. *Semi-manufactured Goods*										
I. Textiles	(5) 11·4	47·5	10·4	31·0	65	91	36·8	66·0	138	322
II. Timber, paper, cork	(7) 6·1	10·0	(8) 13·0	15·5	155	212	14·7	16·8	168	214
III. Metals	—		—		—		—		—	
IV. Chemicals	(9) 37·0	38·5	(10) 22·5	26·0	60	67	45·5	49·0	123	127
Average of B	18·2	32·0	15·3	24·2	76	84	32·3	43·7	136	178
C. *Manufactured Goods*										
I. Textiles	—		—		—		—		—	
II. Paper	—		—		—		—		—	
III. Glass, china, cement	(4) 19·7	19·7	32·0	32·0	162	162	36·0	36·0	182	182
IV. Metal goods	(8) 18·0	30·0	28·5	48·5	158	160	34·0	59·0	188	197
V. Machines	(16) 17·5	22·0	23·0	32·6	130	148	27·6	57·5	157	260
VI. Vehicles	(6) 12·0	14·8	(7) 36·2	101·5	300	680	36·8	95·0	306	640
VII. Apparatuses, instruments	(6) 12·0	12·6	(7) 62·0	62·0	490	520	62·0	62·0	490	520
VIII. Toys and tires	(3) 33·0	33·0	98·0	267·0	295	810	93·0	236·0	280	715
Average of C	18·7	22·0	47·0	90·0	250	410	48·0	91·0	255	410

LIST OF 144 A-PRICES AND A-GOODS
(*In German Mark or Reichsmark (M. or Rm.)*)
(*Comp. pp. 49–55 of text*)

Goods	Export Country	Unit	1913	1927	1931
A. *Foodstuffs*					
AI			M.	Rm.	Rm.
Wheat	Roumania	100 kilos	14·60	22·50	11·80
Rye	Germany	,,	14·20	22·80	8·20
Barley	Roumania	,,	10·50	18·20	6·30
Oats	Germany	,,	14·10	20·10	14·00
Maize	Roumania	,,	9·60	13·50	5·45
Wheat flour . . .	Germany	,,	22·70	23·50	13·20
Rye flour . . .	Germany	,,	17·50	26·80	10·10
AII					
Pigs	Netherlands {	100 kilos	48·60	95·00	74·00
		piece	51·00	125·00	67·60
Cattle	Denmark	,,	368·00	354·00	276·00
Horses	Denmark	,,	885·00	715·00	347·00
AIII					
Eggs	Netherlands	100 kilos	76·00	137·00	101·00
Butter	Denmark	,,	246·00	350·00	244·00
Cheese	Netherlands	,,	59·00	133·00	102·00
Bacon or lard . . . {	Denmark	,,	143·00	190·00	127·00
	Netherlands	,,	76·00	110·00	67·60
Fresh beef . . .	Denmark	,,	104·00	114·00	88·00
Fresh pork . . .	Netherlands	,,	76·00	142·00	88·00
Tins of sardines in oil .	Spain	,,	121·00	77·00	40·00
AIV					
Potatoes	Germany	100 kilos	5·28	10·80	7·15
Hops	Germany	,,	363·00	734·00	167·00
Tomatoes . . .	Italy	,,	8·10	26·40	22·00
Cauliflower . . .	France	,,	32·40	29·70	16·30
Oranges	Spain	,,	9·75	21·60	8·40
Raisins	Greece	,,	32·40	54·00	74·00
Dried figs . . .	Greece	,,	73·00	32·40	26·20
Shelled almonds . .	Spain	,,	186·00	294·00	88·00
Apples	France	,,	28·30	36·20	36·80
Fresh grapes . . .	France	,,	40·50	36·60	36·60
Beans	Roumania	,,	174·00	192·00	86·00
AV					
Unrefined sugar . .	Germany	100 kilos	20·50	31·70	11·50
Refined sugar . . .	Germany	,,	25·60	36·00	14·00
Chocolate . . .	Switzerland	,,	278·00	324·00	296·00
Olive oil . . .	Spain	,,	81·00	138·00	42·00
Margarine . . .	Netherlands	,,	135·00	105·00	79·50
Powdered cocoa . .	Netherlands	,,	186·00	108·00	74·50

Goods	Export Country	Unit	1913	1927	1931
A. *Foodstuffs*—Contd.					
Avi			M.	Rm.	Rm.
Champagne . . .	France	hectol.	356·00	486·00	470·00
Other wines in casks .	France	100 kilos	40·50	66·00	64·60
Liqueurs . . .	France	,,	304·00	314·00	252·00
Leaf tobacco . . .	Greece	,,	158·00	350·00	274·00
B. *Semi-finished Industrial Articles*					
Bi			M.	Rm.	Rm.
Upper leather (cattle, horse)	Germany	100 kilos	1140·00	1780·00	1220·00
Goat leather . . .	Germany	,,	1730·00	4280·00	2930·00
Cotton yarn, single, un-bleached, up to No. 50 .	Great Britain	,,	332·00	321·00	227·00
Cotton yarn, single, un-bleached, over No. 50 .	Great Britain	,,	332·00	620·00	405·00
Raw worsted . . .	Great Britain	,,	454·00	730·00	550·00
Linen yarn, unbleached, up to No. 50 . . .	Belgium	,,	272·00	264·00	232·00
Silk yarn, undyed . .	France	,,	1780·00	4000·00	1980·00
Raw artificial silk yarn .	France	,,	1330·00	582·00	460·00
Cotton tissues, bleached .	Great Britain	,,	346·00	605·00	460·00
Cotton tissues, printed .	Germany	,,	396·00	726·00	492·00
Woollen tissues . .	Germany	,,	856·00	1480·00	1230·00
Bii					
Cellulose, unbleached or bleached . . .	Sweden	100 kilos	14·60	22·40	17·90
Wood pulp . . .	Finland	,,	3·64	4·80	5·30
Timber, hewn, soft . .	Sweden	cu. metre	29·20	52·40	37·20
Planks, soft, not planed .	Sweden	,,	39·00	59·00	44·50
Cork in sheets . .	Spain	100 kilos	36·40	48·00	17·60
Biii					
Pig iron	Germany	100 kilos	6·63	8·18	6·86
Crude steel . . .	Great Britain	,,	29·20	23·20	23·40
Rolled iron . . .	France	,,	10·00	10·40	9·10
Iron sheets, not worked .	France	,,	16·00	15·60	13·20
Iron wire, rough . .	Germany	,,	11·50	11·85	11·40
Iron pipes . . .	Germany	,,	25·40	33·40	41·80
Mould iron . . .	Germany	,,	11·10	10·80	8·60
Tinned sheet . . .	Great Britain	,,	30·00	43·50	34·40
Copper sheets, not worked	Germany	,,	181·00	155·00	114·00
Copper wire, rough . .	Germany	,,	178·00	151·00	112·00
Zinc sheets, not worked .	Germany	,,	57·00	79·00	36·00
Aluminium sheets . .	Germany	,,	161·00	203·00	155·00
Aluminium in blocks .	Switzerland	,,	125·00	200·00	167·00
Rails	Germany	,,	11·50	13·30	13·20

Goods	Export Country	Unit	1913	1927	1931
B. Semi-finished Industrial Articles—Contd.					
B IV			M.	Rm.	Rm.
Potash salts	Germany	100 kilos	7·16	6·26	5·70
Sulphate of ammonia	Great Britain	,,	28·00	20·40	13·20
Sulphurated ammonia	Germany	,,	24·50	20·60	11·20
Superphosphates	Germany	,,	7·60	7·30	5·35
Nitrogen from lime	Norway	,,	20·50	17·00	14·50
Nitrogen from air	Germany	,,	11·50	22·50	21·80
Sulphate of copper	Great Britain	,,	46·00	44·70	37·00
Aniline dyes	Germany	,,	221·00	537·00	450·00
Ordinary soap	France	,,	23·50	66·00	49·00
Non-alcoholic perfumes	France	,,	344·00	577·00	715·00
Medicaments	Germany	,,	918·00	2730·00	2180·00
B V					
Refined oil	Roumania	100 kilos	6·80	8·25	2·70
Petrol	Roumania	,,	22·80	16·80	6·15
Benzol	Great Britain	hectol.	20·60	25·40	34·00
C. Manufactured Industrial Goods					
C I			M.	Rm.	Rm.
Leather shoes	Germany	{100 kilos / pair	982·00 / —	1670·00 / 10·50	1470·00 / 7·56
Leather gloves	France	100 kilos	9200·00	8800·00	9850·00
Fine leather goods	Germany	,,	1080·00	1965·00	1650·00
Cotton yarn, prepared for retail sale	Great Britain	,,	755·00	1600·00	1350·00
Cotton stockings, socks	Germany	,,	926·00	2550·00	2080·00
Cotton hosiery and knitted goods	Germany	,,	536·00	885·00	955·00
Cotton and woollen suits	France	,,	1250·00	775·00	1150·00
Woollen stockings and socks	Germany	,,	1080·00	2520·00	2100·00
Woollen hosiery and knitted goods	Germany	,,	1080·00	2520·00	2100·00
Woollen velvet	Germany	,,	744·00	1310·00	1120·00
Woollen clothing (women)	Germany	,,	1500·00	4280·00	3370·00
Woollen carpets	Germany	,,	423·00	621·00	573·00
Silk stockings and socks	France	,,	10850·00	18000·00	14000·00
Silk crêpes and tulles	France	,,	5750·00	8750·00	6000·00
Artificial silk stockings and socks	Germany	,,	3000·00	3130·00	2200·00
Artificial silk crêpes and tulles	France	,,	5750·00	4200·00	2680·00
Silk ribbons	Switzerland	,,	4910·00	1920·00	1540·00
Galloshes	France	,,	810·00	305·00	260·00
Fur coats	France	,,	10500·00	8500·00	8450·00
C II					
Pasteboard	Germany	100 kilos	20·30	30·80	25·00
Printing paper	Germany	,,	28·60	31·60	23·80
Packing paper	Germany	,,	31·00	47·60	38·00

Goods	Export Country	Unit	1913	1927	1931
C. *Manufactured Industrial Goods*—Contd.					
CIII			M.	Rm.	Rm.
Cement	Germany	100 kilos	3·34	3·32	2·94
Window glass . . .	France	,,	18·60	36·40	39·00
Sheet glass, cut . .	Belgium	,,	61·50	64·50	88·00
Optical glass . . .	Germany	,,	2870·00	2270·00	2030·00
White china . . .	Germany	,,	91·00	138·00	148·00
Coloured china . .	France	,,	121·00	370·00	310·00
CIV					
Iron household utensils .	Germany	100 kilos	116·00	135·00	112·00
Iron cutting-implements .	Germany	,,	266·00	335·00	296·00
Fine iron cutting tools .	Germany	,,	644·00	918·00	946·00
Iron radiators . . .	Germany	,,	41·00	50·00	31·60
Cast-iron lamps . .	Germany	,,	133·00	123·00	110·00
Copper household articles	Germany	,,	462·00	566·00	530·00
CV					
Looms	Great Britain	100 kilos	94·00	157·00	154·00
Spinning machines .	Switzerland	,,	145·00	244·00	197·00
Sewing machines without stand	Germany	,,	283·00	546·00	540·00
Sewing machines with stand	Germany	,,	167·00	278·00	334·00
Hosiery looms . .	Germany	,,	187·00	323·00	334·00
Finishing textile machines	Germany	,,	103·00	180·00	183·00
Internal combustion engines, not movable .	Germany	,,	111·00	183·00	170·00
Steam engines (power machines) . . .	Switzerland	,,	152·00	238·00	260·00
Dynamos . . .	Germany	,,	125·00	197·00	207·00
Metal working machines .	Germany	,,	110·00	184·00	179·00
Wood working machines .	Germany	,,	105·00	158·00	168·00
Milling machines . .	Germany	,,	112·00	169·00	166·00
Paper machines . .	Germany	,,	84·00	131·00	123·00
Mowing machines . .	Germany	,,	64·00	65·00	66·00
CVI					
Locomotives (steam) .	Germany	100 kilos	101·00	155·00	127·00
Private cars . . .	Germany	{ ,,	731·00	485·00	297·00
		piece	9000·00	6120·00	3000·00
Freight motor-cars . .	France	100 kilos	486·00	240·00	236·00
CVII					
Telephone apparatus .	Germany	100 kilos	902·00	840·00	1570·00
Telegraph apparatus .	Sweden	,,	1330·00	1680·00	1770·00
Wireless sets . . .	Germany	,,	594·00	1190·00	965·00
Photographic apparatus .	Germany	,,	2540·00	4870·00	3930·00
Metal thread lamps . .	Germany	,,	2120·00	2510·00	2560·00
Watches (gold cases) .	Switzerland	piece	44·00	67·50	70·00
Watches (silver cases) .	Switzerland	,,	9·50	16·50	18·00
Watches (other cases) .	Switzerland	,,	4·22	5·10	4·00
Pianos	Germany	,,	625·00	1030·00	830·00
CVIII					
Tires	France	100 kilos	810·00	580·00	366·00
Toys	Germany	,,	183·00	252·00	220·00

INDEX TABLE OF A-PRICES

(Comp. pp. 54–55 of text)

1913 = 100, *the group index amounted to :*

Group	1927	1931
A. *Foodstuffs*		
I. Cereals and flour . . .	142·5	67·0
II. Livestock	92·5	53·0
III. Animal foodstuffs . .	140·0	96·5
IV. Fruit and vegetables . .	154·0	59·5
V. Other foodstuffs . . .	102·0	71·0
Average of I–V = average of A^1 .	106·0	69·5
VI. Alcoholic drinks and tobacco .	142·6	123·0
Average of I–VI = average of A^2 .	129·0	78·3
B. *Semi-manufactured goods*		
I. Textiles	172·0	113·0
II. Timber, paper, cork . .	152·0	100·0
III. Metals	112·0	87·5
IV. Chemicals	190·0 *	158·0 *
V. Mineral oils . . .	85·0 †	29·8 †
Average of I–V = average of B .	142·2	97·6
C. *Manufactured Industrial Goods*		
I. Textiles	122·0	102·0
II. Paper	138·0	108·0
III. Glass, china, cement . .	91·2	83·0
IV. Metal goods . . .	128·0	122·0
V. Machines	176·0	177·0
VI. Vehicles	66·6	50·0
VII. Apparatuses, instruments .	161·0	143·0
VIII. Toys, tires . . .	84·0	59·0
Average of I–VIII = average of C .	120·8	105·5
General price level (average of A^2, B, C)	130·6	94·0

* Without medicaments and perfumes as dishomogeneous price elements.

† Without benzol as dishomogeneous price element.

TABLE I: EXPORTS OF EUROPEAN STATES, 1913–34

(Without coins and bullion; in mill. currency units)

For 1913–31 the figures were taken from the official trade statistics and for 1934 from the *Statistische Jahrbuch für das Deutsche Reich,* 1935.

Country	1913	1929	1931	1934	1931 as % of 1929	1934 as % of 1929
Great Britain .	525	729	390	396	45·0	45·5
Germany .	10100	13480	6900	4167	71·2	30·8
France . .	6880	50100	30400	17800	60·6	35·5
Italy . .	2512	14890	10210	5130	67·6	34·5
Belgium . .	3635	31900	23100	13500	72·2	42·3
Switzerland .	1375	2104	1350	835	64·3	39·8
Austria . .	—	2190	1290	855	71·2	39·0
Czechoslovakia	—	20500	13105	7250	63·4	35·3
Netherlands .	(3085)	1990	1320	710	66·0	35·6
Denmark .	637	1616	1260	1170	78·0	72·3
Sweden . .	817	1812	1122	1200	62·0	66·2
Norway . .	381	743	460	570	61·6	76·5
Finland . .	399	6380	4400	6150	68·6	96·5
Esthonia .	—	117	71	69	61·0	59·0
Lettland .	—	274	164	85	59·5	31·0
Lithuania .	—	330	273	147	79·5	44·5
Poland . .	—	2815	1880	980	67·0	34·9
Roumania .	671	29000	22200	13600	76·5	47·0
Hungary .	—	1040	570	278	55·0	26·7
Yugoslavia .	—	7920	4800	3820	61·0	48·0
Bulgaria . .	93	6400	5930	2560	92·6	40·0
Greece . .	119	7000	4200	5460	61·0	78·0
Spain . .	1058	2110	961	1450	45·5	68·6
Portugal . .	35	1073	812	912	76·0	85·0

TABLE II: GOODS CLASSIFICATION OF EUROPEAN EXPORTS, 1913–31

(*Comp. p.* 114, *note* 1, *of text*)

I = Livestock, foodstuffs, and liquids.
II = Raw materials and semi-manufactured goods.
III = Industrial manufactured goods.

In % of Total Exports the exports of I, II, *and* III *amounted to:*

Country	1913 I	II	III	1927 I	II	III	1931 I	II	II
Great Britain	6·2	13·3	78·5	7·3	10·7	79·5	9·1	12·0	75·
Germany	10·4	26·3	63·3	4·4	24·1	71·5	4·2	18·9	76·
France	12·2	27·0	60·8	10·2	30·0	59·8	14·1	23·6	62·
Italy	30·0	38·0	32·0	25·3	34·7	40·0	29·0	28·0	43·
Belgium	10·0	49·1	38·7	8·5	33·7	57·5	9·4	33·9	56·
Switzerland	14·6	11·1	74·3	10·9	9·4	79·5	11·2	11·0	77·
Austria *	27·2	40·4	32·4	3·2	22·7	71·1	4·2	20·3	72·
Czechoslovakia	—	—	—	14·5	19·6	65·8	8·7	15·5	75·
Netherlands	58·1	18·5	23·4	49·3	18·3	30·2	40·6	19·8	31·
Sweden	12·8	63·1	24·1	10·6	52·2	38·3	8·5	43·0	45·
Denmark	83·7	11·0	5·3	82·0	6·3	11·7	84·0	5·3	10·
Norway	36·6	50·5	12·9	28·6	49·9	21·5	25·4	51·2	17·
Finland	14·8	65·3	19·9	8·8	70·4	20·8	10·1	57·1	33·
Poland	—	—	—	28·3	57·8	13·9	32·6	42·6	23·
Esthonia	—	—	—	37·6	29·2	32·8	49·7	26·6	23·
Lettland	—	—	—	23·8	58·0	18·2	32·6	30·4	37·
Lithuania	—	—	—	31·7	63·5	4·7	70·7	24·6	4·
Roumania	71·4	27·7	0·9	42·7	55·1	2·2	no data availabl		
Hungary	—	—	—	68·0	14·0	18·0	57·5	13·7	28·
Yugoslavia †	74·1	24·0	1·9	49·3	41·5	9·2	50·7	42·0	7·
Bulgaria	71·5	18·1	10·4	49·3	46·2	4·5	43·7	53·4	2·
Greece	61·3	38·0	0·7	35·3	63·4	1·3	35·3	61·4	2·
Spain	43·8	30·9	23·3	54·2	25·1	20·3	67·0	16·4	13·
Portugal	68·0	20·4	11·6	61·2	25·2	13·6	68·6	22·7	8·

* Austria, 1913 = figures of Austria-Hungary in 1913.
† Yugoslavia, 1913 = Serbia, 1913.
Sources: (1) Official trade statistics; (2) *Memorandum sur le commerce inter*
national, 1927–29; (3) *Statistiques du commerce extérieur,* 1913–32; (4) Gaedick(
v. Eynern, *Vol. of Tables,* pp. 18–19.

TABLE III: FOREIGN TRADE RELATIONS OF EUROPEAN COUNTRIES WITH EUROPE

(*Comp. pp.* 192–198 *of text and Gaedicke,* Vol. of Text, *p.* 20)

In % *of Total Exports, goods were sent to or received from Europe:*

Country	Exports Average 1909–13	Exports Average 1925–30	Imports Average 1909–13	Imports Average 1925–30
Austria	—	87·6	—	85·1
Austria-Hungary. . .	86·3	—	74·5	—
Belgium—Luxembourg .	80·2	70·5	64·8	61·9
Bulgaria	93·1	90·4	98·6	93·3
Czechoslovakia . . .	—	82·3	—	67·0
Denmark	95·5	96·4	83·5	74·3
Esthonia	—	97·3	—	76·9
Finland	98·0	87·7	99·3	82·0
France	70·1	64·0	52·0	45·5
Germany . . .	75·5	74·4	57·1	52·7
Great Britain . .	36·4	29·9	45·2	39·0
Greece	83·0	73·8	95·3	68·3
Hungary	—	94·1	—	93·7
Italy	66·6	59·2	69·4	51·7
Lettland	—	96·7	—	92·0
Lithuania	—	98·3	—	92·5
Netherlands . . .	74·2	76·4	73·6	64·8
Norway	78·8	72·8	89·9	78·8
Poland—Danzig . . .	—	96·4	—	77·3
Portugal	61·7	66·3	76·3	73·2
Roumania	96·2	89·4	96·0	93·6
Spain	71·3	66·3	65·2	54·9
Sweden	87·9	78·0	86·0	76·8
Switzerland . . .	75·0	68·6	86·1	73·8
Yugoslavia * . . .	95·9	98·0	99·7	90·9

* Yugoslavia, 1913 = Serbia, 1913.

TABLE IVa: POTENTIAL TARIFF LEVELS IN EUROPE

A

Absolute height of potential tariff levels in Europe, 1913–31

(*Comp. pp.* 102 *ff*, 178 *ff*, *of text*)

(*In* % *of Prices*)

Country	Foodstuffs			Semi-manufactured Goods			Industrial Manufactured Goods		
	1913	1927	1931	1913	1927	1931	1913	1927	1931
Germany . .	21·8	27·4	82·5	15·3	14·5	23·4	10·0	19·0	18·3
France .	29·2	19·1	53·0	25·3	24·3	31·8	16·3	25·8	29·0
Italy . . .	*22·0	24·5	66·0	25·0	28·6	49·5	14·6	28·3	41·8
Belgium .	25·5	11·8	23·7	7·6	10·5	15·5	9·5	11·6	13·0
Switzerland .	14·7	21·5	42·2	7·3	11·5	15·2	9·3	17·6	22·0
Austria † .	(29·1)	16·5	59·5	(20·0)	15·2	20·7	(19·3)	21·0	27·7
Czechoslovakia .		36·3	84·0		21·7	29·5		35·8	36·5
Sweden .	‡24·2	21·5	39·0	25·3	18·0	18·0	24·5	20·8	23·5
Finland .	49·0	57·5	102·0	18·8	20·2	20·0	37·6	17·8	22·7
Poland § .	69·4	72·0	110·0	63·5	33·2	40·0	85·0	55·6	52·0
Roumania .	34·7	45·6	87·5	30·0	32·6	46·3	25·5	48·5	55·0
Hungary .	(29·1)	31·5	60·0	(20·0)	26·5	32·5	(19·3)	31·8	42·6
Yugoslavia ‖ .	31·6	43·7	75·0	17·2	24·7	30·5	18·0	28·0	32·8
Bulgaria .	24·7	79·0	133·0	24·2	49·5	65·0	19·5	75·0	90·0
Spain .	41·5	45·2	80·5	26·0	39·2	49·5	42·5	62·7	75·5

* This figure calculated without the tariff level of class Av (comp. p. 71 of text).

† Austria, 1913 = Austria-Hungary, 1913. The same for the figures of Hungary and Czechoslovakia in 1913.

‡ This figure calculated without the tariff level of class Aiv (comp. p. 86 of the text).

§ Poland, 1913 = Russia, 1913.

‖ Yugoslavia, 1913 = Serbia, 1913.

TABLE IVa: POTENTIAL TARIFF LEVELS IN EUROPE

B

Changes in pre-War and post-War tariff levels and duty rates
1913 = 100, tariff levels (T) and duty rates (R) amounted to:

Country	Foodstuffs				Semi-manufactured Goods				Manufactured Industrial Goods			
	1927		1931		1927		1931		1927		1931	
	T	R	T	R	T	R	T	R	T	R	T	R
Germany	125	170	380	250	95	145	153	175	190	225	183	195
France	65·5	107	180	145	96	125	125	125	153	210	178	215
Italy	75	137	188	150	114	180	198	210	193	250	286	275
Belgium	46	90	93	120	138	I	204	I	122	I	137	I
Switzerland	146	290	288	300	157	225	208	335	189	275	236	275
Austria *	56·6	87	204	130	76	120	103	120	109	120	143	130
Czecho-slovakia	125	130	288	160	108	165	148	170	185	220	188	215
Sweden	65	100	117	100	71	75	71	75	85	115	96	115
Finland	117	230	208	260	107	145	106	165	47·5	I	60·5	I
Poland †	103	155	158	160	52·5	65	63	77	65·5	130	61·0	125
Roumania	131	290	252	305	108	210	153	250	190	415	215	270
Hungary	108	170	206	170	132	180	162	195	165	190	220	200
Yugoslavia ‡	138	230	238	260	135	205	180	190	175	160	205	160
Bulgaria	320	400	540	415	204	275	270	300	385	590	465	590
Spain	109	195	193	195	150	240	190	275	148	240	177	250

* Austria, 1913 = Austria-Hungary, 1913. The same for Hungary and Czechoslovakia, 1913.
† Poland, 1913 = Russia, 1913.
‡ Yugoslavia, 1913 = Serbia, 1913.
I = not comparable.

Tariff Levels and the Economic Unity of Europe

[*To face page* 415.]

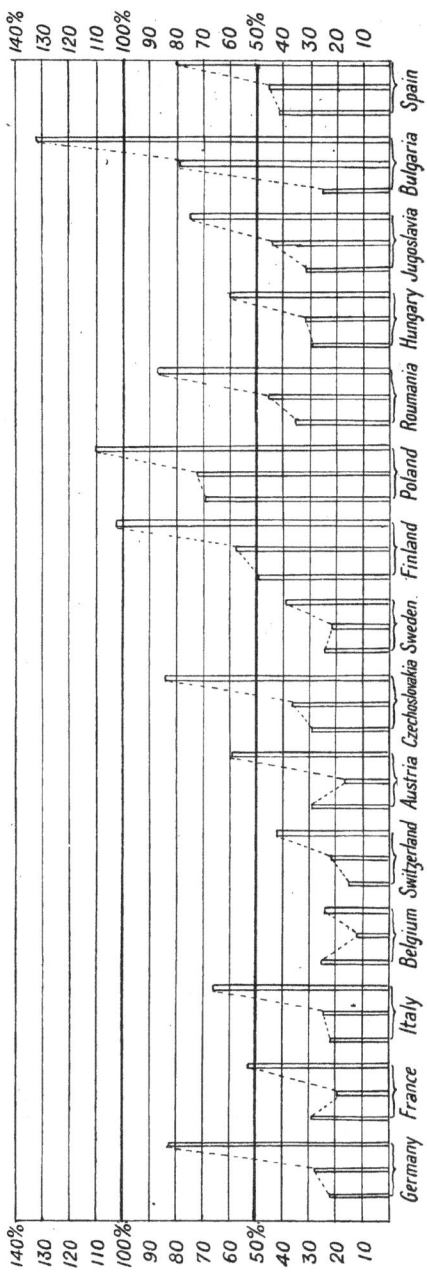

DIAGRAM A

Potential tariff levels in Europe, 1913, 1927, and 1931.
Foodstuffs.

(Comp. p. 102 of text and Table IVA of Appendix.)

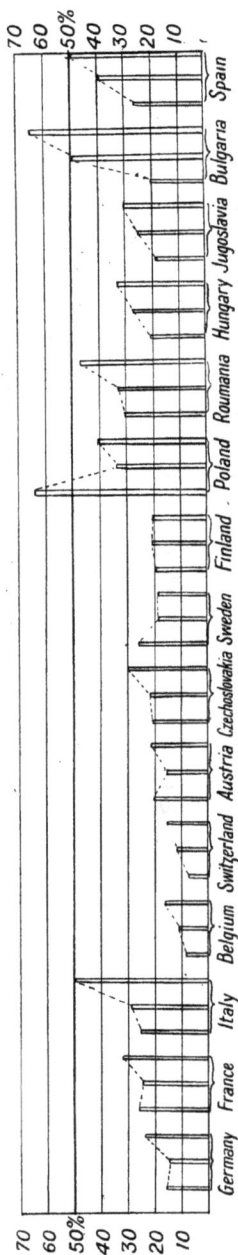

DIAGRAM B

Potential tariff levels in Europe, 1913, 1927, and 1931.
Semi-manufactured goods.

(Comp. pp. 178 ff. of text and Table IVA of Appendix.)

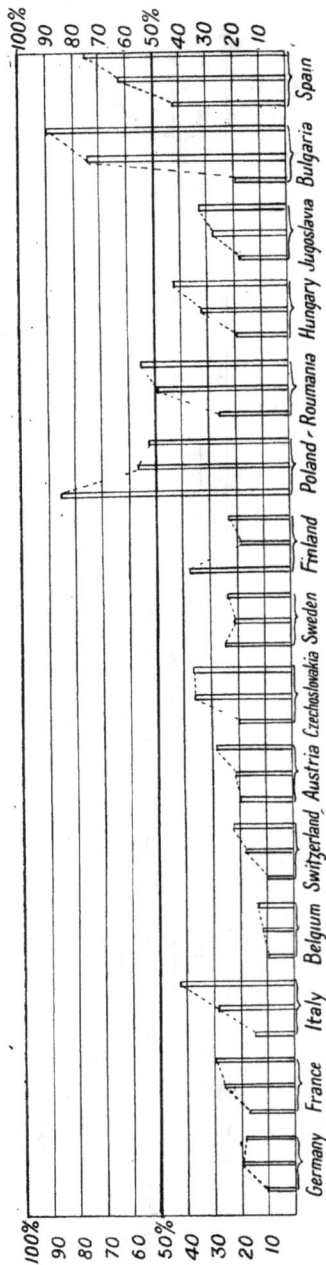

DIAGRAM C

Potential tariff levels in Europe, 1913, 1927, and 1931.
Manufactured goods.

(Comp. pp. 178 ff. of text and Table IVA of Appendix.)

TABLE IVʙ: GENERAL POTENTIAL TARIFF LEVELS IN EUROPE, 1913–31

(*Comp. pp.* 340–345 *of text*)

Country	Absolute Height 1913	1927	1931	1927 as % of 1913	1931 as % of 1913
Germany . . .	16·7	20·4	40·7	122·0	244
France . . .	23·6	23·0	38·0	97·5	160
Italy . . .	24·8	27·8	48·3	112·0	195
Belgium . . .	14·2	11·0	17·4	77·5	122
Switzerland . .	10·5	16·8	26·4	160·0	252
Austria * . .	(22·8)	17·5	36·0	77·0	158
Czechoslovakia †		31·3	50·0	137·0	220
Sweden . . .	27·6	20·0	26·8	72·5	97
Finland . . .	35·0	31·8	48·2	91·0	134
Poland ‡ . .	72·5	53·5	67·5	74·0	93
Roumania . .	30·3	42·3	63·0	140·0	207
Hungary § . .	(22·8)	30·0	45·0	131·0	197
Yugoslavia ‖ . .	22·2	32·0	46·0	144·0	207
Bulgaria . . .	22·8	67·5	96·5	296·0	420
Spain . . .	37·0	49·0	68·5	132·0	185

* Austria, 1913 = Austria-Hungary, 1913.
† Czechoslovakia, 1913 = Austria-Hungary, 1913.
‡ Poland, 1913 = Russia, 1913.
§ Hungary, 1913 = Austria-Hungary, 1913.
‖ Yugoslavia, 1913 = Serbia, 1913.

BIBLIOGRAPHY

A. OFFICIAL STATISTICAL SOURCES

Annuaire statistique de la Lithuanie, 1927, and *Commerce extérieur de la L.*, 1929–31. Kowno, 1927 ff.

Annuaire du commerce extérieur de la republique Polonaise, 1926–27, 1931. Warszawa, 1928, 1932.

Aussenhandel, der tschechoslowakischen Republik, 1927, 1931. Prag, 1928, 1932.

Comertul exterior al Romaniei, 1913, 1927, 1931. Bucuresti, 1914, 1928, 1932.

Commerce extérieur de l'Estonie, 1927–31. Tallin, 1928 ff.

Commerce extérieur de la Hongrie, 1927, 1931. Budapest, 1929, 1933.

Commerce extérieur et transit de la Lettonie, 1927–31. Riga, 1928 ff.

Commerce Yearbook, vol. ii, 1928, 1932. Washington, 1929, 1933.

Danmarks Vareinsforsel og Udforsel, 1913–31. Kopenhagen, 1914, 1932.

Estadistica general del Commercio exterior de Espana, 1913, 1927, 1931. Madrid, 1914, 1928, 1932.

Estatistica commercial, 1913–31. Lisboa, 1914 ff.

Finlands Handel pâ Ryssland och utrikes Oster, 1913. *Ia Ulkomaankauppa*, 1927. *Utrikes Handel*, 1931. Helsingfors, 1915, 1928, 1931.

Handel, der ausw. Deutschlands, 1913, I, 1927, II, Bln. 1914, 1928.

Handels-Archiv, Deutsches, 1919–32. Bln. (Quoted: *H.-A.*)

Jaarstatistiek van den In-Uit-en Doorvoer, 1913–31. Den Haag, 1914–32.

Jahrbuch, Statistisches f. d. Dt. Reich, 1913–14, 1932, 1934, 1935. (Quoted: *Jahrbuch.*)

Memorandum on international trade and balances of payment, vol. iii: "Trade statistics," 1927–29. Geneva, 1931. (Quoted: *Statistiques* I.)

Memorandum sur le commerce extérieur, vol. i, ii. Genève, 1927–29. (Quoted: *Memorandum.*)

Movimento commerciale del regno d'Italia, 1913, 1927, 1931, vol. i. Roma, 1914, 1932 ff.

MÜLLER, ROTH, WEISS: *Der österreichische Zolltarif*, Stand vom 30, xi, 1927.

Nachweise, monatl. über d. ausw. Handel Deutschlands. Dez. 1931, Jan. 1932. Bln., 1932.

NAPOLSKI: *Zollhandbuch f. d. Schweiz.* Stand I, xi, 1927. Bln., 1928.

Norges Handel, 1913–31. Oslo, 1914 ff.

Reichsgesetzblatt f. d. Dt. Reich, 1928, 1929, 1930.

Review of World Trade, 1934. (League of Nations.) Geneva, 1935.
Statements, Annual, of the trade of the United Kingdom. London. 1914, 1931.
Statistik des ausw. Handels Oesterreichs, 1927, 1931. Wien, 1928, 1932.
Statistik des Warenverkehrs der Schweiz mit dem Ausland, 1913, 1927, 1931. Bümpliz, 1914, 1928, 1932.
Statistique du commerce du royaume de Bulgarie avec les pays étrangers, 1913, 1929. Sofia, 1921, 1931.
Statistique du commerce spécial de la Grèce, 1913–31. Athen, 1913–31.
Statistiques de Commerce extérieur du royaume de Yougoslavie, 1927–31. 1928, 1932.
Statistiques du commerce extérieur, 1931–32. Genève, 1933. (Quoted: *Statistiques* II.)
Statistiques du commerce international, 1933. Genève, 1934. (Quoted: *Statistiques* III.)
Sveriges officiella Statistik: Handel, 1913, 1927, 1931. Stockholm, 1915, 1929, 1933.
Tableau général du Commerce de la Belgique avec les pays étrangers, 1913, 1927, 1931. Bruxelles.
Tableau général du commerce extérieur de la France, 1913, 1927, 1931. Paris, 1919, 1928, 1932.
WAERTIG, L. *Allgem. u. vertragsm. Zolltarif für die Tschechoslowakische Republik.* Stand 1928.
WAERTIG, L. *Allgem. u. vertragsm. Zolltarif für die Tschechoslowakische Republik.* 12. Auflage, 1930. Reichenberg, 1927, 1930.
EICHHORN, F.: *Zollhandbuch für Frankreich* (I, iii, 1929). Bln.
Zollhandbuch für das Deutsche Reich, 1925. Nachträge I, II.
Zollhandbuch für das Deutsche Reich, 1931. HERAUSGEG. V. HARTISCH. Bln., 1925–26, 1931.
Zolltarif, allg. u. vertragsm. f. d. Gebiet der Rep. Oesterreich. (Stand Juli, 1931.) Wien, 1931.
Zolltarif für die Schweiz. (Stand 15, viii, 1931.) Bern, 1931.
Zusammenstellung, system. der Zolltarife des In-u. Auslandes. Vol. A–E. Bln., 1910–13.

B. OTHER BOOKS AND ESSAYS

Aussenhandel, der dt. unter der Einwirkung weltwirtschaftlicher Strukturwandlungen, 2 Bände. Bearb. u. herausgeg. im Institut für Weltwirtschaft und Seeverkehr a. d. Universität Kiel. (Quoted: *Enquête* I, II.) Bln., 1932.
BAYER, H.: "Devisenbewirtschaftung als Mittel der Handelspolitik," *Maschinenbau*, 1932, Bd. xi.

2D

418 TARIFFS AND THE ECONOMIC UNITY OF EUROPE

BERGSTRAESSER, A.: "Zur handelspolitischen Lage der Gegenwart." Einleitung zu: Greiff, *Der Methodenwandel der europ Handelspolitik im Jahre* 1931. Bln., 1932.

BEVERIDGE, Sir WILLIAM: *Tariffs: the Case Examined.* London, 1931. (Quoted: Beveridge.)

BRÄUER, K.: Artikel: *Zölle. Handwörterbuch d. Staatsw.*, Bd. viii, S. 1157–1175. Jena, 1928.

Committee on Finance and Industry: Report. London, 1931. (Quoted: Macmillan Report.)

CONDLIFFE: *World Economic Survey*, 1932–33. Geneva, 1933. (Quoted: Survey I.)

CONDLIFFE: *World Economic Survey*, 1933–34. Geneva, 1934. (Quoted: Survey II.)

CONDLIFFE: *World Economic Survey*, 1934–35. Geneva, 1935. (Quoted: Survey III.)

Conférence économique international. Rapport définitif. Genève, 1927.

Considerations on the present evolution of agricultural protectionism. Geneva, 1935. (Quoted: *Considerations.*)

FLACH, H.: "Die intern. Vereinheitlichung des Zolltarifschemas in der europäischen Zollunion," in *Europ-Zollunion*, hrsg. v. H. Heiman. Bln., 1926.

GAEDICKE, H., UND V. EYNERN, H.: "Die produktionswirtschaftliche Integration Europas," *Zum wirtschaftlichen Schicksal Europas*, Teil I. Textband, Tabellenband. Bln., 1933. (Quoted: Gaedicke.)

GRAEVELL, W.: *Scheinbare Widersprüche in der Aussenhandels-Stat. Wirtschafts-Dienst.*, Bd. XIX, Heft 3. Hamburg, 1934.

GREIFF, W.: "Der Methodenwandel der europäischen Handelspolitik im Jahre 1931," *Zum wirtschaftlichen Schicksal Europas*, Teil I. Bln., 1932.

GROSS, H.: *Strukturelle Voraussetzungen wirksamer Industrie-Zölle. Weltwirtschaftl. Archiv.* Bd. 35. 1932.

HABERLER, G.: *Der internationale Handel.* Bln., 1933.

HARMS, B.: *Die Zukunft der deutschen Handelspolitik.* Jena, 1925.

HAUSER, H.: "Des causes économiques de guerre dans le monde actuel," *Rev. Ec. Intern.*, 1934. Bd. IV, pp. 220–243. Bruxelles.

JONES, J.: *Tariff Retaliation.* Philadelphia, 1934.

Journal of the Monetary and Economic Conference. Nr. 1–39. London, 1933. (Quoted: *W.E.C.*, 1933.)

LANGE, K.: "Die Bedeutung des Weltmarktes für die Deutsche Wirtschaft," *Weltwirtschaft*, Febr., 1932.

LEDERER, E.: "European international trade," *The Annals*, July 1934, pp. 107–115. New York.

LEENER: Essai, "Commerce," in Mahaim, E., *La Belgique restaurée.* Bruxelles, 1926.

LOVEDAY, A.: "The measurement of tariff levels," in *The Journal of the Roy. Stat. Society*, vol. i, 112, pp. 487–529. 1929. (Quoted: Loveday.)

MARSHALL, ALFR.: *Die zollpolitische Regelung des Aussenhandels.* Jena, 1925.

NOGARO-MOYES: *La politique douanière de la France.* Paris, 1931.

OHLIN, B.: *The course and phases of the world economic depression.* Geneva, 1931. (Quoted: Ohlin.)

Proceedings of the preliminary conference with a view to concerted economic action. Geneva, 1930. (Quoted: *Proc.* I.)

Proceedings of the second intern. conference with a view to concerted economic action. (First session) Geneva, 1931. (Quoted: *Proc.* II.)

Proceedings of the second intern. conference with a view to concerted economic action. (Second session) Geneva, 1931. (Quoted: *Proc.* III.)

PROIX, J.: *La politique douanière de la France.* Paris, 1931.

REICHLIN, A.: *Der Schweizerische Zolltarif und seine Schutzwirkung.* Zürich, 1932.

Remarks on the present phase of international economic relations. Geneva, 1935. (Quoted: *Remarks.*)

Report and proceedings of the World Economic Conference, Bd. I–II. Geneva, 1927. (Quoted: *W.E.C.* 1927, I, II.)

ROBBINS, L.: *The Great Depression.* London, 1934.

ROBBINS, L.: *The nature of national planning in the sphere of internat. business.* Amsterdam, 1936.

ROOSEVELT, FRANKLIN: *Looking Forward.* London, 1933.

SALTER, Sir ARTHUR: *Recovery: the second effort.* London, 1932.

SALTER, Sir ARTHUR: "Stabilization and Recovery," *Foreign Affairs*, xiv, 1, October 1935.

SCHLIER, O.: "Aufbau der europäischen Industrie nach dem Kriege," *Zum wirtschaftlichen Schicksal Europas*, Teil I. Berlin, 1932.

STOLPER, G.: "Staat—Nation—Wirtschaft," in "*Europäische Zollunion*," Herausgeb. v. H. Heiman. Bln., 1926.

STROHMAYER: "Die deutsche keramische Industrie," *Wirtschafts-Dienst*. März, 1932.

Survey of Overseas Markets (Committee on Industry and Trade). London, 1926. (Quoted: *Balfour Report.*)

Tariff Level Indices. C.E. 1–37. Geneva, 1927. (Quoted: *Tariff Levels.*)

WEBER, ALFRED: "Europa als Weltindustriezentrum u. die Idee der Zollunion," in *Europäische Zollunion*, Hrsg. v. H. Heiman. Bln., 1926.

WEBER, ALFRED: "Die Standortslehre und die Handelspolitik," in *Archiv f. Sozialwissenschaft u. Sozialpolitik*, Bd. 32. 1911.

WEBER, ALFRED: *Kulturgeschichte als Kultursoziologie*. Leiden, 1935.
WILLIAMS, H.: *Through Tariffs to Prosperity*. London, 1931.
Wirtschaft, Die, des Auslandes, 1900–27. (Einzelschriften zur Statistik d. dt. Reiches, Nr. 5.) Bln., 1928. (Quoted: *W.d.A.*)
World Production and Prices, 1925–34. Geneva, 1935.
World Trade Barriers in relation to American Agriculture: Report. Washington, 1933. (Quoted: *Trade Barriers.*)
ZIMMERN, Sir ALFRED: *The Prospects of Democracy*. London, 1929.
ZOLLHÖHEN und WARENWERTE. Wien, 1927. (Quoted: *Wiener Studie.*)

SUPPLEMENTARY BIBLIOGRAPHY

GREGORY, T. E.: "The reports of the experts to the Joint Committee. A personal survey," in *Improvements of commercial relations between nations. Joint Committee, Carnegie Endowment and International Chamber of Commerce*. Paris, 1936. (Quoted: *Carnegie Report*.)
LAYTON, Sir WALTER, and RIST, Professor CH.: *The economic situation of Austria. Report represented to the Council of the League of Nations*. Geneva, 1925. (Quoted: *Layton-Rist Report.*)
OHLIN, B.: "International economic reconstruction," in *Economic Reconstruction. Carnegie Endowment and International Chamber of Commerce*. Paris, 1936.
PASVOLSKY, L.: Memoranda on "The technique of present-day protectionism. Comments on the improvement of commercial relations between nations," in *Carnegie Report*.
RÖPKE, W.: *German commercial policy*. London, 1934.
VINER, J.: Memorandum on "The technique of present-day protectionism," in *Carnegie Report*.

INDEX

(Authors already mentioned in the text or in the bibliography are not included.)

Albania, unimportant as import market, 45.
American Senate Inquiry, 1933 (World Trade Barriers), 110.
American Tariff of 1930—
and Czechoslovakia, 294.
and France, 252, n. 1.
and Germany, 363.
and Italy, 131, 263.
and Spain, 177–178.
and Switzerland, 276.
and international indebtedness, 363.
Austria—
customs tariff, 23.
agrarian tariff policy, 79–81.
industrial tariff policy, 140–142.
and actual tariff levels in Europe, 277–285.
Averages—
problem of, 25–26, 35–36.
of A-prices, 54–55.

Balfour Committee, 239.
Balfour Report, 18.
Belgium—
agrarian tariff policy, 73–76.
industrial tariff policy, 133–136.
"Border Europe" ("Rand-Europa," Agrarian Europe), 46, 146–147.
States of, 48.
Briand, M., and European tariff truce, 1929, 349.
Brunet, M., 26.
Bulgaria—
agrarian tariff policy, 98–99.
industrial tariff policy, 169–173.
law of encouragement of industry, 169–170, 172.
and actual tariff levels in Europe, 321–332.

Capital, dislocation of and protectionism, 372.
"Central Europe" ("Kern-Europa," Industrial Europe), 46, 57.
States of, 47–48.

Chamber of Commerce, International, Vienna Section, and study on tariff levels, 18, 21, 104.
Chamberlain, J., 133.
China, duties of, on cotton tissues, 239.
Colijn, Dr., 351, 352, 353, 355, 361.
Conference, Agrarian, in Warsaw, 1930, 350, 374.
Conference, Economic, 1930 (17/2–24/3), 349.
Conference, Economic, November 1930, 374.
Customs Union between Belgium and Luxemburg, 134.
Customs Union between Austria and Germany, 1931, 353.
Czechoslovakia—
and American Tariff of 1930, 294.
and actual tariff levels in Europe, 285–294.
agrarian tariff policy, 82–85.
industrial tariff policy, 143–146.
and Hungary, 30, 291–292.

Debts, public, and "national recoveries," 7, 358.
Degree of protectionism, 36–37.
Délaisi, Mr., 46.
Denmark—
customs tariff of, 36.
and actual tariff levels in Europe, 296–304.
Duties—
ad valorem d., 23, 27.
autonomous d., 27.
conventional d., 27.
export d., 20.
import d., 20.
prohibitive d., 20 ff.
protective d., 20 ff.
revenue (fiscal) d., 20 ff.
specific d., 23, 27.
on corn, 107.
on sugar, 108.

Duties—
  on iron and steel goods, 179–180.
  on chemical goods, 180.
  on semi-finished textile goods, 179–180.
  on finished textile goods, 180.

Esthonia—
  small import market, 45.
  and actual tariff levels in Europe, 312–315.
  exchange, restrictions of, as trade barriers, 41.
  export statistics, official, as price sources, 24, 27, 31.

Finland—
  agrarian tariff policy, 88–90.
  industrial tariff policy, 150–153.
  and actual tariff levels in Europe, 304–312.
Fordney McCumber tariff, 1922, 239.
France—
  customs tariff, 23.
  agrarian tariff policy, 65–69.
  industrial tariff policy, 120–126.
  compulsory milling regulation, 40.
  prohibition of wine-mixing, 40.
  and actual tariff levels in Europe, 241–253.
  and American tariff of 1930, 252, n. 1.
  as "Empire" State, 377.

Germany—
  agrarian tariff policy, 56–65.
  industrial tariff policy, 113–120.
  and actual tariff levels in Europe, 201–226.
  and American tariff of 1930, 363.
  and tariff war with Poland, 30, 218–219.
  and reparations, 362.
  and compulsory milling regulation, 61.
  as "Regional" State, 377–378.
Goods, finished, definition of, 114–115, n.
Graham, Mr., 350.
Great Britain—
  tariff policy, 6.
  customs tariff, 23, 36.
  industrial tariff policy, 131–133.
  and actual tariff levels in Europe, 227–241.
  and abandonment of Gold Standard, 240–241.
  as "Empire" State, 377.

Greece—
  small import market, 45.
  import taxes beside tariffs, 40.
  and actual tariff levels in Europe, 332–339.
Handels-Archiv, Deutsche, 30.
Hitler, Adolf, 219.
Holland—
  customs tariff, 23, 36.
  and actual tariff levels in Europe, 296–304.
  and Economic Conference of November 1930, 351.
  as "Empire" State, 377.
Hungary—
  agrarian tariff policy, 95–96.
  industrial tariff policy, 162–166.
  and actual tariff levels in Europe, 321–332.
  and Czechoslovakia, 30.

Import statistics, official, as price sources, 27–28, 31.
India—
  tariff level of, 1924, and Great Britain, 239.
  and duties on English cotton manufactures, 239.
Industrialisation of agrarian countries, and tariffs, 113.
  and exports of industrial countries, 184–186.
  and industrial production in industrial countries, 374–376.
Industries of capital goods and tariffs, 182.
Industries of consumers' goods and tariffs, 182.
Industries of consumption orientation and tariffs, 182, 370.
Industries of labour orientation and tariffs, 182, 370.
Industries of transportation orientation and tariffs, 370.
Integration, economic, of Europe, 19, 192–198.
  spheres of, 196–198, 343–345.
  destruction of the spheres of, 376.
  and European protectionism, 381.
Ireland—
  small import market, 45.
  and exports to Great Britain, 340, n. 1.
Italy—
  agrarian tariff policy, 69–73.
  industrial tariff policy, 126–131.
  and actual tariff levels in Europe, 254–263.

Italy—
    and American tariff of 1930, 263.
    subdivision of customs tariff, 32.
    as "Regional" State, 377–378.
    and Abyssinian War, 380.

Kieler investigation (*Enquête*), 47.
    agrarian index of, 105.

Labour orientation, quantitative, of
    industries, 182–183.
Leener, Dr., 73.
Lettland—
    small import market, 45.
    and actual tariff levels in Europe,
    312–315.
List of goods ("A-list"), 24, 49 ff.
Lithuania—
    small import market, 45.
    and actual tariff levels in Europe,
    312–315.
Logie, G. K., Mr., 7.

MacDonald, Mr., 133.
McKenna, Mr., 131.
Macmillan Committee, 240.
Migration—
    European, Sir Walter Layton on,
    364.
    and tariffs, 363–364.
Most favoured nation principle—
    in Europe till 1931, 27.
    destruction of, 354, 356.

Nationalism, economic—
    condemned on World Economic
    Conferences, 1927, 1933, 355,
    359.
Nederbragt, Dr., 352.
Nola, di, Signor—
    on the measurement of tariff
    levels, 37.
    on tariffs and emigration, 364.
Norway—
    customs tariff, 36.
    and actual tariff levels in Europe,
    304–312.

Ottawa, Conference of, 1932, 377.
Ouchy, Convention of, 1933, 354.

Page, Mr., 37.
Poland—
    agrarian tariff policy, 90–93.
    industrial tariff policy, 153–157.
    and actual tariff levels in Europe,
    315–320.
    and tariff war with Germany, 30,
    317–318.
    as "Regional" State, 377.

Portugal—
    small import market, 45.
    and actual tariff levels in Europe,
    332–339.
Preferential treaties between the
    south-east States and Germany,
    Austria, and France, 353.
Prices—
    problem of, 33–35.
    "cif. prices," 27.
    export prices, 33–35.
    "normal" prices, 50.
Progress, technical—
    and tariffs, 360.
    and commercial treaties, 361.
    and price level, 367.
Protection, administrative, 40.

Quotas, as trade barriers, 41, 347.

Rearmament, as cause of "national
    recovery," 7, 358–359.
Riedel, Dr., 284.
Rockefeller Foundation, 7.
Roosevelt, President, 354.
Roumania—
    agrarian tariff policy, 93–95.
    industrial tariff policy, 157–162.
    and actual tariff levels in Europe,
    321–332.
    Act to encourage home industry,
    160–161.
    industrial protectionism, 371–372.
Runciman, Mr., 361.

Sato, Mr., 37.
Scandinavian States, customs tariffs
    of, 23.
Smuts, General, 379–380.
Soviet Russia, foreign trade mono-
    poly, 39.
Spain—
    agrarian tariff policy, 99–102.
    industrial tariff policy, 173–178.
    and actual tariff levels in Europe,
    332–339.
    and French prohibition of wine-
    mixing, 337.
    and American tariff of 1930, 177–
    178.
    and Law to encourage develop-
    ment of industry, 40, 176–177.
State and economics, 39–40.
Stresemann, Dr., 348–349.
Sweden—
    agrarian tariff policy, 85–88.
    industrial tariff policy, 147–150.
    and actual tariff levels in Europe,
    304–312.

Switzerland—
agrarian tariff policy, 76–79.
industrial tariff policy, 136–140.
and actual tariff levels in Europe, 269–277.
and American tariff, 1930, 276.
trade statistics of, 34.

Tariffs—
assimilation of, 31.
and devaluation, 362.
and immigration, 363–364.
decreasing importance of, in post-War time, 38–42.
and military aims, 365–366.
and fiscal needs, 366.
and location of industries, 181–182, 369–370.
and preservation of peasantry, 365.
and reparations, 362.
subdivision of, 32–33.
Tariff levels—
actual, 6, 28 ff., 189–191.
national index of actual tariff levels, 29, 190.
limits of textual analysis of actual tariff levels, 199–200.
height of actual tariff levels, 1860, 369.
potential tariff levels, 22 ff., 29.
Tariff truce—
in Europe, 1929, 349–350.
in world, 1933, 354.
Textile industries in Central Europe, 186.
Theunis, President of World Economic Conference, 1927, 379.
Tournakis, Mr., on emigration and tariff policy, 364.

Trade, foreign (exports), share of, in total output of industry or agriculture—
Austria, 277.
Belgium, 264–265.
Czechoslovakia, 285–287.
Denmark, 298.
France, 243.
Germany, 213–214.
Great Britain, 298.
Greece, 332–333.
Hungary, 322.
Italy, 255.
Netherlands, 298.
Poland, 316.
Portugal, 332.
Roumania, 321.
Spain, 332.
Sweden, 306.
Switzerland, 270.
Trendelenburg, Dr., 35.

World Economic Conference, 1927. 5, 17, 18.
and industrial duties, 104.
against tariffs, 347–348.
World Economic Conference, 1933, 354–355.
World economic crisis (1929 ff.)—
and agrarian tariff levels, 106, 110.
and industrial tariff levels, 184.
and price levels, 342.
World export of important industrial goods and tariffs, 185.
World trade, fall of, 1929–1935, 356–357.

Yugoslavia—
agrarian tariff policy, 96–97.
industrial tariff policy, 166–169.
and actual tariff levels in Europe, 321–332.

For Product Safety Concerns and Information please contact our EU
representative GPSR@taylorandfrancis.com
Taylor & Francis Verlag GmbH, Kaufingerstraße 24, 80331 München, Germany